"This compelling collection offers fresh insights into Vladimir Nabokov's life and artistic legacy. The editor's essay draws on fascinating new archival information to illuminate Nabokov's ties to Boston and environs, while the other wide-ranging essays showcase his brilliance as a literary innovator and cultural icon. Essential reading for scholars and admirers of Nabokov alike."

—Vladimir E. Alexandrov, B. E. Bensinger Professor Emeritus,
Yale University, and author of *To Break Russia's Chains:
Boris Savinkov and His Wars against the Tsar and the Bolsheviks*

"*Nabokov on the Heights* is a tribute both to Nabokov's ability to engage a new generation of readers and to Maxim D. Shrayer's skill in guiding them as they seek to convert their enthusiasm into meaningful scholarship. This volume celebrates Nabokov in Boston, encompassing his life in that city and readings of his work produced by former students and current colleagues of Shrayer at Boston College. The readings, thankfully, do not produce a unified interpretation of the writer, but they bear witness to a shared sense of scholarly community. There are already several books on teaching Nabokov, but this book is different, since it reflects and extends what has already happened in the classroom. A successful class is only the start of a continuing relationship with its teacher and its texts. By retrograde analysis, one can read *Nabokov on the Heights* to discover what can happen when one teaches Nabokov well."

—Eric Naiman, Professor, University of California,
Berkeley, and author of *Nabokov, Perversely*

"In celebration of the role that the colleges and universities of Massachusetts played in the life and work of Vladimir Nabokov, the scholars of Boston College have located and filled in gaps in Nabokov studies, stimulating further thought and discussion."

—Leona Toker, Professor Emerita, The Hebrew University of Jerusalem,
author of *Nabokov: The Mystery of Literary Structures*

NABOKOV ON THE HEIGHTS

New Studies from Boston College

Immigrant Worlds & Texts

For more information on this series, please visit:
https://www.academicstudiespress.com/immigrant-worlds-texts/

NABOKOV ON THE HEIGHTS

New Studies from Boston College

Edited by Maxim D. Shrayer

ACADEMIC STUDIES PRESS

BOSTON

2025

Library of Congress Cataloging-in-Publication Data

Names: Shrayer, Maxim, 1967- editor.
Title: Nabokov on the Heights : new studies from Boston College / edited by
    Maxim D. Shrayer.
Description: Boston : Academic Studies Press, 2025. | Series: Immigrant
    worlds & texts | Includes bibliographical references and index.
Identifiers: LCCN 2024059029 (print) | LCCN 2024059030 (ebook)
    | ISBN 9798887197296 (hardback) | ISBN 9798887197302 (adobe pdf)
    | ISBN 9798887197319 (epub)
Subjects: LCSH: Nabokov, Vladimir Vladimirovich, 1899-1977--Criticism and
    interpretation. | LCGFT: Essays.
Classification: LCC PG3476.N3 Z786 2025 (print) | LCC PG3476.N3
    (ebook) | DDC 813/.54--dc23/eng/20250101
LC record available at https://lccn.loc.gov/2024059029
LC ebook record available at https://lccn.loc.gov/2024059030

Book design by PHi Business Solutions
Cover design by Ivan Grave
On the front cover: Vladimir Nabokov, Loèche-les-Bains, Suisse, 1965.
Photo by Horst Tappe, Fondation Horst Tappe.
On the back cover: Boston College Chestnut Hill campus with a view of
    Gasson Hall and Bapst Library in the background, 2023. Photo by
    Maxim D. Shrayer.

Published by Academic Studies Press
1007 Chestnut St.
Newton, MA 02464, USA
press@academicstudiespress.com
www.academicstudiespress.com

The book is published with the support of Boston College.

Contents

Editor's Introduction: Nabokov on the Heights (and in Boston)

Maxim D. Shrayer

Vladimir Nabokov's connections to the Boston area predate the arrival of the writer and his family to the US as refugees from France in 1940. Peter A. Pertzoff, the Russian-born co-translator of the short stories that established Nabokov's literary reputation in 1940s America, grew up in Cambridge and graduated from Harvard College in 1933. Pertzoff and Nabokov started collaborating in the early 1930s, when Pertzoff was living in the Boston area.[1] In the manifest of the SS *Champlain*, which left Saint-Nazaire on 19 May 1940, less than a month before the fall of Paris to Nazi troops, and arrived in New York on 28 May 1940, the Nabokovs listed under "Whether going to join a relative or friend": "Friend, Serge Koussevitzky, 88 Druce Str. Brookline, Mass."[2] Koussevitzky served as conductor of the Boston Symphony Orchestra in 1924–1949.

Vladimir Nabokov, his wife Véra Nabokov (née Slonim), and their son Dmitri Nabokov lived in the Boston area, in Cambridge and Wellesley, from

*   I would like to express my gratitude to Christian Dupont, Associate University Librarian for Scholarly Resources and The Burns Librarian at Boston College, for his most generous logistical and research assistance, and to the staff of John J. Burns Library for facilitating access to Nabokov-related archival and photographic materials and generously offering information about the materials' provenance.

1   See Maxim D. Shrayer, "Nabokov: Letters to the American Translator," trans. Maxim D. Shrayer, *AGNI* 50 (October 1999): 128–145; Maksim D. Shraer, "V. V. Nabokov i ego amerikanskii perevodchik P. A. Pertsov," *Tallinn* 23 (2001): 157–165.

2   SS *Champlain*, List or Manifest of Alien Passengers, 19–27 May 1940, List 8, Passenger Search, Ellis Island Records, The Statue of Liberty and Ellis Island Foundation, accessed October 23, 2023, https://heritage.statueofliberty.org. Koussevitzky's last name and Nabokov's last name are misspelled in the manifest.

September 1941 to June 1948.[3] Of Nabokov's almost seven years as a Bostonian and a New Englander, for six he resided at the same address, 8 Craigie Circle, in Cambridge—a block and a half west of Concord Street and a short stroll from Cambridge Common. On Sundays, young Dmitri, a future opera basso, would walk to the nearby Christ Church, a Episcopal church where he sang Handel's *Messiah*. On Fridays or Saturdays Dmitri also trained his voice on Ernest Bloch's Jewish liturgical music at a Reform synagogue located across the river in Brookline.[4] After moving to Ithaca, where Vladimir Nabokov assumed a professorship at Cornell University, he and Véra returned to the Boston area for three extensive stays, first in the spring of 1951, as a visiting professor at Harvard, and later on two sabbatical leaves in the spring of 1953 and the spring of 1956. In the 1950s Dmitri Nabokov attended Harvard College and also studied voice at the Longy School of Music. All in all, Nabokov stayed at three addresses in Wellesley and at five addresses in Cambridge, including a two-week disastrous stay in the spring of 1953 at a house that belonged to Robert Frost.[5]

Many of Vladimir Nabokov's big American firsts happened while he was living in the Boston area. He became an American poet, critic, novelist, and translator, a college professor, an entomologist, and an American citizen. It would take another book to detail all of Nabokov's Boston-centered discoveries (and disappointments), so I will only highlight a few of them.

Nabokov visited the Boston area in March 1941 for two weeks of lectures at Wellesley College. It was during that first visit that he met with Edward A. Weeks, editor of the *Atlantic*, where the Englished versions of Nabokov's stories

---

3   I am relying on Brian Boyd's narrative of the Nabokovs' lives in the Boston area. See his *Vladimir Nabokov: The American Years* (Princeton: Princeton University Press, 1991), 35–129, 199–226, and passim. See also Stacy Schiff, *Véra (Mrs. Vladimir Nabokov)* (New York: The Modern Library, 2000), 119–145. Susan Elizabeth Sweeney details Nabokov's Cambridge and Wellesley addresses in "The Nabokovs' Wellesley Addresses; The Nabokovs' Cambridge Addresses; a guide prepared for The Hidden Nabokov Conference," Wellesley College, June 15–19, 2022. See also Dieter E. Zimmer, "Nabokov's Whereabouts," Dieter E. Zimmer 1934–2020, last modified July 9, 2020, http://www.d-e-zimmer.de/HTML/whereabouts.htm. About Nabokov at Wellesley College, see, for instance, Wilma Slaight, "Vladimir Nabokov at Wellesley," Wellesley College, January 8, 2001, https://www.wellesley.edu/russian/history/nabokov-at-wellesley/nabokovslaight.

4   About singing at an Episcopal church and a Reform synagogue, see Maxim D. Shrayer, Interview with Dmitri Nabokov, Montreux, December 11, 2011, https://youtu.be/Yng4Y0LUQ0M?si=ilfOqj7dQ4Pqqxem.

5   On Nabokov and Frost, see Abraham Socher, "The Jack Frost House," *Times Literary Supplement*, July 1, 2005.

"Cloud, Castle, Lake" and "The Aurelian" appeared in 1941.[6] At Wellesley he would teach, with interruptions, until his departure for Cornell, as a "Resident Lecturer in Comparative Literature" and an instructor of Russian subjects. At Wellesley, perhaps the premier women's college, he tasted US academic politics when the college did not rehire him for the academic year 1942–1943, in large measure owing to the principled anti-Soviet views that he refused to dial down even as the US and the USSR were allies fighting Nazi Germany.

While living in the Boston area, Nabokov composed his first English-language short story, "The Assistant Producer" (1943), and conceived of and carried out his first American novel, the dystopian *Bend Sinister*. To quote from his introduction,

> The greater part of the book was composed in the winter and spring of 1945–1946, at a particularly cloudless and vigorous period of life. My daily consumption of cigarettes had reached the four-package mark. I slept at least four or five hours, the rest of the night walking pencil in hand about the dingy little flat in Craigie Circle, Cambridge, Massachusetts, where I lodged under an old lady with feet of stone and above a young woman with hypersensitive hearing. Every day including Sundays, I would spend up to 10 hours studying the structure of certain butterflies in the laboratorial paradise of the Harvard Museum of Comparative Zoology; but three times a week I stayed there only till noon and then tore myself away from microscope and camera lucida to travel to Wellesley (by tram and bus, or subway and railway), where I taught college girls Russian grammar and literature.[7]

During his Boston years, Nabokov produced exemplary metrical translations of some of his favorite Russian poets from the classical age: Pushkin, Lermontov, Afanasy Fet, and Fyodor Tyutchev, as well as translations of his older émigré contemporary Vladislav Khodasevich,[8] who had died in Paris less than three months before the outbreak of World War II. As a recent Russian expatriate

---

6   See Shrayer, "Nabokov: Letters to the American Translator."
7   Vladimir Nabokov, *Bend Sinister*, with an introduction by the author (Alexandria, VA: Time-Life Books, 1981), xi.
8   See V. V. Nabokov, *Stikhotvoreniia*, ed. and with commentary by M. E. Malikova (St. Petersburg: Akademicheskii proekt; Novaia biblioteka poeta, 2002), 415–460; see esp. commentary at 603–610.

and a new Bostonian, Nabokov felt the first pangs of what would become his iconoclastic *Eugene Onegin* translation. Even more importantly, in 1941–1942 Nabokov wrote his first English-language poems. With his first verses written in English, Nabokov debuted in the *New Yorker*,[9] which became the main American port of call for Nabokov's poetry, short fiction, and excerpts from his memoirs and novels. And as a Wellesley instructor, he wrote his only book of English-language literary biography and criticism, *Nikolai Gogol*, which James Laughlin's New Directions put out in 1944. During his early American—that is, Boston—years, Nabokov developed important connections with American authors and intellectuals, among them the writer Sylvia Berkman (at Wellesley) and the literary scholar Harry Levin (at Harvard). While living in Cambridge and teaching at Wellesley, twice a week Nabokov would commute to the western suburb of Boston by a combination of different transports. Nabokov described the commute in a letter to his beloved younger sister Elena (Hélène) Sikorski, who was still living in Prague:

> Not far from Craigie Circle I board a bus, then in the city center I switch to the underground [the Red Line of the T], which takes me to the center of Boston, to the train station. This takes forty minutes. At the train station I get on a real train and an hour later arrive at Wellesley. There I take a taxi cab, which delivers me to the luxurious campus (the college site), somewhat resembling English universities.[10]

We still do not know enough about Nabokov's encounter with urban and suburban parts of the greater Boston area and its many immigrant communities and institutions. Parts of the greater Boston area would serve as an inspiration and setting of Nabokov's literary works, notably Cambridge's fancier apartment blocks in "Double Speak" (1945, retitled "Conversation Piece, 1945") and the Wellesley campus in "The Vane Sisters" (1951). Along with details of his first American years, Nabokov's first postwar letter to his younger sister, mailed from 8 Craigie Circle in Cambridge, communicates a Russian immigrant's gratitude to America for having given shelter to him and his Jewish wife

---

9   See "Vladimir Nabokov, *New Yorker*, accessed November 20, 2023, https://www.newyorker.com/contributors/vladimir-nabokov; see Nabokov, *Stikhotvoreniia*, 393–414, commentary at 598–602.
10 Vladimir Nabokov, letter to Helene Sikorski, January 21, 1946, in *Perepiska s sestroi*, ed. Helene Sikorski (Ann Arbor: Ardis, 1985), 29.

and son during the Shoah: "I love this country. Along with descents into wild *poshlost'*, there are peaks here, on which one can have picknicks with 'understanding' friends."[11] In many of Nabokov's letters from the 1940s, notes of admiration or appreciation mask or hide the festering wounds of American society that tore at his heart—philistinism, consumerism, and above all else, racism and antisemitism. As far as the latter is concerned, Nabokov had his fill of genteel upper-class antisemitism at parlors and cocktail receptions, and of the unabashed, "Hebrews not accommodated" type of anti-Jewish prejudice during the trips he and his family took to the nearby Cape Cod and north of Boston to *N'iu Gempshir*.

Nabokov still lives in the Boston area—in the literary memories he left for posterity, in retellings of his real and imagined adventures and misadventures,[12] and in the memory of his former students and their offspring. Once in the 2000s, I was receiving Versed (what a great name for a sedative to be given to a student of poetry) before a medical procedure at a Wellesley medical clinic. Upon hearing that I taught literature at Boston College, the anesthesiologist asked me if I ever lectured on Nabokov (pronounced with a formidable Boston accent). "Not just lecture, I write about him," I replied. The anesthesiologist[13] proceeded to tell me that his mother had been a student of Nabokov's, whereupon I drifted into sleep. Subsequently I checked and confirmed that Katherine Reese Peebles had indeed been Nabokov's student at Wellesley.[14] In 1943 she wrote a poignant profile of her professor for a college publication: "Fortyish, tall and thin, shoulders hunched forward, he resembles the romantic, American conception of a real artist. His face is like one of those which are often ascribed to geniuses and mad scientists in mystery novels."[15] To Stacy Schiff, who interviewed Peebles in the process of researching Véra Nabokov's biography, Nabokov's former student conjured up a memory of an un(der)consummated campus romance: "I took a course in Russian, and I got sidetracked on a course on Vladimir Nabokov.

11 Nabokov, letter to Helene Sikorski, 25 October 1945, in *Perepiska s sestroi*, 18.
12 For an example, see Maxim D. Shrayer, "A Genius in the Attic: Secrets of a Cape Cod Dacha," *Tablet Magazine*, April 22, 2015, https://www.tabletmag.com/sections/arts-letters/articles/a-genius-in-the-attic.
13 Dr. Douglas C. Peebles, *U. S. News*, accessed November 21, 2023, https://health.usnews.com/doctors/douglas-peebles-216893.
14 Bryan Marquand, "Katherine Reese Peebles, 93; Captured Nabokov in Heart and Words," *Boston Globe*, March 1, 2017, https://www3.bostonglobe.com/metro/obituaries/2017/02/28/katherine-reese-peebles-who-captured-nabokov-heart-and-words-dies/9c4ea1wP109bzbuzdCYbIJ/story.html?arc404=true.
15 Quoted in Marquand.

[. . .] He did like young girls. Just not *little* girls."[16] The writer has a way of becoming mythologically immortal in the minds of his students and readers.

***

What would Nabokov have known about Boston College in the 1940s? Did he ever visit the Boston College campus in Chestnut Hill? Did he ever stroll along the paths of the nearby and historic Houghton Garden?[17] We do not have a record of it, although we should not rule out the possibility that during his years in the Boston area Nabokov ascended the Heights in search of a rare example of local lepidoptera. We do know that in the 1960s, when he was already living in Switzerland, Boston College made two attempts to bring him to the campus for a reading.

Figure 1. Boston College's main campus with a view of Bapst Library (the facing section now houses John J. Burns Library), St. Mary's Hall, Gasson Hall, and Devlin Hall, from Commonwealth Avenue. 1930s. Photo by Clifton Church. Boston College, University Archives.

16 Schiff, *Véra*, 140.
17 "Houghton Garden," Newton Conservators, accessed January 27, 2024, https://newtoncon-servators.org/property/houghton-garden/.

The person who tried to bring Nabokov to the Heights was Francis W. Sweeney, S. J., a legendary campus figure.[18] An educator, poet, and essayist, Rev. Sweeney taught writing and literature at Boston College in 1951–1998. His many contributions included serving as faculty advisor to *Stylus*,[19] one of the oldest college literary magazines in New England, founded in 1883, and curating the Humanities Series (now the Lowell Humanities Series).

In the spring of 1965 Rev. Sweeney wrote to Nabokov care of his American publisher:

April 2, 1965

Vladimir Nabokov, Esq.
c/o G. P. Putnam's Sons
210 Madison Avenue
New York, NY

Dear Mr. Nabokov,

This letter is an inquiry whether it might be possible for you to honor us with a lecture at Boston College one day during the 1965–66 academic year. During the past eight years, the Humanities Series has brought to this University many of the leading writers of England and America. A partial list of these speakers is included on the enclosed flyer.

I would be very grateful if you would let me know whether you might find it convenient to visit us, and if so, what fee we might offer you.

With all good wishes and thanks, I am

Sincerely yours,
Rev. Frencis Sweeney, S. J.
Director[20]

Less than three weeks later, Véra Nabokov replied from Montreux:

---

18 About Sweeney's curatorship of the Humanities Series, see Charles F. Donovan, David R. Dunigan, and Paul A. FitzGerald, S. J., *History of Boston College: From the Beginnings to 1990* (Chestnut Hill, MA: The University Press of Boston College, 1990), 242–243.
    See also *Francis W. Sweeney: Virtual Exhibit Fall 2004—Burns Library*, BC University Libraries, accessed November 21, 2023, https://library.bc.edu/past/libraries/about/exhibits/burnsvirtual/sweeney/2.html; Barbara Adams Hebard, "It Will Take a Lifetime: A New Look at Francis W. Sweeney, S. J.," John Burns Library Blog, June 23, 2014, https://johnjburnslibrary.wordpress.com/2014/06/23/newlookatsweeneysj/.
19 On *Stylus*, see Donovan et al., *History of Boston College*, 82–83.
20 The correspondence between the Nabokovs and Francis W. Sweeney, S. J. is found in the Francis W. Sweeney Papers, John J. Burns Library, Boston College, FWS-HS, MS. 2002.37.

Montreux, April 19, 1965
Palace Hotel

The Reverend Francis Sweeney
Boston College Humanities Series
Chestnut Hill, Mass. 02167

Dear Sir,

My husband asks me to thank you for your kind letter of April 2. He would be very pleased to give some time a reading at the [*sic*] Boston College, but it will not be possible for him to do it in the course of the academic year 1965–1966 because he does not expect to be in the U. S. before summer, 1966.

With best wishes,

Sincerely yours,
Véra Nabokov
(Mrs. Vladimir Nabokov)

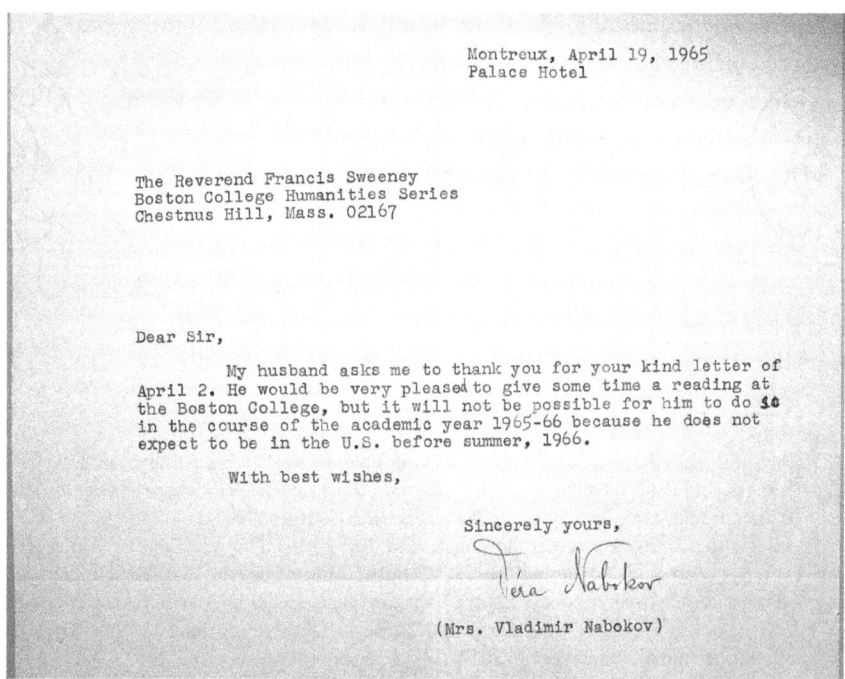

Figure 2. Véra Nabokov's letter to Francis W. Sweeney, S. J. 19 April 1965. The Francis W. Sweeney Papers, John J. Burns Library, Boston College.

Reverend Sweeney refused to give up, and nearly two years later he wrote to Nabokov again:

March 7, 1967

Vladimir Nabokov, Esquire
Care Of G. P. Putnam's Sons
210 Madison Avenue
New York, NY

Dear Mr. Nabokov,
  You may recall that sometime ago I wrote to you with the request that you give a lecture for us one day at Boston College. I know that your crowded work schedule does not permit many engagements of this kind, but I wanted to inquire whether you could see your way clear to visiting us on[e] day in the autumn of 1967 or the spring of 1968. Late October or mid-November would be best for us.
  With every good wish, I am

Yours respectfully,
Francis Sweeney, S. J.

Just under a month later Véra Nabokov replied from Montreux, this time on the stationery of Palace Hotel:

April 3, 1967

The Reverend Francis Sweeney
The Humanities Series
Boston College
Chestnut Hill, Mass. 02167

Dear Sir,
  My husband asks me to thank you for your kind invitation to give a lecture at Boston College. To his regret, he cannot do it either this year or in the spring of 1968 as his plans are still vague, and the first item on his schedule is the writing of a new novel.

Yours truly,
Véra Nabokov
(Mrs. Vladimir Nabokov)

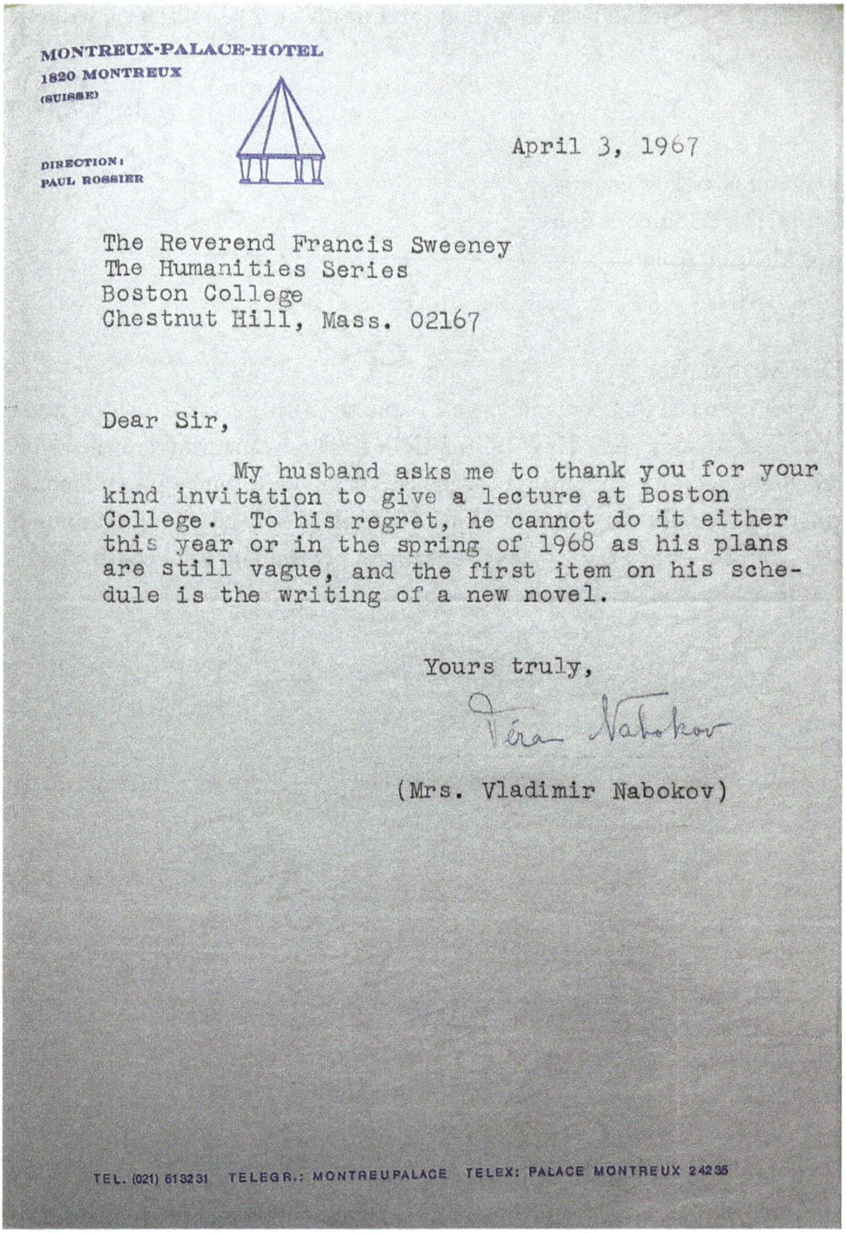

MONTREUX-PALACE-HOTEL
1820 MONTREUX
(SUISSE)

DIRECTION:
PAUL ROSSIER

April 3, 1967

The Reverend Francis Sweeney
The Humanities Series
Boston College
Chestnut Hill, Mass. 02167

Dear Sir,

My husband asks me to thank you for your
kind invitation to give a lecture at Boston
College. To his regret, he cannot do it either
this year or in the spring of 1968 as his plans
are still vague, and the first item on his schedule is the writing of a new novel.

Yours truly,

Véra Nabokov

(Mrs. Vladimir Nabokov)

TEL. (021) 613231   TELEGR.: MONTREUPALACE   TELEX: PALACE MONTREUX 24235

Figure 3. Véra Nabokov's letter to Francis W. Sweeney, S. J., 3 April 1967. The Francis W. Sweeney Papers, John J. Burns Library, Boston College.

Véra Nabokov would travel to the US alone in 1968. The novel that she referred to, *Ada, or Ardor*, Nabokov's longest, most translingual, and also most philosophically complex and pathological, would be published in 1969. And as it happened, Nabokov's last visit to America had been in March–April 1964, on the occasion of the publication of his translation of and commentary to *Eugene Onegin*. Nabokov never visited his adoptive country again, despite some promises and intimations he dispensed in interviews. In the papers of Francis W. Sweeney, S. J., the Nabokov folder is sandwiched between the correspondence with the journalist Edward R. Morrow, whose 12 April 1945 broadcast from Buchenwald, liberated by American troops, Nabokov had likely heard on the wireless,[21] and the correspondence with Ferenc Nagy, the exiled former prime minister of Hungary, who had been living in the United States since 1947.

***

There is a double postscriptum to the story of Nabokov's unrealized visit to Boston College. In 1995, Boston College Libraries acquired Graham Greene's personal library and some of the writer's papers.[22] Greene had played a particularly important role in Nabokov's career and success. It was Greene who chose *Lolita* as one of the three best books of 1955 in the Christmas issue of the *Sunday Times*, thus setting off a scandal that propelled the novel and its author to international stardom. In his weekly column published on January 29, 1956, John Gordon, editor of the *Sunday Express*, went ballistic over the subject of Greene's endorsement: "Without doubt it is the filthiest book I have ever read. Sheer unrestrained pornography. [. . .] Anyone who published it or sold it here would certainly go to prison."[23] Responding with acerbic humor, Greene suggested that a John Gordon Society of cultural censorship be formed. Greene also wanted his publishing venture, The Bodley Head, to release *Lolita* in the UK, but Nabokov ended up going with Weidenfeld & Nicolson. Nabokov remained beholden to Greene, and the first of his two letters in the Greene collection at John J. Burns Library mixes notes of deep appreciation with anxiety over the fate of *Lolita*, at the time only available in the 1955 Paris edition:

---

21 See Maxim D. Shrayer, "Raisa Blokh as an Historical, Literary and Emotional Source for Nabokov's *Pnin*," in *Skreshcheniia sudeb. Literarische und kulturelle Beziehungen zwischen Russland und dem Westen. A Festschrift for Fedor B. Poljakov*, ed. Lazar Fleishman, Stefan Michael Newerkla, and Michael Wachtel, *Stanford Slavic Studies* 49 (Berlin: Peter Lang, 2019), 644–650.

22 See Amy Braitsch, "Graham Greene at the Burns Library," *Boston College Libraries News*, June 23, 2016, https://library.bc.edu/newsletter/?p=41; "Family Life, Friends, and Espionage: The Graham Greene Papers Re-Opened," Boston College Libraries, April 7, 2016, https://library.bc.edu/news/2016/Apr/graham-greene-reopens/. The bulk of Graham Greene's personal papers are at the Harry Ransom Center, University of Texas.

23 Quoted in Boyd, *Vladimir Nabokov: The American Years*, 295, 698n25.

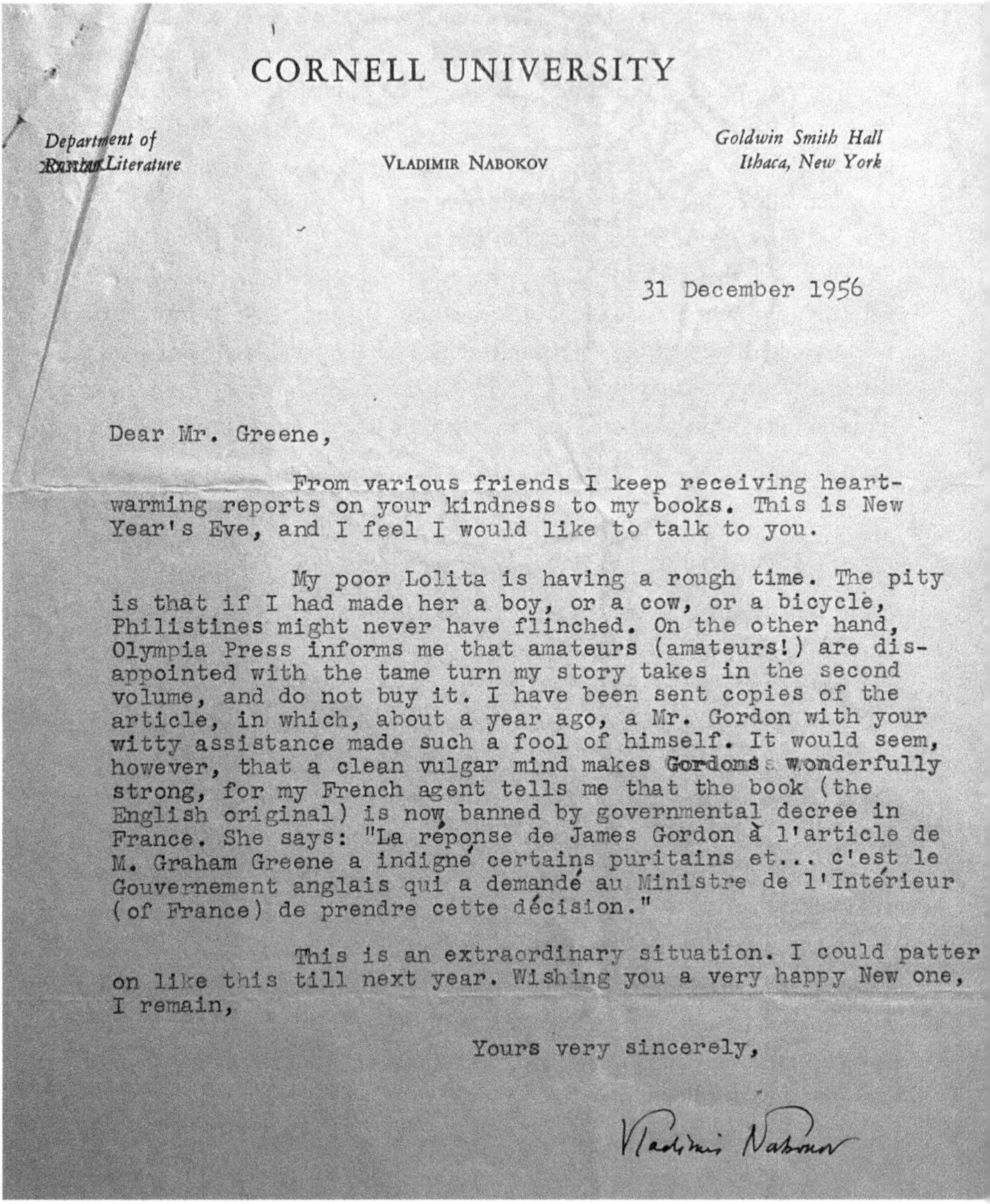

CORNELL UNIVERSITY

Department of
Russian Literature

VLADIMIR NABOKOV

Goldwin Smith Hall
Ithaca, New York

31 December 1956

Dear Mr. Greene,

From various friends I keep receiving heart-warming reports on your kindness to my books. This is New Year's Eve, and I feel I would like to talk to you.

My poor Lolita is having a rough time. The pity is that if I had made her a boy, or a cow, or a bicycle, Philistines might never have flinched. On the other hand, Olympia Press informs me that amateurs (amateurs!) are disappointed with the tame turn my story takes in the second volume, and do not buy it. I have been sent copies of the article, in which, about a year ago, a Mr. Gordon with your witty assistance made such a fool of himself. It would seem, however, that a clean vulgar mind makes Gordons wonderfully strong, for my French agent tells me that the book (the English original) is now banned by governmental decree in France. She says: "La réponse de James Gordon à l'article de M. Graham Greene a indigné certains puritains et... c'est le Gouvernement anglais qui a demandé au Ministre de l'Intérieur (of France) de prendre cette décision."

This is an extraordinary situation. I could patter on like this till next year. Wishing you a very happy New one, I remain,

Yours very sincerely,

Vladimir Nabokov

Figure 4. Vladimir Nabokov's Letter to Graham Greene. December 31, 1956. The Graham Greene Papers, John J. Burns Library, Boston College.

Cornell University
Vladimir Nabokov   Ithaca, New York

31 December 1956

Dear Mr. Greene,

From various friends I keep receiving heart-warming reports on your kindness to my books. This is New Year's Eve, and I feel I would like to talk to you.

My poor Lolita is having a rough time. The pity is that if I had made her a boy, or a cow, or a bicycle, Philistines might never have flinched. On the other hand, Olympia Press informs me that amateurs (amateurs!) are disappointed with the tame turn my story takes in the second volume, and do not buy it. I have been sent copies of the article, in which, about a year ago, a Mr. Gordon with your witty assistance made such a fool of himself. It would seem, however, that a clean vulgar mind makes Gordons wonderfully strong, for my French agent tells me that the book (the English original) is now banned by governmental decree in France. She says: "La réponse de James Gordon á l'article de M. Graham Greene a indigné certains puritains et . . . c'est le Gouvernment anglaise que a demandé au Ministre de l'Intériour (of France) de prendre cette decision."

This is an extraordinary situation. I could patter on like this till next year. Wishing you a very happy New one, I remain,

Yours very sincerely,
Vladimir Nabokov[24]

Nabokov and Greene did not meet in person until the autumn of 1959. On October 28 1959, Véra and Vladimir arrived in London for the official launch of Lolita's British edition. On October 31 Nabokov sent a handwritten note to Greene, on the stationery of Stafford Hotel, located a short distance from Buckingham Palace:

---

24   The Nabokov-related materials are located in two folders of the Graham Greene Papers, John J. Burns Library, Boston College (Graham Greene MS. 1995.003): Lolita controversy, correspondence 1956–1982 and Lolita controversy, articles 1958–1959. Cf. the text of Nabokov's 1956 letter to Greene as published in Vladimir Nabokov, Selected Letters 1940–1977, ed. Dmitri Nabokov and Matthew J. Bruccoli (New York: Vintage, 1989), 187–198.

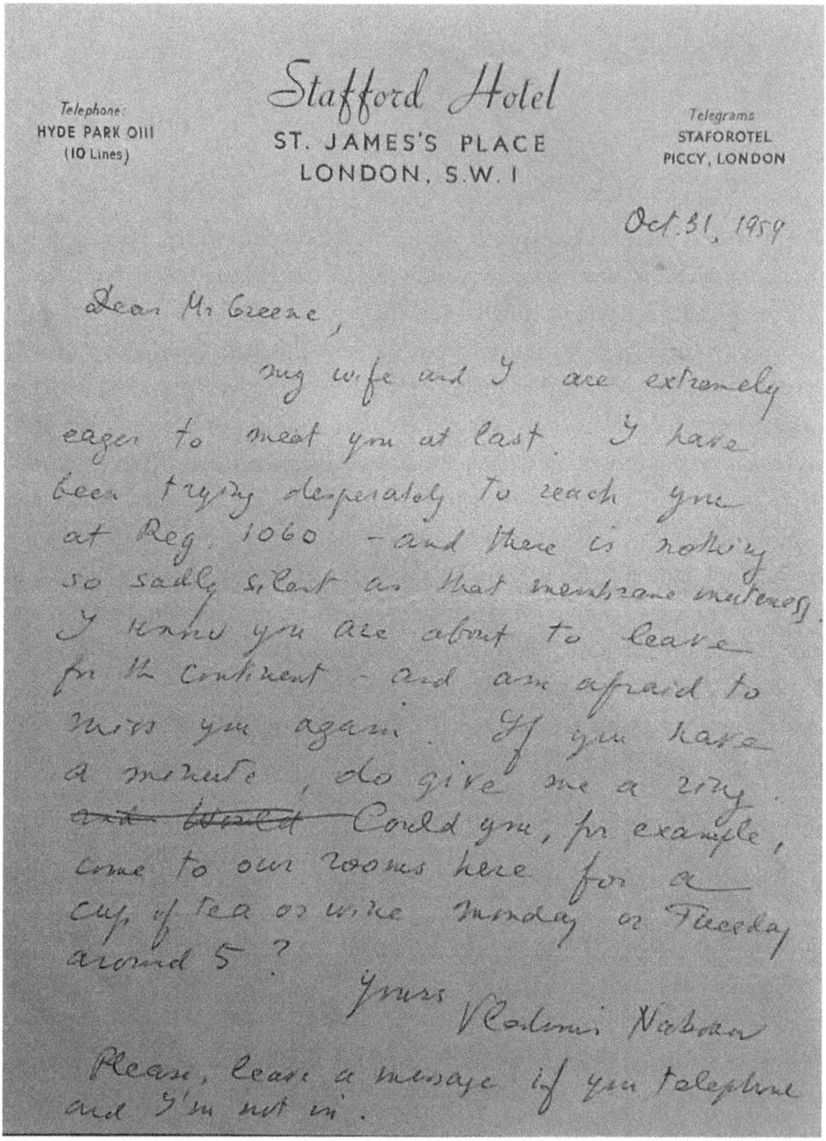

Figure 5. Vladimir Nabokov's Letter to Graham Greene. 31 October 1959. The Graham Greene Papers, John J. Burns Library, Boston College.

Stafford Hotel
St. James's Place
London, S. W. I

Oct. 31, 1959

Dear Mr. Greene,

My wife and I are extremely eager to meet you at last. I have been trying desperately to reach you at Reg. 1060—and there is nothing so sadly silent as that
membrane muteness. I know you are about to leave for the Continent—and
am afraid to miss you again. If you have a minute, do give me a ring. ~~And Would~~
Could you, for example, come to our rooms here for a cup of tea or wine Monday
or Tuesday around 5?

Yours
Vladimir Nabokov

Please, leave a message if you telephone and I'm not in.

Neither of the dates that Nabokov proposed apparently worked, and so Nabokov
ended up dining with Greene on November 1, 1959.[25] As a surviving note from
Greene's secretary to Nabokov indicates, Greene wanted Nabokov to autograph
a copy of the first edition of *Lolita* and left it at the hotel for the author to sign;[26]
Nabokov also signed a copy of the Olympia Press edition with the words: "for
Graham Greene November 1959 from Vladimir Nabokov." He also drew a butterfly, and beneath it, slantwise, added, "Green swallowtail dancing waisthigh."[27]

---

25 Vladimir Nabokov, Diary Entry, November 1, 1959, Vladimir Nabokov Papers, the Henry
W. and Albert A. Berg Collection of English and American Literature, New York Public
Library. On Nabokov's visit to London in 1959, see Boyd, *Vladimir Nabokov: The American
Years*, 398–399. I am grateful to Brian Boyd for clarifying the date of Nabokov's meeting with
Greene in a series of email communications on November 26, 2023.
26 Letter from Graham Greene's secretary to Vladimir Nabokov, November 5, 1959, The
Graham Greene Papers, John J. Burns Library, Boston College.
27 Christie's Live Auction 1098, Masterpiece of World Literature from the Library of Roger
Rechler, 2002, Nabokov Lots, Vladimir Nabokov, *Lolita* (Paris: The Olympia Press, 1959),
2 vols., Graham Greene's copy with vol. 2 autographed by Nabokov, accessed February 7,
2024, https://www.christies.com/lot/lot-3984253?ldp_breadcrumb=back&intObjectID=
3984253&from=salessummary&lid=1. Christian Dupont generously shared this information.

Greene also owned a signed copy of the 1959 Weidenfeld & Nicolson edition with the following autograph: "To Graham Greene whose courageous support of this book will be always gratefully remembered by Vladimir Nabokov Nov. 2, 1959. London."[28] Greene subsequently sold his 1955 copy of *Lolita* to the London bookseller R. A. Gekoski.[29] Both editions of *Lolita* from Greene's personal library eventually ended up in the collection of Roger Rechler, which was auctioned by Christie's in 2002.[30]

The Graham Greene Collection at Boston College also contains a trove of clippings detailing the controversy around *Lolita* and its British publication, some of them provided by a clipping service.

The Burns Library also owns seven books by Nabokov from Greene's personal library, six of them with the bookplates "From the Library of Graham Greene."

They include unsigned copies of *Mary; King, Queen, Knave; The Defense; Despair; Laughter in the Dark; Invitation to a Beheading; and Speak, Memory*, all British editions from the 1960s–1980s, but not the 1955 Olympia Press or 1959 Weidenfeld & Nicolson British editions of *Lolita* with Nabokov's autographs.

Greene would outlive Nabokov by almost fourteen years, and he remained a reader of Nabokov's fiction and nonfiction. His copies of the 1968 clothbound Weidenfeld & Nicolson edition of *King, Queen, Knave* and of the 1969 Penguin Books paperback of *Speak, Memory* contain notes that await their investigator. In his copy of *Speak, Memory*, Greene marked, in Chapter Six, the famous passage on beauty and patterning in nature, which begins this way: "The mysteries of mimicry had a special attraction for me. Its phenomena showed an artistic perfection usually associated with man-wrought things."[31]

***

28 Christie's Live Auction 1098, Masterpiece of World Literature from the Library of Roger Rechler, 2002, Nabokov Lots, Vladimir Nabokov, *Lolita* (London: Weidenfeld & Nicolson, 1959), 2 vols., Graham Greene's copy autographed by Nabokov, accessed February 7, 2024. https://www.christies.com/lot/lot-3984254?ldp_breadcrumb=back&intObjectID=3984254&from=salessummary&lid=1.

29 *Tolkien's Gown and Other Stories of Great Authors and Rare Books*, chapter 1, "Lolita," R. A. Gekoski, accessed February 7, 2022. https://gekoski.com/tolkiens-gown-and-other-stories-of-great-authors-and-rare-books/.

30 Christie's Live Auction 1098, Masterpiece of World Literature from the Library of Roger Rechler, 2002, accessed February 7, 2024. https://www.christies.com/en/auction/masterpieces-of-modern-literature-library-of-roger-rechler-17472/.

31 Vladimir Nabokov, *Speak, Memory: An Autobiography Revisited* (Harmondsworth: Penguin Books, 1969), 98; Graham Greene's Personal Library, John J. Burns Library, Boston College.

Figure 6. *Lolita*-related clippings. Graham Greene's Papers, John J. Burns Library, Boston College.

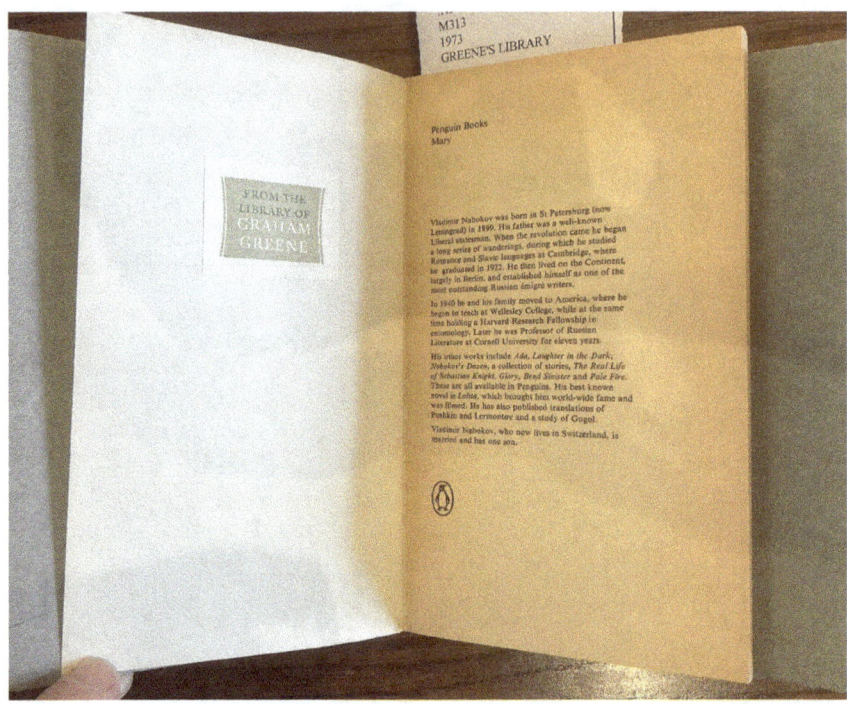

Figure 7. Copy of the 1973 Penguin Books edition of *Mary* from Graham Greene's library. John J. Burns Library, Boston College.

Figure 8. Books by Nabokov from Graham Greene's personal library. John J. Burns Library, Boston College.

Yet there is still more to Vladimir Nabokov's presence on the Boston College campus. In the autumn of 2023 I participated in a literary event at John J. Burns Library. I arrived early, entered the building from the Commonwealth Avenue side, and walked up the steps and down the corridor in the direction of the main reading room. The first door on the left is the O'Brien Fine Print Room. I went in, and on the left side wall, in the last of the middle section of five bookcases, I was surprised to see a trio of painted terracotta sculptures by Michael de Lisio, the American sculptor and poet and son of Italian immigrants best known for his three-dimensional enactments of famous photographs of artists and writers.[32] In the O'Brien Fine Print Room, three artists—not the likeliest bedfellows on the postwar art scene—share the same shelf. All three of them appear to resist having been forced into a group portrait: Sarah Caldwell, conductor and visionary leader of the Opera Company of Boston; Pablo Picasso; Vladimir Nabokov.[33]

De Lisio's 1968 bust of Nabokov was based on a 1962 photograph that Horst Tappe took in Zermatt, Switzerland, where Nabokov was hunting for butterflies. Part of the earliest sequence in a long series of photos Tappe would take in the 1960s and 1970s, the Zermatt picture of a mirthful Nabokov wearing a hooded rain jacket became one of the writer's most famous images. How did this Nabokov bust end up at Boston College?

In June–September 1998 Boston College's McMullen Museum of Art held a retrospective titled *Artists and Writers: Sculptures by Michael de Lisio*.[34] On display were fifteen individual sculptures, among them Henry James, Gertrude Stein, W. H. Auden, Evelyn Waugh (whose *Brideshead Revisited* carries echoes of Nabokov's *The Real Life of Sebastian Knight*),[35] a sculpture of Sarah Caldwell almost identical to the one currently on display at the Burns Library, and a

32 Roberta Smith, "Michael de Lisio, 91, Sculptor Who Turned Photos into Statues," *New York Times*, February 2, 2003, https://www.nytimes.com/2003/02/02/nyregion/michael-de-lisio-91-sculptor-who-turned-photos-into-statues.html.

33 Michael de Lisio, *Sarah Caldwell*; *Pablo Picasso*; *Vladimir Nabokov*. Painted terracotta. McMullen Museum of Art 2018.37; 2018.36; 2018.32. On display at John J. Burns Library.

34 See "Michael de Lisio: Artists & Writers," Boston College Libraries, accessed November 27, 202, https://library.bc.edu/past/libraries/about/exhibits/burns/delisio.html; Alston Conley, ed., *Artists and Writers: Sculpture by Michael de Lisio*, (Chestnut Hill: McMullen Museum of Art, Boston College 1998), https://catalog.hathitrust.org/Record/102132295.

35 On Nabokov and Waugh, see Margarit Tadevosyan and Maxim D. Shrayer, "Thou Are Not Thou": Vladimir Nabokov and Evelyn Waugh," *Nabokovian* 50 (Spring 2003): 24–39.

Figure 9. Sculptures of Sarah Caldwell, Pablo Picasso, and Vladimir Nabokov, by Michael de Lisio. O'Brien Fine Print Room, John J. Burns Library, Boston College, 2023. Photo by Maxim D. Shrayer.

Figure 10. Sculpture of Vladimir Nabokov, by Michael de Lisio. O'Brien Fine Print Room, John J. Burns Library, Boston College, 2023. Photo by Maxim D. Shrayer.

Figure 11. Photo of Vladimir Nabokov, by Horst Tappe. Zermatt, Switzerland, 1962. Fondation Horst Tappe.

different sculpture of Pablo Picasso. Of the ten participants in de Lisio's group portrait *Shakespeare and Company*, James Joyce and Ernest Hemingway make the most appearances in Nabokov's life and works.[36]

While the 1998 retrospective did not include a sculpture of Nabokov, twenty years later Boston College acquired de Lisio's bust of the author for its collections.[37] And while de Lisio's 1968 Nabokov greets the curious visitor and the impatient researcher with a half-smile and a countenance more skeptical than does the poet of winged nymphets in Tappe's 1962 photograph, one thing is certain: Nabokov is here to stay. Hence the main motivation behind this collection of essays *Nabokov on the Heights: New Studies from Boston College*.

***

In December 1995, when I was visiting Boston College as part of an on-campus job interview, my senior colleague Michael J. Connolly, then the chair of what used to be the Department of Slavic and Eastern Languages and Literatures, which has since grown to encompass Eastern, Slavic, and German Studies, floated the idea of offering a course on Vladimir Nabokov. A brilliant linguist and a student of Roman Jakobson, Professor Connolly proceeded to impersonate Jakobson making his deal-breaking comment at a 1957 meeting, when Harvard was considering Nabokov for a professorship of literature. Nabokov and Jakobson had planned to collaborate on an annotated English-language

---

36 On Nabokov and Joyce, See Nina Khaghany's essay in this volume. On Nabokov and Hemingway, see Yuri Leving, "Nabokov and Hemingway: The Fish That Got Away," in *Revising Nabokov Revising*, ed. Mitsuyoshi Numano and Tadashi Wakashima (Kyoto: The Nabokov Society of Japan, 2010), 137–144.

37 De Lisio's sculpture of Nabokov was acquired via the New York-based art critic Sanford Schwartz in May 2018. I am grateful to Christian Dupont for sharing this information and giving me close access to the three de Lisio sculptures at the Burns Library.

Figure 11. Boston Elevated Railway System Map, 1940. Wikimedia.[38]

---

38   See "1940 Boston Elevated Railway System Map," Wikimedia Commons, last modified April 4, 2023, https://commons.wikimedia.org/wiki/File:1940_Boston_Elevated_Railway_system_map.png.

edition of *The Tale of the Igor Campaign*, but later feuded.[39] Jakobson opposed Nabokov's candidature, and when others pointed out that Nabokov was a great writer, Jakobson remarked, all his consonants palatalized beyond recognition: "An elephant may be a great animal, but would you make him a professor of zoology?" Professor Connolly had heard the anecdote from the late Lawrence G. Jones, Jakobson's former graduate student and research collaborator. It was Professor Jones who had established Slavic studies at Boston College in 1969.

With Professor Connolly's support, we have made Nabokov a regular feature of Boston College's course offerings in Slavic and English, and I could not be happier. Having first taught a Nabokov course in the spring semester of 1997, I have had the pleasure of offering lecture courses and seminars on him over the past twenty-seven years. Other colleagues in the English Department, notably the late Andrew von Hendy, have also taught works by Nabokov, and I was also delighted in welcoming new Boston College colleagues who have research interests in Nabokov studies: Kevin Ohi and Eric Weiskott. Both of them have contributed to this volume.

The idea for a collection of essays by Boston College students and faculty originated during the spring semester of 2023, when I was teaching a seminar on Nabokov. It was a remarkable group of undergraduate, MA, and PhD students, and from the very beginning it became apparent that the participants not only enjoyed unusual intellectual synergy but also wanted to make a contribution to Nabokov studies.

The present volume includes of a baker's dozen of essays by eight former participants of my Nabokov courses and three Boston College faculty members who work on Nabokov. Brief comments are therefore in order on the book's scope, structure, and themes. The collection opens with an essay by Eric Weiskott, a Boston College professor, who examines Nabokov's entire career through the prism of the "success motif," which finds its greatest articulation in Nabokov's first English-language novel, *The Real Life of Sebastian Knight*. In his provocative approach to reading Nabokov as a "gustatory" experience, Brendan McCourt provides a compelling argument for eating Nabokov's literary fruits and having them, too. Three scholars— Megumi DeMond, Nicholas Adler, and Katie Pelkey—investigate key aspects of Nabokov's sui generis poetics by looking at the figurations of painting, chess, death, and immortality in the writer's

39 On Nabokov and Jakobson, see Boyd, *Vladimir Nabokov: The American Years*, 145, 167, 215–217, 288, 302–303, 311. For a recent assessment, see Victoria A. Baene, "Past Tense: Nabokov and Jakobson," *Harvard Crimson*, 4 October 2012, https://www.thecrimson.com/article/2012/10/4/nobokov-jakobson-harvard-academy/.

Russian- and English-language works. Ciara Spencer and Fiona Steacy, whose chapters also originated in the 2023 Nabokov seminar, offer new perspectives on the interconnected themes of marriage, companionship, and authorship in Nabokov's art and life. Nina Khaghany, a recent graduate, and Kevin Ohi, a Boston College professor, zoom in on Nabokov's very famous works by giving us comprehensive studies of Nabokov's profound debt to Joyce in *Invitation to a Beheading* and of Nabokov's aesthetic fashioning of the "erotic child" in *Lolita*. The essays by Jared Hackworth, a recent MA student, and Samuel Peterson, a senior, add compelling layers of evidence to our growing understanding of Nabokov's postwar American contexts—suburbia, the Cold War, McCarthyism, and the civil rights era. In my own essay, I look at Nabokov's shifting views of and attitudes to religious apostasy from the interwar émigré years to the post-Shoah American years. And I am very pleased to include the photo essay by Matthew Lyberg, who took the first Nabokov course that I offered at Boston College. This nostalgic photo essay has its roots in Lyberg's senior honors thesis (in itself a tribute to a bygone era of Boston College's intellectual history), and it is heartening to see that after almost twenty-five years Lyberg, who learned photography in Nabokov's native St. Petersburg, is still drawn to the writer's Boston-area haunts.

***

I would like to dedicate this volume to the memory of Vladimir, Véra, and Dmitri Nabokov, a translingual family of immigrant artists who remained Russians and Jews and became Americans while living only a few short miles from the Heights.

M. D. S.
November 2024
Chestnut Hill, Mass.

Angst and Asymptote: The *Success* Motif in Nabokov's Fiction

Eric Weiskott

Introduction: Sebastian Knight's *Success* in *The Real Life of Sebastian Knight*

In Nabokov's *The Real Life of Sebastian Knight* (1941), the title character's second novel is *Success*. In it, a godlike narrator traces the universe's struggle to cause a certain man and woman to meet for the first time. *The Real Life of Sebastian Knight* is, significantly, Nabokov's first novel written directly in English after nine in Russian. He wrote the novel in Paris during lean years for his family and entered it (unsuccessfully) in a London literary competition, an attempt to translate his prowess in Russian fiction into another linguistic domain.[1] As such, *The Real Life of Sebastian Knight* may be expected to reflect obliquely on methods of novel writing and on the second acts (second novels, second languages, second halves) of literary careers. In the novel's most literary-critical chapter, Sebastian's half-brother V. summarizes the structure of *Success* this way:

> if [Knight's] first novel is based on methods of literary composi-
> tion,—the second one deals mainly with the methods of human
> fate. With scientific precision in the classification, examination
> and rejection of an immense amount of data (the accumulation

I thank my colleague Maxim D. Shrayer for commenting on an earlier version of this essay.

1   Brian Boyd, *Vladimir Nabokov: The Russian Years* (Princeton, NJ: Princeton University Press, 2016), 496. On the Nabokov family's situation in those years see ibid., 480, 485–489, 492–496.

of which is rendered possible by the fundamental assumption that an author is able to discover anything he may want to know about his characters, such capacity being limited only by the manner and purpose of his selection in so far as it ought to be not a haphazard jumble of worthless details but a definite and methodical quest), Sebastian Knight devotes the three hundred pages of *Success* to one of the most complicated researches that has ever been attempted by a writer. We are informed that a certain commercial traveller Percival Q [. . .] meets the girl [. . .] with whom he will be happy ever after . . . This is the formula: quite uninteresting if viewed as an actual happening, but becoming a source of remarkable mental enjoyment and excitement, when examined from a special angle . . .

We learn a number of curious things. The two lines which have finally tapered to the point of meeting are really not the straight lines of a triangle which diverge steadily towards an unknown base, but wavy lines, now running wide apart, now almost touching. In other words there have been at least two occasions in these two peoples' lives when unknowingly to one another they all but met. In each case fate seemed to have prepared such a meeting with the utmost care . . . But, every time, a minute mistake (the shadow of a flaw, the stopped hole of an unwatched possibility, a caprice of free will) spoils the necessitarian's pleasure and the two lives are diverging again with increased rapidity.[2]

The motif is of "two lives" tracing "two lines" that asymptotically approach one another numerous times over. Nabokov casts *Success* as Sebastian Knight's breakout literary success. (*Nomen est omen.*) Albeit displaced into the unreal realm of unreadable because fictitious novels, a favorite theme of Nabokov's (the eponymous novel at issue in the short story "The Admiralty Spire," 1933, Van Veen's *Letters from Terra* in *Ada or Ardor: A Family Chronicle*, 1969, and many more), *Success* is an otherworldly double of several actual fictions by Nabokov that appeared both before and after *The Real Life of Sebastian Knight*. This essay surveys the forebodings and reverberations of this motif across Nabokov's fiction, with particular attention to *The Gift* (1952; serialized 1937–1939) and *Ada or Ardor*. I argue that the *Success* motif exemplifies Nabokov's playful metaphysics,

2   Vladimir Nabokov, *The Real Life of Sebastian Knight* (Norfolk, CT: New Directions, 1941; repr. New York: Vintage, 1992), 93–95.

his theory of the absolute value of the literary work, his inclination toward self-reference, and the exacting aesthetic economy of his moral universe. If Nabokov takes ecstatic pleasure in playing God ("an author is able to discover anything he may want to know about his characters"), he equally derives morbid satisfaction from painting blemishes ("a minute mistake") into his own designs.[3] It is for Nabokov literature, and in particular the novel with its wide scope for multiple focalization and multidirectional to-ings and fro-ings, that can contain both gestures.

Earlier Fiction: Russian

The first articulation of the *Success* motif in Nabokov's fiction may be the short story "A Matter of Chance" (1924), in which a suicidal Russian émigré husband, unbeknownst to him, comes agonizingly close to a reunion with his recently expatriated wife after a five-year absence. The action takes place on a fast train bound from Berlin to Paris. As we shall see, most iterations of the *Success* motif in Nabokov involve a man and a woman who were, are, or are to become romantically involved. Fate strives "with the utmost care" to effect the reunion in "A Matter of Chance," but best-laid plans are spoiled by a series of inconveniences and human shortcomings: the husband Aleksey's cocaine-induced neglect to place a familiar face (that of Princess Ukhtomski, known to the couple from prerevolutionary Russia, and now by chance sharing a compartment with Aleksey's wife Elena); the abrupt uncoupling of the diner car in which Aleksey works from the carriage in which Elena dozes; the failure of Aleksey's German colleague to understand the Cyrillic-alphabet inscription on Elena's misplaced wedding ring. Like one part of *Success*, "A Matter of Chance" anatomizes a missed connection. "[T]he necessitarian's pleasure" is obstructed by human frailty and negligence of the meaningful detail—"He could not understand why the face of the old lady with the sandwich had disturbed him so deeply"—but also by an axiom concerning exile that Nabokov upheld in literature as in life, namely that there is no going back.[4] The curtain of exile can be pressed into the

---

3   Cf. ibid. 88, V.'s description of the day on which Sebastian Knight completed *Success*: "The door opens. Sebastian Knight is disclosed lying spread-eagled on the floor of his study. Clare is making a neat bundle of the typed sheets on the desk. The person who entered stops short. / 'No, Leslie,' says Sebastian from the floor, 'I'm not dead. I have finished building a world, and this is my Sabbath rest.'"

4   Vladimir Nabokov, *The Stories of Vladimir Nabokov*, [ed. and trans. Dmitri Nabokov] (New York: Knopf, 1995; repr. New York: Vintage, 1997, with additions 2002, 2006, 2008), 58.

thinnest, nearly diaphanous fabric in "A Matter of Chance" yet, with a fatality that is the trick of literary design, can never be torn. This is the *Success* motif at its most asymptotic. Neither Aleksey nor Elena realize how close they had come. The never-realized consummation of fate's design becomes sublated into the short story form. Only readers, not the characters, appreciate the full import of what has transpired.

Nabokov's handling of the *Success* motif illustrates his non-utilitarian conception of literary value. The literary work possesses value, for Nabokov, insofar as it eschews concerted philosophical, political, or other didactic commitments and transcends its historical conditions.[5] "'[R]eality,'" he permits Charles Kinbote to aver in *Pale Fire* (1962), "is neither the subject nor the object of true art which creates its own special reality having nothing to do with the average 'reality' perceived by the communal eye."[6] On this particular topic, not much daylight separates Kinbote from Nabokov.[7]

Completion of "A Matter of Chance" preceded publication of the first of Nabokov's novels. As Maxim D. Shrayer observes with reference to "A Matter of Chance" and "The Seaport" (1924), "the early short stories frequently served as test-sites for future explosions of style and theme."[8] "A Matter of Chance" has an affinity with Nabokov's first novel, *Mary* (1926). Here again the axiom that exile is forever thwarts a hoped-for reunion of man and woman by a trick of literary design. In this case the pair are not husband and wife but the title character and the protagonist, her ex-lover Lev Glebovich Ganin, who intends to intercept her on her way to meet her husband in Berlin. (*That* reunion presumably does succeed, after all, off-stage.) When the title character Mary (Mashen'ka in the original Russian) is on the point of arriving, Lev Glebovich abruptly departs Berlin

---

In "The Visit to the Museum" (1939), the narrator inadvertently returns via a tortuous museum and finds Soviet Russia all too real but himself a "semiphantom" there. See ibid., 284–285 (quotation at 285). In *Look at the Harlequins!* (1974), Vadim Vadimovich does choose to go back, incognito, and finds his hometown of St. Petersburg unrecognizable. The ending of the novel casts doubt on Vadim's reliability as a narrator and concrete reality as a person.

5   These attitudes, which react against the utilitarian/historicist theories of human being advanced by Charles Darwin in biology, Karl Marx in economics, and Sigmund Freud in psychoanalysis, have their own historical and political partiality. See generally Dana Dragunoiu, *Vladimir Nabokov and the Poetics of Liberalism* (Evanston, IL: Northwestern University Press, 2011), and Will Norman, *Nabokov, History and the Texture of Time* (New York: Routledge, 2012).

6   Vladimir Nabokov, *Pale Fire* (New York: Putnam, 1962; repr. New York: Vintage, 1989), 130.

7   Maxim D. Shrayer points out to me that the two full names Charles Kinbote (cf. V. Botkin) and Vladimir Nabokov share most letters, although they fall short of being anagrams.

8   Maxim D. Shrayer, *The World of Nabokov's Stories* (Austin: University of Texas Press, 1999), 28.

and *Mary* ends. The difference from "A Matter of Chance" is that this outcome is no contingent mistake:

> As Ganin looked up at the skeletal roof in the ethereal sky he realized with merciless clarity that his affair with Mary was ended forever. It had lasted no more than four days—four days which were perhaps the happiest days of his life. But now he had exhausted his memories, was sated by them, and the image of Mary [...] now remained in the house of ghosts, which itself was already a memory.
>   Other than that image no Mary existed, nor could exist.
>   [...]
>   Then he picked up his suitcases, hailed a taxi and told the driver to go to a different station at the other end of the city. He chose a train...[9]

Whereas in "A Matter of Chance" Nabokov indulges in the perverse desire to muddy fate's grand design, in *Mary* he takes the motif a step further, redirecting readers' frustration from fate to an individual character's "caprice of free will." There is no intrinsic reason for Ganin's decision not to meet Mary, and that is the point. This is the concluding page of *Mary*. Ganin's change of mind is not marked within the novel as a "mistake," minute or otherwise; it emerges as the surprising culmination, retrospectively inevitable, of Nabokov's study of exile, longing, and malice. Ganin has learned, and the novel teaches, a "merciless" lesson about the irreversibility of loss and the pricelessness of memory.

Nabokov's first novel, published when the author was twenty-seven years old, lacks something of the inwoven intricacy of his later fiction. Even his second novel, *King, Queen, Knave* (1928; revised in translation 1968) is markedly more sophisticated and multidimensional. *Mary* bares the *Success* motif, first tried out in "A Matter of Chance," on its very surface, bending the trick of the narrowly missed connection into the form of the novel as such. In a sense, then, when many years later Nabokov's creation and transitional representative V. was to praise *Success*, this was also Nabokov alluding to his own entry into novel writing. There are other indications of mutual resonance between the young Knight and the young Nabokov. V.'s description of Sebastian's first

---

9   Vladimir Nabokov, *Mary*, trans. Michael Glenny (New York: McGraw-Hill, 1970; repr. New York: Vintage, 1989), 114.

novel, *The Prismatic Bezel*, resembles Nabokov's first, *Mary*, as Priscilla Meyer has observed.[10] *Mary* is uncharacteristic of Nabokov, and of his *Success* motif, in staging a purposefully missed connection, one that is evident in real time to characters themselves.

The extraordinarily vivid short story "Spring in Fialta" (1936) deserves mention in connection with the *Success* motif, although it works differently from the other fictions discussed in this essay.[11] The narrator Victor meets his lover Nina by chance over many years on no fewer than eleven separate occasions, the last of which unfolds in the present-tense frame of reference, while the other rendezvous subsist as Victor's memories.[12] Unlike the authoritative narrator of Sebastian Knight's *Success*, Victor is not in the omnipotent position of examining fate's inner workings dispassionately. And unlike in "A Matter of Chance" and *Mary*, there is no suspense about whether a meeting will come to pass. In "Spring in Fialta," which ends with Nina's death by traffic accident, fate is all too proficient a plotter. Victor wishes that fate had spared Nina in preference to her insufferably talented novelist/dramatist husband Ferdinand and his foppish friend Segur, "those salamanders of fate, those basilisks of good fortune,"[13] but the story discloses, in the end, a morose rather than jocose metaphysical economy, just as Victor's final interview with Nina reveals that she does not reciprocate his feelings for her.

Nabokov wrote "Spring in Fialta" amid his largest novel project to date, *The Gift*.[14] *The Gift* was self-consciously the summation of Nabokov's career as a Russophone fiction writer.[15] The liaison between Fyodor Konstantinovich

10 Priscilla Meyer, *Nabokov and Indeterminacy: The Case of "The Real Life of Sebastian Knight"* (Evanston, IL: Northwestern University Press, 2018), 42. Meyer points to the surreal coalescence of country house and boardinghouse in *Mary* and in V.'s description of *The Prismatic Bezel*. *The Gift*, too, contrasts country house and boardinghouse.

11 The story was a favorite of Nabokov's. On its Chekhovian subtext, see Shrayer, *World of Nabokov's Stories*, 207–237.

12 Nabokov, *Stories of Vladimir Nabokov*, 415–416 (no. 1), 418–420 (nos. 2–4), 424–425 (nos. 5–9), 428 (no. 10). Cf. Nabokov, *Stories of Vladimir Nabokov*, 423: "I still wonder what exactly she meant to me [. . .] and still less do I understand what was the purpose of fate in bringing us constantly together."

13 Ibid., 429.

14 Shrayer, *World of Nabokov's Stories*, 220.

15 For example, characters from Nabokov's prior novels sit on the Committee of the Society of Russian Writers in Germany: Podtyagin (*Mary*), Luzhin (*The Defense*, 1930), and Zilanov (*Glory*, 1932). See Vladimir Nabokov, *The Gift*, trans. Michael Scammell (New York: Putnam, 1963; repr. New York: Vintage, 1991), 317, and Alexander Dolinin, "*The Gift*," in *The Garland Companion to Vladimir Nabokov*, ed. Vladimir E. Alexandrov (New York: Garland, 1995), 135–169, at 151–152. In addition to the three exact correspondences noticed by Dolinin, I would claim the seedy Gurman in *The Gift* as a garbled revenant of Hermann Karlovich, the

Godunov-Cherdyntsev and Zina Mertz occupies the center of the novel's action, transpiring over the course of the long Chapter 3 (of five). Fyodor could have met Zina in Chapter 1, wrapping *The Gift* up in no time, as it were, but he declines an all-important yet apparently mundane invitation:

> "Listen," he said, spitting at my chin, "why don't you let me introduce you to Margarita Lorentz—she has told me to bring you over some night—do come, we hold little soirées at the studio—you know, with music, sandwiches, red lampshades—a lot of young people come—the Polonski girl, the Shidlovski brothers, Zina Mertz ..."
>
> These names were unknown to me; I felt no desire to spend evenings in the company of Vsevolod Romanov, nor did Lorentz's pug-faced wife interest me in any way—so not only did I not accept the invitation, but since that time I began avoiding the artist.[16]

The name Zina Mertz is unknown to the reader, too, at this point. The passage acquires an ironic and fatidic tinge only retroactively, upon reaching Chapter 3. There, Zina reappears as the one confirmed reader of Fyodor's *Poems*. Concurrently, she resurfaces in the person of Fyodor's landlady's daughter, whom Fyodor first overhears through the wall and then views in the flesh. He had rented the room despite the disagreeableness of the landlady's new husband Boris Shchyogolev, because of a glimpse of what Fyodor took to be the daughter's shimmering "pale bluish" dress.[17] At table, Fyodor catches her "graceful languor" but not her name, as on this occasion she remains silent, so he is as yet unable to connect her with Romanov's invitation.[18] First named but unheard of, then heard but unseen, then seen but unheard, Zina comes to Fyodor in waves, like

---

murderous narrator of *Despair*. The Slavic form of *Herman* is *German*. Russian *gurman*, so spelled, corresponds to English/French gourmand. In the company of three of Nabokov's characters, *Gurman* could be read or heard as a playful interlingual blending of Hermann and gourmand. Gratitude to Maxim D. Shrayer for advice on Slavic phonology.

16 Nabokov, *The Gift*, 59. Cf. Nabokov, *The Gift*, 177: "When he had first moved in with the Shchyogolevs and seen her for the first time he had had the feeling that he already knew a great deal about her, that even her name had been long familiar to him, and certain characteristics of her life, but until he spoke to her he was unable to make out whence and how he knew it."

17 Ibid., 144.

18 Ibid., 158.

reality does for one awakening from a dream.[19] Finally, with the suddenness of a revelation, she is his girlfriend, whom he is to meet where they "usually met."[20]

As in *Success*, it emerges that fate had furnished the young couple with several other early opportunities for a meeting, as when Zina hears Fyodor read at an "evening of poetry," or when Fyodor is asked to help her with a German translation.[21] The very opening scene of the novel expresses a never-surmounted single degree of social separation between the two lovers, the Lorentzes, who own the belongings depicted in loving detail being loaded into a house. Such is the bounty of Fyodor's destiny that he pays no price for his prejudgment of Romanov and the Lorentzes or his inattention during a poetry reading. Zina "was [...] cleverly and elegantly made to measure for him by a very painstaking fate."[22] Many of Nabokov's characters sense that "there glimmered in the mist some exquisite event which was just about to happen";[23] Fyodor is practically unique in being correct that the promised event will be exquisite.

Stephen H. Blackwell has argued that Zina functions as an avatar of Nabokov's ideal reader.[24] If so, in *The Gift* Nabokov causes the *Success* motif to play out a drama of readerly cooperation.[25] As opposed to the bitterness of *Mary* or the desperate deaths capping off "A Matter of Chance" and "Spring in Fialta," the repeated identification of Zina with the encouragement of a brilliant young writer suffuses the motif of the missed connection in *The Gift* with redemptive warmth. There is very little angst here.[26] Nevertheless, it remains recognizably a

---

19 Possibly relevant to Zina's narrative function is the fact that *Zina* forms the final syllables of *Mnemozina*, "Mnemosyne" (goddess of memory) in Russian. Nabokov's first choice of a title for his memoir was *Speak, Mnemosyne*.

20 Nabokov, *The Gift*, 176.

21 Ibid., 70 (translation help), 180 (quotation), 182 (translation help), 363 (translation help).

22 Ibid., 177.

23 Ibid., 179.

24 Stephen H. Blackwell, *Zina's Paradox: The Figured Reader in Nabokov's "Gift"* (New York: Lang, 2000).

25 Rather than restricting his focus to Fyodor's diegetic relationship with Zina, Blackwell claims for Zina the position of implied co-creator of *The Gift*, venturing onto shakier interpretive ground. See Jane Grayson, review of *Zina's Paradox*, by Stephen Blackwell, *Slavonic and East European Review* 80 (2002): 122–124, at 124, and Paul D. Morris, review of *Zina's Paradox*, by Stephen Blackwell, *Nabokov Studies* 6 (2000/2001): 209–212, at 212. Blackwell reads Zina in relation to Fyodor and his book as one would read Ada Veen in relation to Van Veen and his book in *Ada or Ardor*. See Blackwell, *Zina's Paradox*, 171n16, and Priscilla Meyer, review of *Zina's Paradox*, by Stephen Blackwell, *Slavic Review* 60 (2001): 684–685, at 684. *See also Fiona Steacy's essay in this volume (M.D.S.)*

26 In an unpublished continuation of *The Gift*, Nabokov meant to kill off Zina, however. The mode of death, a traffic accident, was the same as for (the rhymingly named) Nina in "Spring in Fialta." See Jane Grayson, "Washington's Gift: Materials Pertaining to Nabokov's *Gift* in the

version of the same motif. Because Fyodor partly is, and partly is not, the author of *The Gift* itself, the fated-encounter motif in this novel is less clinical than V. describes *Success* to be.

An even deeper metafictional self-reference joins *The Gift* to *The Real Life of Sebastian Knight*, Nabokov's immediately subsequent novel.[27] In the final scene of *The Gift*, Fyodor and Zina discuss how many times their first meeting had been thwarted by "a hitch that almost ruined everything."[28] "Fate made a second attempt, simpler this time but promising better success . . ."[29] The trick that finally worked, the bluish dress glimpsed by Fyodor while touring Shchyogolev's apartment, turns out to have been a false façade, for the dress was not Zina's. Given that the match has already succeeded, the exchange has a playful tone with exultant undertones. Fyodor marvels at what an inept novelist fate is and declares to Zina that he will make this theme, that is, the *Success* motif, the subject of his first novel. In the first instance, *The Gift* itself answers to purpose. The ending, if read analeptically alongside the central scenes from Chapter 3 and Fyodor's earlier contiguities to Zina known to the reader, retroactively reveals the *Success* motif to be the novel's main thread.[30] The author-protagonist who concludes the work by beginning to write it is a device familiar from, for example, Geoffrey Chaucer's *Book of the Duchess* and *Parliament of Fowls* and William Langland's *Piers Plowman*, not to mention Marcel Proust's *À la recherche du temps perdu*,[31] with the difference that Fyodor's authorship of *The Gift* is never explicitly claimed, except in a dream reunion with his late/missing father.[32] Nabokov followed through on Fyodor's plans a second time when conjuring up *Success* for Sebastian Knight. Fyodor's "chess idea for his as yet hardly planned 'novel'" in

---

Library of Congress," *Nabokov Studies* 1 (1994): 21–67, at 42–46; Yuri Leving, *Keys to "The Gift": A Guide to Nabokov's Novel* (Boston, MA: Academic Studies Press, 2011), 172–177; and Boyd, *Vladimir Nabokov*, 505–506, 516–517.

27 I pass over the Russian novella *The Enchanter* (1986; written 1939).

28 Nabokov, *The Gift*, 364.

29 Ibid., 363.

30 On analeptic reading, see Lauren Elizabeth Wilwerding, "Singular Plots: Female Vocation and Radical Form in the Nineteenth-Century Novel" (PhD diss., Boston College, 2017). See also Dolinin, *"The Gift,"* 163; Tom Whalen, "'And so the password is—?': Nabokov and the Ethics of Rereading," in *Nabokov and the Question of Morality: Aesthetics, Metaphysics, and the Ethics of Fiction*, ed. Michael Rodgers and Susan Elizabeth Sweeney (New York: Palgrave, 2016), 21–32; and Meyer, *Nabokov and Indeterminacy*, 4–5. Nabokov famously decreed, "The good reader [. . .] is a rereader." See Vladimir Nabokov, *Lectures on Literature*, ed. Fredson Bowers, with an introduction by John Updike (New York: Harcourt Brace Jovanovich/ Bruccoli Clark, 1980), 3.

31 See Nabokov, *Lectures on Literature*, 210–211.

32 Nabokov, *The Gift*, 355.

his creator's last Russian novel became a set piece in Nabokov's chess-infused first English novel through "a knight's move, a change of shadows, a shift that displaces the mirror."[33]

Later Fiction: English

The Gift inculcates in more vivid tones than any other Nabokov novel a sensation its author always claimed to be able to feel, a novel as yet unrealized but "specifically promised" to perception as a textural whole.[34] *Success* resembles *The Real Life of Sebastian Knight* itself as well as Nabokov's earlier Russian novels, and also, eerily, his future English ones, as if Sebastian's resume were Nabokov's recipe for a career as an English novelist.[35] Three English novels stand out in the present context.

Pale Fire is tantamount to *Success* comically subjectivized. The chance meeting between the poet John Shade and the assassin Jakob Gradus alias Jack Grey occurs in the mind of deranged commentator Charles Kinbote alias Charles II of Zembla. It is a missed connection, both for Kinbote, who believes Gradus means to assassinate him on behalf of a revolutionary organization, and for readers, who infer that a psychotic Grey killed Shade because he mistook him for the judge who had him locked away. Substitution of voluntary manslaughter, man to man, for the heterosexual romance of the other *Success* narratives suits *Pale Fire*'s preoccupation with untimely death and the novel's anxious imaginative response to queer desire, a response mirrored more than analyzed by some Nabokovian critics.[36]

---

33 Ibid., 239 (second quotation), 363 (first quotation); Grayson, "Washington's Gift," 51 (*The Gift* and *The Real Life of Sebastian Knight* connected by a knight's move); and Meyer, *Nabokov and Indeterminacy*, 49 (*The Real Life of Sebastian Knight* and chess). See also Nick Adler's chapter in this volume.

34 Nabokov, *The Gift*, 55. Intimations of yet-to-be-written works, by Nabokov and by his characters, include: Nabokov, *Stories of Vladimir Nabokov*, 225, *The Defense*, trans. Michael Scammell (New York: Putnam, 1964; repr. New York: Vintage, 1990), 82, *Invitation to a Beheading*, trans. Dmitri Nabokov (New York: Putnam, 1959; repr. New York: Vintage, 1989), 209, *The Gift*, 171, 194, 199–200, *Lectures on Literature*, 379, *Bend Sinister* (New York: Holt, 1947; repr. New York: Vintage, 1990), 157, *Strong Opinions* (New York: McGraw-Hill, 1973), 69, 178, 309–310, and *Look at the Harlequins!* (New York: McGraw-Hill, 1974), 120–123.

35 For the strange habit Knightian characters have of invading V.'s reality, see Susan Fromberg, "The Unwritten Chapters in *The Real Life of Sebastian Knight*," *Modern Fiction Studies* 13 (1967–1968): 427–442, at 432–440.

36 See Kevin Ohi, "Narcissism and Queer Reading in *Pale Fire*," *Nabokov Studies* 5 (1998/1999): 153–178. Ohi criticizes, as illustrative of a larger critical tendency, the work of Brian Boyd.

The space in which Gradus's asymptotic approach unfolds is less reality than Shade's "Pale Fire" as expounded by Kinbote.[37] Commenting on lines 17 and 29 of the poem, Kinbote remarks on the "extraordinary coincidence" of Shade's having subtextually referred to his own future killer.[38] The secret passages scoring King Charles's Zembla are always also secret passages of Shade's verse purportedly elucidated in Kinbote's prose. If in *The Gift* the *Success* motif traces a socially generative, straight (so to speak) writer-reader relation, in *Pale Fire* Nabokov inverts the zone of literary imagination. *Pale Fire* ends with Kinbote's feverish prediction of the recursion of its assassination plot, carried out by "a bigger, more respectable, more competent Gradus": the literary critic?[39]

Just as Victor in "Spring in Fialta" is powerless to deflect Nina's destiny, so Kinbote can only record, but can never alter, Gradus's gradual approach.[40] "And all the time he was coming nearer."[41] There are other points of similarity to Nabokov's previous *Success*-like plots. Gradus is comically bad at embodying the implacability of fate, as with destiny's halting efforts to bring Fyodor and Zina together in *The Gift*. A half-forgotten chance encounter with Gradus, belatedly recalled, lies in Kinbote's prerevolutionary past,[42] a flaw in historical memory comparable to Aleksey's puzzlement over Princess Ukhtomski's familiar face in "A Matter of Chance" or Fyodor's initial failure to recognize the Zina-shaped invitation fate was sending him. *Pale Fire* picks up the medievalizing overtones of the plot of *Success*, Sebastian Knight's "definite and methodical quest"

See esp. Ohi, "Narcissism and Queer Reading," 162: "A phobic reaction to homosexuality [...] allows Boyd to reduce the novel's difficulties of reading to a mere question of personal pathology." Imbricated within the question of the novel's processing of queerness is the controversy over whether (as Boyd initially held, before revising his views) Shade invented Kinbote, or vice versa, or neither.

37 Nabokov, *Pale Fire*, 78 ("We shall accompany Gradus in constant thought, as he makes his way from distant dim Zembla to green Appalachia, through the entire length of the poem, following the road of its rhythm, riding past in a rhyme, skidding around the corner of a run-on, breathing with the caesura . . ."), 136 ("The force propelling him is the magic action of Shade's poem itself"). Gradus's mission is synchronized with Shade's composition, down to the minute. See ibid., 151.

38 Ibid., 77.

39 Ibid., 301.

40 Cf. Vladimir Nabokov, *Transparent Things* (New York: McGraw-Hill, 1972), 92: "Direct interference in a person's life does not enter our scope of activity, nor, on the other, tralatitiously speaking, hand, is his destiny a chain of predeterminate links: some 'future' events may be likelier than others, O. K., but all are chimeric, and every cause-and-effect sequence is always a hit-and-miss affair, even if the lunette has actually closed around your neck, and the cretinous crowd holds its breath."

41 Nabokov, *Pale Fire*, 273.

42 Ibid., 293–294.

(note the hero's Arthurian name Percival) for metaphysical knowledge trans-lated into Gradus's "quest" to hunt down and assassinate the King of Zembla.[43] *The Gift* and *Pale Fire* stand apart from Nabokov's other novels in thrusting the *Success* motif into the foreground of the design. It is the note on which they both end and the theme that reverberates backwards through their "immense amount of data": but what a difference between the two novels in the handling! The kinds of metafictional/metaphysical fun *The Gift* and *Pale Fire* have are quite distinct.[44]

A fateful meeting between incestuous lovers Van and Ada Veen, preceded by near misses, makes up one strand of the substantial weft of *Ada or Ardor*. Around the midpoint of the massive Part 1, a novel unto itself, Ada and Van classify and examine their accumulated asymptotic approaches.[45] At first meet-ing, fate affords six-year-old Ada only a "charming glimpse" of eight-year-old Van.[46] In keeping with Nabokov's leading men's forgetfulness (as Aleksey forgets Princess Ukhtomski in "A Matter of Chance," or as Fyodor forgets having heard Zina's name before meeting her in *The Gift*, or as Kinbote forgets having waved to Gradus once), Van remembers nothing of this glimpsed moment. A second encounter preceding the years covered by Part 1 is even less certain:

> After carefully matching memories, Van and Ada concluded that it was not impossible that somewhere along a winding Riviera road they passed each other in rented victorias that both remem-bered were green, with green-harnessed horses, or perhaps in two different trains, going perhaps the same way, the little girl at the window of one sleeping car looking at the brown sleeper of a parallel train which gradually diverged toward sparkling

43 Ibid., 282. See Priscilla Meyer, *Find What the Sailor Has Hiden: Vladimir Nabokov's "Pale Fire"* (Middletown, CT: Wesleyan University Press, 1988), 41–98, and *Nabokov and Indeterminacy*, 30 (*Success*). More particularly, both novels reflect the genre conventions of the medieval romances that Nabokov studied at the University of Cambridge.

44 See Vladimir E. Alexandrov, *Nabokov's Otherworld* (Princeton: Princeton University Press, 1991), 108–136 (*The Gift*), 187–212 (*Pale Fire*). Alexandrov sought to prioritize metaphys-ics over metafiction, a corrective that made sense in Nabokov studies in the 1990s. However, Nabokov consistently interweaves the two topics, or rather metafiction comes to be the signature mode of his (and some of his more enlightened characters') access to metaphys-ics—as Alexandrov intermittently allowed himself to recognize. See Alexandrov, *Nabokov's Otherworld*, 18: "the metaliterary [in Nabokov] is camouflage for, and a model of, the meta-physical." What Alexandrov really opposed, and rightly so, was "the purely metaliterary view of Nabokov." See Alexandrov, *Nabokov's Otherworld*, 16.

45 Vladimir Nabokov, *Ada or Ardor: A Family Chronicle* (New York: McGraw-Hill, 1969), 149–153.

46 Ibid., 150.

stretches of sea that the little boy could see on the other side of the tracks. The contingency was too mild to be romantic, nor did the possibility of their having walked or run past each other on the quay of a Swiss town afford any concrete thrill. But as Van casually directed the searchlight of backthought into that maze of the past where the mirror-lined narrow paths not only took different turns, but used different levels (as a mule-drawn cart passes under the arch of a viaduct along which a motor skims by), he found himself tackling, in still vague and idle fashion, the science that was to obsess his mature years—problems of space and time, space versus time, time-twisted space, space as time, time as space—and space breaking away from time, in the final tragic triumph of human cogitation: I am because I die.[47]

The image of the diverging trains recalls the denouement of "A Matter of Chance." Tucked away in the vastness of Van's mega-memoir and referring to a year that falls outside the chronological scope of its romance narrative proper, the passage is subtly central to *Ada*. The indeterminacy of Ada and Van's 1881 crossing of paths establishes the overall method of composition of Part 1: the unaccountable contingency of romance, that is to say, the *Success* motif. A meeting "not impossible" yet unconfirmable can occur only in the space of imaginative writing, only for the reader's benefit. It can occur, moreover, only in mental retrospect, and the passage is Nabokov's most overt theorization of the analeptic reading that all his novels demand. The alert reader of Nabokov has no choice but to riffle the pages in search of an earlier detail flown from the mind's coop. This is most especially the case in *Ada*, where hundreds of pages of print and decades of narrative time can separate interlinked references.[48]

Whereas V. appoints Sebastian Knight to the role of godlike surveyor of an entirely coherent literary domain of Sebastian's own device, in practice, as we have seen, Nabokov's iterations of the *Success* motif frequently imagine a more fallible operation of "the searchlight of backthought." What Sebastian masters in the form of his *Success*, Van experiences as a convoluted "maze of the past." The risk that a character's or the narrator's memory might already have failed in some all-important particular is what lends a sense of risk to any collision of two lives in Nabokov.

---

47   Ibid., 153.
48   Cf. Nabokov, *Transparent Things*, 94: "Enforced re-creation of irrecoverable trivia."

In anatomizing a chance meeting between a man and a woman with suave omniscience, *Transparent Things* (1972) resembles V.'s description of *Success*. Here the *Success* motif bends back again, as it did in *Pale Fire*, from warmth into darkness. Early on, the novel's protagonist Hugh Person hires a prostitute, and while the encounter itself is sordid, is not described, and has no apparent auratic glow about it, unbeknownst to both of them the room where they lie hosted "a Russian novelist" in the previous century.[49] The novelist commands the narrator's attention in this short chapter ("the night-shirted, bare-necked, dark-tousled traveler whom we catch in the act of deciding what to take out of the valise").[50] His writings and personal manners are entirely gratuitous to this novel, except as a demonstration of the narrator's ability to "sin[k] into the history" of objects and persons at will.[51] (Recall V. on Sebastian Knight: "an author is able to discover anything he may want to know about his characters . . .")[52]

Subtextually composed by the Switzerland-based novelist R., *Transparent Things* reclaims, or pretends to reclaim, the omniscience characterizing *Success*.[53] Hugh and the Russian novelist miss their connection by a century. Meanwhile, Hugh will meet his ill-fated love interest Armande Chamar after boarding a train "by mistake," yet another staging of the *Success* motif aboard a locomotive (compare "A Matter of Chance," *Mary*, and *Ada or Ardor*). Fate flies under the radar: "The mechanism of their first acquaintance was ideally banal."[54] R.'s novel *Three Tenses* juxtaposes past, present, and future through—what else—a meeting of the protagonist's three girlfriends. The presence of the future beau ("Claire" / "C.," "his future wife")[55] imputes to R. again a Knightian omniscience about happenstance, an ability to pose a lifetime at a "special angle" for total examination. Armande "was [. . .] little aware of the future (which the author, of course, knew in every detail),"[56] and reading the novel analeptically one is invited to identify this author as R. Both Armande and R. perish over

---

49 Ibid., 17.
50 Ibid., 18.
51 Ibid., 1.
52 Nabokov, *The Real Life of Sebastian Knight*, 93.
53 The self-reference in *Transparent Things* to V.'s description of *Success* in *The Real Life of Sebastian Knight* may become overt in Armande's dubbing Hugh "Percy," which enhances the similarity to Knight's Percival. See Nabokov, *Transparent Things*, 43–49.
54 Both quotations since the previous note are from Nabokov, *Transparent Things*, 25. Cf. Nabokov, *Look at the Harlequins!* 137: "by a banal miracle of synchronization she came dancing down those very steps."
55 Nabokov, *Transparent Things*, 46.
56 Ibid., 47.

the course of *Transparent Things*, R. of liver disease and Armande at the hands of Hugh who murders her in *his* sleep, so that R.'s foreknowledge of Armande's fate acquires a spooky metaphysical aspect which it suits Nabokov to play up more in this novel than in any other, especially at the end when Hugh dies too. Hugh, who toils away for a publisher, has less literary aptitude or emotional insight than Sebastian in *The Real Life of Sebastian Knight*, Fyodor in *The Gift*, or Van in *Ada or Ardor*, more akin to Kinbote in *Pale Fire* in both respects—and he pays the price for it.

Nabokov's last complete novel, *Look at the Harlequins!* (1974), begins by sending up the *Success* motif that he had auditioned fifty years earlier in "A Matter of Chance":

> I met the first of my three or four successive wives in somewhat odd circumstances, the development of which resembled a clumsy conspiracy, with nonsensical details and a main plotter who not only knew nothing of its real object but insisted on making inept moves that seemed to preclude the slightest possibility of success. Yet out of those very mistakes he unwittingly wove a web, in which a set of reciprocal blunders on my part caused me to get involved and fulfill the destiny that was the only aim of the plot.[57]

This passage is the first of the novel's many red herrings. Vadim Vadimovich's fictitious memoir does not hinge on the circumstances of his meeting any of his wives, not even the unnamed last of them, "you," to whom he addresses the memoir. The *Success* motif never comes to the fore again, except, in quotation marks, in the supposed blurb of Vadim's *Lolita*-like novel *A Kingdom by the Sea*.[58] *Look at the Harlequins!* burlesques all of Nabokov's previous novels and has a particular affinity for the atmosphere and humor of *The Real Life of Sebastian Knight*. But the 1974 novel can never quite descend from parody long enough to become invested in any asymptotic relations.

---

57 Nabokov, *Look at the Harlequins!* 3.
58 Ibid., 216: "*All seems to end honky-donky* [sic!] [. . .] *had there not been running its chaotic course, in a sheef* [sheaf?] *of parallel lives beyond our happy couple's ken, the tragic tiny* [destiny?] *of Virginia Garden's inconsolable parents, Oliver and* [?]*, whom the clever author by every means in his power, prevents from tracking their daughter Dawn* [sic!!]." Bracketed commentary in the original.

Conclusion: Reading Nabokov at the Scale of the Career

The methodology tried out on Nabokov in this essay differs from how critics usually read him. Taking the span of his whole career and his use of a single motif as the parameters for analysis has justified a focus on *The Gift, The Real Life of Sebastian Knight*, and *Ada or Ardor*. The last of these I leave aside as having already ascended to a position of prominence in Nabokov studies and requiring no ex parte advocacy. *The Gift* has long been recognized as special, though its belated complete publication in Russian (1952) and its density of allusion to the Russian émigré literary scene in mid-century Berlin have impeded its full evaluation.[59] *The Real Life of Sebastian Knight* is a distinctly second-tier novel in critical estimation, with the honorable exception of Meyer's book-length study.[60] Although one might have expected Nabokov's oeuvre to be picked over by this late date, in fact the proportion of Anglophone scholarship directed toward the apical sequence *Lolita—Pnin—Pale Fire* (1955–1962), and to a lesser extent the next link in the chain, *Ada or Ardor*, to the detriment of the fourteen earlier and later novels (to say nothing of the plays, poetry, and short stories) is difficult to overstate.[61] Processes of canon-formation, with an unmistakable Anglocentric bias, have been hard at work in Nabokov studies. Now I obviously think the prevailing judgment that *The Real Life of Sebastian Knight* is second-rate Nabokov is wrong, but that is not really the point. Like an L-shaped move in chess, to centralize the sequence *The Gift—The Real Life of Sebastian Knight* changes the whole field of play, suggesting new emphases.

Furthermore, instead of delivering a traditional essay-length close reading of *The Real Life of Sebastian Knight*, I have traced a motif it introduces explicitly but which it shares with several of Nabokov's other novels. Nabokov, in a sense, wrote only one novel, but he wrote it eighteen different ways (nine times in Russian and nine in English). A shared form, like a fault line in a rock formation, renders apprehensible the shape a career has taken. Whatever else they are about, such as "the methods of human fate," Nabokov's novels are about methods of literary

---

59 Dolinin, "*The Gift*," 137–138.
60 Meyer, *Nabokov and Indeterminacy*.
61 The present collection forms an exception. But for example, of thirty-eight presentations whose titles announced or alluded to a Nabokovian text at the "Hidden Nabokov" conference in Wellesley, MA in June 2022, twenty-four dealt with *Lolita, Pale Fire, Pnin*, or *Ada or Ardor*. Papers on *The Gift*: one. Papers on all of Nabokov's other Russian novels combined: four. Papers on *The Real Life of Sebastian Knight*: zero. I recognize that, lacking Russian, I cannot fully profit from the significant Russian-language body of criticism on Nabokov's Russian fiction.

reading, a topic on which he held dogmatic and eccentric opinions. Of all his novels, the pivotal pair *The Gift—The Real Life of Sebastian Knight* are least coy about the methodological implications of his fictional making. The two novels emblematize Nabokov's determination to exalt the inutility of literature and to use the affordances of the career to do so. Thus I read Nabokov's novels and stories as a creative series, as self-revision, which can only be decomposed into constituent expressions ("novels") at the expense of interrupting the continuity and fluidity of reading at the scale of the career. In retracing the moves by which he arrived at each new articulation of self ("Artistic originality has only its own self to copy," he once opined—a characteristically double-edged assertion),[62] I have been working through the submerged stylistic correspondences between early and late, Russian and English. Read through the less-familiar chord change, *The Gift / The Real Life of Sebastian Knight / Ada, or Ardor*, with grace notes contributed by stories and other novels, Nabokov's career evokes "A feeling of fantastically planned, / Richly rhymed life."[63] Readers who focus only on one or two novels, or only on the Russian ones, or only the English ones, or who enforce a linguistic periodization of Nabokov's life, will miss the rhyme.

Bibliography

Primary Sources
Nabokov, Vladimir. *Ada or Ardor: A Family Chronicle*. New York: McGraw-Hill, 1969.
———. *Bend Sinister*. New York: Holt, 1947; repr. New York: Vintage, 1990.
———. *The Defense*. Translated by Michael Scammell in collaboration with the author. New York: Putnam, 1964; repr. New York: Vintage, 1990.
———. *The Gift*. Translated by Michael Scammell. New York: Putnam, 1963; repr. New York: Vintage, 1991.
———. *Invitation to a Beheading*. Translated by Dmitri Nabokov in collaboration with the author. New York: Putnam, 1959; repr. New York: Vintage, 1989.
———. *Lectures on Literature*. Edited by Fredson Bowers, with introduction by John Updike. New York: Harcourt Brace Jovanovich/Bruccoli Clark, 1980.
———. *Look at the Harlequins!* New York: McGraw-Hill, 1974.
———. *Mary*. Translated by Michael Glenny. New York: McGraw-Hill, 1970; repr. New York: Vintage, 1989.
———. *Pale Fire*. New York: Putnam, 1962; repr. New York: Vintage, 1989.
———. *The Real Life of Sebastian Knight*. Norfolk, CT: New Directions, 1941; repr. New York: Vintage, 1992.

62 Nabokov, *Strong Opinions*, 95.
63 Nabokov, *Pale Fire*, 68.

———. *The Stories of Vladimir Nabokov*. [Edited and translated by Dmitri Nabokov]. New York: Knopf, 1995; repr. New York: Vintage, 1997, and with additions 2002, 2006, 2008.

———. *Strong Opinions*. New York: McGraw-Hill, 1973.

———. *Transparent Things*. New York: McGraw-Hill, 1972.

Secondary Sources

Alexandrov, Vladimir E. *Nabokov's Otherworld*. Princeton, NJ: Princeton University Press, 1991.

Blackwell, Stephen H. *Zina's Paradox: The Figured Reader in Nabokov's "Gift."* New York: Lang, 2000.

Boyd, Brian. *Vladimir Nabokov: The Russian Years*. Princeton, NJ: Princeton University Press, 2016.

Dolinin, Alexander. "*The Gift*." In *The Garland Companion to Vladimir Nabokov*, edited by Vladimir E. Alexandrov, 135–169. New York: Garland, 1995.

Dragunoiu, Dana. *Vladimir Nabokov and the Poetics of Liberalism*. Evanston, IL: Northwestern University Press, 2011.

Fromberg, Susan. "The Unwritten Chapters in *The Real Life of Sebastian Knight*." *Modern Fiction Studies* 13 (1967–1968): 427–442.

Grayson, Jane. Review of *Zina's Paradox*, by Stephen Blackwell. *Slavonic and East European Review* 80 (2002): 122–124.

———. "Washington's Gift: Materials Pertaining to Nabokov's *Gift* in the Library of Congress." *Nabokov Studies* 1 (1994): 21–67.

Leving, Yuri. *Keys to "The Gift": A Guide to Nabokov's Novel*. Boston, MA: Academic Studies, 2011.

Meyer, Priscilla. Review of *Zina's Paradox*, by Stephen Blackwell. *Slavic Review* 60 (2001): 684–685.

———. *Find What the Sailor Has Hidden: Vladimir Nabokov's "Pale Fire."* Middletown, CT: Wesleyan University Press, 1988.

———. *Nabokov and Indeterminacy: The Case of "The Real Life of Sebastian Knight"*. Evanston, IL: Northwestern University Press, 2018.

Morris, Paul D. Review of *Zina's Paradox*, by Stephen Blackwell. *Nabokov Studies* 6 (2000/2001): 209–212.

Norman, Will. *Nabokov, History and the Texture of Time*. New York: Routledge, 2012.

Ohi, Kevin. "Narcissism and Queer Reading in *Pale Fire*." *Nabokov Studies* 5 (1998/1999): 153–178.

Shrayer, Maxim D. *The World of Nabokov's Stories*. Austin: University of Texas Press, 1999.

Whalen, Tom. "'And so the password is—?': Nabokov and the Ethics of Rereading." In *Nabokov and the Question of Morality: Aesthetics, Metaphysics, and the Ethics of Fiction*, edited by Michael Rodgers and Susan Elizabeth Sweeney, 21–32. New York: Palgrave, 2016.

Wilwerding, Lauren Elizabeth. "Singular Plots: Female Vocation and Radical Form in the Nineteenth-Century Novel." PhD diss., Boston College, 2017.

Unlimited Time: Visual Art and Temporality in Vladimir Nabokov's "La Veneziana" and "The Visit to the Museum"

Megumi DeMond

Introduction: Painting into the Otherworld

Vladimir Nabokov had a peerless gift for molding language into a picture on the page and constructing an altered sense of reality. Many scholars have written about the nature and role of time in his work as a key to unlocking his metaphysics.[1] Theorizing Nabokov's views of temporality has mainly concentrated on novels that present narrators or protagonists as writers, such as Fyodor

1   The specific works which examine Nabokov's metaphysics, at least in part through discussions of temporality, include: Gennady Barabtarlo, "Artistic Time," in *Insomniac Dreams: Experiments with Time by Vladimir Nabokov*, ed. Gennady Barabtarlo (Princeton: Princeton University Press, 2018), 159–192; Leonid Bilmes, "Description and Narration in Vladimir Nabokov's *Ada or Ardor*," in *Ekphrasis, Memory and Narrative after Proust: Prose Pictures and Fictional Recollection* (New York: Bloomsbury Academic, 2023), 87–116; Brian Boyd, "Nabokov, Time, and Timelessness: A Reply to Martin Hägglund," *New Literary History* 37, no. 2 (2006): 469–478, accessed March 29, 2023, doi:10.1353/nlh.2006.0032; Conall Cash, "Picturing Memory Puncturing Vision: Vladimir Nabokov's *Pale Fire*," in *The Goalkeeper: The Nabokov Almanac*, ed. Yuri Leving (Boston, MA: Academic Studies Press, 2010), 124–151, accessed March 29, 2023, https://doi.org/10.2307/j.ctt1zxsk4n; Martin Hägglund, "Chronophilia: Nabokov and the Time of Desire," *New Literary History* 37, no. 2 (2006): 447–467, accessed March 29, 2023, doi:10.1353/nlh.2006.0036; Lacy Mattison, "Nabokov's Aesthetic Bergsonism: An Intuitive, Reperceptualized Time," *Mosaic: An Interdisciplinary Critical Journal* 46 no. 1 (2013): 39, accessed March 29, 2023, http://www.jstor.org/stable/44030114; Leona Toker, "Philosophers as Poets: Reading Nabokov with Schopenhauer and Bergson," *Russian Literature TriQuarterly* 24 (1991): 185–196; "Nabokov and Bergson on Duration and Reflexivity," in *Nabokov's World: The Shape of Nabokov's World*, vol. 1, ed. Jane Grayson, Arnold McMillin, and Priscilla Meyer (New York: Palgrave, 2002), 132–140.

Godunov-Cherdyntsev in *The Gift* or Van Veen in *Ada, or Ardor* (originally, and aptly, titled *The Texture of Time*—still the title of the treatise Van Veen composes within the novel). Yet studies of the nature and texture of Nabokov's time have not focused extensively on the works that foreground visual arts—particularly painting, for which Nabokov possessed a lifelong passion.

Two of Nabokov's short stories of the interwar Russian émigré years, the early "La Veneziana" (1924; pub. 1995) and the late "The Visit to the Museum" (1938), demonstrate the connections between temporal theories and visual art that are present within the worlds of his fiction. The paintings in these stories play a central role in opening up their textual spaces to an otherworld. I use the term in keeping with Véra Nabokov's famous admission of "a key undercurrent . . . which permeates all that [Nabokov] has written and characterizes it like a kind of watermark . . . a strange otherworldliness, the 'hereafter' (*potustoronnost'*)," and to Vladimir E. Alexandrov's detailed exploration of the subject in *Nabokov's Otherworld*.[2] I will also lean on Maxim D. Shrayer's further elucidation of the term "otherworld," defined as "a sui generis dimension which exists simultaneously within the author's mundane reality and which is both a source and an addressee of artistic creation."[3] This otherworld comprises a distorted temporality, itself an inextricable element of reality.

Desire for Time and Art: Nabokovian Temporality

Understanding the influence of Bergsonian metaphysics on Nabokov's writing—and Nabokov's molding of Henri Bergson's theories into his own distinct metaphysics—is critical to grasping the puzzling layers of visual art in his texts.[4] In "La Veneziana" and "The Visit to the Museum," works of visual

---

2   Passage translated by Dmitri Nabokov in his essay, "Translating with Nabokov," in *The Achievements of Vladimir Nabokov*, ed. George Gibian and Stephen Jan Parker (Ithaca, NY: Cornell Center for International Studies, 1984), 174; see Vladimir Alexandrov's *Nabokov's Otherworld* (Princeton NJ: Princeton University Press, 1991).

3   Maxim D. Shrayer, "Writing and Reading the Otherworld," in *The World of Nabokov's Stories* (Brookline: Ladispoli Books, 2015; originally published in 1999 by University of Texas Press), Kindle; Shrayer focuses more on the role of spatiality in this otherworld.

4   I first encountered the connection between Nabokov and Bergson by way of Laci Mattison's article "Nabokov's Aesthetic Bergsonism: An Intuitive, Reperceptualized Time," *Mosaic: An Interdisciplinary Critical Journal* 46, no. 1 (March 2013), accessed March 29, 2023. Mattison draws on Leona Toker's seminal work on Nabokov and Bergson: "Philosophers as Poets: Reading Nabokov with Schopenhauer and Bergson" and "Nabokov and Bergson on Duration and Reflexivity." In doing so, Mattison argues the intricacies of how Nabokov "refines and extends Bergson," rather than focusing narrowly

art function as subversive temporal markers that demonstrate a distinctly
Bergsonian concept: the simultaneous existence of multiple realities, worlds
that cannot be intellectualized. Bergson's stance involves seeing time not
through the scientific lens—as discrete, measured units—but through an intuitive lens—as flowing together.[5] Like Bergson, whom Nabokov names among
thinkers who never "lost the glamour and thrill they held for me,"[6] Nabokov
recognized an unsegmented temporality achieved through intuition, which he
called the "pure element of time" and "time's common flow."[7] Yet Nabokov
the author and thinker departed from and extended Bergson's theories in
important ways. Leona Toker contends that Nabokov likely saw Bergson as a
"rival poet" rather than a "neutral spokesman."[8] Nabokov integrated the idea
of an unsegmented temporality *with space*, a decidedly non-Bergsonian category, through what Lacy Mattison calls "temporal layering"—a collapsing
and folding together of different moments in time (past, present, future), thus
creating multiple durations within one space.[9] This intuitive, temporal-spatial

---

on how Bergson influenced Nabokov. I draw on the work of Mattison and Toker, and also
on Hilary Lynn Fink's comprehensive interpretations of Bergson and Nabokov's theoretical cross-pollinations, as the basis for my interpretations of Nabokov's metaphysics in "La
Veneziana" and "The Visit to the Museum." Fink establishes Henri Bergson's influence on
the wider Russian modernist literary movement in "Bridging the Kantian Gap: Bergson
and Russian Modernism, 1900–1930" (PhD diss., Columbia University, 1996); she
argues that Russian modernists found particular resonance in Bergson's theories due to
their "theurgic impulse to transform reality through art," paralleling Bergson's emphasis
on "philosophical intuition—made manifest through art—in the process of self-creation
and participation in existence" (vi).

5   Bergson's notion of time calls for avoiding the spatialization of time—which he considers a
scientific treatment—but rather conceiving of time intuitively as "durée réelle" (real time)
or "time as a fluctuating, non-spatial continuum" (ibid., 6). Mattison paraphrases Bergson's
intuition versus science argument as "[having] turned affective time into representational
time because we have, following science, applied the rules of space to time: science, philosophy, and linguistics are all disciplines that Bergson critiques for spatializing time" (Mattison,
"Nabokov's Aesthetic Bergsonism," 39).

6   Nabokov, *Strong Opinions* (New York: Vintage, 1973), 43. Mattison draws a more concrete
connection between the two thinkers in citing this Nabokov's statement.

7   Vladimir Nabokov, *Speak, Memory* (New York: Vintage International, 1989), 21–22. Michael
Glynn outlines numerous parallels between Nabokov's and Bergson's ideas on the nature of
reality (see Michael Glynn, *Vladimir Nabokov: Bergsonian and Russian Formalist Influences in
His Novels* [New York: Palgrave Macmillan, 2007]). Most relevant to my study is Glynn's proposal that the writer and philosopher agreed that intellection only enables a partial, deluded
apprehension of reality and that art—being deautomatizing—serves as an antidote to this
deluded view (54–63; 71–77).

8   Leona Toker, "Philosophers as Poets: Reading Nabokov with Schopenhauer and Bergson,"
Russian Literature TriQuarterly 24 (1991): 185.

9   While Nabokov's integration of space into the idea of intuitive time may appear to contra-
dict Bergson's philosophy, Nabokov actually *combines* the notions of intuition, temporality,

condition of opening up to multiple realities figures prominently in the inter-woven fictional worlds within "La Veneziana" and "The Visit to the Museum."

Both stories foreground modes of inscribing time that reflect Nabokov's temporal layering of space whereby the inscribed object contains the past in the present and carries the possibility of a future.[10] An intimate relationship of the verbal and visual arts permeated Nabokov's writing and thinking, fueling his image-driven mode of perceiving the world.[11] In interviews and lectures, Nabokov stated that he "think[s] in images" and believes that "[l]iterature is not a pattern of ideas but a pattern of images. Ideas do not matter much in compari-son to a book's imagery and magic."[12] Nabokov's valuing of the "two sister arts" (the words of Gerard de Vries and D. Barton Johnson) manifests in his term "word-picture," which the writer used to "denote delightful images, like those presented by himself: images of light and shade, actions, gestures or landscapes, but most often of scenes in which people are caught in a way they have never been portrayed before."[13] Nabokov's use of the term "word-picture" emphasizes his method of using words to create painting-like images and the centrality of visual art in his exploration of "worlds in regression."[14]

---

and space into a form of nonlinear, nonrational experience. Mattison explains this concept succinctly: "For Nabokov, this ability to embody multiple durations and to connect with other experiences through the method of intuition is also how space is temporally layered" (Mattison, "Nabokov's Aesthetic Bergsonism," 40).

10　The idea of inscribing time into a material object arises in Martin Hägglund and Brian Boyd's public exchange regarding Nabokov's notions of time (Hägglund, "Chronophilia" and Boyd, "Nabokov, Time, and Timelessness"). Despite their disagreement on many points related to Nabokov's temporality, their foundational interpretations align—that Nabokov exhibited a double bind in his relationship with time wherein the fear of losing time ("chronophobia") is intrinsic to the desire to have time ("chronophilia"). Hägglund extends this notion, con-tending that Nabokov used writing as a mode of inscribing a moment in time and thereby rendering it into memory and preventing its loss. Continuing this line of logic, visual art is also an inscription of time—a physical artifact that preserves an image seen in a once-existing present.

11　From childhood, Nabokov, who had a gift for drawing, practiced remembering images in great detail during his lessons with Mstislav Dobuzhinsky of the World of Art (Mir iskusstva) group (Gerard de Vries and D. Barton Johnson, "Nabokov and the Two Sister Arts," in *Nabokov and the Art of Painting* [Amsterdam: Amsterdam University Press, 2006], 11). For a comprehensive, thematic study of the European and American artists who influenced Nabokov's lifelong artistic sensibilities, see Gavriel Shapiro, *The Sublime Artist's Studio: Nabokov and Painting* (Evanston, IL: Northwestern University Press, 2009).

12　De Vries and Johnson, "Nabokov and the Two Sister Arts," 11.

13　Ibid., 12.

14　The title of D. Barton Johnson's classic study, *Worlds in Regression: Some Novels of Vladimir Nabokov* (Ann Arbor, MI: Ardis, 1985).

Yet Nabokov believed that the visual arts, specifically painting rather than plastic arts, enable a different form of temporality from that of the verbal arts, and thus a different reality—because they are not confined within the boundaries of time. In his university lectures, Nabokov famously held that the act of reading inherently involves the element of time while regarding a painting does not:

> When we read a book for the first time the very process of laboriously moving our eyes from left to right, line after line, page after page . . . the very process of learning in terms of space and time what the book is about, this stands between us and artistic appreciation. When we look at a painting we do not have to move our eyes in a special way even if, as in a book, the picture contains elements of depth and development. The element of time does not really enter in a first contact with a painting.[15]

In Nabokov's view, the eye's movement "from left to right" involves space and time, a linear, scientific, non-Bergsonian (con)figuration of time. Paintings are time-less; as an inscription of the past in the present for the future,[16] they present the opportunity for what Nabokov termed "Consciousness without Time."[17] Considering the painting as a type of instantaneous imprinting of the image on the mind betokens a Bergsonian concept of intuition, or the Nabokovian concept of temporal layering. Nabokov's use of visual art *within* the world of his prose fiction—despite, or perhaps because of, the linear, written mode that breathes it into existence—profoundly enables the reader to surrender to this alternate, non-mundane version of reality.

---

15 Nabokov, *Lectures on Literature*, ed. Fredson Bowers (San Diego, CA: Harcourt Brace Jovanovich/Bruccoli Clark, 1980), Kindle.

16 Gennady Barabtarlo writes on Nabokov's views of time prior to his dream experiments (in the 1960s) as "somewhat simplistic" in Barabtarlo, "Artistic Time," in *Insomniac Dreams: Experiments with Time by Vladimir Nabokov*, ed. Grennady Barabtarlo (Princeton, NJ: Princeton University Press, 2018), 161. He references Nabokov's comment that art requires "'the perfect fusion of the past and the present [. . .] the inspiration of genius adds a third ingredient: it is the past and the present and the future [. . .] that come together in a sudden flash; thus the entire circle of time is perceived, which is another way of saying that times ceases to exist'" (Nabokov, *Lectures on Literature*).

17 As Boyd mentions, Nabokov uses this term in his 1951 yearbook. Boyd expounds that this term encompasses "consciousness *not restricted to present time* as human consciousness is: consciousness operating in a time that allows direct access to the past" (Boyd, "Nabokov, Time, and Timelessness)."

Temporal Layering through Portraiture in "La Veneziana"

In "La Veneziana," written in 1924 in Berlin but unpublished in the writer's lifetime, Nabokov showcases his own understandings of time in a way that becomes
less labored in his later work. The story centers around a gathering at an English
Colonel's summer home, with visitors Frank (the Colonel's son), Simpson
(Frank's friend), McGore (an art dealer), and Maureen (McGore's wife).[18]
Frank/Maureen/McGore and Frank/Maureen/Simpson form two interconnected love triangles. While Frank and Maureen actively pursue an amorous
affair, Simpson pines for Maureen from afar—and through the verisimilar
Venetian woman pictured in what is initially presented as a Renaissance-era
portrait. This affair and Simpson's varied attempts to interact with the painted
Venetian woman drive the story's plot, until it is ultimately revealed that the
portrait's provenance was itself a deception.

This early short story is thus valuable for examining the inner workings of the
connections among visual art, time, and the fictional worlds of Nabokov's texts.
Notably, this story layers and intertwines the scientific and measurable data
with the intuitive and uncognizable, thus echoing Bergson's metaphysics, while
the initial presentation of the *Veneziana* painting hints at Nabokov's treatment
of these ideas. (The prototype for this fictionalized painting is Sebastiano del
Piombo's "Ritratto femminile ['Dorotea']," which young Nabokov would have
seen at a Berlin museum.)[19] The last sentence of the initial description reads:
"On the left the black was interrupted by a large right-angled opening straight
into the twilight air and the bluish-green chasm of the cloudy evening."[20]

After the initial description, with details pointing skyward within the world
of the painting, Nabokov writes, "Yet it was not in those details of stupendous
umbral interplay, nor the dark-hued warmth of the entire painting, that struck
Simpson."[21] The original Russian version uses the adjective "tenevoi," which
can be literally translated as pertaining to a shadow cast by an object.[22] Dmitri
Nabokov's decision to translate his father's adjective as "umbral" here is
highly deliberate, as among other relatively prosaic descriptive terms of the

---

18 Nabokov, "La Veneziana," trans. from the Russian by Dmitri Nabokov, in *The Stories of Vladimir Nabokov*, [ed. Dmitri Nabokov] (New York: Vintage Books, 1997), 90–115. *Also see Ciara Spencer's discussion of "La Veneziana" in her essay in this volume (M. D. S.).*
19 See Dmitri Nabokov's note to the story in Nabokov, *The Stories of Vladimir Nabokov*, 668, as well as Shrayer's discussion of the story in "Writing and Reading the Otherworld."
20 Nabokov, "La Veneziana" 94.
21 Ibid.," 94; *emphasis mine* (M. D. M.).
22 I thank Maxim D. Shrayer for this insight.

Figure 1. Sebastiano del Piombo, *Bildnis einer jungen Römerin (Dorothea)*, 1512. Gemäldegelerie, Staatliche Museen zu Berlin—Preußicher Kulturbesitz. Wikimedia.

English-language version of the text ("prominent," "tender," "dark-hued," "elongated," "yellow"), this term stands out as rather technical, referring to the umbra, the central and darkest portion of a cast shadow. The term is used in algebra, astronomy, and geology; as an astronomical term, it is defined as "Pertaining to the umbra of sun-spots or eclipses."[23] This specific technical term serves as a distraction to Simpson's true realization, that the Venetian woman in the portrait strikingly resembles Maureen McGore: "It was something else

---

23 OED Online, s.v. "umbral, adj.2," accessed April 26, 2023, https://www.oed.com/dictionary/umbral_adj?tab=meaning_and_use; see also "Umbra, penumbra and antumbra," Wikipedia, last modified August 13, 2024, https://en.wikipedia.org/wiki/Umbra,_penumbra_and_antumbra.

[...] he said, 'God, how she resembles—'/ 'My wife,' finished McGore."[24] Here one observes the start of a pattern within the story, in which logic and rationality contrast with, but ultimately contribute to, the sense of distorted time and reality.

In a later significant scene, Nabokov, through his narrator, directly expresses the arbitrariness of the linear notion of time and relates it to astronomy. This moment occurs just before Simpson visits the *Veneziana* painting for the second time, tempted by its enchanting contours amid the prosaics of everyday life:

> The distinctive feature of everything extant is its monotony. We partake of food at predetermined hours because the planets, like trains that are never late, depart and arrive at predetermined times. The average person cannot imagine life without such a strictly established timetable. But a playful and sacrilegious mind will find much to amuse it imagining how people would exist if the day lasted ten hours today, eighty-five tomorrow, and after tomorrow a few minutes. [...] The planets would become like racehorses, and what excitement would be aroused by some sorrel Mars as it tackled the final celestial hurdle! Astronomers would assume bookmakers' functions, the god Apollo would be depicted in a flaming jockey cap, and the world would merrily go mad.[25]

The "predetermined hours" invoke the idea of measured time, while the description of a "mad" world, in which one day lasts ten hours and another lasts a few minutes, invokes the same measuredness and turns it on its head. The comparison of planets to "trains that are never late" parallels Nabokov's observation in his journals concerning what the true nature of time *is not*—that "We feel [time] as moving only because it is a medium where growth and change take place *or where things stop, like stations*."[26] Thus in this passage, Nabokov details his comprehension of the mechanistic core of such scientific, linear time. He characterizes this interpretation through Simpson's fear of this version of the measurable time in which he is living. Simpson "was particularly conscious of this monotony. He found it somehow terrifying that today, too, breakfast would be followed by

---

24 Nabokov, "La Veneziana," 94.
25 Ibid.," 105.
26 Nabokov quoted in Barabtarlo, "Artistic Time," 160–161; emphasis mine (M. D. M.).

lunch, tea by supper, with inviolable regularity."[27] It is fitting, then, that Simpson is nominated to be the character who interacts most intimately with the painting and enters into its otherworld.

The *Veneziana* painting presents an inscription of time—the confluence of past, present, and future—that leads to a new dimension of reality. Nabokov fashions the Venetian lady within the portrait as someone whose motion was suddenly rendered still: "With the elongated fingers of her right hand spread in pairs, she seemed to have been on the point of adjusting the falling fur but to have frozen motionless, her hazel, uniformly dark eyes gazing fixedly, languidly from the canvas."[28] These hints of a sudden cessation of movement ("whose motion was suddenly rendered still," "on the point of adjusting") suggest a painter rendering a living person in all her activity and life, for posterity.[29] McGore even puts this very phenomenon into words: "The impression of antiquity can be evoked as easily as the impression of color by pressing one's upper eyelid. On occasion I allow myself the luxury of imagining today's world, our machines, our fashions, as they will appear to our descendants four or five hundred years hence."[30]

McGore's comment also leads one to imagine one's present being regarded by a future person looking into the past and, perhaps, anticipates Nabokov's own notion of a "future recollection."[31] When Simpson regards this inscription of time, he comprehends multiple realities—again set against the backdrop of scientific facts. The narrator notes:

> [...] the one thing that fascinated [Simpson]—apart, of course,
> from the purely physiological effect of the splendid colors on his
> optic nerves—was the resemblance he had immediately noticed,

---

27   Nabokov, "La Veneziana," 106.

28   Ibid., 94.

29   Shrayer similarly notes the portrait's contents rendered into infinitude, contending that both Frank and Simpson "perceive [the painting] through a prism of eternity." His analysis thus concords with the idea of the inscription of time in a material object—rendering it into memory and preventing its loss—that results from a dual chronophobia-chronophilia: "For Frank [...] creating the portrait was [...] a way of immortalizing his beloved" ("Writing and Reading the Otherworld").

30   Nabokov, "La Veneziana," 98.

31   Nabokov develops this notion of "future recollection" in multiple works, such as in the Russian short story "A Guide to Berlin": "How can I demonstrate to him that I have glimpsed somebody's future recollections?" ("A Guide to Berlin," trans. from the Russian by Dmitri Nabokov and Vladimir Nabokov, in *The Stories of Vladimir Nabokov*, 160). He expresses his personal endeavor to observe and preserve future memory in *Speak, Memory*: "The idea consisted of parodizing a biographic approach projected, as it were, into the future and thus transforming the very specious present into a kind of paralyzed past" (248).

even though he was seeing Maureen for the first time. And the remarkable thing was that the Veneziana's face . . . clarified for him the real beauty of that other Maureen."[32]

Later Simpson declares that the Venetian woman "looks absolutely real."[33] His observation of the painting flips the answer to the question "Which Maureen is real?" from the Maureen in the world of "mundane reality,"[34] to the Venetian beauty in the world that Simpson later enters and inhabits. The idea that the Veneziana within the portrait is the "real" Maureen is momentarily confirmed when Simpson enters the painting: "Simpson [...] moved toward her and effortlessly entered the painting [...] at his very side stood a real, Venetian, Maureen— tall, gorgeous, all aglow from within."[35] No longer the two-dimensional woman whose motion was frozen in time, she "stood half-facing him, alive and three-dimensional."[36] Simpson has stepped directly into the past, now having become the present.

Significantly, this different conception of time, intuitive and not logical, resides within the same physical space as the everyday temporal dimension: the hallway within the Colonel's summer residence: "Simpson looked about the room in which he was standing, but without any awareness of a floor beneath his feet. In the distance, instead of a fourth wall, a far, familiar hall glimmered like water, with the black island of a table at its center."[37] The room contains no fourth wall and is therefore not a separate addition to the hallway, but rather an expansion of it; it is a space that has always existed within the otherworld of the painting. Under certain conditions, which require an effort of imagination, the space may be accessed by people, such as Simpson, for whom "impressionability [takes] the place of intellect."[38] After Simpson first observes the painting, he exits to the garden and experiences an "auditory hallucination that had afflicted him since childhood." During these "hallucinations," Simpson "would involuntarily begin to wonder if, through this silence, he might hear the entire, enormous world traversing space with a melodious whistle, the bustle of distant cities, the pounding of sea waves, the singing of telegraph wires above the deserts."[39] This passage

---

32 Nabokov, "La Veneziana," 95.
33 Ibid., 100.
34 Shrayer, "Writing and Reading the Otherworld."
35 Nabokov, "La Veneziana," 110–111.
36 Ibid., 110.
37 Ibid., 111.
38 Ibid., 107.
39 Ibid., 97.

presents space as instantaneously traversable, with concomitant sounds from disparate spaces sensed by one person positioned in one place.

Once Simpson enters the painting and stays therein, he is no longer within the *part* of the space that is the original hallway in the Colonel's house, while the reader is no longer able to access the layers of reality within the painting itself. The story notes, that "directly in front of [Simpson], even more distinct than before, stretched the hall, filled with live, terrestrial air that, henceforth, he would not breathe."[40] The hallway is filled with "terrestrial air," an earthly dimension to which Simpson, now living within the painting, no longer has access. He is inscribed in the painting, having joined the Venetian lady. The next time the reader encounters Simpson, it is only through his absence, while the story has returned to its original prosaic plane of being. The servant, who is checking on the visitors' whereabouts, notes that Simpson has disappeared; meanwhile, McGore and the Colonel admire a recent addition to the *Veneziana*: "It was an excellent, if hastily executed, portrait of Simpson. Gaunt, his black jacket strongly highlighted by the lighter background, his feet turned oddly outward, he extended his hands as if in supplication, and his pallid face was distorted by a pitiful, frantic expression."[41] This expression and position reflect the emotions of terror and the "ridiculous pose" that the three-dimensional Simpson experienced just prior to this scene.[42] Yet McGore and the Colonel's immediate, rational conclusion is that Frank had painted the figure of Simpson onto the Renaissance Italian canvas. It is only when McGore scrapes the painted Simpson off the portrait and throws the rags out of the window that Simpson is returned to the mundane reality of the story.

When Simpson "disappears," three main narrative questions arise. Did Simpson really only fall asleep in the garden, or did he actually enter the painting? Was the figure of Simpson on the canvas really Frank's hasty painting job, or did Simpson really freeze into the painting? Is the intuitive, temporally layered perspective or the logical, cerebral perspective of the story's temporality inherently correct? The point of confusion for these questions lies in a number of narrative developments. Prior to what appears to be Simpson's entry into the painting, he becomes very sleepy, "collaps[ing] like an empty suit of clothes onto the grass in the narrow interstice between flower bed and castle wall. A wave of drowsiness came over him."[43] It is possible that Simpson really did fall

---

40 Ibid., 111.
41 Ibid., 112.
42 Ibid., 111.
43 Ibid., 110.

asleep there in his bout of drowsiness, and his entry into the hallway and painting was merely a dream. In that vein, if Simpson only dreamt the experience and
was asleep the entire night in the garden, then he would have only been able to
emerge on the painting by Frank's own artistic hand. Frank even admits to having painted Simpson onto the canvas.[44]

Yet three important clues confound this line of thinking. The first is the old
watchman who saw the light on in the hallway on the night when Simpson's purportedly fell asleep. Simpson actually turned on the light after the wave of drowsiness, indicating that this action was not a dream.[45] The second clue is the lemon
that the gardener finds, which has transcended the confines of the painting's otherworld and entered the mundane reality. The lemon from the painting "[bore]
the imprint of five fingers," suggesting the physical trace of Simpson's strong grip.
Finally, the timing is fortuitous: McGore scrapes off Simpson from the canvas,
throws the rag with the remains of the painted Simpson out of the window, and
Simpson's physical body is discovered.

These clues all indicate that Simpson has transcended linear time and entered
into the past captured and frozen within the painting. However, the habitual
intellectualization of reality is the very thing that traps the keen reader within the
bounds of human consciousness. If space is temporally layered, then both of the
story's realities could be true: Simpson could have fallen asleep in the garden, *and*
he could have entered the painting. In his works, from the early Russian stories to
the late American novels, Nabokov continued to explore the process of stepping
outside the bounds of human consciousness, and the short story "The Visit to
the Museum" represents a particularly telling example of his explorations.

The Museum Space as Temporal Maëlstrom in "The Visit to the Museum"

For Nabokov, the simultaneous existence of fictional realities mirrors the layering of different durations of and points in time. In tracing the influence of

---

44 Frank writes in the letter to his father, "'*You also wanted to see a sample of my art. That is why I
made you a portrait of my former friend*'" (ibid., 114); italics in original.

45 The old watchman appears in a section devoted to his observation of the light in the window;
a "giant of an old fellow with venerable gray side-whiskers, which, incidentally, the gardener's
children liked to tug" and akin to a "guardian angel," the description of the old watchman
is mystical and fairytale-like, evoking the image of Father Time (ibid., 109). Simpson was
"unaware of how he had got up, gone indoors, and switched on the lights," but as the old
watchman confirms, the lights were indeed on (ibid., 109).

Bergsonian metaphysics on Nabokov's notion of temporality, Mattison emphasized that Nabokov's fiction represents a departure from the idea of a cognizable, "representational" time (Mattison borrows this term from Bergson). Both the early "La Veneziana" and late "The Visit to the Museum" bring to life the apparent and yet unresolved tension between scientific and artistic cognition of reality—quite literally in the material objects' interactions with human characters.

"The Visit to the Museum," one of Nabokov's last Russian-language short stories, came to life in 1938 in Paris, about fourteen years after "La Veneziana."[46] As Shrayer notes, "The Visit to the Museum" prominently features what by the late 1930s had become two hallmark aspects of Nabokov's poetics: entering the otherworld and archeology of memory.[47] Entry into the otherworld is evident as an element of "La Veneziana," as previously explored. It may be fitting that Nabokov set a story with elements so central in his later fiction within a museum—a space where pieces of visual art are kept and displayed.

The painting that drives the events of the story (set in France) is the portrait of the grandfather of the protagonist's friend. This friend tasks the protagonist (also the story's first-person narrator) with finding and purchasing the portrait on his behalf. While at the museum, the narrator meets M. Godard, the museum director, and discusses with him essential questions about the portrait: whether or not it exists within the museum and at what price he could purchase it. This discussion leads nowhere, except to the protagonist becoming lost in the maze-like space and eventually—apparently—exits to the Russia he no longer knows.

The portrait captures an element of the friend's exilic nostalgia—a simulacrum of his connection to the prerevolutionary Russian past. When the friend requests that the narrator look for the portrait of his grandfather in the provincial museum, he "smil[es] and spread[s] out his hands" as he simultaneously shares historical information about the grandfather and about the painting. The narrator explains:

> It went more or less as follows: after the grandfather died in their St. Petersburg house back at the time of the Russo-Japanese War, the contents of his apartment in Paris were sold at auction. The portrait, after some obscure peregrinations, was acquired by the museum of Leroy's native town. My friend wished to know if the portrait was really there; if there, if it could be ransomed; and if it

46 Boyd, "Chronology of Nabokov's Life and Main Works," *Nabokovian*, accessed May 3, 2023, https://thenabokovian.org/chronology.
47 Shrayer, "Writing and Reading the Otherworld."

could, for what price. When I asked why he did not get in touch with the museum, he replied that he had written several times, but had never received an answer.[48]

This passage adumbrates a number of points that become important throughout the story: a spatial connection between Russia and France, where the Russian émigré narrator lives in exile, and a temporal connection between the time of the Russo-Japanese war, 1904–1905, and the 1930s, the present time in the narrative. The narrator notably introduces the question of the nature of reality— both within and without the portrait—in the story's opening, commenting that his friend may not possess the ability to "remain this side of fantasy."[49]

The chosen setting of a museum, a space that houses numerous artifacts from the past in the present, erases the traditional confines of time while still exhibiting objects that inscribe time. The size of the museum and the number of objects it contains complicate the notions of time that the young Nabokov first elaborates in "La Veneziana." Furthermore, the museum is presented as a space where prescriptive versus intuitive approaches to art are in counterpoint, similar to the dynamic that already exists in "La Veneziana," yet subtler. The protagonist's initial observations of the museum seek to rationalize the selection of objects on display. Regarding "an assortment of strange black lumps of various sizes," he comments with a scientific eye that he was "quite at a loss to guess their nature, composition, and function." When he asks the custodian what these objects are, the custodian simply replies, "'Science has not yet determined,'" and goes onto explain the referential contexts in which the objects were found (when and by whom).

The protagonist continues his attempts to understand the logic of the museum collection, asking "who decided, and why, that they merited a place in the museum" and "what they are made of."[50] The custodian's final response leads nowhere: "'Science . . .' he began anew, but stopped short and looked crossly at his fingers, which were soiled with dust from the glass." As the protagonist continues to examine items on display, his mode of interacting with the museum's collection begins to change. When the protagonist sees "a spade, a mattock, and a pick," he thinks "absentmindedly": "To dig in the past [. . .] but this time did

---

48 Nabokov, "The Visit to the Museum," trans. from the Russian by Dmitri Nabokov and Vladimir Nabokov, in *The Stories of Vladimir Nabokov*, 277.

49 See also Shrayer's discussion of this point, for which he provides the original Russian version of this sentence; he explains that the original Russian, "*[p]o siu storonu fantazii*" (this side of the fantasy) is easily recognized as the opposite of *po tu storonu fantazii* (the other side of fantasy)" (Shrayer, "Writing and Reading the Otherworld").

50 Nabokov, "The Visit to the Museum," 278.

not seek clarification from the custodian."[51] The phrase "to dig in the past" is a temporal signal, and it calls to mind two temporal interpretations: to dig *into* the past, as in the present person exploring the past, or to muse about what it was like to be a person digging in the past. Here the shift in the protagonist's mindset marks one of the story's subtle gestures in the direction of the otherworld.

The complexity of the temporal layering increases as the visitors' interactions with the museum's artifacts becomes more and more absurd. As M. Godard, the museum director, guides the protagonist through the museum halls, a group of visiting young people play with the old objects. One of them holds up a cigarette to the portrait of the protagonist's friend, which shows "a glowing cigar" from which the youth "prepared to borrow a light." Here the present engages with the frozen past. Another irreverent visitor wears an ancient helmet: "one of [the merry crowd of youths] had put on his head a copper helmet with a Rembrandtesque gleam [. . .] and someone's shove made the helmet fly off the hooligan's head with a clatter."[52] This action is literally a compression of time, a fusion of the past and present. The museum's temporally layered space enables this interaction between the apparently static—though "La Veneziana" teaches differently—object from the past and a living human in the present.

The portrait of the grandfather, with its increasingly problematic provenance, creates further cracks in the façade of the story's logical, rational reality. Because the portrait underpins the entire plot, its very questionable existence carries significant implications for the exilic world of the story. The first time the narrator sees the painting, he exclaims that he had "found the very object whose existence had hitherto seemed to me but the figment of an unstable mind."[53] The protagonist thinks, "Frankly, I enjoyed the thought that the portrait existed. It is fun to be present at the coming true of a dream."[54] Rather than a definitive, "I enjoyed that the portrait existed," the protagonist's language invokes indeterminacy, stating he "enjoyed the *thought*" of the portrait's existence.

This indeterminacy is emphasized further when the protagonist meets with the museum director. When the narrator offers the "substantial sum" his friend is willing to pay for the portrait, M. Godard denies the portrait's existence outright: "there is no such picture in our museum." This response prompts the narrator's response that "no power on earth could make me doubt its existence." M. Godard disagrees, having no doubt that the piece *does not* exist; he invokes both

---

51 Ibid., 279.
52 Ibid., 282.
53 Ibid., 279.
54 Ibid.

logic and divinity to support his belief: "[B]ut I am not crazy either. I have been curator of our museum for almost twenty years now and know this catalogue as well as I know the Lord's Prayer [. . .] I cannot conceive of this portrait's existence in our museum."[55] At this moment, M. Godard and the protagonist are at a hermeneutic stalemate. The protagonist has his memory as evidence of the portrait's existence, and M. Godard has the museum catalog.

The question of the portrait's existence deepens the cracks in the façade of mundane reality. The protagonist walks through an exit that he had not previously noticed[56]—or perhaps that did not previously exist at all. The narrator and M. Godard "thrust [their] way through it," a forceful passage, as the verb "thrust" suggests, into a space that is still in the same museum as before but now holds a sense of expansion and distortion. This entry into the otherworld presents a striking similarity to Simpson's entry into the painting in "La Veneziana." The protagonist loses himself in transition, at various points describing the hall as "one of considerable dimensions" and the museum as "unnecessarily spreading."[57] This experience is punctuated by the protagonist's rapid movement through tiers and layers of time. According to Shrayer, "the narrator proceeds through a section of Ancient sculpture into a room with Oriental fabrics and then into rooms with paintings that bespeak their High Renaissance or Baroque origins. [. . .] The change of exhibits along the narrator's way suggests a history of human civilization from antiquity to modernity."[58] The protagonist then encounters "a crowd of gray-haired people with umbrellas examining a gigantic mock-up of the universe."[59] This scene warrants close attention. Shrayer underscores the absurdism of this scene,[60] which I would like to examine further.

This moment presents a double-layered mimesis, in which the story does not weave the universe into the seams of its fictional world, but instead captures a "mock-up" that exists *within* this world. The containment of a universe within the museum space is reminiscent of Simpson's hallucination in "La Veneziana," albeit through sight rather than hearing. Just as Simpson "might hear the entire, enormous world traversing space," this display of the universe contains the entire world, thus becoming a work of visual art that one comprehends beyond the element of time.

---

55   Ibid., 280.
56   Shrayer, "Writing and Reading the Otherworld."
57   Nabokov, "The Visit to the Museum," 282.
58   Shrayer, "Writing and Reading the Otherworld."
59   Nabokov, "The Visit to the Museum," 283.
60   Shrayer, "Writing and Reading the Otherworld."

As in the case of "La Veneziana," the indeterminacy of reality intensifies in the finale of "The Visit to the Museum," transcending readers' ability to make sense of it through rational or intellectual contemplation. Nabokov presents his protagonist as having found the exit from the museum, at which point the "reality" of this provincial museum, of the fictional town of Montisert, of France, is subordinated to a newly found reality. The protagonist exclaims: "when I flung the door open, there was no theater, but only a soft opacity and splendidly counterfeited fog with the perfectly convincing blotches of indistinct streetlights. More than convincing! [. . .] [I]mmediately a joyous and unmistakable sensation of reality at last replaced all the unreal trash amid which I had just been dashing to and fro. The stone beneath my feet was real sidewalk."[61] The narrator finds himself in Bolshevik Russia, "the factual Russia of today." He comments that he has previously experienced a similar feeling in his sleep, but now this spatial and temporal positioning is his actual reality.[62]

Was the museum all a dream? Or is Russia—be it czarist Russia of the émigré's past or Bolshevik Russia of the present—the dream? Perhaps both dream and reality, the otherworld and mundane world, exist simultaneously? Nabokov's readers may not reach a neat understanding of their coexistence, but perhaps that itself is both the pleasure of his art and a working conclusion to this investigation.

Bibliography

Primary Sources

Nabokov, Vladimir. "A Guide to Berlin." Translated by Dmitri Nabokov and Vladimir Nabokov. In *The Stories of Vladimir Nabokov*, [edited by Dmitri Nabokov], 155–160. New York: Vintage Books, 1997.

———. "La Veneziana." Translated by Dmitri Nabokov and Vladimir Nabokov. In *The Stories of Vladimir Nabokov*, [edited by Dmitri Nabokov], 90–115. New York: Vintage Books, 1997.

———. *Lectures on Literature*. Edited by Fredson Bowers. San Diego: Harcourt Brace Jovanovich/ Bruccoli Clark, 1980. Kindle. Rpt. of 1980 Harcourt print edition.

———. *Speak, Memory: An Autobiography Revisited*. New York: Vintage International, 1989.

———. *Strong Opinions*. New York: Vintage, 1973.

———. "The Visit to the Museum." Translated by Dmitri Nabokov and Vladimir Nabokov. In *The Stories of Vladimir Nabokov*, [edited by Dmitri Nabokov], 277–285. New York: Vintage Books, 1997.

---

61   Nabokov, "The Visit to the Museum," 284.
62   Ibid., 285.

Secondary Sources

Alexandrov, Vladimir E. *Nabokov's Otherworld*. Princeton, NJ: Princeton University Press, 1991.

Barabtarlo, Gennady. "Artistic Time." In *Insomniac Dreams: Experiments with Time by Vladimir Nabokov*, edited by Grennady Barabtarlo, 159–192. Princeton, NJ: Princeton University Press, 2018. Accessed March 29, 2023. https://doi.org/10.2307/j.ctvc7720g.9.

Bilmes, Leonid. "Description and Narration in Vladimir Nabokov's *Ada or Ardor*." In *Ekphrasis, Memory and Narrative after Proust: Prose Pictures and Fictional Recollection*, 87–116. New York: Bloomsbury Academic, 2023. Accessed March 29, 2023. https://ebookcentral.proquest.com/lib/bostoncollege-ebooks/detail.action?docID=7101480.

Boyd, Brian. "Chronology of Nabokov's Life and Main Works." *Nabokovian*. Accessed May 3, 2023. https://thenabokovian.org/chronology.

———. "Nabokov, Time, and Timelessness: A Reply to Martin Hägglund." *New Literary History* 37, no. 2 (2006): 469–478. Accessed March 29, 2023. doi: 10.1353/nlh.2006.0032.

Cash, Conall. "Picturing Memory Puncturing Vision: Vladimir Nabokov's *Pale Fire*." In *The Goalkeeper: The Nabokov Almanac*, edited by Yuri Leving, 124–151. Boston, MA: Academic Studies Press, 2010. Accessed March 29, 2023. https://doi.org/10.2307/j.ctt1zxsk4n.

De Vries, Gerard, and D. Barton Johnson. "Nabokov and the Two Sister Arts." In *Nabokov and the Art of Painting*, 11–29. Amsterdam: Amsterdam University Press, 2006.

Fink, Hilary Lynn. "Bridging the Kantian Gap: Bergson and Russian Modernism, 1900–1930." PhD diss., Columbia University, 1996. Accessed September 4, 2023. https://go.openathens.net/redirector/bc.edu?url=https://www.proquest.com/dissertations-theses/bridging-kantian-gap-bergson-russian-modernism/docview/304247907/se-2.

Glynn, Michael. *Vladimir Nabokov: Bergsonian and Russian Formalist Influences in His Novels*. New York: Palgrave Macmillan, 2007. Kindle. Rpt. of the 2007 Palgrave Macmillan print edition.

Hägglund, Martin. "Chronophilia: Nabokov and the Time of Desire." *New Literary History* 37, no. 2 (2006): 447–467. Accessed March 29, 2023. doi: 10.1353/nlh.2006.0036.

Johnson, D. Barton. *Worlds in Regression: Some Novels of Vladimir Nabokov*. Ann Arbor, MI: Ardis, 1985.

Mattison, Laci. "Nabokov's Aesthetic Bergsonism: An Intuitive, Reperceptualized Time." *Mosaic: An Interdisciplinary Critical Journal* 46, no. 1 (2013): 39. Accessed March 29, 2023. http://www.jstor.org/stable/44030114.

Nabokov, Dmitri. "Translating with Nabokov." In *The Achievements of Vladimir Nabokov*, edited by George Gibian and Stephen Jan Parker, 145–177. Ithaca, NY: Cornell Center for International Studies, 1984.

Shapiro, Gavriel. *The Sublime Artist's Studio: Nabokov and Painting*. Evanston, IL: Northwestern University Press, 2009.

Shrayer, Maxim D. "Writing and Reading the Otherworld." In *The World of Nabokov's Stories*. Brookline, MA: Ladispoli Books, 2015. Kindle. Rpt. of the 1999 University of Texas print edition.

Toker, Leona. "Philosophers as Poets: Reading Nabokov with Schopenhauer and Bergson." *Russian Literature TriQuarterly* 24 (1991): 185–196.

———. "Nabokov and Bergson on Duration and Reflexivity." In *Nabokov's World: The Shape of Nabokov's World*, vol. 1, edited by Jane Grayson, Arnold McMillin, and Priscilla Meyer, 132–140. New York: Palgrave, 2002.

Marriage and Its Discontents: Infidelity and Unhappiness in Vladimir Nabokov's Life and Art

Ciara Spencer

Introduction: Nabokov, Marriage, and the Spirit of Modernism

Portrayals of unhappy marriages flit across Vladimir Nabokov's fiction like a slideshow on the theme of failed domesticity. Throughout the entirety of Nabokov's literary corpus, one would be hard-pressed to identify even a handful of fulfilling marriages. Yet relationships scarred by any number of insults and errors abound. This essay will attempt to unravel some of the patterns that arise in Nabokov's numerous depictions of unhappy or unsuccessful marriages. In these texts, marriage itself becomes a literary device for depicting characters' instabilities. By way of examining those areas and zones in Nabokov's fiction, where a marital bond appears warped or insufficient, I will discuss Nabokov's commentary on the fragility of human romantic connection in the face of unstable or otherwise anomalous personal existence. I will then turn to a discussion of the author's own marriage to Véra Nabokov (née Slonim). In doing so, I will follow the threads of Nabokov's biographical inspiration for his fiction.

Modernist literature often concerns itself with deconstructing the institution of marriage. A protean artist whose career spanned the 1910s–1970s, Nabokov bridged modernism and postmodernism. However, Nabokov's early decades show him engaged in conversation with the works of major early twentieth-century modernists, including Franz Kafka, James Joyce, and Ezra Pound.[1] Students of modernism typically regard the focus on love and marriage as highly paradoxical.[2] In *Unmaking Love: The Contemporary Novel and the Impossibility of Union*, Ashley T. Shelden proposes that "modernist writers attempted to imagine love in ways that resisted conservative, redemptive fantasies about attachment. However, modernists remained ambivalent about love: they rejected fusion and continued to strive for it at the same time."[3] This critical perspective provides an important backdrop for the exploration of marriage within Nabokov's fiction. Nabokov frequently portrays romantic relationships that simultaneously reflect an uneasiness around the attachments of marriage and a deeply rooted connection to the idea of marriage as a symbol of social and personal security. Nabokov's Russian works, composed during the 1920s and 1930s and attuned to contemporary questions of love and marriage, are emblematic of the deeply contradictory and contentious spirit of modernism.

Instability and Abuse within Marriage

Nabokov frequently allows failed or dysfunctional marital relationships to mirror a protagonist's instabilities and aberrancies—whether these instabilities are sexual, psychological, or social. Several of Nabokov's novels, notably *The Defense* (1930) and *Lolita* (1955), and numerous short stories reflect this authorial tendency. In each case, although the specifics of the couple's marriage and the protagonist's personal aberrancies vary, Nabokov uses the marriage as a literary device that reflects the married subjects' internal instabilities.

Of course, we see hints of sexual instability throughout Nabokov's works.[4] One of the most interesting, minor flashes of this theme as it intersects with marriage occurs in the short story "Perfection" (1930), which follows destitute Russian émigré Ivanov eking out a living as a tutor in Berlin. Ivanov's sexuality is

---

1 For more on Nabokov's European period and his early modernist influences, see John Burt Foster, *Nabokov's Art of Memory and European Modernism* (Princeton, NJ: Princeton University Press, 1993), 11.
2 See Debrah Raschke, *Modernism, Metaphysics, and Sexuality* (Selinsgrove, PA: Susquehanna University Press, 2006).
3 Ashley T. Shelden, *Unmaking love: The Contemporary Novel and the Impossibility of Union* ((New York: Columbia University Press, 2017), 2.
4 See Maxim D. Shrayer, "Nabokov's Sexography," *Russian Literature* 48, no. 4 (2000): 495–516, accessed May 10, 2023, https://doi.org/10.1016/S0304-3479(00)80033-2.

difficult to unpack within the text, but Nabokov's text alludes to several facets of
its instability in this passage:

> Ten years before, in Serbia, the only woman he had ever loved—
> another man's wife—had become pregnant by him. She suffered
> a miscarriage and died the next night, deliring and praying. He
> would have had a son, a little fellow about David's age. When
> in the morning David prepared to pull on his swimming trunks,
> Ivanov was touched by the way his café-au-lait tan . . . abruptly
> gave way to a childish whiteness below the waist.[5]

Here Nabokov reveals Ivanov's rapt attention on the naked body of his young
charge, ten-year-old David, and hints at Ivanov's infrequent romantic attachment to women. While Nabokov does not clarify Ivanov's attraction to David's
body, it is certainly possible to read into the man's gaze on the young boy.[6]

In other of his early works, Nabokov's exploration of sexual instability is far
more elaborate and overt. Nabokov's 1930 novel *The Defense* portrays sexual
uncertainty through the lens of a dysfunctional marriage. Protagonist Luzhin's
sexual and social development is both directly and indirectly stunted in favor of
his development as a chess prodigy. The theme of failed marriages arises early in
the text, as Luzhin's early childhood is marked by the dissolution of his parents'
marriage after an affair between Luzhin's father and a young aunt. The fact of this
affair is never stated outright, but is rather revealed with progressively greater
clarity as the young protagonist ages and becomes aware of the circumstances.
The first mention of the affair occurs with Luzhin's childhood realization that
"Up until just recently his aunt has been at their place every day, but now she had
stopped coming and there was something in the air, some elusive interdiction,
that prevented him from asking about it at home."[7]

Luzhin's early introduction to infidelity, despite its later associations with
his budding chess genius, leads to a spiral of further harm against both himself
and his parents. Because Luzhin's parents do not communicate with their son

---

5 Vladimir Nabokov, "Perfection," trans. Dmitri Nabokov, in *The Stories of Vladimir Nabokov*,
   [ed. Dmitri Nabokov] (New York: Vintage Books, 1995), 343.
6 Shrayer discusses Ivanov's homoerotic desire as reminiscent of the writer Aschenbach's in
   Thomas Mann's *Death in Venice*; see Shrayer, "Saving Jewish-Russian Émigrés," in *Revising
   Nabokov Revising. The Proceedings of the International Nabokov Conference*, ed. Mitsuyoshi
   Numano and Tadashi Wakashima, 123–130 (Kyoto: The Nabokov Society of Japan, 2010).
7 Vladimir Nabokov, *The Defense*, trans. Michael Scammell in collaboration with the author
   (New York: Vintage Books, 1990), 51.

about the sudden disappearance of his aunt, his subsequent urge to seek out his old companion eventually leads to the continuation of the father's affair and to his mother's choice to leave the family.[8] A more important consequence of this affair, however, through its direct impact on Luzhin's fate and his own eventual development as a sexual and social being, is Luzhin's initiation to chess at the hands of his aunt and one of her intimate male friends.

Because of the setting in which Luzhin learns the game that will become his métier, his genius as a chess player is linked from its inception to the downfall of a marriage. The narrative ties Luzhin's sexual development directly to his professional development with the introduction of Valentinov, Luzhin's impressario and the progenitor of a "peculiar theory that the development of Luzhin's gift for chess was connected with the development of the sexual urge."[9] In keeping with his theory, Valentinov "kept [his prodigy] at a distance from women and rejoiced over his chaste moroseness."[10] Here, readers learn that Luzhin's professional success comes at the expense of his ability to form conventional sexual and romantic relationships. The consequences of Luzhin's stunted sexual development impact his future love life as much as they do his chess career.

In fact, the novel's plot splits its focus almost equally between the course of Luzhin's decline as a chess player and the development of his relationship with the unnamed Russian émigré woman who will become his wife. Not only does the couple meet during a chess tournament, but it is Luzhin's genius that initially attracts his partner, who views him as "an artist, a great artist." The future Mrs. Luzhin recognizes Luzhin's talent as a connection to a social sphere which she has always admired but never had access to—"a mysterious art equal to all the recognized arts. She had never been in close contact with such people."[11] Like Valentinov, Luzhin's wife views proximity to our protagonist's chess career as a symbol of her own success, and, after Luzhin's breakdown, slips neatly into a mirror of Valentinov's role as Luzhin's caretaker. But there is also a difference: where Valentinov had encouraged Luzhin's chess skills at the expense of his sexual maturity, Luzhin's wife acts as an enforcer of her husband's prescribed ban on engaging with chess, instead attempting to mold Luzhin into the image of the perfect, eccentrically brilliant husband.[12]

---

8   Ibid., 74.
9   Ibid., 94.
10   Ibid.
11   Ibid., 88.
12   See especially "'I shall stop loving you' [. . .] 'if you start thinking about chess, and I can see every thought, so behave yourself,'" in ibid., 162.

One can only assume that Luzhin's genius contributes to her enthusiasm for what is portrayed to be a marriage not free of eroticism yet free of conventional sex. Nabokov hints at Luzhin's discomfort with physical intimacy numerous times throughout the text; in a particularly descriptive domestic portrait, the couple undertakes a ritualistic series of kisses across the face, "observing a strict sequence that had once been approved by him," before Luzhin rewards his wife with a simple kiss on the hand and earns the response, "'What tenderness' [...] 'ah, what sweet tenderness.'"[13] When it is time for the wife to undress, the couple separates and Luzhin returns to his mission of hiding a pocket chess set from the prying eyes of his spouse. Here, the impacts of Valentinov's seclusion of his former charge are seen most clearly. Luzhin's marriage, like each of his other interpersonal relationships, fosters an addiction to chess, the one outlet for which Luzhin has consistently received praise and attention.[14] Further, while Luzhin's marriage is not scarred by infidelity like his parents' relationship, the development of his chess genius has contributed to the termination of two respective sets of marital bonds in the novel. First Luzhin's mother's physical separation from Luzhin's father and, later, a lack of emotional fulfillment, leads Luzhin to seek dissolution at the end of the novel. Nabokov's depiction of marriage in *The Defense* suggests an incompatibility between traditional constructions of bourgeois marriage and sexual instability, which Luzhin exhibits through stifled and underdeveloped sexuality.

Lolita (1955; American edition 1958) might be the most obvious example of a sexually pathological marriage in Nabokov's corpus. In America, Humbert Humbert marries Charlotte Haze in order to gain access to young Dolores (Lolita), Charlotte's twelve-year-old daughter and the object of his desire. Humbert Humbert derives his own forbidden desire for Lolita from the condition he refers to as nympholepsy. This marriage is centered around Humbert Humbert's lust—not towards his new American wife but towards a sexualized child—and is intended to excuse "all the casual caresses her mother's husband would be able to lavish on his Lolita."[15] Of course, Mrs. Haze's well-timed death allows Humbert Humbert to unleash the full scope of his sexual abuse, leading to a quasi-marital/parental relationship with Lolita.

---

13 Ibid., 220–221.
14 See especially, "During the whole time that [Valentinov] lived with Luzhin he unremittingly encouraged and developed his gift, not bothering for a second about Luzhin as a person" in ibid., 92.
15 Vladimir Nabokov, *Lolita* (New York: Random House, 1997), 70.

However, while much of *Lolita*'s plot focuses on Humbert Humbert's relationship with the youngest Haze, it is worth noting his deliberate manipulation of marriage to exercise his pathological desire while also gaining—or maintaining—societal respect. Humbert Humbert's marriage to Mrs. Haze serves a dual purpose in harboring Humbert Humbert's sexual aberrancies. The marriage both enables, masks, and legitimizes a level of proximity to Lolita that American middle-class society would otherwise deem improper.

Within the performance of his middle-class American marriage to Mrs. Haze, Humbert Humbert's attempts to conjure up feelings of lust or affection for his bride only augment his nympholepsy. He encourages Charlotte to unearth photos from her youth, to "see how Lotte had looked as a child."[16] He finds that, "even though the light was wrong and the dresses graceless, [he] was able to make out a dim first version of Lolita's outline, legs, cheekbones, bobbed nose."[17] Humbert Humbert's nympholepsy colors the rituals and rites of his marriage; the traditionally innocent act of looking at a spouse's childhood photos becomes an attempt to situate Charlotte as an object of desire both by viewing her as a young girl and by locating the specter of Lolita within her mother's image.

Nympholepsy was similarly central to Humbert Humbert's first marriage to Valeria, in Paris some fifteen years prior to the time when he meets Lolita. Humbert Humbert is unabashed in his recognition that "what really attracted me to Valeria was the imitation she gave of a little girl."[18] Yet he immediately clarifies, "I appealed to her stale flesh very seldom, only in cases of great urgency and despair. The grocer had a little daughter whose shadow drove me mad; but with Valeria's help I did find after all some legal outlets to my fantastic predicament."[19] While Valeria's youthful style was insufficient to detract Humbert Humbert from his enduring attraction to young girls, the pair's relationship did provide him with the outward appearance of sexual normalcy within a French bourgeois marriage.[20]

Humbert Humbert's self-awareness as a nympholept—an aberrant—pushes him to marriage as an institution of acceptable sexuality. Of his sexual

16   Ibid., 76.
17   Ibid.
18   Ibid., 27.
19   Ibid., 28.
20   For more on *Lolita* and how "the protagonists' ideals and aspirations of sexual harmony go against the grain of the bourgeois marriage," see Maxim D. Shrayer, "Nabokov's Sexography," *Russian Literature* 48 (2000): 495–516.

relationships prior to coming to America and meeting Lolita, Humbert Humbert writes:

> No wonder, then, that my adult life during the European period of my existence proved monstrously twofold. Overtly, I had so-called normal relationships with a number of terrestrial women having pumpkins or pears for breasts; only, I was consumed by a hell furnace of localized lust for every passing nymphet whom as a law-abiding poltroon I never dared approach. The human females I was allowed to wield were but palliative agents.[21]

Hiding behind the façade of his conventional marriages yet disgusted by the women he uses to gain legitimacy, Humbert Humbert is free to enact his true desires without philistine suspicion. Humbert Humbert's inability to form conventional marital or sexual bonds is deliberately pushed to the foreground of the novel. Humbert's dysfunctional marriage to Mrs. Haze is mirrored and mimicked in his relationship with Lolita. Yet it is precisely this marriage that enables, masks, and legitimizes Humbert Humbert's abusive treatment of Lolita.

Infidelity

I will now turn to the topic of infidelity as a narrative landscape for Nabokov's fictional exploration of marital discontent. Nabokov's early short story "La Veneziana" (1924; pub. 1995)[22] showcases an impotent husband and an unfaithful wife. In this text, Maureen McGore runs off with Frank, a young son of the wealthy art collector hosting the McGores. As the affair develops, the text reveals that Maureen and her husband "had had no conjugal relations for more than a year, but he nevertheless visited her every morning and watched with powerless excitement while she did her hair."[23] Here, Nabokov establishes McGore's sexual impotence and powerlessness; however, Nabokov does not stop at this revelation of sexlessness in the couple's marriage. Rather, he further

---

21 Nabokov, *Lolita*, 18.
22 Vladimir Nabokov, "La Veneziana," in *The Stories of Vladimir Nabokov*, 111. See Nabokov, *The Stories of Vladimir Nabokov*, 646 for more context on the work's origin. *In her essay in this volume, Megumi DeMond investigates the poetics of "La Veneziana" (M. D. S.).*
23 Nabokov, "La Veneziana," 111.

sexualizes Frank's power over Maureen's husband, as Mr. McGore claims, "I produced the canvas and paints for him. He seduced me with his talent."[24] While McGore's seduction is figurative rather than literal, Nabokov's use of the term "seduced" suggests intentionality. Within "La Veneziana," an early story that remained unpublished in Nabokov's lifetime the anxiety of cuckoldry might be portrayed with the utmost clarity, directly linking a wife's affair with having a powerless and impotent husband.

In *Invitation to a Beheading*, originally serialized in Paris in 1935–1936, Nabokov's focus on heteronormative sexuality intersects again with portrayals of marital infidelity. The novel's protagonist and partial narrator Cincinnatus C. is awaiting his execution for the crime of "gnostical turpitude,"[25] a charge that, while undefined, is suggestive of a dissent from the prescribed norms of the dystopian society where he lives. Nabokov's narrator indicates that "[f]rom his earliest years Cincinnatus, by some strange and happy chance comprehending his danger, carefully managed to conceal a certain peculiarity."[26]

During the course of his imprisonment, Cincinnatus C. attempts to cope not only with his impending execution but also with the flagrant infidelity of his wife, Marthe. Cincinnatus C. narrates numerous, graphic accounts of her extra—and intra—marital sexual liaisons.[27] As in the following passage, Cincinnatus C. often depicts himself as powerless against the lust of Marthe and her lovers:

> Count how many she had [. . .] endless torture: to talk at dinner
> with one or another of her lovers, appear cheerful, crack nuts,
> crack jokes, and all the while to be mortally afraid to bend down,
> and chance to see the nether half of the monster whose upper half
> was quite presentable, having the appearance of a young woman

---

24 Ibid., 114.
25 Vladimir Nabokov, *Invitation to a Beheading*, trans. Dmitri Nabokov in collaboration with the author (New York: Vintage Books, 1989), 72.
26 Ibid., 24.
27 For the sake of space, I have not attempted to elucidate any possible Joycean inspiration for Marthe's behavior and the novel's *Ulysses*-esque narration of adultery. However, Joyce's impact on Nabokov cannot be overstated. For more context on Nabokov's relationship with and reading of Joyce, see Geert Lernout, "Nabokov on Joyce and Ulysses," in *Vladimir Nabokov's Lectures on Literature: Portraits of the Artist as Reader and Teacher*, ed. Jürgen Pieters and Ben Dhooge (Leiden: Brill Rodopi, 2018), 101–120. Also, while one might attempt to connect the Marthe of *Invitation* to Joyce's mistresses of the same name, recipient of Joyce's famed "dirty letters," note that *Invitation* was written decades before the publication of Joyce's letters to his mistress. For more on Joyce's Marthe, however, see Janine Utell, *James Joyce and the Revolt of Love: Marriage, Adultery, Desire* (New York: Palgrave Macmillan, 2010), 17–32. *For a detailed examination of Joyce's influence on Nabokov, see Nina Khaghany's essay in this volume (M. D. S.).*

and a young man visible down to the waist at table, peacefully feeding and chatting; and whose nether half was a writhing, raging quadruped.[28]

Cincinnatus C. plays an unusual role in his wife's infidelities. Despite having full knowledge of Marthe's sexual escapades, Cincinnatus C. still attempts to maintain the façade of a happy bourgeois marriage. He includes his wife's lovers in their domestic mealtime rituals and plays the welcoming host, all the while aware of the other men's power to cuckold and humiliate him, often under Cincinnatus C.'s gaze. Yet, while Cincinnatus C. claims to be terrified of Marthe's infidelity, it does not prohibit him from hosting and witnessing her sexual escapades. Furthermore, Cincinnatus C.'s complex sexual landscape lends itself to speculation that his imprisonment is meant as punishment for queerness, though this is not directly established in the text.

In fact, Cincinnatus C.'s response to Marthe's affairs and sexual "calisthenics" (to borrow the term from Cincinnatus C.'s jailer M'sieur Pierre) entirely diverges from one's expected reaction. While aspects of her adultery border on humorous, the protagonist nevertheless maintains his emotional devotion to his wife. In the midst of his imprisonment, he thinks, "In spite of everything I loved you, and will go on loving you [...] I shall love you, and one day we shall have a real, all-embracing explanation, and then perhaps we shall somehow fit together, you and I, and turn ourselves in such a way that we form one pattern and solve the puzzle."[29] Reading Cincinnatus heteronormatively thus clarifies that Cincinnatus C. and his wife Marthe are operating under two different definitions of what constitutes an acceptable marriage.

One might suggest that Cincinnatus C.'s sexual and psychological weakness renders him incapable of recognizing the futility of his relationship with Marthe. From this perspective, his belief that a simple "all-embracing explanation" would be capable of rectifying their marital troubles, or that such a conversation would even occur at all, becomes a further example of his profound naivety. If one takes seriously the notion of Cincinnatus C.'s queerness, however, his enduring love for unfaithful Marthe reflects the inherent instability of his sexuality in a homophobic totalitarian environment.[30] Leaving in the background numerous other

---

28 Nabokov, *Invitation to a Beheading*, 64.
29 Ibid., 60.
30 *The question of the homophobia of the society where Cincinnatus C. lives has its roots in a very productive discussion of the topic by members of the Nabokov seminar at Boston College in the spring semester of 2023 (M. D. S.).*

instances of infidelity within Nabokov's corpus, I will now turn to an examination of death within marriage.

Death within Marriage

A number of Nabokov's works portray death as a major theme in conjunction with both sexual heteronormalcy and marital infidelity. Nabokov's short stories "Revenge" (1924) and "The Aurelian" (1930), in particular, focus on a husband's violence and virulence resulting from a perceived insult on the part of a wife, and both end in the death of one partner.

"Revenge" follows an unnamed English professor as he navigates the assumed infidelity of his young wife. The wife, who "despite her husband's capricious disposition, his frequent outbursts of unjustified jealousy, his silences, sullenness, and incomprehension [. . .] felt happy, for she loved and pitied him,"[31] writes a romantic letter to an old (spectral) lover after seeing him in a dream. The fact that the wife "lied to poor Jack"[32] with her romantic language in this letter is of no consequence, as the professor "realized with utter clarity that he would murder his wife."[33] Nabokov again contrasts two partners' varying ideas of love and marriage. Where the professor's wife is satisfied within her marriage solely through the act of providing her husband with love and pity, the professor is possessed with morbid, violent jealousy.[34] The professor's murder of his wife provides an alternate ending to the extramarital affairs that plague Nabokov's other characters. There is irony in this wife's being innocent of adultery, and this dramatic irony, stemming from the two characters' versions of reality, only further emphasizes the fragility of their partnership.

In the early "Revenge," readers instead witness the fulfillment of the homicidal spousal rage that would receive a subtler treatment in Nabokov's later fiction. In the masterpiece story "The Aurelian," readers meet the deeply unlikeable Paul Pilgram, a shop owner and lepidopterist who "belonged, or rather was meant to belong (something—the place, the time, the man—had been ill-chosen) to a special breed of dreamers, such dreamers as used to be called in the old days

---

31 Vladimir Nabokov, "Revenge," trans. Dmitri Nabokov, in *The Stories of Vladimir Nabokov*, 72.
32 Ibid., 70.
33 Ibid., 68.
34 It is worth noting that this marriage is also coded with infrequent sexual intimacy and with sexual violence, as Nabokov notes that the wife enjoyed her husband's "infrequent, forceful caresses," in ibid., 72.

'Aurelians.'"[35] This self-identification as a dreamer and lover of the otherworldly beauty of butterflies and moths, or Aurelian, places Pilgram outside of society's psychosocial norms. This passion for the lepidoptera infects Pilgram with a disdain for the ordinary world in which he is forced to live. Pilgram's chosen outlet for this disdain, and for domestic abuse, is Eleanor, his wife of nearly twenty-five years.[36] From Pilgram's perspective, marriage is incompatible with his particular form of genius. After a personal disappointment leaves him with the idea that he will not be able to abandon the woman who ties him to a mundane existence and travel abroad on a butterfly collecting expedition, Pilgram "for several minutes, with his eyes closed, nagged his wife, thinking she was still standing near; then he heard her sobbing softly in the kitchen, and toyed with the idea of taking an ax and splitting her pale-haired head."[37] However, it is not Eleanor who meets her end in this story, and her response to the absence of her husband reveals the contradictory ways in which the two partners conceive of their marriage.

Eleanor's mental turmoil upon realizing that her husband has left her[38] (although yet unaware of his death) reflects the duality of the spouses' partnership. Although "she felt like howling, running to the police, showing her marriage certificate, insisting, pleading," Eleanor nevertheless "kept on sitting, her hair slightly ruffled, her hands in white gloves."[39] Eleanor's initial instinct is to seek the help of the authorities; she feels that proof of her marriage alone should be sufficient evidence for the reestablishment of her domestic comfort. To Eleanor, the nuptial bond exists as proof of societal stability regardless of the relationship's actual unhappiness. This concept is thwarted, however, by her recognition that to act as if her marriage certificate were proof of any inherent right to stability would not accomplish anything.

Perhaps surprisingly, Nabokov also employs the device of spousal death in works where a marriage might otherwise have been happy and fulfilling. We see this in both the short story "The Return of Chorb" (1925) and in Nabokov's unfinished 1940 sequel to his novel *The Gift* (serialized in 1937–1938; complete book edition 1952). "The Return of Chorb"[40] features the recently widowed émigré writer Chorb, whose brief but happy marriage ended with his wife's

---

35 Vladimir Nabokov, "The Aurelian," trans. Peter A. Pertzoff and Vladimir Nabokov, in *The Stories of Vladimir Nabokov*, 250.

36 Ibid.

37 Ibid., 256.

38 Note that Pilgram announces his departure through a letter which reads, "'*Off to Spain. Don't touch anything till I write. Borrow from Sch. or W. Feed the lizards,*'" in ibid., 258.

39 Nabokov, "The Aurelian," 258.

40 See Nabokov, *The Stories of Vladimir Nabokov*, 648, for more context on the work's origin.

accidental death by electric shock midway through the couple's honeymoon. In his grief, Chorb retraces the couple's steps, "pass[ing] in reverse through all the spots they had visited together on their honeymoon journey."[41] Chorb is haunted by his deceased wife on this slow journey; his days are punctuated by the memory of their time together, and "night imbued with sudden terror her irrational presence."[42] The Chorbs' fleeting, happy marriage thus becomes the stuff of nightmares, culminating with Chorb's return to the hotel in which the couple began their marriage. Chorb hires a prostitute who vaguely resembles his dead spouse to sleep beside him in the hotel room and reenact his brief happiness.

Nabokov nods to Orpheus as a parallel figure to Chorb; a stone sculpture of the mythological Thracian poet-singer stands outside of the hotel.[43] Chorb's journey through the places he and his wife visited during their honeymoon bears a deliberate resemblance to the myth of Orpheus and Eurydice. Like Orpheus descending into the underworld to retrieve his beloved Eurydice, Chorb retraces his steps in a futile attempt to reclaim what he has lost.[44] However, while Orpheus sought to bring Eurydice back from death, Chorb's journey is a quest of mourning and introspection rather than an attempt at resurrection.

The haunting presence of Chorb's deceased wife throughout his journey echoes the spectral presence of Eurydice in Orpheus's life. Just as Orpheus was burdened with the memory of Eurydice, Chorb is tormented by the memory of his wife's absence, which permeates both his waking hours and his nightmares. Furthermore, the transformation of the Chorbs' memory of a happy marriage into a nightmarish reality underscores the tragic aspect of their relationship. This transformation, too, parallels the myth of Orpheus and Eurydice, where the blissful union of the lovers is shattered by the cruel hand of fate. In both narratives, the idealized image of marital happiness is juxtaposed with the harsh reality of

---

41 Vladimir Nabokov, "The Return of Chorb," trans. Dmitri Nabokov, in *The Stories of Vladimir Nabokov*, 148.

42 Ibid., 149.

43 Ibid., 153. For a discussion of Chorb's Orphic journey, see Maxim D. Shrayer, *The World of Nabokov's Stories* (Austin: University of Texas Press, 1999), 95–99; Matthew Roth, "'Together into the Tomb': Orphic Undercurrents in 'The Return of Chorb,'" *Nabokovian* 83 (2022), accessed March 16, 2024, https://thenabokovian.org/sites/default/files/2022-07/Roth_Fall_2022.pdf.

44 For a discussion of how Nabokov merges the real world with the "otherworld" of Chorb's journey, see Priscilla Meyer, "Nabokov's Short Fiction," in *The Cambridge Companion to Nabokov*, ed. Julian Connolly (Cambridge: Cambridge University Press, 2005), 123, accessed March 16, 2024, https://digitalcollections.wesleyan.edu/_flysystem/fedora/2023-03/28671-Original%20File.pdf.

mortality, highlighting the fragility of human relationships and the inevitability of loss. As Shrayer states in his analysis of Chorb's journey, "[Chorb's] tragic mistake lies in his having confused the immortality of memory and the physical irreversibility of death."[45] Chorb's obsession with holding onto the vestiges of his wife, his belief that "if he recreated thus the near past—her image would grow immortal and replace her forever,"[46] reflects a disconnect between mundane reality and the idealism of romance.

In the unfinished sequel to *The Gift*, however, this portrait of love cut short by death looks somewhat different. At the conclusion of the published part one of novel, protagonists Fyodor and Zina are heading for marital happiness. Nabokov characterizes this couple's fulfilling relationship in several key ways that differ from the unhappy or dysfunctional marriages we have so far examined. First, Fyodor and Zina believe that they are highly compatible partners. Nabokov's narrator, capturing Fyodor's perspective as he falls in love with his future wife, claims, "not only was Zina cleverly and elegantly made to measure for him by a very painstaking fate, but both of them, forming a single shadow, were made to the measure of something not quite comprehensible, but wonderful and benevolent and continuously surrounding them."[47] With the frequent inclusion of such highly deliberate, ardent prose, Nabokov implies an underlying cohesion between the two halves of this couple. In fact, he suggests they are fated for a marriage that reflects both ideals of sexual harmony and societal expectations of domestic bliss.

Yet, while the pair may be able to escape the traps of Nabokov's many other fictional marriages, riddled as they are with miscommunication and disagreement over the meanings of love and matrimony, we also see hints of these same problems within the origin of Fyodor's and Zina's relationship. Almost immediately after waxing poetic about the couple's fateful cohesion, Nabokov hints at the failings of Fyodor's love for Zina:

> He would scarcely have decided to say that he loved her—for he
> had long since realized that he was incapable of giving his entire
> soul to anyone or anything: its working capital was too necessary
> to him for his own private affairs; but on the other hand, when he
> looked at her he immediately reached (in order to fall off again a

---

45   Shrayer, *The World of Nabokov's Stories*, 90.
46   Nabokov, "The Return of Chorb," 149.
47   Nabokov, *The Gift*, 177.

minute later) such heights of tenderness, passion and pity as are reached by few loves.[48]

Even while Nabokov outlines an emotional formula for maintaining a successful romantic relationship—tenderness, passion, and pity—he suggests that Fyodor cannot sustain these emotions. Further, Nabokov clarifies that despite the pair's supposed fate as two halves of a "single shadow," Fyodor may not be constitutionally capable of valuing another human being above his literary work.

This idea finds reinforcement at the novel's finale, as the pair's palpable happiness arises out of Zina's willful obfuscation of the extent of Fyodor's self-centeredness. Zina encourages Fyodor's writing ambitions, stating, "'That's all marvelous, [. . .] like it all immensely. I think you'll be such a writer as has never been before, and Russia will simply pine for you—when she comes to her senses too late." Yet Zina immediately follows her praise with the question, "'But do you love me?'"[49] Here, Nabokov shows that, unlike for Luzhin's wife in *The Defense*, Fyodor's genius is not enough to sustain Zina's satisfaction in the relationship. In fact, Fyodor's response of "'What I am saying is in fact a kind of declaration of love'" is met with Zina's candid retort, "'A 'kind of' is not enough. You know at times I shall probably be wildly unhappy with you. But on the whole it does not matter, I'm ready to face it.'"[50] Zina's willingness to embrace these intimations and pangs of unhappiness might signal an understanding of the sacrifices necessary within an enduring marriage. At the same time, this passage establishes an unequal dynamic within the foundation of Zina and Fyodor's relationship, and this dynamic, framed by Nazism, World War II and the approaching Holocaust, emerges as the couple's downfall in Nabokov's unfinished sequel to the novel.

This abandoned text of part two, which is currently only available in Russian, has been summarized in the work of Jane Grayson and Maxim D. Shrayer. In Shrayer's summary, "the half-Jewish Zina and her husband Fyodor are living in Paris in the late 1930s; they are childless and poverty-stricken. Their marriage is strained; Fyodor sees a French prostitute. Zina dies in Paris, run over by a car—perhaps more of an authorial rescue from encroaching history than it is an authorial punishment."[51] Of course, Nabokov's intentions for Zina's death are

---

48 Ibid., 178.
49 Ibid., 364.
50 Ibid., 364–65.
51 Maxim D. Shrayer, "'I Am Talking to You Like King Solomon,'" *Jewish Review of Books*, Fall 2015, accessed May 10, 2024, https://jewishreviewofbooks.com/articles/1870/i-am-talking-to-you-like-king-solomon/.

unclear. What is suggestive, however, is that historicizing the unfinished pages reveals the challenges Zina might have faced even if Nabokov had attempted to give her an alternative trajectory. At Nabokov's time of writing, 1940,[52] the full scope of Zina's endangerment as a Jewish woman and a refugee in Nazi-occupied Paris would have been unknown. While Zina's death would have spared her the horrors that would soon overtake Europe, it also releases her from what by now is an unhappy marriage with Fyodor.

One section of Nabokov's sequel is dedicated to Fyodor's relationship with "Yvonne," a prostitute working in Paris. Grayson's description of the affair examines Fyodor's sexual and aesthetic investment in the relationship, which transcends in duration and emotional gravity beyond the simple procurement of a sex worker's services.[53] Further, as Grayson explicates, immediately after Zina's death Fyodor visits a café, where "he meets a young woman he already knows slightly and senses to be attracted to him. They have a casual affair, lasting through the spring."[54] In Nabokov's draft of Fyodor's and Zina's future, the instabilities in their relationship have overpowered Zina's hopeful naivety towards Fyodor's self-obsession. While readers may finish part one of *The Gift*—the only one available to Anglophone readers—with a sense that the couple's early union reflects mutual understanding and productive communication, is it impossible to read Nabokov's plans for the couple without returning to Fyodor's own recognition of the fleetingness which characterizes his feelings of love for Zina?

We do not know if Nabokov intended for part two of *The Gift* to end with Zina's death. One cannot help but wonder where Nabokov might have carried Fyodor's story past the death of his wife.[55] Stressing the instability in Fyodor's romantic and professional affairs, Grayson states that the "last chapter" of Nabokov's draft can be summed up by Fyodor's experiencing "a loss of direction, a sense of futility. Everywhere the sketches end in a dead-end, an impasse, or in stalemate."[56] Perhaps, where many of Nabokov's characters have demonstrated marriage's incompatibilities with personal happiness and fulfillment, Fyodor's fate after the dissolution of his marriage with Zina, the biggest supporter of his artistic ambitions, reveals the devastating consequences of losing a supporter who both recognizes and accepts one's failings.

---

52   Ibid.; Jane Grayson, "Washington's Gift: Materials pertaining to Nabokov's *Gift* in the Library of Congress," *Nabokov Studies* 1 (1994): 27, accessed May 16, 2023, https://doi.org/10.1353/nab.2011.0094.
53   Ibid., 35.
54   Ibid., 43.
55   Question posed by Maxim D. Shrayer in conversation on May 4, 2023.
56   Grayson, "Washington's Gift," 45.

The Modernist Marriage of Vladimir and Véra Nabokov

Of course, Vladimir Nabokov's personal history with infidelity is well-documented. His most notorious affair, the one that nearly ended his marriage, began in 1937 with the introduction of the Russian émigrée Irina Guadanini.[57] Vladimir and Irina met in Paris; Vladimir was living separately from Véra Nabokov and their son, Dmitri, as he desperately searched for work that would allow him to take his Jewish wife and child out of Nazi Germany. Irina, a divorcée and an aspiring poet, was a great fan of Nabokov's writing. (Unlike Véra, however, Irina was not Jewish, and no apparent danger awaited her during the Nazi occupation of France.)[58]

Nabokov's letters to his wife during the months of his affair with Guadanini fluctuate garishly between outpourings of love for his wife and scorn for any references to the rumors of his extramarital affair. On 7 April 1937, Vladimir writes, "I dreamt of you this night [...] and, all morning long, have been going around in a sort of cloud of tenderness for you. I felt your hands, your lips, hair, everything—and if I'd been able to dream such dreams more often, my life would've been easier. You are my love."[59] Just one month later, on 10 May 1937, Nabokov tells his wife that the writer Ivan Bunin is jealous not of his writing but rather of "'the success with women' that the gutter gossip attributes to me."[60] For the last several decades, critics and biographers have attempted to reconcile the man who could so elegantly lie about this affair with the man who so clearly loved his wife. What makes Nabokov's 1937 affair even more difficult to forgive is that, despite the serious professional and existential circumstances that brought him to Paris, he made minimal attempts to hide his affair with Guadanini. Vladimir Nabokov's letters to Véra Nabokov during the course of this affair remained full of deflection, denial, and . . . tenderness.[61]

Eventually, Véra Nabokov would receive an anonymous letter, probably from a concerned Parisian acquaintance, tipping her off about her husband's relationship with Irina Guadanini.[62] The affair played out dramatically and even publicly.

---

57 For information on the affair between Nabokov and Irina, see Andrea Pitzer, *The Secret History of Vladimir Nabokov* (New York: Pegasus Books, 2013), 130–135. See also Brian Boyd, *Vladimir Nabokov: The Russian Years* (Princeton, NJ: Princeton University Press, 1990), 433.
58 Pitzer, *The Secret History of Vladimir Nabokov* 130–135.
59 Vladimir Nabokov, *Letters to Véra*, ed. and trans. Olga Voronina and Brian Boyd (New York: Alfred A. Knopf, 2015), 345.
60 Nabokov, *Letters to Véra*, 372.
61 See Schiff, Stacy, *Véra: Mrs. Vladimir Nabokov* (New York: Random House, 1999), 90.
62 Pitzer, *The Secret History of Vladimir Nabokov*, 133.

Vladimir's eventual admission to Véra of the truth of his infidelity began the couple's process of reconciliation. While Vladimir's letters to his wife in the coming months prove that the couple fought continuously, Véra would later deny that her marriage had undergone such turmoil. Yet evidence remains that she threatened to take Dmitri away from her husband. Further, months after the affair had ended, Vladimir still kept in contact with his former mistress.[63]

How much of Nabokov's writing about marriage and infidelity was informed or inspired by his own experiences? Biographers and critics have already pointed to links between Véra and Zina, some even calling *The Gift* an "ode to [Nabokov's] fidelity."[64] Yet Nabokov himself was certainly not consistently faithful to Véra, and his unfinished sequel to *The Gift* reveals the same of Fyodor, who has been called Nabokov's partial alter ego. While the connections between the two women, both of them their partners' most supportive readers and intellectual equals, are ponderous, consideration of the sequel to *The Gift* puts Véra's denial of her inspiration for Zina's character into context.[65] While Nabokov was working on the published version of *The Gift* during his affair with Guadanini, he wrote its unfinished sequel only three short years after the finale of his marriage's most difficult period. Véra, of course, would not want to be connected to a woman whose death, in what survives of part two of *The Gift*, barely interrupts her husband's bouts of sexual exploration.

Eventually, however, the marriage of Véra and Vladimir Nabokov regained its stability. By the time of the author's death, Véra had become totally committed to preserving a public image of their marriage's unfailing happiness.[66] This attempt at damage control, however, could not erase biographers' curiosity about Nabokov's extramarital relationships. How are we to understand the couple's desire to erase the memory of their marital struggles against available evidence, especially when their story ended in the kind of reconciliation that Nabokov granted so few of his fictional characters?

Perhaps Véra Nabokov, like the wives of many of her husband's protagonists who were geniuses, viewed the appearance of a happy marriage primarily as a

---

63   On Véra's response to the affair, see Schiff, *Véra*, 90.

64   Ibid., 91. See also Shrayer "I Am Talking to You Like King Solomon" for more on connections between Véra and Zina, especially in context of the unfinished sequel. Also see Maxim D. Shrayer, "Nabokov, Religion, and the Holocaust," *Tablet Magazine*, September 7, 2023, https://www.tabletmag.com/sections/arts-letters/articles/nabokov-religious-conversion-holocaust.

65   For more information, see Yuri Leving, *Keys to "The Gift": A Guide to Nabokov's Novel* (Boston, MA: Academic Studies Press, 2011), 172–177.

66   Schiff, *Véra*, 349.

symbol of security and stability within a highly unstable world.[67] Or perhaps the couple, experiencing their romance over the span of many decades rather than the spread of a few hundred pages, was an example of two people who manage to reach a mutual understanding of what it means to exist within, and narrate, their own marriage and connection.

Bibliography

Primary Sources

Nabokov, Vladimir. *Invitation to a Beheading*. Translated by Dmitri Nabokov in collaboration with the author. New York: Vintage Books, 1989.

———. *Lolita*. New York: Random House, 1997.

———. *Letters to Véra*. Edited and translated by Olga Voronina and Brian Boyd. New York: Alfred A. Knopf, 2015.

———. *The Stories of Vladimir Nabokov*. [Edited by Dmitri Nabokov]. New York: Vintage Books, 1995.

———. *The Defense*. Translated by Michael Scammell in collaboration with the author. New York: Vintage Books, 1990.

———. *The Gift*. Translated by Michael Scammell in collaboration with the author. New York: Vintage Books, 1991.

Secondary Sources

Boyd, Brian. *Vladimir Nabokov: The Russian Years*. Princeton, NJ: Princeton University Press, 1990. http://www.jstor.org/stable/j.ctt1btc5v8.

———. *Vladimir Nabokov: The American Years*. Princeton, NJ: Princeton University Press, 1991. http://www.jstor.org/stable/j.ctt1btc5pp.

Foster, John Burt, Jr. *Nabokov's Art of Memory and European Modernism*. Princeton, NJ: Princeton University Press, 1993. http://www.jstor.org/stable/j.ctt7rg65.

Grayson, Jane. "Washington's Gift: Materials pertaining to Nabokov's *Gift* in the Library of Congress." *Nabokov Studies* 1 (1994): 21–67. Accessed May 16, 2023. https://doi.org/10.1353/nab.2011.0094.

Lernout, Geert. "Nabokov on Joyce and Ulysses." In *Vladimir Nabokov's Lectures on Literature: Portraits of the Artist as Reader and Teacher*, edited by Jürgen Pieters and Ben Dhooge, 101–20. Leiden: Brill Rodopi, 2018.

Leving, Yuri. *Keys to "The Gift": A Guide to Nabokov's Novel*. Boston, MA: Academic Studies Press 2011.

Meyer, Priscilla. "Nabokov's Short Fiction." In *The Cambridge Companion to Nabokov*, edited by Julian Connolly, 119–134. Cambridge: Cambridge University Press, 2005. Accessed

---

67 *In her essay in this volume, Fiona Steacy examines Véra Nabokov's co-creative relationship with her husband (M. D. S.).*

March 16, 2024. https://digitalcollections.wesleyan.edu/_flysystem/fedora/2023-03/28671-Original%20File.pdf.

Pitzer, Andrea. *The Secret History of Vladimir Nabokov*. New York: Pegasus Books, 2013.

Raschke, Debrah. *Modernism, Metaphysics, and Sexuality*. Selinsgrove, PA: Susquehanna University Press, 2006.

Roth, Matthew. "'Together into the Tomb': Orphic Undercurrents in 'The Return of Chorb.'" *Nabokovian* 83 (2022). Accessed March 16, 2024. https://thenabokovian.org/sites/default/files/2022-07/Roth_Fall_2022.pdf.

Schiff, Stacy. *Véra: Mrs. Vladimir Nabokov*. New York: Random House, 1999.

Shelden, Ashley T. *Unmaking Love: The Contemporary Novel and the Impossibility of Union*. New York: Columbia University Press, 2017.

Shrayer, Maxim D. "'I Am Talking to You Like King Solomon.'" *Jewish Review of Books*, Fall 2015. Accessed May 10, 2023. https://jewishreviewofbooks.com/articles/1870/i-am-talking-to-you-like-king-solomon/#.

———. "Nabokov's Sexography." *Russian Literature* 48, no. 4 (2000): 495–516. Accessed March 16, 2024. https://doi.org/10.1016/S0304-3479(00)80033-2.

———."Saving Jewish-Russian Émigrés." In *Revising Nabokov Revising. The Proceedings of the International Nabokov Conference*, edited by Mitsuyoshi Numano and Tadashi Wakashima, 123–130. Kyoto: The Nabokov Society of Japan, 2010.

———. *The World of Nabokov's Stories*. Austin: University of Texas Press, 1999.

———. "Nabokov, Religion, and the Holocaust." *Tablet Magazine*, 7 September 2023. Accessed November 15, 2023. https://www.tabletmag.com/sections/arts-letters/articles/nabokov-religious-conversion-holocaust.

Utell, Janine. *James Joyce and the Revolt of Love: Marriage, Adultery, Desire*. New York: Palgrave Macmillan, 2010.

Joyce's L. Bloom to Nabokov's Cincinnatus C.: The Influence of Joyce's *Ulysses* on Nabokov's *Invitation to a Beheading*

Nina Khaghany

Introduction: Nabokov and Joyce

It requires little imagination to picture university students smuggling contraband into their dormitories. It is amusing, however, to picture that around 1922, one of these items of contraband was a blue, goatskin cover copy of Joyce's *Ulysses,* brought from Paris to Cambridge University by Peter Mrosovsky, friend of the young Vladimir Nabokov.[1] Banned in England in 1922, *Ulysses* introduced Nabokov to the literary use of sexually explicit if metaphorical language; Mrosovsky read the more explicit sections of Molly Bloom's soliloquy to Nabokov during finals week. Nabokov's initial, small interactions with *Ulysses* grew into great esteem for Joyce's novel, which Nabokov praised many times as one of the greatest literary works of the twentieth century. Nabokov commented in 1977 that "Joyce's *Ulysses* is set apart from all modern literature, not only by the force of his genius, but also by the novelty of his form."[2]

Already during his interwar European years of exile, Nabokov was an admirer of Joyce, so much so that when first saw the great Irishman in the late 1930s in Paris, he described him as a wonder-like figure "sitting [. . .] arms folded [. . .]

---

1   Brian Boyd, *Vladimir Nabokov: The Russian Years* (Princeton, NJ: Princeton University Press, 1990), 194.
2   Robert Robinson, "Nabokov's Butterflies, Four Interviews," in *Conversations with Vladimir Nabokov,* ed. Robert Golla (Jackson: University Press of Mississippi, 2017), 223.

glasses glinting" among a team of Hungarian soccer players.[3] Nabokov admitted in 1954 that even though he and Joyce shared an entire dinner, he remembers "not one word of it."[4]

When Nabokov suggested his list of the greatest literary works of the twentieth century, he placed, "in this order: Joyce's *Ulysses*, Kafka's [*The Metamorphosis*], Bely's *Petersburg*, and the first half of Proust's fairy tale, *In Search of Lost Time*."[5] He taught these works in his "Masters of European Fiction" at Cornell University and spent a large part of the course on *Ulysses*; out of all his lecture notes, the only manuscripts of Nabokov lectures that were published in facsimile were his lectures on Joyce.[6] Even in his final exam, questions on Joyce's *Ulysses* occupied ninety minutes of the allotted time, whereas Proust and Kafka were only given thirty minutes each. As Geert Lernout remarks, "it seems safe to say Joyce was worth three Kafkas or three Prousts."[7]

In a *Vogue* interview in 1969, Nabokov explained that he urged his students to read beyond the novel's classical allusions: "Instead of perpetuating the pretentious nonsense of Homeric, chromatic, and visceral chapter headings, instructors should prepare maps of Dublin with Bloom's and Stephen's intertwining itineraries clearly traced."[8] Joyce himself was often annoyed with his early interpreters' preoccupation with *The Odyssey*, and he ultimately refrained from publishing chapter titles, originally named after characters and events in *The Odyssey*.[9] Nabokov referenced Joyce's decision as support for his own teaching method: "There is nothing more tedious than a protracted and sustained allegory based on a well-worn myth; and after the work had appeared in parts, Joyce promptly deleted the pseudo-Homeric titles of his chapters when he saw

3   Alfred Appel Jr., "Nabokov's Interview," *Wisconsin Studies in Contemporary Literature* 8, no. 2 (1967), accessed September 15, 2023, http://lib.ru/NABOKOW/Inter06.txt_with-big-pictures.html.
4   Appel Jr., "Nabokov's Interview." Also see M. H Bengal, "Joyce, Nabokov, and the Hungarian National Soccer Team," *James Joyce Quarterly* 31, no. 4 (1994): 519–25, accessed September 15, 2023, http://www.jstor.org/stable/25473589.
5   Geert Lernout, "Nabokov on Joyce and Ulysses," in *Vladimir Nabokov's Lectures on Literature,* ed. Ben Dhooge and Jürgen Pieters (Leiden: The Netherlands: Brill, 2017), 99–120, accessed September 15, 2023, https://doi.org/10.1163/9789004352872_008.
6   Ibid., 101–102.
7   Ibid., 99.
8   Sadie Stein, "Nabokov on Joyce," *Paris Review*, August 23, 2013, accessed September 15, 2023, https://www.theparisreview.org/blog/2013/08/23/nabokov-on-joyce/.
9   Litz Walton, "Joyce's Notes for the Last Episodes of 'Ulysses,'" *Modern Fiction Studies* 4, no. 1 (1958), accessed September 15, 2023, http://www.jstor.org/stable/26277074.

what scholarly and pseudoscholarly bores were up to."[10] After Joyce, Nabokov emphasized that *Ulysses* is beyond a parody of Homer, and its modernist novelty leaves a magnitude of impressions in the mind of the reader.[11]

And yet, despite his praise of *Ulysses*, Nabokov denied any influence of Joyce directly on his writing. In keeping with his common practice of deflecting claims of influence, Nabokov maintained that he had failed to study *Ulysses* fully until the late 1930s, already after having completed and published *Invitation to a Beheading* in 1935–1936.[12] The 1959 forward to the English translation of *Invitation to a Beheading* offers a glaring example:

> Incidentally, I could never understand why every book of mine invariably sends reviewers scurrying in search of more or less celebrated names for the purpose of passionate comparison. During the last three decades they have hurled at me (to list but a few of these harmless missiles) Gogol, Tolstoevski, Joyce, Voltaire, Sade, Stendhal, Balzac, Byron, Beerbohm, Proust, Kleist, Makar Marinski, Mary McCarthy, Meredith (!), Cervantes, Charlie Chaplin, Baroness Murasaki, Pushkin, Ruskin, and even Sebastian Knight.[13]

Scholars of Nabokov often disregard his disclaimers or denials of influence. For instance, Maxim D. Shrayer questions Nabokov's rejection of Kafka's influence.[14] Gavriel Shapiro offers a comparison of *Invitation to a Beheading* to Kafka's *The Castle*.[15] Pace Nabokov, critics have drawn parallels between Nabokov and Joyce, notably, between *Finnegans Wake* and *Pale Fire*, and between *Ulysses* and both *Lolita* and *The Real Life of Sebastian Knight*.[16]

---

10 Vladimir Nabokov, *Lectures on Literature*, ed. Fredson Bowers (San Diego, CA: Harcourt/ Bruccoli Clark, 2002), 442.

11 See James Joyce, letter to Carlo Linati, September 21, 1920, in *Letters of James Joyce*, comp. Danis Rose and John O'Hanlon, accessed September 15, 2023, https://jjda.ie/main/JJDA/u/FF/ubiog/ulett.htm.

12 Appel Jr., "Nabokov's Butterflies."

13 Vladimir Nabokov, *Invitation to a Beheading*, trans. Dmitri Nabokov in collaboration with the author (New York: Vintage Books, 1989), 6.

14 Maxim D. Shrayer, "A Dozen Notes to Nabokov's Short Stories," *Nabokovian* 40 (1998): 42–63.

15 Gavriel Shapiro, *Delicate Markers: Subtexts in Vladimir Nabokov's Invitation to a Beheading* (New York: Peter Lang, 1998).

16 For further reading, see: Gennady Barabtarlo, "Within and Without Cincinnatus's Cell: Reference Gauges in Nabokov's Invitation to a Beheading," *Slavic Review* 49, no. 3 (1990): 390–97; Mary Bellino, "Nabokov's Ada: The Place of Consciousness" [review of Boyd,

Nabokov composed *Invitation to a Beheading* while working on his longest Russian-language novel *The Gift*, which has been compared to *Ulysses*. In his

---

Vladimir Nabokov: The Russian Years], *Nabokov Studies* 7, no. 1 (2002): 223–229, accessed September 15, 2023, https://doi.org/10.1353/nab.2010.0010; Anat Ben-Amos, "The Role of Literature in 'The Gift,'" *Nabokov Studies* 4, no. 1 (1997): 117–49, accessed September 15, 2023, https://doi.org/10.1353/nab.2011.0038; Anna Brodsky, "Homosexuality and the Aesthetic of Nabokov's 'Dar,'" *Nabokov Studies* 4 (1997): 95–115, accessed September 15, 2023, https://doi.org/10.1353/nab.2011.0026; Leland De la Durantaye, "Lolita in *Lolita*, or the Garden, the Gate and the Critics," *Nabokov Studies* 10, no. 1 (2006): 175–97, accessed September 15, 2023, https://doi.org/10.1353/nab.2007.0003; Alexander Dolinin, "Art of the Execution: Notes on the Theme of Capital Punishment in Nabokov," *Nabokov Online Journal* 8 (2014), accessed September 15, 2023, https://www.academia.edu/10744602/Art_of_the_Execution_Notes_on_the_Theme_of_Capital_Punishment_in_Nabokov; Penelope Gilliatt, "Penelope Gilliatt interview with Vladimir Nabokov, for American *Vogue*," in Vladimir Nabokov, *Conversations with Vladimir Nabokov*, ed. Robert Golla (Jackson: University Press of Mississippi, 2017), 103; Herbert Gold, "Vladimir Nabokov, The Art of Fiction no. 40," in Nabokov, *Conversations with Vladimir Nabokov*, 151; Neil Hickey, "The Author of *Lolita*," in Nabokov, *Conversations with Vladimir Nabokov*, 27; Erwin R. Steinberg, "James Joyce and the Critics Notwithstanding, Leopold Bloom Is Not Jewish," *Journal of Modern Literature* 9, no. 1 (1981), accessed September 15, 2023, http://www.jstor.org/stable/3831274; Donald B. Johnson, "Vladimir Nabokov" [review of Jane Grayson's book], *Nabokov Studies* 9, no. 1 (2005): 215–16, accessed September 15, 2023, https://doi.org/10.1353/nab.2005.0011; Thomas Karshan, "December 1925: Nabokov between Work and Play," *Nabokov Studies* 10, no. 1 (2006): 1–25, accessed September 15, 2023, https://doi.org/10.1353/nab.2007.0005; Nassim Balestrini, "Nabokov Criticism in German-Speaking Countries: A Survey," *Nabokov Studies* 5, no. 1 (1998): 185–234, accessed September 15, 2023,, https://doi.org/10.1353/nab.2011.0030; Will Norman, "The Real Life of Sebastian Knight and the Modernist Impasse," *Nabokov Studies* 10, no. 1 (2006): 67–97, accessed September 15, 2023,https://doi.org/10.1353/nab.2007.0014; Ole Nyegaard, "Uncle Gustave Is Present: The Canine Motif in Lolita," *Nabokov Studies* 9, no. 1 (2005): 133–55, accessed September 15, 2023, https://doi.org/10.1353/nab.2005.0016; J. H. Raleigh, "Bloom as a Modern Epic Hero," *Critical Inquiry* 3, no. 3 (1977): 583–98, accessed September 15, 2023, http://www.jstor.org/stable/1342941; Robinson, "Nabokov's Butterflies," 224; Rudolf Sardi, "Nabokov's Cold Pudding: The Stylistic and Structural Impact of *Finnegans Wake* on *Lolita*, *Pale Fire*, and *Bend Sinister*," *AnaChronist* (2009), accessed September 15, 2023, https://link.gale.com/apps/doc/A225938542/AONE?u=mlin_m_bostcoll&sid=googleScholar&xid=9ea54719; Philipp Schweghauser, "Metafiction, Transcendence, and Death in Nabokov's Lolita," *Nabokov Studies* 5, no. 1 (1998): 99–116, accessed September 15, 2023, https://doi.org/10.1353/nab.2011.0035; Franklin Sciacca, "Sacrificing the Maiden's Head: Decoding Nabokov's Burlesque of Sex and Violence in *Invitation to a Beheading*," in *The Goalkeeper: The Nabokov Almanac*, ed. Yuri Leving (Boston: Academic Studies Press, 2010), 28–47, accessed September 15, 2023, https://doi.org/10.2307/j.ctt1zxsk4n.7; Savely Senderovich, "Dickens in Nabokov's *Invitation to a Beheading*: A Figure of Concealment," *Nabokov Studies* 3, no. 1 (1996): 13–32, accessed September 15, 2023, https://doi.org/10.1353/nab.2011.0037; Shapiro, *Delicate Markers*; Anna Sharudenko, "Joyce's Criticism of Sexism and Anti-Semitism through the Use of Bloom's 'Femininity' in *Ulysses*," *Macksey Journal* 2 (2021), accessed September 15, 2023, https://www.jstor.org/stable/26285792; Erik Simpson, "Bloom's Perversion in Ulysses," *Prairie Bloom: Studies of Ulysses at Grinnell*, November 15, 2016, accessed September 15, 2023, https://eriksimpson.sites.grinnell.edu/Ulysses16/uncategorized/blooms-perversion-in ulysses/.

biography, Brian Boyd draws a connection between *Ulysses* and *The Gift*: "In *Ulysses*, Joyce compresses all the swarming life of Dublin into a single book. In *The Gift*, as if in reply, Nabokov offers us a capital and a contingent [. . .]."[17] Furthermore, John Burt Foster Jr. argues that Nabokov's experimentation with "Circean" techniques in *Bend Sinister* served as a stepping stone to the whirlwind plot of *Invitation to a Beheading*.[18] Just as in these cases, Nabokov's denial or obfuscation of influence often yields the opposite results by auguring further investigation. The trace of Joyce in *Invitation to a Beheading* has not received sufficient attention, and this essay attempts to remedy this situation.

The Voices of Cincinnatus C. and Leopold Bloom

In *Lectures on Literature*, Nabokov critiques Joyce's stream of consciousness technique in Molly Bloom's soliloquy, explaining that Joyce emphasizes verbal thought over images: "One can comment here that it exaggerates the verbal side of thought. Man thinks not always in words but also in images, whereas the stream of consciousness presupposes a flow of words that can be notated: it is difficult, however, to believe that Bloom was continuously talking to himself."[19]

Foster Jr. believes that Nabokov's opinion of Molly's prose "should not be understood as making a blanket condemnation of Joyce."[20] Nabokov's praise of Bloom's voice, specifically the impression that Bloom is not just "talking" but thinking, may also be construed as a commentary on the creation of the voice of Cincinnatus C., the protagonist of *Invitation for a Beheading*. In Cincinnatus, Nabokov utilizes Joyce-style stream of consciousness monologue along with images from the character's past to create what Foster Jr. has called "two-tiered memory."[21]

Leopold Bloom is introduced in Chapter 4, "Calypso." In contrast to the verbose and overly intelligent mind of Stephen Dedalus, the voice of Bloom is fragmentary and unpretentious. In comparison to Dedalus, Bloom's pedestrian tone supports the mundane nature of his opening scene, which features Bloom setting up breakfast for himself, his wife, and his cat: "Another slice of bread

---

17   Boyd, *Vladimir Nabokov: The Russian Years*, 464–466. See also John Burt Foster Jr., *Nabokov's Art of Memory and European Modernism* (Princeton, NJ: Princeton University Press, 1993), 233–254, accessed September 15, 2023, http://www.jstor.org/stable/j.ctt7rg65.16.
18   Foster, *Nabokov's Art of Memory and European Modernism*, 177.
19   Nabokov, *Lectures on Literature*, 289.
20   Foster, *Nabokov's Art of Memory and European Modernism*, 246n7.
21   Ibid., 41

and butter. Three four, right. She didn't like her plate full. Right [. . .] Cup of tea soon. Good. Mouth dry."[22] Bloom's stream of consciousness narrates his current actions as he butters his wife's toast while also giving a broader context of Bloom's life—his past with his wife and a hint towards his future. The use of the first-person stream of consciousness inherently immerses the reader in Bloom's perspective, but Annalisa Volpone ventures that Joyce's use of unfinished fragmentary speech involves the reader further, as a co-participant in Bloom's memory.[23] Volpone argues that Joyce's "silence" and "unwillingness to continue" Bloom's thoughts forces the reader to try and fill in the gaps of the narrative,[24] an example of which can be seen later in the same chapter of the novel: "Bone them young so they metempsychosis. That we live after death. Our souls. That a man's soul after he dies, Dignam's soul . . . / Did you finish it? He asked."[25]

More commonly, however, Bloom's unfinished thoughts end in periods. Throughout *Ulysses*, a phrase circulates pertaining to a letter Bloom receives from a potential suitor: "What perfume does your wife wear?"[26] It is repeated in fragmented form throughout the text: "What perfume?"; "What perfumes does your?"[27] Paired with repetition, the changing forms of the phrase invite the reader to return to their own memory of the letter to understand why Bloom is recalling its message.

At other times, Bloom's fragmented thoughts are not repetitions, but censored thoughts: "Molly fondling him in her lap. O the big doggybowowosywowsy! [. . .] Then about six o'clock I can. Six. Six. Time will be gone then. She . . ."[28] Bloom is aroused by the memory of his wife and begins to think about the time when she will be alone at home. Blazes Boylan, with whom Molly is having an affair, arrives at four in the evening and therefore will be gone by six. This logic is confirmed by the wordplay of "six" and sex as well as of "time" and "him" (surely Blazes Boylan). The fragment "she," however, leaves the reader without answers. "[S]he" is, presumably Molly, but nothing further can be deduced, leaving the reader to hypothesize.

---

22 James Joyce, *Ulysses*, ed. Hans Walter Gabler, Wolfhard Steppe, Claus Melchior, and Michael Groden (New York: Vintage Books, 1993), 45.
23 Annalisa Volpone, "The Poetics of the Unsaid: Joyce's Use of Ellipsis between Meaning and Suspension," in *Doubtful Points: Joyce and Punctuation* (Leiden: Brill, 2014), 87–108, accessed September 15, 2023, https://doi.org/10.1163/9789401211833_007.
24 Volpone, "The Poetics of the Unsaid," 93.
25 Joyce, *Ulysses*, 53.
26 Ibid., 63.
27 Ibid., 219, 227, 487, 489.
28 Ibid., 143.

Cincinnatus's thoughts, like those of Bloom, are often fragmentary, and he offers the reader an explanation for his disjointed thinking: "I have in my head many projects that were begun and interrupted at various times."[29] Much like Annalisa Volpone argues for Bloom, Stephen Blackwell comments on how "ruptures" in *Invitation to a Beheading* increase the necessity of the reader to fill in the gaps of Cincinnatus's thoughts: "These ruptures heighten the reader's uncertainty about the narrated world. [. . .] The reader becomes a character in the work of art, but one with a role that is open and flexible."[30]

Chapter Two of *Invitation to a Beheading* provides one of the instances where Nabokov utilizes a "Bloom-like" laconic stream of consciousness for the voice of Cincinnatus C.:

> "In any case I have been measured," said Cincinnatus, resuming his journey and rapping lightly with his knuckles on the walls. "But how I don't want to die! My soul has burrowed under the pillow. Oh, I don't want to! It will be cold getting out of my warm body. I don't want to . . . wait a while . . . let me doze some more."[31]

Like Leopold Bloom, Cincinnatus C. recounts his current actions of falling asleep ("doze some more") but also prompts the reader to investigate the workings of his memory.[32] Furthermore, his stream of consciousness displays Nabokov's experimentation with "two-tiered" memory.[33] Consider another example, also from Chapter Two:

> Childhood on suburban lawns. They played ball, pig, daddy-longlegs, leapfrog, rumpberry, poke. He was light and nimble, but they did not like to play with him. In winter the city slopes were covered with a smooth sheet of snow, and what fun it was to hurtle down on the so-called "glassy" Saburov sleds. How quickly night would fall, when one was going home after sledding.[34]

---

29 Nabokov, *Invitation to a Beheading*, 16.
30 Stephen Blackwell, "Reading and Rupture in Nabokov's *Invitation to a Beheading*," *Slavic and East European Journal* 39, no. 1 (1995): 38, accessed September 15, 2023, https://doi.org/10.2307/308691.
31 Nabokov, *Invitation to a Beheading*, 26.
32 Ibid.
33 Foster, *Nabokov's Art of Memory and European Modernism*, 41.
34 Ibid., 25.

Nabokov introduces images of Cincinnatus's past in concise fragments. The author provides small details that evoke intimate memories of a child's experience at playing, such as the names of certain made-up games: "ball, pig, daddy-longlegs, leapfrog, rumpberry, poke."[35] The fragmented thoughts even feel childish, lacking correct grammar. After this memory, Cincinnatus admits, a bit randomly, *"That which does not have a name does not exist.* Unfortunately everything had a name."[36] The text then jumps to his perspective in the present: "'Nameless existence, intangible substance,' Cincinnatus read on the wall where the door covered it when open."[37] Reading the sign on the door triggered a memory of his childhood. Nabokov has constructed a stream of consciousness based on a "two-tiered" memory. The reader is first immersed in the images in Cincinnatus's head before they are given a verbal translation of his present. In *Ulysses*, the reader is left to piece together Bloom's train of thought as he attempts to avoid Blazes Boylan. Similarly, by inverting the order of Cincinnatus's flashback and his current actions, Nabokov's reader must piece together both the conscious mind and current reality of Cincinnatus C.

Authorship for Bloom and Cincinnatus C.

Another hallmark of Bloom's stream of consciousness is self-censorship of thought. While Cincinnatus also censors his thought, unlike Bloom who remains in public throughout *Ulysses*, Cincinnatus is alone in a jail cell for most of the novel. Not only are his thoughts private, but so too are many of his spoken words. In one instance, he speaks to his short-lived view of the hills and mountains outside the jail cell: "Bewitching! I have never seen those hills look exactly like that, so mysterious. Somewhere among their folds, in their mysterious valleys, couldn't I . . . No, I had better not think about it."[38]

The placement of ellipses leads the reader to make inferences about Cincinnatus's experience. We associate his desire to censor his imagination with a rejection of hopeless simulations of freedom. We also come to a similar conclusion as Cincinnatus censors his thoughts when thinking about Little Emmie:

---

35 Ibid.
36 Ibid., 26.
37 Ibid.
38 Ibid., 43.

"No—this was only self-deception, nonsense. The child had doodled aimlessly . . . Let us copy out the titles and lay the catalogue aside. Yes, the child . . . With the tip of her tongue showing at the right corner of her mouth, tightly holding the stubby pencil, pressing down upon it with a finger white with effort . . . And then, after connecting a particularly successful line, leaning back, rolling her head this way and that, wriggling her shoulders, and, going back to work on the paper, shifting her tongue to the left corner . . . so painstakingly. . . . Nonsense, let's not dwell on it anymore."[39]

Little Emmie is a figure of both hope and perversion for Cincinnatus C., as he engages in intimate acts with her and believes that she could tell him the date of his death sentence.[40]

Like Bloom, Cincinnatus censors his thoughts to prevent the development of hope for the future and to avoid dwelling on current issues. Unlike Bloom, however, Cincinnatus begins un-censoring his thoughts through writing. In one particular instance, he transfers his direct thoughts to paper, beginning with a small portion of his thinking and expanding on it as his writes:

"But then perhaps," thought Cincinnatus, "I am misinterpreting these pictures. Attributing to the epoch the characteristics of its photograph. The wealth of shadows, the torrents of light, the gloss of a tanned shoulder, the rare reflection, the fluid transitions from one element to another—perhaps all of this pertains only to the snapshot, to a particular kind of heliotypy, to special forms of that art, and the world really never was so sinuous, so humid and rapid-just as today our unsophisticated cameras record in their own way our hastily assembled and painted world."

"But then perhaps" (Cincinnatus began to write rapidly on a sheet of ruled paper) "I am misinterpreting . . . Attributing to the epoch . . . This wealth . . . Torrents . . . Fluid transitions . . . And the world really never was . . . Just as . . . But how can these ruminations help my anguish? Oh, my anguish—what shall I do with you, with myself?"[41]

39 Ibid., 62.
40 Ibid., 47. For more about "Little Emmie," see my discussion below.
41 Ibid., 51.

Here, we note elements of Bloom-like stream of consciousness not in the thoughts of Cincinnatus C., which appear to be in order, but in Cincinnatus's writing. The un-censoring of Cincinnatus's emotions is marked by his "rapid" writing and exasperated cries of "anguish."[42] As the novel progresses, we begin to hear Cincinnatus's story directly through his writing, which maintains the first-person voice.

The voice of Cincinnatus C. feels most authentic in his writing, and is also marked by a greater sense of authorship. Censorship in Bloom's thought is in itself a kind of authorship, and his stream of consciousness does not depict the entire truth. Bloom's voice invites the reader to fill in the gaps and omissions and restore meaning. Cincinnatus's writing works in a similar way, which he even acknowledges with his image of the "umbilical cord" connecting him to other worlds.[43] Interestingly enough, one gets a similar image of the umbilical cord in *Ulysses* not from Bloom, but from Stephen Dedalus. Stephen remarks on the image of the "omphalos" (navel) that connects all living things to Eve.[44] He imagines reaching down into his navel and picking up a phone to speak to his past mothers.[45] With the idea of the navel, Stephen suggest that speech connects the subject to the rest of the world. Both Joyce and Nabokov call on the imagery of words that do not belong solely to a privileged speaker, thus rendering the search for an "authentic" voice in Cincinnatus C. and Bloom as ultimately futile.

In order to facilitate this "artistic harmonious balance between the reader's mind and the author's mind," Nabokov creates the unique voice of a third person omniscient narrator.[46] Nabokov's highly personalized narrator has access to Cincinnatus's direct thoughts and can speak to the reader, a technique Joyce uses as well. On its own, the stream of consciousness writing of Bloom seeks to eliminate boundaries between his mind and that of *Ulysses*'s reader. However, it was another goal of Joyce's to depict Bloom in the broader world of Dublin, and thus not all of these boundaries could be dropped. As Joyce put it, "I want to give a picture of Dublin so complete that if the city one day suddenly disappeared from the earth it could be reconstructed out of my book."[47] Bloom's life is

---

42 Ibid.
43 Ibid., 53.
44 Joyce, *Ulysses*, 32.
45 Ibid., 32.
46 Vladimir Nabokov, "Good Readers and Good Writer" [1948], accessed September 15, 2023, http://moodyap.pbworks.com/f/nbkv.GoodReaders_Writers.pdf.
47 Irene Topher, "Joyce's Dublin," Irish Culture and Customs, accessed September 15, 2023. https://www.irishcultureandcustoms.com/AWriters/JoyceDublin.html.

described by a third person omniscient narrative entity, which is referred to by Joyceans as the "arranger."[48] After Joyce, Nabokov bridges the final gap between his protagonist's world of fiction and his reader's through his own use of metaliterary devices.

The Arrangers

David Hayman describes the device of Joyce's arranger: "The arranger should be seen as something between a persona and a function, somewhere between the narrator and the implied author."[49] The intersection of the arranger's narratorial capabilities and the authorial intent is especially visible in Chapter 7 of *Ulysses*, "Aeolus," which describes Bloom at work as an advertisement writer for the *Freeman's Journal* and is organized by a variety of subsection headings (as in a newspaper). Although the form of the chapter differs from those before it, the narrative voice maintains its ability to depict Bloom's thoughts as well the world around him.

However, when looking at titles such as "We see the Canvasser at work" or "Short but to the point" (which describes the subsection itself as short in length) one questions the identity of "we."[50] Here the narrative voice does not represent Bloom's perspective but that of the reader. Thus, Hayman's Joycean arranger emerges: an entity that has one foot in the mind of the author, one that is aligned with the audience, and yet another in the mind of Bloom as he works on his advertisement for "Alexander Key(es)."[51] John Somer argues that the emergence of the arranger's metaliterary voice in "Aeolus" is not sudden but part of an increasing presence that continues to grow until its peak in Chapter 11, "Sirens."[52]

Hayman's term, "the arranger," applies to the narratorial entity of *Invitation to a Beheading*. I am not the first to draw a connection between one of Nabokov's narrators and Joyce's arranger; John Somer compares Nabokov's narrator in the originally Russian short story "The Leonardo" (1933) to the arranger.[53] Unlike

---

48 David Hayman, *"Ulysses": The Mechanics of Meaning*, revised and expanded (Madison, WI: University of Wisconsin Press, 1982), 122–123. For further reading, see John Somer, "The Self-Reflexive Arranger in the Initial Style of Joyce's 'Ulysses,'" *James Joyce Quarterly* 31, no. 2 (1994): 65–79, accessed September 15, 2023, http://www.jstor.org/stable/25485420.
49 Ibid., 65.
50 Joyce, *Ulysses*, 32.
51 Ibid.
52 Somer, "The Self-Reflexive Arranger in the Initial Style of Joyce's 'Ulysses,'" 67.
53 Ibid., 71.

Joyce's arranger who emerges after seven episodes, Nabokov's announces itself with a metaliterary power already in the second paragraph of *Invitation to a Beheading*.

> So we are nearing the end. The right-hand, still untasted part of the novel, which, during our delectable reading, we would lightly feel, mechanically testing whether there were still plenty left (and our fingers were always gladdened by the placid, faithful thickness) has suddenly, for no reason at all, become quite meager: a few minutes of quick reading, already downhill, and—O horrible![54]

Here, the pronouns "we" and "our" reveal that the arranger's perspective is united with the reader's.[55] The arranger and the reader are both engaged in "our delectable reading," just as they both feel the "faithful thinkness" of the remaining pages of the book in "[their] fingers."[56] Moreover, the arranger echoes the typical emotions of a reader, admitting that they were once "gladdened" to begin the novel, yet upon hearing about Cincinnatus's execution, they suddenly exclaim, "O horrible!"[57]

However well this passage unifies the perspective of the reader and the arranger, the latter's knowledge is always superior to the former's. The arranger knows the details of Cincinnatus's past as it tells the story in Chapter Two of the novel.[58] Furthermore, the arranger knows more about Cincinnatus's current experience. In one instance, Cincinnatus stares in wonder at a "painting" on his wall. The arranger (in parenthesis) corrects him: "(Actually it was a parchment sheet hanging on the wall with two columns of detailed 'rules for prisoners'; the bent corner, the red letters of the heading, the vignettes, the ancient seal of the city—namely, a furnace with wings—provided the necessary materials for the evening illumination.)"[59] Here, the use of parentheses separates Cincinnatus's thoughts of the "painting" from the voice of the arranger interjecting the truth about the "parchment."

---

54 Nabokov, *Invitation to a Beheading*, 12.
55 Ibid.
56 Ibid.
57 Ibid.
58 Ibid., 13.
59 Ibid., 14.

The arranger can also speak to Cincinnatus: "Cincinnatus, your criminal exercise has refreshed you" and also "Cincinnatus, what anguish!"[60] The arranger distinguishes his voice from Cincinnatus's but also separates himself from audience: "(the double, the gangrel, that accompanies each of us—you, and me, and him over there—doing what we would like to do at that very moment, but cannot [. . .])."[61] The use of "you," "me," and "him over there" solidifies the arranger as an entity with its own selfhood. The arranger makes a funny point about the tension between his experiences and those of Cincinnatus. The description of the end of Cincinnatus's first day is interrupted by parentheses: "It was then and only then (that is, lying supine on a prison cot, after midnight, after a horrible, horrible, I simply cannot tell you what a horrible day) that Cincinnatus C. clearly evaluated his situation."[62] While parentheses often separate the arranger's voice from Cincinnatus's, here the pronoun "I" confuses this logic, as it implies that the arranger understands Cincinnatus's "horrible" situation as if he had experienced it. The statement "I simply cannot tell you" further confuses the perspective of the arranger. Here he is both a separate individual who cannot understand Cincinnatus's day and one who is using the statement idiomatically, denoting that he, more than words can express, understands Cincinnatus.

In some instances, however, the arranger's voice becomes that of Cincinnatus C., notably facilitated through Cincinnatus's writing. The arranger and Cincinnatus engage in "mimicry," a technique, Hayman argues, that is central to Joyce's arranger.[63] In Chapter Four, the arranger proclaims, "Cincinnatus, what anguish!" which is later picked up in Cincinnatus's writing: "But how can these ruminations help my anguish? Oh, my anguish—what shall I do with you, with myself?"[64] What is more interesting, however, is what accompanies "mimicry": the progression of thought. In this same instance as Cincinnatus begins to write, the narrative transitions from the arranger's voice first to Cincinnatus's thoughts, and later to his written words:

> Reveling in all the temptations of the circle, life whirled to a state of such giddiness that the ground fell away and, stumbling, falling, weakened by nausea and languor—ought I to say

---

60 Ibid., 48.
61 Ibid., 25.
62 Ibid., 20.
63 Somer, "The Self-Reflexive Arranger in the Initial Style of Joyce's 'Ulysses,'" 70.
64 Nabokov, *Invitation to a Beheading*, 49–51.

it?—finding itself in a new dimension, as it were . . . Yes, matter has grown old and weary, and little has survived of those legendary days—a couple of machines, two or three fountains—and no one regrets the past, and even the very concept of "past" has changed. / "But then perhaps," thought Cincinnatus, "I am misinterpreting these pictures. Attributing to the epoch the characteristics of its photograph . . . "But then perhaps" (Cincinnatus began to write rapidly on a sheet of ruled paper)[65]

In the beginning, it is unclear which thoughts belong to the arranger and which to Cincinnatus. The arranger has used "I" previously, but one could argue that this usage enables a transition to Cincinnatus's voice.[66] Indeed, the presence of the ellipses, a hallmark of Cincinnatus's voice, morphs an incomplete thought into the next statement. The most obvious distinction can be made through use of the terms "thought" and "wrote."[67] Although parentheses bring back the third-person omnipresent voice of the arranger (a separate entity from Cincinnatus C.), this transition of thought shows the arranger's words becoming a part of Cincinnatus's own writing.

As *Invitation to Beheading* progresses, the voice of Cincinnatus's writing grows in power, and the reader begins to see less of the arranger. For example, Chapter Five is devoted to Cincinnatus's letter. His writing begins to take over the arranger's voice in Chapter Nine. The voice of the arranger at the end of the chapter is cut off ("only a moment ago").[68] In the preceding chapters, Cincinnatus's actions are halted when the arranger explains that the lights went out.[69] The inversion of the positions of Cincinnatus and the arranger signals that, while Cincinnatus's voice strengthens in his writing, he also begins to affect the voice of the arranger.

Both Joyce's and Nabokov's arrangers serve as intermediaries between the reader, the protagonist, and the implied author. However, while in *Ulysses* the voice of the arranger fluctuates in presence, in *Invitation to a Beheading* the arranger and Cincinnatus's voice begin to blend. Nabokov's play with the arranger is different than Joyce's, which also correlates to *Invitation to a Beheading's* metaliterary ending. In *Ulysses*, the world of fictional Dublin is one Leopold Bloom continues to inhabit, despite his hardships throughout his day.

65 Ibid., 53.
66 Ibid.
67 Ibid.
68 Ibid., 107.
69 Ibid., 67, 97.

For Cincinnatus C., the daily, mundane world is unbearable, and he escapes this fictional world by destroying it. In contrast to Joyce, Nabokov gives Cincinnatus C. access to the arranger's voice in order to break the boundaries between fiction and reality, thus allowing his protagonist to free himself.

Bloom and Cincinnatus C. as "Feminine" Jews

Among scholars of *Ulysses*, the physical appearance of Leopold Bloom, who is of Jewish descent on his father's side, is not a highly debated topic. He is five feet nine and one-half, mustached, wears a bowler hat, and carries a cane.[70] He notably has a distinct air of femininity to his physical appearance; described as a "new womanly man" in "Circe" (Chapter 15), he is the "submissive, feminine partner" in his sexual relationship with his wife Molly.[71] There are many interpretations of Joyce's reasoning behind his description of Bloom's physical appearance. There are those who believe that Bloom is based on a real person, those who attribute Bloom's femininity to Joyce's modernist interest in hermaphroditism, and those who argue that the author put a bit of himself into his novel's protagonist.[72] Joyce embraced certain feminine elements of his own physique, notably his small feet, an attribute he gives to Stephen Dedalus, his alter ego in *Ulysses* and elsewhere.[73]

Some aspects of Bloom's appearance and characterization may be tied back to his "Jewishness."[74] Specifically, Bloom embodies aspects of the antisemitic ste-

---

70   Patrick Hastings, "'Stork's Legs' and 'The Step of a Pard': Bloom's Gait," Ulysses Guide, July 24, 2011, accessed September 15, 2023, https://www.ulyssesguide.com/essay-blooms-gait#:~:text=Still%2C%20a%20few%20precise%20details,and%20is%20referred%20to%20as%20; Thomas F. Staley, "The Search for Leopold Bloom: James Joyce and Italo Svevo," *James Joyce Quarterly* 1, no. 4 (1964): 59–63, accessed September 15, 2023, http://www.jstor.org/stable/25486462.

71   Joyce, *Ulysses*, 403; Joseph Allen Boone, "A New Approach to Bloom as 'Womanly Man': The Mixed Middling's Progress in 'Ulysses,'" *James Joyce Quarterly* 20, no. 1 (1982): 67–85, accessed September 15, 2023, http://www.jstor.org/stable/25476481.

72   See Hastings, "'Stork's Legs' and 'The Step of a Pard'; Boone, "A New Approach to Bloom as 'Womanly Man.'"

73   See Fintan O'Toole, "Samuel Beckett: The Private Voice," *New York Review of Books* 65, no. 5 (2015), accessed September 15, 2023, https://www.nybooks.com/articles/2015/03/19/samuel-beckett-private-voice/. Steven Dedalus in Episode 3, "Proteus," is described as having small feet: "But you were delighted when Esther Osvalt's shoe went on you: girl I knew in Paris. Tiens, quel petit pied!" (Joyce, *Ulysses*, 43.) A similar event occurs as Marthe explains the size of Cincinnatus's shoe; see Nabokov, *Invitation to a Beheading*, 21.

74   The term "Jewishness" is used by Erwin R. Steinberg in discussing Bloom's Jewish heritage. In this article, Steinberg argues that Bloom should not be considered Jewish based on

reotypes that were particularly alive in Joyce's time. Joyce's biographer Richard Ellmann suggests that in Leopold Bloom, Joyce criticized Otto Weininger's concept of the "womanly." Ellmann proposes that Joyce had a particular affinity with Weininger's view of the womanly man as "the premise of non-existence," which Joyce supported in his writing by "laboring to isolate female characteristics, from an incapacity for philosophy to a dislike for soup."[75]

Otto Weininger (1990–1903), who was born in Vienna to a Jewish family and converted to Christianity in 1902, had a complex and largely self-hating relationship with his own Jewishness. His legacy played a part in shaping modern notions of racialized antisemitism.[76] In his treatise *Sex and Character: An Investigation of Fundamental Principles* (1903), Weininger describes Jewish men who are traditionally circumcised as "men who have become women."[77] He also alleges the "perversity" of Jewish men by claiming that they are "more absorbed in sexual matters than the Aryan, although he is notably less potent sexually and less liable to be enmeshed in a great passion."[78] In Joycean circles, Bloom is often regarded as a perverse figure. Erik Simpson writes that Bloom engages in voyeurism and has an odd complicity with his wife's adultery as seen in "Circe," where Bloom imagines Molly and Blazes Boylan having sex and urges them on shouting, "Show! Hide! Show! Plough her! More! Shoot!"[79] Bloom also sends erotic letters and photographs and allegedly engages in masochism.[80] At the same time, he does not have sexual intercourse with his wife. Weininger points to the widespread belief, well known to students of Christian Judeophobia, that Jews are "seducers of the soul" and that foreigners, specifically Jewish men, corrupt Christian

---

tenets of the Jewish faith. However, in view of Joyce's depiction of Bloom, as well as how Bloom is perceived by those around him, Bloom comes to embody antisemitic stereotypes assigned to Jewish men in twentieth-century Europe. See Steinberg, "James Joyce and the Critics Notwithstanding, Leopold Bloom Is Not Jewish," *Journal of Modern Literature* 9, no. 1 (1981): 27–49, accessed September 15, 2023, http://www.jstor.org/stable/3831274.

75   Richard Ellmann, *James Joyce*, new and rev. ed. (New York: Oxford University Press, 1982), 463.

76   About Weininger, see "Otto Weininger," Wikipedia, last modified August 20, 2024, https://en.wikipedia.org/wiki/Otto_Weininger.

77   Otto Weininger, *Sex and Character: Authorized Text from the 6th German Edition* (New York City: G. P. Putnam's Sons, 1906), 302. Steinberg argues that it is possible that Joyce referenced this antisemitic (and self-hating) text because of how widely discussed it was in his time. Additionally, there is mention of Joyce discussing Weininger with Frank Budgen; see Steinberg, "The Source(s) of Joyce's Anti-Semitism in 'Ulysses,'" *Joyce Studies Annual* 10 (1999): 63–84, accessed September 15, 2023, http://www.jstor.org/stable/26285792.

78   Weininger, *Sex and Character*, 311.

79   Joyce, *Ulysses*, 403.

80   Erik Simpson, "Bloom's Perversion in Ulysses."

women.[81] Joyce specifically portrays Bloom as a victim of this antisemitic anxiety in Chapter 12 of *Ulysses*, where a character known as the Citizen tells Bloom that "strangers [do not belong in] Ireland" and also refers to a Christian "dishonored wife."[82] (I will discuss this further in the section that follows.)

Cincinnatus C. is described as feminine in ways that recall Bloom. The narrator points out that Marthe remarks that her husband's shoes were so small, they were even "tight on her feet."[83] The introduction to Cincinnatus's small and delicate body is offered in comparison to the physique of Rodion the jailer while they dance a waltz. The narrator remarks on Rodion's weight and might while making it clear that Cincinnatus was definitely the "smaller partner"—traditionally the feminine one—and "light as a leaf."[84]

Cincinnatus's "perversion" is seen through his interactions with Little Emmie.[85] Franklin Sciacca remarks that the twelve-year-old Emmie's is an "Ur-Lolita" figure (aged twelve when Humbert Humbert meets her), as she is pictured with "a piece of brilliant barberry-red hard candy" on her tongue: "the extended symbol of that ripe, but as yet innocent, female sexuality."[86]

Furthermore, in an extended metaphor of a peach, Cincinnatus's engages in voyeurism akin to Bloom's. In Cincinnatus's recollection, he writes to Marthe that he saw her with another man:

> Or when you, with eyes closed tight, devoured a spurting peach and then, having finished, but still swallowing, with your mouth still full, you cannibal, your glazed eyes wandered, your fingers were spread, your inflamed lips were all glossy, your chin trembled, all covered with drops of the cloudy juice, which trickled down onto your bared bosom, while the Priapus who had nourished you suddenly, with a convulsive oath, turned his bent back

---

81 Among his sources, Steinberg references Joan Young Gregg's book *Devils, Women, and Jews* (New York: SUNY, 1997); see Steinberg, "The Source(s) of Joyce's Anti-Semitism in 'Ulysses,'" 68–69.

82 Joyce, *Ulysses*, 266.

83 Nabokov, *Invitation to a Beheading*, 13.

84 Ibid.

85 In the Preface to the English version of the novel, Nabokov includes one of his caustic caveats to the reader, in which he attempts to head off any odious comparisons by flatly stating that it is "the evil-minded who will perceive in little Emmie a sister of little Lolita." See ibid., 7–8.

86 Sciacca, "Sacrificing the Maiden's Head," 37.

to me, who had entered the room at the wrong moment. "All kinds of fruit are good for Marthe," you would say [. . .].[87]

Here Cincinnatus spectates Marthe performing fellatio, which he describes through the metaphor of a dripping peach. At the end of Chapter 18 of *Ulysses*, "Penelope," through the similar metaphor of a pear, Molly describes an episode where she wishes to perform fellatio, notably, in an obvious way for Bloom's enjoyment:

> I might go over to the markets to see all the vegetables and cab-bages and tomatoes and carrots and all kinds of splendid fruits all coming in lovely and fresh who knows whod be the 1st man Id meet theyre out looking for it in the morning [. . .] Id love a big juicy pear now to melt in your mouth like when I used to be in the longing way then Ill throw him up his eggs and tea in the moustachecup she gave him to make his mouth bigger I suppose hed like my nice cream too [. . .] Ill let him know if thats what he wanted that his wife is fucked yes [. . .] theres the mark of his spunk on the clean sheet I wouldnt bother to even iron it out that ought to satisfy him"[88]

Molly metonymizes men as "vegetables" and "splendid fruits" before using the euphemism of a "juicy pear" to describe fellatio. Indeed, she describes that Bloom would have "wanted" his wife "fucked" and would feel "satisfaction" viewing the evidence.

Perhaps more significantly, however, Cincinnatus's relationship with his wife signals a debt to Joyce's construction of the marriage of Leopold and Molly Bloom. Cincinnatus and Marthe do not have conventional sexual relations. Instead, Marthe seeks out suitors who are domineering men in Cincinnatus's life, in a way reminiscent of Molly's choice of Blazes Boylan as a lover.[89]

While neither Molly nor Marthe engages in sexual intercourse with their hus-bands, they both praise their men for their gentleness and lack of abusiveness.

---

87 Nabokov, *Invitation to a Beheading*, 141. *In his essay featured in this volume, Brendan McCourt explores the connections between "sex and eating" in Nabokov's works and discussed the peach-eating scene in Invitation to a Beheading (M. D. S.).*
88 Joyce, *Ulysses*, 654.
89 *In a footnote to her essay in this volume, Ciara Spencer speculates about a connection between the Marthe of Invitation and Joyce's mistresses of the same name, recipient of Joyce's famed "dirty let-ters" (M. D. S.).*

Molly's relationship with Leopold Bloom is the final issue addressed in Chapter 18, "Penelope." This chapter is unlike any other in *Ulysses* as Molly's thoughts are also carried by her stream of consciousness. Molly admits that she liked—loved—Leopold Bloom because she saw "he understood or felt what a woman is."[90] Because of "Bloom's" nature as a "womanly man," he is able to connect to Molly in a way that other men cannot. Through Molly's deep appreciation of her husband, a Jew and an outsider for his detractors, Joyce communicates his authorial sympathy toward Bloom while perhaps debunking antisemitic stereotypes.

Not only does Molly admit that being with her Jewish husband makes her feel "understood," she is able to recall exactly when she felt his love—during their trip to Spain: "then I asked him with my eyes to ask again yes and then he asked me would I yes to say yes my mountain flower and first I put my arms around him yes and drew him down to me so he could feel my breasts all perfume yes and his heart was going like mad and yes I said yes I will Yes."[91] Here, Molly's sexual satisfaction comes from Bloom's gentleness of both spirit and touch.

Marthe, unlike Molly—which is significant—betrays her husband not just by way of the flesh but also by collaborating with the oppressive system. She thus breaks the highest moral bonds of their union. And yet, in a fashion that recalls Molly, Marthe values Cincinnatus C. because he understands her and is gentle with her. In her last visit to her husband in jail, Marthe admits that she received a marriage proposal but plans to reject it: "Anyway I feel it's time I had a good, long rest—you know, close my eyes, stretch out, not think about anything, and relax, absolutely alone of course or else with someone who would really care, and understand everything, everything."[92] Marthe's words prove that she does not simply wish to be left "alone." Rather, she wishes to be "understood" and "cared" for. Dominated by violent men, Marthe feels misunderstood. In the next few lines of the scene, she tells Cincinnatus to "repent" and exclaims that she was ready to give him "everything."[93] While Marthe's last visit with Cincinnatus may be rife with textual irony, one still hears echoes of Molly's soliloquy in Marthe's nostalgia for a relationship in which she is treated kindly, can "relax," and finally be "understood."

---

90   Joyce, *Ulysses*, 654.
91   Ibid., 655.
92   Nabokov, *Invitation to a Beheading*, 198.
93   Ibid., 13.

Nabokov (Re)Turns to the Joycean Other

Why does Nabokov's Cincinnatus C. inherit some of the antisemitic stereotypes with which Joyce endows Leopold Bloom even as he also valorizes Bloom's Jewishness? What the reader knows about Cincinnatus's origins pertains largely to his mother, and there is no reason to believe she is Jewish. At the same time, little is known of Cincinnatus's father, and this could this suggest an obfuscation of his origins. Leopold Bloom himself is not Halachically Jewish: his mother was Irish Catholic, and his father, a Hungarian Jew.[94] He knows little Hebrew and in one instance forgets the story and tradition of Passover.[95] And yet, however Bloom's "Jewishness" is conceived, it is an important component of Joyce's characterization of him as the other in the novel. Bloom openly claims to be a Jew, and, more importantly to Joyce, most of the people around Bloom treat him with contempt and derision.[96] These instances of prejudice are most seen specifically in Chapter 7, "Aeolus," where Bloom is continually interrupted and belittled by his coworkers, and Chapter 12, "Cyclops." As mentioned earlier, Chapter 12 is narrated by a character known as the Citizen. The Citizen describes Bloom in terms that ooze antisemitism: "And his old fellow before him perpetrating frauds, old Methusalem Bloom, the robbing Bloom, the robbing bagman, that poisoned himself with prussic acid after he swamping the country with his baubles and his penny diamonds."[97]

It is not only the Citizen who mistreats Bloom, but all the drinkers in Barney Kiernan's. They "laugh" at Bloom, continually cutting him off: "What I mean is . . . [/]—*Sinn Fein*! says the Citizen. *Sinn Fein amhain!* The friends we love are by our side and the foes we hate before us."[98] Later, they chase Bloom out of the pub.[99] Joyce is less concerned about Bloom's faith than about the way his Jewish roots provoke those around him. Bloom eventually becomes fed up with his mistreatment, and in Chapter 12 he states indignantly: "'I was born here. Ireland [. . .] I belong to a race too [. . .] That is hated and persecuted. Also now. This very moment [. . .] But it's no use, says he. Force, hatred, history, all that. That's not life for men and women, insult and hatred. And everybody knows that it's the very opposite of that that is really life [. . .] Love.'"[100]

---

94   Steinberg, "James Joyce and the Critics Notwithstanding, Leopold Bloom Is Not Jewish."
95   Ibid., 30.
96   Ibid., 33.
97   Joyce, *Ulysses*, 275.
98   Ibid., 251.
99   Ibid., 275.
100 Ibid., 272–273.

In Chapter 12, "Cyclops," we finally hear Bloom address his feelings towards his mistreatment. He rejects "hatred" and "force," and in a lighthearted moment, proclaims "love" as the solution. However, this moment is short-lived and Bloom has to flee the bar. Despite Molly's appreciation of Bloom in Chapter 18, the reader finishes *Ulysses* unsure if Bloom and Molly will reunite. As the narrative concludes, the husband and wife remain together, but alone, at their house on 7 Eccles Street.

Cincinnatus C. faces many forms of contempt, abuse, and prejudice. It is ultimately because of his "turpitude," his indeterminable "otherness," that he is sentenced to death. Although both protagonists are victimized, Bloom and Cincinnatus respond differently to their "othering"—Bloom with the desire to assimilate, Cincinnatus by leaving behind his unaccepting world. While Joyce recognizes that Jews in Dublin encounter antisemitism, he draws on classical mythology to construct—that is, fabricate—a historical world, one day in Dublin in 1904, during which Bloom can peacefully return to his home. In contrast to Joyce, and writing at a very different time in history, Nabokov creates a dystopian world in *Invitation to a Beheading*. However, many aspects of this composite world have led critics to believe that Nabokov is commenting on both Hitlerism and Stalinism.[101] In fact, much of the scholarship on *Invitation to a Beheading* circles around this idea.[102]

If the Nabokov of the late 1930s is indeed using a character of Jewish origin, partially modelled on Bloom, to comment on the atmosphere in Nazi Germany with its legalized persecution of Jews, it is hardly surprising that escape is the only viable option left to Cincinnatus C. Hence Nabokov's decision to send Cincinnatus to a better reality, one where he can be with people who will understand and accept him—and not persecute him for being himself.[103]

---

101 See note 103.
102 For some examples, see Charles Baxter, "Nabokov, Idolatry, and the Police State," *Boundary 2*, 5, no. 3 (1977): 813–28, accessed September 15, 2023, https://doi.org/10.2307/302565; Walter Cohen, "The Making of Nabokov's Fiction," *Twentieth Century Literature* 29, no. 3 (1983): 333–50, https://doi.org/10.2307/441470; Dana Dragunoiu, "Vladimir Nabokov's 'Invitation to a Beheading' and the Russian Radical Tradition," *Journal of Modern Literature* 25, no. 1 (2001): 53–69, accessed September 15, 2023, http://www.jstor.org/stable/3831866; Will Norman, "Nabokov and Benjamin: A Late Modernist Response to History," *Ulbandus Review* 10 (2007): 79–100, accessed September 15, 2023, http://www.jstor.org/stable/25748166; Gavriel Shapiro, *Delicate Markers*.
103 For Further reading, see Dragunoiu, "Vladimir Nabokov's 'Invitation to a Beheading," 9.

In Closing: The Art of Suffering and the Suffering of Art

Not only did Nabokov claim *Ulysses* as one of the greatest literary works and a stylistic gamechanger, but he also asserted *Invitation to a Beheading* as the work for which he "had the highest esteem."[104] One wonders if Nabokov's "esteem" was a nod towards his debt to Joyce.

Joyce transformed the novel and revolutionized techniques of narrating a world of multiple realities surrounding his characters. At the same time, Joyce holds a particularly important place among Anglo-American modernists in his depiction of the dangers of modern racialized antisemitism. Although Nabokov would have probably objected to a comparative investigation of *Invitation to a Beheading* and *Ulysses*, bringing these novels together opens up questions that go far beyond matters of aesthetics. Thinking of the echoes of Joyce in Nabokov's *Invitation to a Beheading* also helps us reconstruct both Nabokov's artistic vision and his historical foresight, on the eve of World War II and the Holocaust, when intolerance and prejudice were about to erupt in the biggest genocide in history.[105] In loving his Cincinnatus C. in much the same way that Joyce loves the half-Jewish Leopold Bloom, Nabokov the creator puts him through suffering in art while also coddling and sheltering him from a much greater suffering.

Bibliography

Primary Sources

Joyce, James. *Ulysses*. Edited by Hans Walter Gabler, Wolfhard Steppe, Claus Melchior, and Michael Groden. New York: Vintage Books, 1993.

Nabokov, Vladimir. *Invitation to a Beheading*. Translated by Dmitri Nabokov in collaboration with the author. New York: Vintage Books, 1989.

———. *Lectures on Literature*. Edited by Fredson Bowers, introduction by John Updike. San Diego: Harcourt/Bruccoli Clark, 2002.

---

104 Appel Jr., "Nabokov's Butterfly."

105 About Nabokov's protection of his characters, especially his Jewish characters, from the calamities of history, see Maxim D. Shrayer, "Saving Jewish-Russian Émigrés," in *Revising Nabokov Revising. The Proceedings of the International Nabokov Conference*, ed. Mitsuyoshi Numano and Tadashi Wakashima (Kyoto: The Nabokov Society of Japan, 2010), 123–130; Maxim D. Shrayer, "Nabokov, Religion and the Holocaust," *Tablet Magazine*, September 7, 2023, accessed September 15, 2023, https://www.tabletmag.com/sections/arts-letters/articles/nabokov-religious-conversion-holocaust.

Secondary Sources

Appel, Alfred, Jr. "Nabokov's Interview." *Wisconsin Studies in Contemporary Literature* 8, no. 2 (1967). Accessed September 15, 2023. http://lib.ru/NABOKOW/Inter06.txt_with-big-pictures.html.

Balestrini, Nassim "Nabokov Criticism in German-Speaking Countries: A Survey." *Nabokov Studies* 5 (1998): 185–234. Accessed September 15, 2023. https://doi.org/10.1353/nab.2011.0030.

Barabtarlo, Gennady. "Within and Without Cincinnatus's Cell: Reference Gauges in Nabokov's Invitation to a Beheading." *Slavic Review* 49, no. 3 (1990): 390–97.

Baxter, Charles. "Nabokov, Idolatry, and the Police State." *Boundary* 2, 5. no. 3 (1977): 813–28. https://doi.org/10.2307/302565. Accessed 15 September 2023.

Bellino, Mary. "Nabokov's Ada: The Place of Consciousness [review of Brian Boyd's book]." *Nabokov Studies* 7, no. 1 (2002): 223–29. Accessed September 15, 2023. https://doi.org/10.1353/nab.2010.0010.

Ben-Amos, Anat. "The Role of Literature in 'The Gift.'" *Nabokov Studies* 4, no. 1 (1997): 117–49. Accessed September 15, 2023. https://doi.org/10.1353/nab.2011.0038.

Bengal, M. H. "Joyce, Nabokov, and the Hungarian National Soccer Team." *James Joyce Quarterly* 31, no. 4 (1994): 519–25. Accessed September 15, 2023. http://www.jstor.org/stable/25473589.

Blackwell, Stephen. "Reading and Rupture in Nabokov's Invitation to a Beheading." *Slavic and East European Journal* 39, no. 1 (1995): 38–53. Accessed September 15, 2023. https://doi.org/10.2307/308691.

Boone, Joseph Allen. "A New Approach to Bloom as 'Womanly Man': The Mixed Middling's Progress in 'Ulysses.'" *James Joyce Quarterly* 20, no. 1 (1982): 67–85.

Boyd, Brian. *Vladimir Nabokov: The Russian Years.* Princeton, NJ: Princeton University Press, 1990.

———. "Words, Works and Worlds in Joyce and Nabokov: Or Intertextuality, Intratextuality, Supratextuality, Infratextuality, Extratextuality and Autotextuality in Modernist and Prepostmodernist Narrative Discourse." *Cycnos* 12, no. 2 (1995): 3–12.

Brodsky, Anna. "Homosexuality and the Aesthetic of Nabokov's 'Dar.'" *Nabokov Studies* 4 (1997): 95–115. Accessed September 15, 2023. https://doi.org/10.1353/nab.2011.0026.

Cohen, Walter. "The Making of Nabokov's Fiction." *Twentieth Century Literature* 29, no. 3 (1983): 333–50. Accessed September 15, 2023. https://doi.org/10.2307/441470.

De la Durantaye, Leland. "Lolita in *Lolita*, or the Garden, the Gate and the Critics." *Nabokov Studies* 10 (2006): 175–97. Accessed September 15, 2023. https://doi.org/10.1353/nab.2007.0003.

Dolinin, Alexander. "Art of the Execution: Notes on the Theme of Capital Punishment in Nabokov." *Nabokov Online Journal* 8 (2014). Accessed September 15, 2023. https://www.academia.edu/10744602/Art_of_the_Execution_Notes_on_the_Theme_of_Capital_Punishment_in_Nabokov.

Dragunoiu, Dana. "Vladimir Nabokov's 'Invitation to a Beheading' and the Russian Radical Tradition." *Journal of Modern Literature* 25, no. 1 (2001): 53–69. Accessed September 15, 2023. http://www.jstor.org/stable/3831866."

Ellmann, Richard. *James Joyce.* New and rev. ed. New York: Oxford University Press, 1982.

Foster, John Burt. *Nabokov's Art of Memory and European Modernism.* Princeton: Princeton University Press, 1993. Accessed September 15, 2023. http://www.jstor.org/stable/j.ctt7rg65.16.

Gilliatt, Penelope. "Penelope Gilliatt Interview with Vladimir Nabokov for American *Vogue*." In *Conversations with Vladimir Nabokov*, edited by Robert Golla, 100–109. Jackson: University Press of Mississippi, 2017.

Gold, Herbert. "Vladimir Nabokov, The Art of Fiction no. 40." In *Conversations with Vladimir Nabokov*, edited by Robert Golla, 143–154. Jackson: University Press of Mississippi, 2017.

Hastings, Patrick. "'Stork's Legs' and 'The Step of a Pard': Bloom's Gait." Ulysses Guide. Last modified 2016. Accessed September 15, 2023. https://www.ulyssesguide.com/essay-blooms-gait#:~:text=Still%2C%20a%20few%20precise%20details,and%20is%20referred%20to%20as%20.

Hayman, David. *"Ulysses": The Mechanics of Meaning*. Revised and expanded ed. Madison, WI: University of Wisconsin Press, 1982.

Hickey, Neil. "The Author of Lolita." In *Conversations with Vladimir Nabokov*, edited by Robert Golla, 27–29. Jackson: University Press of Mississippi, 2017.

Johnson, Donald B. Review of *Vladimir Nabokov*, by Jane Grayson. *Nabokov Studies* 9 (2005): 215–16. Accessed September 15, 2023. https://doi.org/10.1353/nab.2005.0011.

Karshan, Thomas. "December 1925: Nabokov between Work and Play." *Nabokov Studies* 10 (2006): 1–25. Accessed September 15, 2023. https://doi.org/10.1353/nab.2007.0005.

Lernout, Geert. "Nabokov on Joyce and Ulysses." In *Vladimir Nabokov's Lectures on Literature* (Leiden: Brill, 2017). Accessed September 15, 2023. https://doi.org/10.1163/9789004352872_008.

Nabokov, Vladimir. "Good Readers and Good Writers." Accessed September 15, 2023. http://moodyap.pbworks.com/f/nbkv.GoodReaders_Writers.pdf.

Norman, Will. "Nabokov and Benjamin: A Late Modernist Response to History." *Ulbandus Review* 10 (2007): 79–100. Accessed September 15, 2023. http://www.jstor.org/stable/25748166.

———. "*The Real Life of Sebastian Knight* and the Modernist Impasse." *Nabokov Studies* 10 (2006): 67–97. Accessed September 15, 2023. https://doi.org/10.1353/nab.2007.0014.

Nyegaard, Ole. "Uncle Gustave Is Present: The Canine Motif in Lolita." *Nabokov Studies* 9 (2005): 133–55. Accessed September 15, 2023. https://doi.org/10.1353/nab.2005.0016.

O'Toole, Fintan. "Samuel Beckett: The Private Voice." *New York Review of Books* 65, no. 5 (2015). Accessed September 15, 2023. https://www.nybooks.com/articles/2015/03/19/samuel-beckett-private-voice/.

Raleigh, J. H. "Bloom as a Modern Epic Hero." *Critical Inquiry* 3, no. 3 (1977): 583–98. Accessed September 15, 2023. http://www.jstor.org/stable/1342941.

Robinson, Robert. "Nabokov's Butterflies, Four Interviews." In *Conversations with Vladimir Nabokov*, edited by Robert Golla, 221–224. Jackson: University Press of Mississippi, 2017.

Sardi, Rudolf. "Nabokov's Cold Pudding: The Stylistic and Structural Impact of *Finnegans Wake* on *Lolita*, *Pale Fire*, and *Bend Sinister*." *AnaChronist* (2009). Accessed September 15, 2023. https://link.gale.com/apps/doc/A225938542/AONE?u=mlin_m_bostcoll&sid=googleScholar&xid=9ea54719.

Schweghauser, Philipp. "Metafiction, Transcendence, and Death in Nabokov's Lolita." *Nabokov Studies* 5, no. 1 (1998): 99–116. Accessed September 15, 2023. https://doi.org/10.1353/nab.2011.0035.

Sciacca, Franklin. "Sacrificing the Maiden's Head: Decoding Nabokov's Burlesque of Sex and Violence in *Invitation to a Beheading*." In *The Goalkeeper: The Nabokov Almanac*, edited by Yuri

Leving, 28–47. Boston: Academic Studies Press, 2010. Accessed September 15, 2023. https:// doi.org/10.2307/j.ctt1zxsk4n.7.

Senderovich, Savely. "Dickens in Nabokov's *Invitation to a Beheading*: A Figure of Concealment." *Nabokov Studies* 3 (1996): 13–32. Accessed September 15, 2023. https://doi.org/10.1353/ nab.2011.0037.

Shapiro, Gavriel. *Delicate Markers: Subtexts in Vladimir Nabokov's Invitation to a Beheading.* New York: Peter Lang, 1998.

Sharudenko, Anna. "Joyce's Criticism of Sexism and Anti-Semitism through the Use of Bloom's 'Femininity' in *Ulysses*." *Macksey Journal* 2 (2021). Accessed September 15, 2023. https://www. jstor.org/stable/26285792.

Shrayer, Maxim D. "Saving Jewish-Russian Émigrés." In *Revising Nabokov Revising. The Proceedings of the International Nabokov Conference*, edited by Mitsuyoshi Numano and Tadashi Wakashima, 123–130. Kyoto: The Nabokov Society of Japan, 2010.

————. "Nabokov, Religion and the Holocaust." *Tablet Magazine*, September 7, 2023. Accessed September 15, 2023. https://www.tabletmag.com/sections/arts-letters/articles/ nabokov-religious-conversion-holocaust.

Simpson, Erik. "Bloom's Perversion in Ulysses." *Prairie Bloom: Studies of Ulysses at Grinnell*. Accessed September 15, 2023. https://eriksimpson.sites.grinnell.edu/Ulysses16/uncategorized/blooms- perversion-in-ulysses/.

Somer, John. "The Self-Reflexive Arranger in the Initial Style of Joyce's 'Ulysses.'" *James Joyce Quarterly* 31, no. 2 (1994): 65–79. Accessed September 15, 2023. http://www.jstor.org/ stable/25485420.

Staley, Thomas F. "The Search for Leopold Bloom: James Joyce and Italo Svevo." *James Joyce Quarterly* 1, no. 4 (1964): 59–63. Accessed September 15, 2023. http://www.jstor.org/ stable/25486462.

Steinberg, Erwin R. "James Joyce and the Critics Notwithstanding, Leopold Bloom Is Not Jewish." *Journal of Modern Literature* 9, no. 1 (1981): 27–49. Accessed September 15, 2023. http://www.jstor.org/stable/3831274.

————. "The Source(s) of Joyce's Anti-Semitism in 'Ulysses.'" *Joyce Studies Annual* 10 (1999): 63–84. Accessed September 15, 2023. http://www.jstor.org/stable/26285792.

Stein, Sadie. "Nabokov on Joyce." *Paris Review*, August 23 2013. Accessed September 15, 2023. https://www.theparisreview.org/blog/2013/08/23/nabokov-on-joyce/.

Topher, Irene. "Joyce's Dublin." Irish Culture and Customs, March 4, 2011. Accessed September 15, 2023. https://www.irishcultureandcustoms.com/AWriters/JoyceDublin.html.

Volpone, Annalisa. "The Poetics of the Unsaid: Joyce's Use of Ellipsis between Meaning and Suspension." In *Doubtful Points: Joyce and Punctuation, 87–108*. Leiden: Brill, 2014. Accessed September 15, 2023. https://doi.org/10.1163/9789401211833_007.

Walton, Litz. "Joyce's Notes for the Last Episodes of 'Ulysses.'" *Modern Fiction Studies* 4, no.1 (1958): 3–20. Accessed September 15, 2023. http://www.jstor.org/stable/26277074.

Weininger, Otto. *Sex and Character: Authorized Text from the 6th German Edition*. New York: G. P. Putnam's Sons, 1906.

"That Skip-Space Piece": Positioning the Knight in Nabokov's Poetics

Nicholas Adler

Introduction: Working on Our Knight Moves

In *Knight's Move*, a collection of essays published in Berlin in 1923,[1] Viktor Shklovsky explains that the chess knight moves in a strange "L-shape" for two reasons: "the conventionality of art" and the fact that "it is forbidden to take the straight road."[2]

The L-shaped move comes from the figure of the knight in chess, but for Shklovsky, it represents the defamiliarizing prerogative of the artist to see and depict the beyond the "straight road" that constitutes blind adherence to convention. Vladimir Nabokov, who would have read Shklovsky's collection with interest as a Berlin-based young émigré author,[3] takes up this knight metaphor in *The Gift* (ser. 1937–1938; complete book edition 1952), where Fyodor Godunov-Cherdyntsev, his protagonist, writes disparagingly of the nineteenth-century Russian author

*   I am grateful to Maxim D. Shrayer for directing my attention, as I prepared the final version of this essay, to Olga Voronina's recent Russian-language book, *Tainopis': Nabokov. Arkhiv. Podtekst* (St. Petersburg: Izdatel'stvo Ivana Limbakha, 2023), and for translating a summary of Chapter 4, "Spiral Galaxies, or the Cosmic 'Knight's Move' in the Novel *Bend Sinister* and the Short Story 'Lance.'" Voronina examines the connection between Viktor Shklovsky's concept of the knight's move and the otherworldly travel of Nabokov's protagonists. Her engaging work, while thematically related to this essay, centers around two Nabokov texts which I do not address and builds outward toward a cosmology with the medieval knight as its key figure.

1   Dale Peterson, "Knight's Move: Nabokov, Shklovsky and the Afterlife of Sirin," *Nabokov Studies* 11, no. 1 (2007): 1.

2   Viktor Shklovsky, *Knight's Move*, trans. Richard Sheldon (London: Dalkey Archive Press, 2005), 3.

3   For an exploration of the connection between Shklovsky's work and Nabokov, see Maxim D. Shrayer, *The World of Nabokov's Stories* (Austin: University of Texas Press, 1999), 76–81.

Figure 1. Cover of Victor Shklovsky's collection of essays *Khod konia* (Berlin: n.p., 1923).

Nikolai Chernyshevski that the man "saw everything in the nominative [...] when in truth] any genuinely new trend is a knight's move, a change of shadows, a shift that displaces the mirror."[4] By drawing attention to Chernyshevski's inability to see past the nominative, Fyodor fashions himself as a writer who can see beyond the obvious and make "knight's moves" in his creation of art.

Association between Nabokov's protagonists and knights is not limited to explicit mentions like those in *The Gift* or obvious signals such as the title of *The Real Life of Sebastian Knight*. To make a knight's move is to enjoy—or suffer, as the case may be—privileged access to Nabokov's otherworld.[5] Following

---

4   Vladimir Nabokov, *The Gift*, trans. Michael Scammel (New York: Vintage International, 1991), 293.

5   This essay follows Vladimir E. Alexandrov's use of the term "otherworld" as a transcendent realm of idealized love and memory; see Vladimir E. Alexandrov, *Nabokov's Otherworld* (Princeton, NJ: Princeton University Press, 1991).

this thread through a number of Nabokov's prewar and postwar works accords further understanding of what it means to be a knight on the chessboard of a text's constructed reality while also contributing to the study of Nabokov's otherworldly poetics.

A Solution in *The Defense*

In *The Defense* (1930), a novel about an émigré chess grandmaster by the name of Aleksandr Ivanovich Luzhin, Nabokov claims to "introduce a fatal pattern into Luzhin's life" by planting "chess effects [...] in separate scenes [... as well as in] the basic structure of this attractive novel."[6] This claim, taken from Nabokov's 1964 foreword to the English-language version of the text, positions the novel as a starting point for this essay's investigation into the chess knight's capacity to act as a cipher for the governing logic of Nabokov's fictional worlds. Although the term "fatal pattern" implies a certain teleological force, his description of this pattern soon afterwards in the text as "the semblance of a game of skill" implies that parallels between the novel and a game of chess may only be superficial.[7]

Strother B. Purdy picks up on this implication, noting that chess analogies abound in *The Defense* yet their inconsistent nature limits their interpretive potential.[8] Purdy concludes that the chess content of the novel is characterized by "dullness and incoherence" but that a significant connection can be drawn between the symmetry of a chessboard and the theme of symmetry within the novel.[9] Brian Boyd, highlighting *The Defense* in particular, asserts that "within his novels Nabokov creates puzzles as precise as the chess problems he liked to compose."[10] At the same time, Boyd does not engage fully with the idea that the rules of chess could be employed to solve the problems of Nabokov's novels. Boyd and Purdy, then, both understand overarching attributes of chess play as significant in the structure of *The Defense* while undervaluing the possibility that any particular rules of chess can be mapped onto the novel. Earl D.

---

6   Vladimir Nabokov, *The Defense* (New York: Vintage International, 1990), 8.
7   Ibid.
8   For an essay which uses a chess analogy to interpret Luzhin's life, and which Purdy recognizes as failing to rigorously apply the rules of chess, see John Updike, "Grandmaster Nabokov," in *Assorted Prose* (New York: Alfred A. Knopf, 1965), 318–327.
9   Strother B. Purdy, "Culture in Action: Symbols and Strategies," *Modern Fiction Studies* 14, no. 1 (1968–1969): 384.
10   Brian Boyd, "The Problem of Pattern: Nabokov's *Defense*," *Modern Fiction Studies* 33, no. 4 (1987): 577.

Sampson represents this critical position concisely when he writes that "none of Nabokov's novels [. . . is] planned as a whole to reproduce the pattern of any actual game; rather, his overall approach to literary composition follows the *principles* of game playing."[11]

While the thematic connections that critics uncover between chess and Nabokov's novel are compelling, it is also possible to trace a line between the rules of chess and the action of the novel. A chess novel with strikingly few depictions of actual chess play, *The Defense* contains only two instances of a specifically designated piece capturing another piece. One of those instances occurs in Luzhin's realization of the novel's titular defense. When his fiancée's finger touches his eyelid, "the slight pressure on his eyeball causes a strange black light to leap there, to leap like a black Knight which simply took the Pawn if Turati moved it out on the seventh move."[12] The other instance is a more abstract application of chess to life. As Luzhin's fiancée—before she becomes his fiancée— sits waiting for him to answer a question about his childhood, he loses the thread of the conversation, gazing out at the lawn in front of him and "thinking that with a Knight's move of this lime tree standing on a sunlit slope one could take that telegraph pole over there."[13] Knight's move has two meanings in this instance. At the literal level, one could move in an L-shape from the lime tree to the telegraph pole. At both the metaphysical and the metaliterary level, making a knight's move in the Shklovskian sense allows one to find in the mundane realities of a hotel lawn the artistic intricacies of a chess problem. This knight's move in this instance is the first of many in which the world of chess pulls Luzhin away from the comfortable yet mundane world that his fiancée and her family inhabit. The other knight's move, the one which Luzhin imagines employing against Turati, is the titular defense itself, the move (or meta-move) which would have provided Luzhin "the key to indisputable victory."[14] In both scenes, Luzhin is the character making the move. And in both scenes, the move is simultaneously linked to his inability to connect with reality and to his chess-playing. Not every artistic (and therefore defamiliarizing in the Shklovskian sense) knight's move in *The Defense* is signposted with the literal figure of a chess knight, but each

---

11 Earl D. Sampson, "Games Nabokov's Characters Play," *Russian Language Journal* 36 (Winter–Spring 1982): 196.

12 Nabokov, *The Defense*, 116. *Tura*, in Russian, means rook. And while the character of Turati could be discussed in the context of his namesake piece—just as *The Real Life of Sebastian Knight*'s Claire Bishop could be discussed in the context of hers—this paper will leave such discussions to other critics.

13 Ibid., 99.

14 Ibid., 154.

appearance of Luzhin's artistic prowess is accompanied by a loss of contact with reality. This sets the stage for the novel's two overt knight's moves to serve as models for the abstract, artistic knight's moves which follow in the text.

These artistic knight's moves remain grounded in the movement of the chess knight, allowing them to serve in critical investigations of the novel as a chess problem. Both Janet Gezari[15] and D. Barton Johnson engage in such investigations, with Johnson notably claiming that Luzhin "is not a player in a chess game but a pawn in a chess problem [because] in problems, all pieces are in a sense pawns, for all moves are foreordained by the composer."[16] Conflating pawn as puppet with pawn as chess piece exemplifies the tendency—understandably common in scholarship on *The Defense*—to use chess terminology allegorically, with insufficient attention paid to the implications of specific chess terms.

If the novel is a chess problem, one should be able to pinpoint a solution— either a true solution or one of the false solutions Nabokov delights in using to trick overconfident readers. This essay takes up the challenge of reading *The Defense* as a chess problem and proposes that a straight line is the ostensible solution. Luzhin more than once describes inspired gameplay as harmony. Critics make note of the idea of symmetry in the context of the novel's structure and the structure of chess. [17] But it is Luzhin's father, an author, who overtly expresses the answer to what making a harmonious, symmetric move will bring about. When he finally breaks free from the clichés and recycled plots that have dominated his stories up until this point, the elder Luzhin feels that his incredible new story would come together instantly if only he could find "a definite design, a sharp line."[18] He never finds this line, just as Luzhin never finds lasting harmony in chess and never masters the secrets of the straight lines that entrance him first in his childhood math books and later the cubes he sketches after retiring from professional chess. He cannot effectively wield these straight lines for the same reason that he cannot engage straightforwardly with the other people in his life; knights do not have the capacity to do so.

---

15   For an essay which does not figure Luzhin as a particular chess piece but does brilliantly pursue the analogy of Luzhin's suicide as a *sui-mate*, or self-mate, see Janet Gezari, "Chess and Chess Problems," in *The Garland Companion to Vladimir Nabokov*, ed. Vladimir E Alexandrov (New York: Routledge, 1995), 44–53.

16   D. Barton Johnson, "Text and Pretext in Nabokov's *The Defense* or 'Play It Again, Sasha,'" *Modern Fiction Studies* 30, no. 2 (1984): 287.

17   See Purdy, "Culture in Action: Symbols and Strategies" or Gezari, "Chess Problems and Narrative Time in *Speak, Memory.*"

18   Nabokov, *The Defense*, 82.

If this essay takes the world of *The Defense* to be a chess problem, its solution may involve other characters moving in a straight line. But it could not involve Luzhin moving in a straight line because knights are functionally and structurally unable to do so. The straight lines that others follow in conversations, in advancement through career and society, and even in shaving their beards, all elude him. The move of a chess knight involves both an asymmetrical route and a temporary elevation, jumping over pieces that would otherwise block its path. Both the asymmetry and the elevation are incomprehensible within the logic of movement followed by any other chess piece. Fittingly, the novel ends with Luzhin jumping out of his bathroom window in a fit of activity that baffles and traumatizes his family and acquaintances. Purdy, already frustrated with potential chess references not borne out by the rules of chess, comments that as Luzhin despairs of "constructing [a defense], he commits suicide—which is hardly, of course, playing the game."[19] An alternative reading is that rather than pursuing symmetry or attempting to move within the reality of the novel, Luzhin makes a knight's move, leaving that plane of existence in order to end up somewhere inconceivable to others and enacting the genuine solution to the chess problem that is the novel.

A Present Absence in *The Real Life of Sebastian Knight*

The prospect of a Nabokovian protagonist making "knight's moves" can also be observed, albeit for a different reason, in Nabokov's first English-language novel, *The Real Life of Sebastian Knight* (1941). Literally speaking, every move made by novelist Sebastian Knight, the half-brother of the narrator (who is simply called V.) and the subject of the biography V. researches and reconstructs, is a Knight's move. Those moves are linked to the moves of the chess piece in the novelist's embrace of the connection between his name and the chess piece, since "the signature under each poem [he writes is] a little black chess-knight drawn in ink." [20] Chess imagery aside, the link is evident in the V.'s assertion that his brother "used parody as a kind of springboard for leaping into the highest region of serious emotion," thus repurposing certain tricks of the literary trade in order to create a work of transcendent art.[21] This sort of "Knightian twist" epitomizes Shklovsky's conception of artists who make revivifying,

19   Purdy, "Culture in Action: Symbols and Strategies," 383.
20   Vladimir Nabokov, *The Real Life of Sebastian Knight* (New York: Vintage Books, 1992), 15.
21   Ibid., 89.

defamiliarizing knight's moves.[22] Dale Peterson not only makes a compelling case for these linkages between Sebastian, chess knights, and the Shklovskian knight's move; he also expands the chess connection to include other pieces: "The match that the plot plays out features a Knight, a Bishop, and a Rook (Nina's birthname is Toorovetz, from *tura*)."[23] But, once again, there is no critical consensus. Gennady Barabtarlo describes the text as "a vaguely developed chess-planted landscape [. . . in which,] however, chess turns out to be a diversion, small game in a big hunt."[24] He cites a letter from Vladimir Nabokov to Edmund Wilson, dated October 21, 1941, in which the former writes, "except for the sketchy chess-game alluded to in one chapter there is no 'chess-idea' in the development of the whole book. Sounds attractive, but it is not there."[25]

Though Nabokov himself warns against trying to apply the rules of chess to the entire structure of *The Real Life of Sebastian Knight*, this does not mean that all the novel's allusions to chess are diversionary. Focusing on the moves of a knight, specifically in the way such moves differ from those of other pieces, is not a "chess-idea." If anything, it is an anti-chess-idea, highlighting the way in which the moves of the knight differ from other pieces and occur beyond the plane of the board. This fits with the critical interventions of Peterson and Barabtarlo since, regardless of their disagreement over the employment of other chess figures, the two scholars agree that that both Sebastian and V. are characters who sometimes act as uneasy inhabitants of reality while at other times move through a surreal plane of artistic creation. With Sebastian, this is apparent in descriptions of his writing, while for V., it is revealed as the novel progresses and he describes his engagement with the world around him: "My quest had developed its own magic and logic and though I sometimes cannot help believing that it had gradually grown into a dream . . . using the pattern of reality for the weaving of its own fancies."[26] A knight-idea is different from a chess-idea because the knight, each time it moves, is separated from the chessboard.[27]

---

22 Ibid., 156.
23 Peterson, "Knight's Move: Nabokov, Shklovsky and the Afterlife of Sirin," *Nabokov Studies* 11 (2007): 32.
24 Gennady Barabtarlo, "Taina Naita. Narrative Stance in Nabokov's *The Real Life of Sebastian Knight*," *Partial Answers* 6, no. 1 (2008): 64.
25 Simon Karlinsky, ed., *Dear Bunny, Dear Volodya: The Nabokov-Wilson Letters (1940–1971)* (Berkeley: University of California Press, 2001), 58.
26 Nabokov, *The Real Life of Sebastian Knight*, 135.
27 The knight is able to move to spaces even when its path to those spaces is entirely blocked by other pieces. Since this movement would be impossible on the plane of the chessboard, the knight can be understood to move by temporarily jumping above that plane. No other chess piece has this ability.

Thus, when Barabtarlo says, "since the characters who cause [Knight's] identity to fade and flicker are themselves shown to be unworthy of complete trust, the reader tends to ignore their evidence," one can understand this double distrust in terms of the fact that, as a jumping knight flickers in and out sight for pieces confined to the plane of the chess board, other pieces flicker in and out of sight for the knight.[28] As one regards the world through V.'s narrative lens, the logic of other characters' placement as rooks and bishops will not appear consistent.

This lack of consistency is the key to this essay's approach to *The Real Life of Sebastian Knight* and other Nabokov works. Rather than argue either for or against a formulaic application of chess rules to all the actions of every character, I argue specifically for the application of knight rules to the artistic heroes of Nabokov's texts. While *The Real Life of Sebastian* may figure other characters as rooks or bishops, an analysis of those characters would be fundamentally different from the analysis this essay applies to its knight figures—just as the moves of those chess pieces are fundamentally different from the knight's. When V. tells readers that "[t]he keynote of Sebastian's life was solitude and [...] he was aware of his inability to fit into the picture—into any kind of picture," he may close the door on the possibility of a cohesive chess-idea, but the prospect of a knight-idea (or Knight-idea) is only strengthened.[29]

Outcasts on the plane of the chessboard and phantasmatic creations when they leap above it, the artistic transcendence of Nabokov's protagonists lines up with Barabtarlo's anagrammatic solution to *Sebastian Knight*, the "vibrant nothingness" indicated by his formulation "a knight is absent."[30] To pass through the plane above the chess board is to disappear temporarily into an indeterminate space. Knights draw lines between squares on the board but, in doing so, they depart from the board. The resulting present-absence allows one to visualize a Knight at the core of a text in which "a knight is absent."

Knight's Move as Otherworldly Travel

While the movement of the knight has not been used as a key to understanding artistic transcendence in Nabokov, the transcendence itself has been extensively theorized. The poetics of the knight's move, thus far explored in the context of *The Defense* and *The Real Life of Sebastian Knight*, operates within the

28 Barabtarlo, "Taina Naita," 73.
29 Nabokov, *The Real Life of Sebastian Knight*, 42.
30 Barabtarlo, "Taina Naita," 73.

larger framework of Nabokov's metaphysics. In *Nabokov's Otherworld* (1991), Vladimir E. Alexandrov lays out the view that Nabokov's novels are both infused with and shaped by the author's "sui generis faith in a transcendent realm."[31] Maxim D. Shrayer expands on this notion, demonstrating that the otherworld is a dimension which "exists simultaneously with the author's mundane reality and is both a source and an addressee of artistic creation."[32] Nabokov makes the realm of idealized love, exalted memory, and artistic freedom accessible only temporarily—and only to his protagonists and narrators.

Making a knight's move—as I have previously suggested it in the context of *The Defense* and *The Real Life of Sebastian Knight*—entails leaving this plane of existence and entering the otherworld. In a recent book, Priscilla Meyer makes the case that the attempts both Sebastian and V. make to deal with loss, memory, and artistic inspiration manifest as forays into the otherworld. Meyer emphasizes that, for Sebastian, exilic status plays a privileged role in such moves: "His lifelong quest for the otherworld becomes in exile a counter to the irrevocability of his loss of Russia and all it represents."[33] V., on the other hand, is represented as an otherworldly traveler driven forward by the loss of his brother and the gradual realization of his own artistic prowess.

Similarly, the knight's moves in *The Defense*—moments in which Luzhin allows artistic impulses to transport him away from his material reality and into a transcendent world suffused with chess imagery—fall squarely in the domain of scenes which Alexandrov references to construct his theory of the otherworld in this novel. In his elucidation of the "way[s] that chess appears to put Luzhin in contact with a realm transcending the mundane,"[34] Alexandrov specifically calls attention to the instances in which Luzhin's insights into the world of chess correspond with a striking "blindness with regard to the physical world around him."[35] My earlier assertion that Luzhin's suicide does not complicate a positioning of the novel as a chess problem but rather provides the knight's move required to solve the said problem therefore finds common ground with Alexandrov's conclusion: "one can infer that according to the novel's logic the otherworld is preferable to this world [and that] in this light, Luzhin's suicide is a return to a realm to which he had journeyed temporarily during his unconsciousness."[36] Alexandrov's assertion that, "if through death Luzhin enters the same world

31   Alexandrov, *Nabokov's Otherworld*, 4.
32   Maxim D. Shrayer, *The World of Nabokov's Stories* (Austin: University of Texas Press, 1999), 21.
33   Priscilla Meyer, *Nabokov and Indeterminacy: The Case of The Real Life of Sebastian Knight* (Evanston, IL: Northwestern University Press, 2018), 149.
34   Ibid., 67.
35   Ibid., 65.
36   Ibid., 77.

he touched during the peak moments of his games, then even suicide does not allow him to escape from the chess that is his fate," validates the interpretation of Luzhin's defenestration as a move into another plane of existence—a knight's move that carries him above the chessboard of his mundane reality into a plane of artistic creation, which uncannily resembles a chessboard itself.

Negative Knights in *Pale Fire*

The connection of knights with the otherworld provides a framework for engaging with the figure of the knight in Nabokov's other texts. Unpacking the figure of the chess knight, Janet K. Gezari and William K. Wimsatt relate it to the mysterious character of Gradus in *Pale Fire* (1962). The passage they explore in detail comes from the commentary part *of Pale Fire* and imagines Gradus on the brink of committing a murder after the fashion of a knight poised to move on the chessboard:

> I contemplate him with quiet surprise: here he is, the creature ready to commit a monstrous act-and coarsely enjoying a coarse meal! We must assume, I think, that the forward projection of what imagination he had, stopped at the act, on the brink of all its possible consequences, comparable to the squares which a chess knight (that skip-space piece), standing on a marginal file, "feels" in phantom extensions beyond the board, but which have no effect whatever on his real moves, on the real play.[37]

When Gezari and Wimsatt argue that "the knight has eight moves, but in the 'real' realm established by the board, the number of moves will depend on the knight's position," they gloss over the fact that the number of moves any chess piece can make is dependent on that piece's position in the "real" realm of the board.[38] That is to say, they fail to explain why Gradus is envisioned as a knight rather than a bishop, a rook, or a queen. If phantom extensions are significant only insofar as they connote impossible endpoints beyond the boundaries of the chessboard, there would be no reason to employ a "skip-space piece" as opposed to any other piece in order to illustrate those extensions.[39]

---

37 Vladimir Nabokov, *Pale Fire* (New York: Vintage Books, 1962), 195.
38 Janet K. Gezari and William K. Wimsatt, "Vladimir Nabokov: More Chess Problems and the Novel," *Yale French Studies* 58, no. 1 (1979): 104.
39 Nabokov, *Pale Fire*, 276

Recognizing the importance of the knight in this scenario requires one to understand the components of its movement as they relate to Gradus. The assassin's "here," the square currently attributed to Gradus, is that seat at which he is "coarsely enjoying a coarse meal." [40] The "possible consequences [resulting from the murder are] comparable to the squares which a chess knight [. . .] 'feels.'" [41] This means that the act of murder itself occurs between the knight's current location and the squares to which it could potentially move. The act of murder—which Gradus can imagine but cannot imagine beyond—exists in the "skip-space," the region about the board through which the knight alone can travel as it moves from one square to another. The result of such a reading is a surprising positioning of Shade's prospective murder within the otherworld, the significance of which I will examine below.

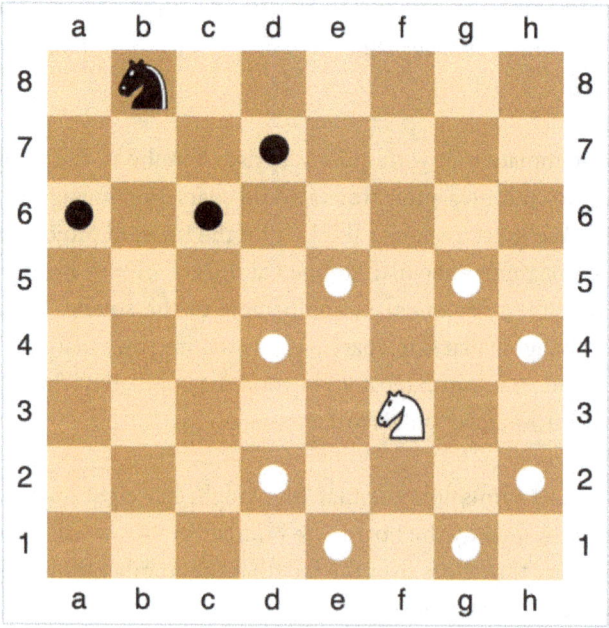

Figure 2. Possible moves shown for a black knight and a white knight on an otherwise unoccupied chessboard. Wikipedia.[42], [43]

---

40 Ibid.

41 Ibid.

42 "Knight (chess)," *Wikipedia*, accessed 10 November, 2023, https://en.wikipedia.org/wiki/Knight_(chess).

43 If Gradus enjoying his meal is the black knight on a marginal file, and the possible consequences of the murder are either the three possible moves shown in the image (if one distrusts Kinbote's derisive account of Gradus's imagination) or the five moves rendered

Such a reading also positions Gradus as a privileged otherworldly traveler, a surprising status since he is not "the estranged protagonist of a given story" and is certainly not portrayed as being "able to see otherworld beatitude and love despite the *poshlost'* [. . .] of existence," the usual precondition for otherworld access.[44] In fact, Gradus is described as a crude man who makes limited "concessions to intellectual curiosity."[45] He would be an unusual subject to be granted access to a Nabokovian otherworld. But subjecthood in *Pale Fire* is itself an unusual issue. Meyer frames the issue succinctly: "In John Shade's poem 'Pale Fire,' Shade finds some 'faint hope' that he may find his daughter Hazel in an otherworld, while his neighbor Kinbote hopes to find his own lost otherworld, Zembla, immortalized in Shade's poem."[46] Regardless of whether I follow the lead of some critics in viewing Shade and Kinbote as the same person, Zembla itself—sensual, beautiful, evanescent, and inextricably tied to memory—represents the otherworld for whichever man is depicting it. Thus, the figure of Gradus, portrayed while journeying from Zembla to New Wye, is not only a part of this otherworld but a figure who can travel between the otherworld and this world (even if the direction of his travel is unusual).

That said, even if Gradus were to be understood as a character in his own right—a man who is not invented by Kinbote or Shade and hails from a country that exists in the real world—a case can be made for his movement beyond the chessboard plane of reality. Martine Hennard's assertion that Kinbote "literalizes the analogy between writing and the evasion of death [while] Gradus is his antithesis" and that Gradus "may well be the dark side of Kinbote" crystallizes this case, positioning Gradus as someone whose otherworld has a destructive potential to match Kinbote's constructive potential.[47] Gradus's otherworld, then, is conceivable as the photonegative of Kinbote's, tied to ugliness, violence, and death but nevertheless representing a distinct plane of existence from his material reality, a downwardly transcendent plane in which he may enact Kinbote's murder and enjoy the corruption of everything beautiful and pure in Zembla.

---

impossible by the boundary of the board (if one trusts Kinbote's account), the murder is in both cases positioned within the nebulous space between the knight's current position and the endpoints of its prospective moves.

44   Shrayer, *The World of Nabokov's Stories*, 22
45   Nabokov, *Pale Fire*, 232
46   Meyer, *Nabokov and Indeterminacy*, 124
47   Martine Hennard, "Playing a Game of Worlds in Nabokov's 'Pale Fire,'" *Modern Fiction Studies* 40, no. 2 (1994): 310.

Dustin Condren echoes Meyer's attribution of two separate otherworlds to Kinbote and Shade. While he sees Kinbote as accessing the otherworld through Zembla, he views Shade's creation, the long poem *Pale Fire*, as a "meditation of the otherworldly."[48] With Hazel lost to the otherworld (possibly during her lifetime but definitely in death), Shade can ponder the distance between them, but cannot satisfyingly bridge it. His inability to cross over to this otherworld is illustrated in Canto 3 with a passage that also supports this essay's reading of knights in *Pale Fire*. A lament that no phantom presence of Hazel would come to greet Shade and his wife, Sybil, feeds into a brief imagined dialogue with Sybil. This dialogue concludes with the line, "And now what shall I do? My knight is pinned."[49] Since the knight is the figure that can move temporarily about the plane of the board and into the otherworld, the tragedy of a pinned knight is the tragedy of one who can recognize a path to the otherworld but can be prevented from traversing that path by forces greater than itself. Shade tells us what has pinned his knight:

> Later came minutes, hours, whole days at last.
> When she'd be absent from our thoughts, so fast
> Did life, the woolly caterpillar run.
> We went to Italy. Sprawled in the sun
> On a white beach with other pink or brown
> Americans. Flew back to our small town.
> Found that my bunch of essays The Untamed
> Seahorse was "universally acclaimed"
> (It sold three hundred copies in one year).
> Again school started, and on hillsides [...] [50]

Shade loses access to the otherworld occupied by Hazel for longer and longer periods of time because vacation, publication, occupation—the minutiae of life, that woolly caterpillar—fully engross his attention. He is able to glimpse the otherworld through composition of the poem *Pale Fire*, writing at the end of Canto 4 that he understands "[e]xistence, or at least a minute part /Of [his]

48   Dustin Condren, "John Shade Shaving: Inspiration and Composition in a Selection from Pale Fire," *Nabokov Studies* 10 (2006): 141.
49   Nabokov, *Pale Fire*, l. 661.
50   Ibid., ll. 665–674.

existence, only through [his] art" and that he suspects "the verse of galaxies divine" to be contained within "a single line."[51] Still, his fear of death ("it's not bedtime yet")[52] and his attachment to the pleasures and responsibilities of the mundane world prevent him from fully entering the otherworld during his lifetime.[53]

Defeating the Whole Brilliant Affair in *Speak, Memory*

As a Russian émigré in interwar Europe, Nabokov was a prolific composer of chess problems. His comparisons between writing novels and composing chess problems come from a foundation of concrete experience. Tracing the impact of that experience leads me to one particular point in Nabokov's oeuvre.[54] The composition of a specific chess problem—as well as the meaning Nabokov ascribes to it—is fleshed out in the penultimate chapter of his autobiographical work *Speak, Memory* (1966).[55] If one takes Nabokov at his word when he concludes this chapter by writing, "it is only now [...] that the information concealed in my chess symbols [...] may be, and in fact is, divulged," then probing the import of this chess problem is pivotal for uncovering the significance of chess symbolism, including the knight's move, throughout his works.[56]

---

51 Ibid., ll. 971–976
52 Ibid., l. 985
53 For an example of how Nabokov's protagonists can immerse themselves in the otherworld at the expense of their mundane life (and even their mundane aliveness), see Shrayer, "Memory, Pilgrimage, and Death in 'The Aurelian' (1930)," in *The World of Nabokov's Stories*, 108–134. Vladimir Nabokov, *The Gift*, trans. Michael Scammel (New York: Vintage International, 1991), 293.
54 While Nabokov's *Poems and Problems* (1970) contains eighteen chess problems composed by the author, it does not ascribe significance to any one problem in the manner that *Speak, Memory* does. Nevertheless, it is of some relevance that Nabokov credits the final problem in *Poem and Problems* with "mild magic" born out in the promotion of pawn to knight, which simultaneously achieves checkmate. For this passage, see Vladimir Nabokov, *Poems and Problems* (New York: McGraw-Hill, 1970), 209.
55 Originally published in the United States under the title *Conclusive Evidence* in 1951, the 1966 text represents a revised and extended version.
56 Nabokov, *Speak Memory: An Autobiography Revisited* (New York: Vintage International, 1989), 293.

Figure 3. Vladimir Nabokov. White to move and mate in two moves. Composed in Paris in 1940. ChessBase.[57]

While critics have previously taken up this challenge, their focus has tended to be on the symbolism of the game of chess as a whole rather than the function of specific pieces on the board. Gezari, in an analysis of the *Speak, Memory* chess problem, writes that "the enactment of the solution, the actual line of play on the board, is only interesting in relation to the try or false key."[58] That is to say, she finds the solution of the problem relevant only insofar as it highlights folly of an alternative route that some arrogant solvers might pick. Purdy examines the problem in a similar light. After describing both the problem and both its false lead and correct solution, Purdy concludes, "Nabokov emphasizes the element of deception in his introduction to this interesting, if not altogether accurately described, problem"[59] before transitioning to a discussion of Nabokov's

---

57 "Nabokov: Poems and Problems," ChessBase, October 23, 2014, accessed November 10, 2023, https://en.chessbase.com/post/nabokov-poems-and-problems; cf. Nabokov, *Poems and Problems*, 182 [Problem 1].

58 Janet Gezari. "Chess Problems and Narrative Time in *Speak, Memory*," *Biography* 10, no. 2 (1987): 156.

59 Purdy, "Culture in Action: Symbols and Strategies," 381

"obsessive impulse"[60] to deceive his readers. Like Gezari's, Purdy's reading emphasizes the element of deception within the problem without noting that a single piece, knight, is the agent of this deception.

If White begins by advancing their b7 pawn to b8, promoting it to a knight, Black may underestimate the significance of this move and respond with Pd6+ or Pd5+. White can answer this with Kxd7# in the first case or Qc7# in the second case, securing a "beautiful mate" with either their newly minted knight or their queen.[61] On the other hand, if Black understands the knight to be a piece that can capture the c7 pawn and bring about a checkmate through its skip-space ability, they will respond to White making a knight at b8 by simply leaving their c7 pawn protected and making a different move, thus "defeat[ing] the whole brilliant affair."[62] That is all to say, if Black understands the knight's potential to secure a mate, they can easily foil White's hoped-for, brilliant mate in two. A less formal reading of this problem would be that in the *Speak, Memory* chess problem, knights are powerful when underestimated but, when treated like any other attacking piece, their brilliance falls away.

Here lies a potential key to Nabokov's knights. However brilliant Luzhin is as a chess player, his talent falls away to reveal weakness and incompetence when he is held to conventional standards of conversation and hygiene. Similarly, regardless of Sebastian's and V.'s abilities to transgress boundaries of identity, confrontations with the necessity of organizing business affairs or flirtation divert them from their loftier paths and leave them mired in insecurity. And however sublime Fyodor's romance with Zina (Mnemosyne) may be, the fact that they do not have the apartment key jeopardizes the physical consummation of their romance in the final pages of *The Gift*.

Coda: A Silent Knight

Recognizing the chess knight as integral to Nabokov's poetics sets the stage for innovative readings of the author's work. In the rather saturated field of scholarship on *Lolita* (1955), hardly enough attention has been paid to the character of Kenneth Knight.[63] Considering the fact that this boy, a classmate of Lolita's,

---

60 Ibid., 382
61 Nabokov, *Speak Memory*, 293
62 Ibid.
63 For an article which examines the significance of Kenneth Knight's name, though only in the context of Lolita's entire class list, see Gavriel Shapiro, "*Lolita* Class List," *Cahiers du Monde russe* 37, no. 1 (1996): 325.

is only mentioned three times in passing over the course of the novel, this is not surprising. While the scope of this essay disallows a detailed analysis of Kenneth Knight, viewing him as a Nabokovian knight charges his brief appearances with much more interpretive potential. Two of his appearances yield a striking conclusion.

The reader of *Lolita* learns, during an elucidation of the sexual exploits of Ramsdale children, that "Kenneth Knight who was the brightest [of the boys] used to exhibit himself wherever and whenever he had a chance"[64] This reference to Kenneth's exhibitionism, combined with a brief parenthetical mention of his position as delivery boy for the Ramsdale *Journal*,[65] appears to be of little importance until one assesses him and Humbert Humbert as two knights of different hue. Humbert's engagement with a sensual and literary otherworld yields destruction and sorrow because he imposes the conditions of his otherworld onto characters who could not possibly understand it.[66] In chess terms, if Kenneth's moves are those of a knight, they are not performed at a sufficient distance above the plane of the board, resulting in collisions with the other pieces. Granting that Kenneth Knight, like Humbert Humbert, is a privileged liaison to a literary and sensual otherworld (albeit one whose interiority is not depicted), his method of engagement with the otherworldly realm may present an alternative to Humbert's. If access to the otherworld is to be found through language, the Ramsdale *Journal* provides a potential portal to the otherworld for everyone (at least, everyone in Ramsdale) since the *Journal* is written and published for and about them. Thus, one can imagine a scenario in which the otherworld is rendered accessible to the residents of the town—though this access route would likely present a tortuous reading experience for Humbert. And while exhibitionism is certainly now recognized as potentially traumatic to onlookers, it is an expression of individual sensuality that does not actively seek to engage others. This offers an illustration of engagement with a sensual otherworld, the conditions of which Kenneth Knight does not impose on anyone else. Considering newspaper delivery and exhibitionism in this context,

---

64   Vladimir Nabokov, *Lolita* (New York: Vintage International, 1997), 136–137

65   Ibid., 54

66   For a reading of Humbert Humbert as a privileged traveler to a transcendent realm which is both aesthetic and literary, and also a tyrant in his solipsistic (re)creation of Lolita, see Matthew Winston, "Lolita and the Dangers of Fiction," *Twentieth Century Literature* 21, no. 4 (1975): 421–427. For a similar reading which focuses on the dehumanizing aspect of this (re)creation, also see Christina Tekiner, "Time in *Lolita*," *Modern Fiction Studies* 25, no. 3 (1979): 463–469.

Kenneth's two short scenes within *Lolita* provide the seeds of two potential alternatives to the violence Humbert brings about through his rapture. As far as privileged, plane-jumping characters go, Kenneth Knight may not be the most romantic or the best elucidated, but a shrewd reader may well recognize him as "the brightest."

In tracing the knight-idea though Nabokov's works, I take a formalist approach by remaining concerned with the knight's move as a literary function rather than a key to the psychological or cultural conditions under which those texts came into being. In doing so, I have remained ironically faithful to the conditions under which the knight's move may have first entered Nabokov's writing. Irina Paperno suggests that Nabokov makes purposeful allusion to Shklovsky's *Knight's Move* within *The Gift*. [67] And while Michael Glynn challenges her assumption that Nabokov's chess references are indebted to Shklovsky, noting that the novelist's expertise in chess was independent of his familiarity with Shklovsky, he maps out a different path of indebtedness. Writing about Nabokov's connection to Russian Formalism, Glynn contends that "Nabokov absorbed Shklovsky's ideas on the automatizing mind and the role of art,"[68] which "makes the familiar unfamiliar [. . . and] seeks to distort and estrange reality."[69] Although Glynn does not credit Shklovsky with Nabokov's use of the term "knight's move," he does credit Shklovsky with Nabokov's use of temporary, art-induced jumps above the plane of reality, the very phenomena which this essay understands to be the essence of Nabokovian knight's moves.

Nabokov's protagonists are chess knights, disconnected and dysfunctional when held to the standards of their fellow pieces, able to rise temporarily above the regular plane of existence as they track routes to unexpected destinations, and ultimately a staple of the game—however unique their role may appear in any given match. Whether they are reading literature, writing literature, dreaming of another country, playing a game, or committing a murder, the artistic transcendence of these knightly characters finds a common form in the movement of the knight in chess. While this essay investigates only some notable examples, the quest to theorize the Nabokovian knight's move has only just begun.

---

67 Irina Paperno, "How Nabokov's *Gift* Is Made," *Stanford Slavic Studies* 4, no. 2 (1992): 295–322.

68 Michael Glynn, "Nabokov and Russian Formalism," in *Vladimir Nabokov: Bergsonian and Russian Formalist Influences in His Novels* (London: Palgrave Macmillan, 2007), 43.

69 Ibid., 45.

Bibliography

Primary Sources
Nabokov, Vladimir. *The Defense*. New York: Vintage International, 1990.
———. *The Gift*. Translated by Michael Scammell. New York: Vintage International, 1991.
———. *Lolita*. New York: Vintage International, 1997.
———. *Pale Fire*. New York: Vintage International, 1989.
———. *Poems and Problems*. New York: McGraw-Hill, 1970.
———. *The Real Life of Sebastian Knight*. New York: Vintage International, 1992.
———. *Speak, Memory: An Autobiography Revisited*. New York: Vintage International, 1989.

Secondary Sources
Alexandrov, Vladimir E. *Nabokov's Otherworld*. Princeton, NJ: Princeton University Press, 1991.
Barabtarlo, Gennady. "Taina Naita. Narrative Stance in Nabokov's *The Real Life of Sebastian Knight*." *Partial Answers* 6, no. 1 (2008): 57–80.
———. "Nabokov's Trinity (On the Movement of Nabokov's Themes)." In *Nabokov and His Fiction: New Perspectives*, edited by Julian Connolly, 109–138. Cambridge: Cambridge University Press, 1999.
Boyd, Brian. "The Problem of Pattern: Nabokov's Defense." *Modern Fiction Studies* 33, no. 4 (1987): 575–604.
Condren, Dustin. "John Shade Shaving: Inspiration and Composition in a Selection from *Pale Fire*." *Nabokov Studies* 10, no. 1 (2006): 129–146.
Gezari, Janet. "Chess Problems and Narrative Time in *Speak, Memory*." *Biography* 10, no. 2 (1987): 151–162.
———. "Chess and Chess Problems. *The Garland Companion to Vladimir Nabokov*, 44–53. Ed. Vladimir E Alexandrov. New York, Routledge, 1995.
Gezari, Janet K., and William K. Wimsatt. "Vladimir Nabokov: More Chess Problems and the Novel." *Yale French Studies* 58, no. 1 (1979): 102–115.
Glynn, Michael. "Nabokov and Russian Formalism." In *Vladimir Nabokov: Bergsonian and Russian Formalist Influences in His Novels*, 23–51. New York: Palgrave Macmillan, 2007.
Hennard, Martine. "Playing a Game of Worlds in Nabokov's *Pale Fire*." *Modern Fiction Studies* 40, no. 2 (1994): 299–317.
Johnson, D. Barton. "Text and Pretext in Nabokov's The Defense or 'Play It Again, Sasha.'" *Modern Fiction Studies* 30, no. 2 (1984): 278–87.
Karlinsky, Simon, ed. *Dear Bunny, Dear Volodya: The Nabokov-Wilson Letters (1940–1971)*. Berkeley: University of California Press, 2001.
Kuzmanovich, Zoran. "'Just as it was, or perhaps a little more perfect': Notes on Nabokov's Sources." *Nabokov Studies* 7 (2002): 13–32.
Meyer, Priscilla. *Nabokov and Indeterminacy: The Case of The Real Life of Sebastian Knight*. Evanston, IL: Northwestern University Press, 2018.
Paperno, Irina. "How Nabokov's *Gift* is Made." *Stanford Slavic Studies* 4, no. 2 (1992): 295–322.
Peterson, Dale. "Knight's Move: Nabokov, Shklovsky and the Afterlife of Sirin." *Nabokov Studies* 11 (2007): 25–37.

Purdy, Strother B. "Culture in Action: Symbols and Strategies." *Modern Fiction Studies* 14, no. 1 (1968–1969): 379–395.

Sampson, Earl D. "Games Nabokov's Characters Play." *Russian Language Journal* 36, no. 123/124 (1982): 193–203.

Shapiro, Gavriel. "*Lolita* Class List." *Cahiers du Monde russe* 37, no. 1 (1996): 317–335.

Shklovsky, Viktor. *Knight's Move*. Trans. Richard Sheldon. London: Dalkey Archive Press, 2005.

Shrayer, Maxim D. *The World of Nabokov's Stories*. Austin: University of Texas Press, 1998.

Tekiner, Christina. "Time in *Lolita*." *Modern Fiction Studies* 25, no. 3 (1979): 463–469.

Updike, John. "Grandmaster Nabokov." In *Assorted Prose*, 318–328. New York: Alfred A. Knopf, 1965.

Winston, Mathew. "*Lolita* and the Dangers of Fiction." *Twentieth Century Literature* 21, no. 4 (1975): 421–427.

Sharing Other Worlds: Companionship and Coauthorship in *Glory and The Gift*

Fiona Steacy

Nabokov's Model of Romantic Coauthorship

"The years are passing, my dear, and presently nobody will know what you and I know," Vladimir Nabokov writes in the final chapter of his autobiography *Speak, Memory* (1966).[1] He is addressing his wife, Véra Nabokov (née Slonim), the transcriber, reader, dedicatee, and, I would argue, a coauthor of most of his works. Nabokov goes on to describe the birth of their son Dmitri in 1934 in Berlin, the joy of raising him as contrasted with the horror of Hitler's rise to power, the "federation of light and shade" formed by the numerous parks visited during their time in 1930s Europe and no longer distinguishable in memory.[2] Here in the final chapter of *Speak, Memory*, where Nabokov directly addresses his lifelong intimate partner and coauthor, students of Nabokov may find keys to the writer's understanding of romantic coauthorship.

Two of Nabokov's novels written during his interwar European exile are the focus of this essay. I will explore the ways in which his protagonists in *Glory* (1932) and *The Gift* (ser. 1937–1938; complete Russian book edition 1952) coauthor worlds along with their respective intimate partners—exceptions to

1   Vladimir Nabokov, *Speak, Memory: An Autobiography Revisited* (New York: Vintage International, 1989), 295.
2   Ibid., 305.

the typically solipsistic and solitary other worlds of Nabokov's characters.[3] The presence of other worlds within Nabokov's texts is well recognized by scholars, though conceptions of these other worlds vary. Vladimir E. Alexandrov uses the compound "otherworld," an admittedly imperfect translation of the Russian *postustoronnost'*, meaning something akin to the othersidedness or the hereafter.[4] He further explains that the term approximately describes "a transcendent, non-material, timeless, and beneficent ordering and ordered realm of being that seems to provide for personal immortality, and that affects everything that exists in the mundane world." While Alexandrov notes the necessity of definitions for the purpose of analysis, he cautions that "all one can have is intuitions of what it may be like; no certainty about it is possible."[5] D. Barton Johnson observes that Nabokov's novels "contain more than one world in varying degrees of presence."[6] Nabokov, Johnson notes, derives many of his "aesthetic and philosophical views" from the Russian Symbolist movement, a core belief of which "is that there exists, beyond the scope of the intellect, another, more real world, and that what man sees before him is but a shadow and echo of true reality."[7] Thus, when I refer to other worlds, I mean the fictive worlds within the fictive worlds of the novels that are ostensibly the characters' creations. These worlds are coauthored not only by the novels' protagonists and their intimate partners, but, paradoxically, by Nabokov and these protagonists, blurring and coalescing the layers of Nabokov's metafiction as he and his characters jointly author other worlds.

Both the protagonist's romantic relationship and the coauthorial creations are most fully realized in *The Gift*, the longest and the most overtly metaliterary of Nabokov's Russian novels. *The Gift* is also Nabokov's most fully realized version of a coming-of-age story in which a protagonist attains artistic self-certainty. Stephen H. Blackwell notes, echoing Nabokov's earlier critics, that *The Gift* might accurately be called a *Künstlerroman*, a variation on the Bildungsroman in which the ultimate achievement is creative rather than maturational.[8] The earlier

---

3   For a pioneering examination of Nabokov's otherworlds, see Vladimir E. Alexandrov, *Nabokov's Otherworld* (Princeton, NJ: Princeton University Press, 1991).

4   Ibid., 3.

5   Ibid., 5.

6   D. Barton Johnson, *Worlds in Regression: Some Novels of Vladimir Nabokov.* (Ann Arbor, MI: Ardis, 1985), 1.

7   Ibid., 2–3.

8   Stephen H. Blackwell, *Zina's Paradox: The Figured Reader in Nabokov's "Gift"* (New York: Peter Lang Publishing), 38. *Also see Eric Weiskott's essay in this volume (M.D.S.).*

Glory, on the other hand, initially resembles a traditional coming-of-age story in which a dreamy young adult seeks acceptance from his peers (and, as the name would suggest, glory)—only to toss the script in the finale. The novel's émigré protagonist, Martin Edelweiss, instead of acclimating to adulthood like Darwin, his Cambridge classmate and romantic rival, vanishes into the other world of his own cocreation. *Glory* thus prefigures the romantic and metafictional coauthorship that takes place within *The Gift*.

Existential and Artistic Coming of Age in Nabokov's Novels

Many of Nabokov's works feature characters with outlandishly antisocial personalities and obsessions. As compared with other protagonists in Nabokov's oeuvre, *Glory*'s Martin Edelweiss and *The Gift*'s Fyodor Godunov-Cherdyntsev are relatively well-adjusted. *Glory* follows a deceptively simple trajectory until its surreal departure from expectation at the end.[9] It depicts glimpses of Martin's childhood, his escape from Russia, and his transformative university years at Cambridge, yet it culminates in Martin's abrupt disappearance in place of his expected maturation. Superficially, *The Gift* is Nabokov's "nearest approach to the tradition of the classical [nineteenth] century Russian novel."[10] It quickly reveals itself, however, to be much more than a development narrative of a young émigré writer desperate for recognition. Like *Glory*, *The Gift* follows a wistful male protagonist. This time however, Nabokov's protagonist is slightly older, more self-assured, and, notably, an author by profession and vocation. Nabokov wrote these novels at either end of the turbulent 1930s, *Glory* when he was entering the period of his interwar Russian émigré stardom, and *The Gift* as Europe was heading for another world war.[11]

Both Martin and Fyodor share a relative sociability and involvement in their communities. They stand in contrast to the protagonists of Nabokov's other novels of the 1930s, such as *The Defense*'s monomaniacal chess player, Luzhin, or *Invitation to a Beheading*'s Cincinnatus C., whose opacity is intolerable to

---

9   Leona Toker argues that *Glory* "masks eschatological anxiety with apparent simplicity." See her "Nabokov's *Glory*: 'One Example of How Metaphysics Can Fool You,'" in *Nabokov: The Mystery of Literary Structures* (Ithaca, NY: Cornell University Press, 1989), 88.

10   Johnson, *Worlds in Regression*, 93.

11   For more on the development of Russian émigré culture, see Marc Raeff's *Russia Abroad: A Cultural History of the Russian Emigration, 1919–1939* (New York: Oxford University Press, 1990).

others.[12] The protagonists of *Glory* and *The Gift* always have one foot firmly in reality, self-conscious of their place in the real world (despite their frustrations with it) and seeking validation—Martin primarily from his peers and Fyodor from literary colleagues like the older émigré writer Koncheyev. While both Martin and Fyodor display an inclination toward lone ventures into their personal worlds, Nabokov allows for an intermittent, if not always lasting, joint creative consciousness, a coauthorship of worlds with their respective intimate companions.

While Fyodor experiences degrees of collaboration with non-romantic companions, including his mother and his émigré acquaintance Mrs. Chernyshevski, both Fyodor and Martin collaborate most generatively with their romantic interests, Martin with Sonia, and Fyodor with Zina. Sonia and Martin cocreate Zoorland,[13] an absurdist and anti-utopian parody of Bolshevik Russia, into which Martin arguably dissolves[14] at the end of *Glory*. Zina and Fyodor coauthor Fyodor's book *Life of Chernyshevski*, and as some critics have argued based on Nabokov's imperfect clues, they coauthor *The Gift*, a version of the novel in which the two of them exist as characters. In this way, the characters' coauthored worlds materialize within the novels, making the characters themselves both metaliterary and metaphysical collaborators with Nabokov. Inversely, Nabokov's authorial presence looms over the texts, a reminder (at times ominous) that the characters are, after all, his creations, his deliberately crafted literary devices.

Authoring through Dreams in *Glory*

Structurally, *Glory* differs drastically from *The Gift*. It is significantly shorter and faster in pace, and it follows its protagonist through his formative years via a limited third person perspective. Martin is not a writer by profession, and *Glory* is not expressly about literary creation. Where, then, is the evidence that Martin constructs worlds with both Sonia and Nabokov? As Leona Toker points out, *Glory* masks Nabokov's complex metaphysics in simplicity; it is an "involution" that "[erodes] the border between the 'inside' and the 'outside,' between

---

12 Vladimir Nabokov, *Invitation to a Beheading*, trans. Dmitri Nabokov in collaboration with the author (New York: Vintage International, 1989), 72.
13 Maxim D. Shrayer, "The Perfect Glory of Nabokov's Exploit," *Russian Studies in Literature* 35, no. 4 (1999): 29–41.
14 Toker, "Nabokov's *Glory*," 99.

the fictional world and the mind of its author." [15] Martin's defining characteristic, if one goes along with what Nabokov established in his American foreword to *Glory*, is his lack of talent:

> [A]mong the many gifts I showered on Martin, I was careful not to include talent. How easy it would have been to make him an artist, a writer; how hard not to let him be one, while bestowing on him the keen sensitivity [...] how cruel to prevent him from finding in art [...] relief from the itch of being! [16]

Despite Nabokov's insistence, Martin's imaginative capability *is* a creative talent, but he does not materialize his creations in published text (although the writer Sergei Bubnov imperfectly does it for him). Martin's "keen sensitivity," coupled with his metamorphosing aspiration to commit an act of valorous or artistic glory (an exploit), makes him an avid dreamer, and as Nabokov cryptically notes, again in the foreword, "he is a rarity—a person whose 'dreams come true.'" [17] Indeed, Martin authors worlds through his dreams, even though the dreams' corrupted realization brings him less satisfaction than what the premonitions themselves accord. In Martin's youth, he dreamt about competing in soccer matches. As a Cambridge student preparing for a soccer game, however, he presciently observes

> a certain peculiarity about his life: the property that his reveries had of crystallizing and mutating into reality, as previously they had mutated into sleep. This seemed to him a guarantee that the new series of reveries he had recently evolved—about an illegal, clandestine expedition—would also grow solid and be filled with life. [18]

Without an outlet of artistic expression, Martin's dreams permeate his everyday life, blurring the boundary between his real and imagined worlds. [19] As with Nabokov's other protagonists, Martin's dreams often develop on the brink of

---

15 Ibid., 88.
16 Nabokov, *Glory*, xiii.
17 Ibid., xii.
18 Ibid., 109.
19 Toker argues that Martin receives an anticipation of death in exchange for the talent he is not given.

sleep or amid an indifferent crowd of strangers, in "opulent" and "purifying" solitude.[20] Martin's anonymity, and the unknowability of his thoughts to strangers, are "indispensable to [his] complete happiness."[21] Despite his delight in solitude and aloneness, however, Martin's greatest imaginative work is a product of intimate collaboration.

Sonia and Martin as Artistic Collaborators

Aspects of Sonia and Martin's nascent collaborative relationship prefigure Zina and Fyodor's fruitful coauthorship. As Maxim D. Shrayer observes, Sonia and Martin coauthor the fictional—and only partly textualized—territory of Zoorland.[22] Martin hopelessly pursues Sonia, and his love, mostly unrequired in romantic terms, is a burden to his beloved. Nevertheless, their relationship is intimate in its own sui generis fashion, allowing at least the potential for their coauthorship, even if the collaboration remains underdeveloped in comparison to Fyodor and Zina's.

When Martin returns to Cambridge after a summer away, his London-based émigré friends, the Zilanovs, house him in the former room of their recently deceased daughter, Nelly. At night Sonia sneaks into the room that is now Martin's and explains to him in excitement her belief that fulfilling one's personal "duty" in life is the most important thing one can do. Martin, too thrilled with Sonia's presence in his room to interpret her exact intentions, attempts to kiss her. Sonia pulls away and says, "how couldn't you see that this is the way I used to come to Nelly, and we talked and talked till dawn."[23] The bed, for Sonia, is a conspiratorial space, an opening to an imaginative world that she shared with Nelly and wants to share with Martin, but Martin disrupts this intention by trying to transform their authorial union into a physical one.

Their romance, to the extent that it is anything more than just Martin's one-sided fantasy, is physical only briefly, on a Berlin city street—the external imaginative space complementary to the private imaginative space of the bedroom. Martin, under the influence of "Swedish punch" and the "infectious [...] gaiety and whispering" of couples in doorways, talks animatedly about the Roman

---

20 Nabokov, *Glory*, 49, 152.
21 Ibid., 49.
22 Shrayer," The Perfect Glory," 32.
23 Nabokov, *Glory*, 94.

poet Horace, prompting Sonia to kiss him.[24] Although the physicality is only momentary, Sonia recognizes in this moment Martin's potential for imaginative thinking, which sparks a coauthorial relationship between them.[25] The next time they meet, Martin, recalling games from his childhood, draws Sonia into the act of coauthorship by inviting her to collaborate on his creation of Zoorland, the fictitious territory into which he intends to cross. To Martin's surprise, Sonia plays along, and he is "astounded by her unexpectedly revealed capacity for daydreaming."[26] The intimacy of their relationship, which has thus far been stifled by the one-sidedness of Martin's romantic interest, blossoms through the creation of their shared other world:

> [. . . F]rom that day on she occasionally condescended to play Zoorland with him [. . .] They studied Zoorlandian customs and laws [. . .] Sometimes during the general conversation—at table for instance—Sonia would turn to him and quickly whisper, "Have you heard, there's a new law forbidding caterpillars to pupate."[27]

Joint world-building is depicted as a kind of play, a return to childhood. This process is enabled by secrecy and exclusivity, as evidenced by Sonia's turning to Martin to whisper new developments while apparently in the presence of others. Although the product of their coauthorship is a fictional territory that is authoritarian to the point of absurdity (issuing laws for caterpillars to follow), its creation allows them to display unrestrained romantic imaginativeness and verbal artistry.

It is, however, possible to interpret Zoorland as more than just Martin and Sonia's fictional other world. Zoorland as text-within-text is materialized in a corrupted form by Bubnov, a professional writer and Martin's romantic rival. When Martin discovers that Bubnov has published a story about Zoorland in a Russian émigré paper, he perceives it as the ultimate romantic betrayal: "In it Martin recognized with disgust and embarrassment (as if he were witnessing some dreadfully obscene act) much of what he and Sonia used to think up—now oddly illumined by the imagination of an intruder."[28] Bubnov is not, to

---

24 Ibid., 143–44.
25 Shrayer," The Perfect Glory," 32.
26 Ibid., 147.
27 Nabokov, *Glory*, 148.
28 Ibid., 166. For a detailed discussion of Bubnov's literary theft from Martin, see Maxim D. Shrayer, "Bunin's Tambourine: Echoes of the Old Master in His Disciple's Fourth Novel,"

Martin, yet another coauthor of Zoorland, but rather an "intruder," a plagiarist and a voyeur sharing his titillating discovery with other outsiders. Martin's disturbance at this violation of privacy underscores that to him Zoorland is much more than a fantasy.

The text's unresolved ending, in which Martin's fate is left unknown to both characters and readers, allows for the possibility that Martin has not crossed the border into Russia but rather entered the realm—text—of Zoorland.[29] Martin *is*, therefore, an author by Nabokov's own definition: "Every true author emigrates to his art and stays therein."[30] Just as Martin's other, more mundane dreams have materialized, the dream of a world that he coauthored with Sonia materializes at the end of *Glory*. Furthermore, while Martin and Sonia cocreate the territory into which Martin disappears at the end, it is Nabokov who textualizes it thereby coauthoring the world that he gives his characters agency to create. When Martin enters Zoorland, it becomes material in the world of the text—a place so real that it can obliterate the protagonist.

Zina as Coauthor

The coauthorship among characters and with the author is more obviously present in the complex structure and metaliterary commentary on writing in *The Gift* than in the narrative of *Glory*. Blackwell extensively analyzes the role of love in Zina and Fyodor's coauthorship in *The Gift*, arguing that the novel itself is "both the story of their love and its issue," and that, through "reading lovingly," Zina models how a reader can "breach the isolation" of the text.[31] Although Blackwell acknowledges that Zina's involvement results in a kind of coauthorship, he focuses primarily on Zina's relationship to Fyodor as his ideal reader and, in turn, a model of Nabokov's own ideal reader.[32] While Blackwell also acknowledges the ambiguity of *The Gift*'s authorship due to the text's unmarked shifts between third-and-first-person narration, he ultimately concludes that

Nabokov Studies 16 (2019): 1–11, accessed March 25, 2024, https://muse.jhu.edu/article/747613.

29 Shrayer, "The Perfect Glory," 32.

30 Vladimir Nabokov, "Definitions," quoted in Maxim D. Shrayer, *The World of Nabokov's Stories* (Austin: University of Texas Press, 1999), 161.

31 Blackwell, *Zina's Paradox*, 119, 101.

32 Paul D. Morris has critiqued Blackwell's case for Zina as "a creative force," essentially arguing that Blackwell overstates her role in shaping the text. Paul D. Morris, "Zina's Paradox: The Figured Reader in Nabokov's *Gift*" [review of *Zina's Paradox*, by Stephen Blackwell], *Nabokov Studies* 6 (2000–2001): 209–212.

Fyodor is the narrator all along, with the shifts occurring between past and present Fyodor rather than between him and a separate coauthor. Blackwell provides an in-depth examination of Zina's pivotal role in the shaping of the text of *The Gift*, and so to avoid redundancy with his work, I will present only the most essential evidence of Zina's collaboration. Nevertheless, Zina's active authorial role should not be overshadowed by her role as attentive reader, nor should Nabokov's looming coauthorial presence be overshadowed by the tidy cyclicality of the novel's ending, rather in concert with Nabokov's own notion that "one can only reread" a book.[33]

Two particular moments within *The Gift* indicate Zina's role as coauthor: that in which Fyodor first determines to write his biography of Chernyshevski and the passage that depicts the writing process of that biography. In the first, Zina reassures Fyodor after his failure to write his father's biography, saying, "Oh, I have a thousand plans for you."[34] This brief statement, easy to miss within the ample text of *The Gift*, reveals Zina to be not only the generative force behind Fyodor's *Life of Chernyshevski*, but also the dominant author in their life together. More than just encouraging Fyodor, she anticipates and guides his trajectory as both a writer and her companion. Later, when Fyodor has embarked on the composition of *Life of Chernyshevski*, Zina corrects Fyodor's phraseology, feels ownership over Chernyshevski, and leaves lingering traces of her corrections even when Fyodor later changes them. As Fyodor writes, Zina interjects with comments like, "Wonderful, but I'm not sure you can say it like that in Russian," often winning out in their disagreements: "[A]fter an argument he would correct the expression she had questioned. Chernyshevski she called Chernysh for short and got so used to considering him as belonging to Fyodor, and partly to her, that his actual life in the past appeared to her as something of a plagiarism."[35]

Zina views Chernyshevki, a nineteenth-century Russian radical, as a character in a world of their own creation more than an actual historical figure. Based on the comical inventiveness of the work she and Fyodor produce, the Chernyshevski of their text is, indeed, a wholly different being. In a passage focused so keenly on the particularity of phrasing, it is worth noting the slightly unusual wording of "his actual life in the past." The inclusion of "in the past" suggests that the facts of Chernyshevski's life are irrelevant to the present moment. Zina and Fyodor

---

33   Vladimir Nabokov, *Lectures on Literature*, ed. Fredson Bowers (New York: Harcourt Brace Jovanovich, 1980), 3.

34   Vladimir Nabokov, *The Gift*, trans. Michael Scammel in collaboration with the author (New York: Vintage International, 1991), 193–94.

35   Ibid., 204

have undertaken the creation of a new Chernyshevski, modeled roughly on the
real Chernyshevski, yet wholly their own. Zina "took [it] on trust" that Fyodor
"clung assiduously to historical truth," but "the least clumsiness or fogginess
in his words seemed to be the germ of a falsehood, which had to be immediately exterminated."[36] Unconcerned with Fyodor's fidelity to the facts of the real
Chernyshevski's life, Zina is nevertheless fastidious in her efforts to help Fyodor
choose his words. Her partial ownership of the text of *The Life of Chernyshevski* is
further indicated by another moment in the same compositional scene, in which
Zina guides Fyodor's writing through her persistent presence:

> Gifted with a most flexible memory, which twined like ivy around
> what she perceived, Zina by repeating such word-combinations
> as she particularly liked ennobled them with her own secret con-
> volution, and whenever Fyodor for any reason changed a turn of
> phrase [. . .] the ruins of the portico stood for a long time [. . .]
> reluctant to disappear. There was an extraordinary grace in her
> responsiveness which imperceptibly served him as a regulator, if
> not as a guide.[37]

Zina's own "gift" is her subtle ability to influence Fyodor's composition by
dwelling on and repeating the phrases she likes until their mark is so prevalent
that they remain indelibly on the text even when Fyodor *thinks* he has extracted
them. Zina's authorial control over the direction of *The Life of Chernyshevski*
shows her to be far more than just an astute and responsive reader. At minimum,
she acts as Fyodor's "regulator," overseeing the process as he chooses his words.
As the text suggests, however, she might more correctly be called a "guide," leading Fyodor down her own avenues of thought but doing so "imperceptibly."

Lesser Collaborators in *The Gift*

Fyodor's romantic relationship with Zina is ultimately the most productive of
his close relationships, culminating in at least two completed works—*The Life
of Chernyshevski* (embedded in the text of Nabokov's novel) and *The Gift* (presumably the title of the novel Fyodor will have written). It is not, however, the
only relationship in which Fyodor collaborates with the novel's other characters.

---

36 Ibid., 205.
37 Ibid.

His prior collaborative relationships are primarily familial, taking place between him and his sister, Tanya, as well as between him and his mother, Elizaveta Pavlovna. The novel's first instance of Fyodor's sharing in creative coauthorship with another character is in his childhood play with his sister. Interspersed with excerpts from Fyodor's book of poems about childhood are reminiscences often involving Tanya. In young Fyodor's insomniac state (a Nabokovian affliction that he conferred on his protagonist), he "subsist[ed] on conversations with Tanya [. . .] exchang[ing] conundrums from room to room [. . .] she to guess mine, I to think of another."[38] Rejecting the prefabricated fun of the toys "[f]rom indifferent givers on the outside," brother and sister engage in their own creative play that requires a carefully calibrated understanding of one another, a mind-melding capacity for solving each other's riddles.[39] Fyodor "subsists" on their conversation, nourished by this collaboration. Still, their collaboration is not tantamount to his coauthorship with Zina. Teasing the reader who expects a predictable account of a writer's childhood, Nabokov writes, "little Fedya and his sister Tanya [. . .] would even write plays themselves for their performances [. . .] That, my good man, may be true of other poets but in my case it is a lie."[40] Likely indicative of the fact that for Nabokov non-romantic collaborative authorships are inherently limited, Fyodor's relationship with Tanya does not generate a textualized world.

Fyodor's relationship with his mother is also collaborative and perhaps more vital to the composition of his works in the novel, yet still not textually generative to the extent of his relationship with Zina. Not only does Elizaveta Pavlovna urge Fyodor to write a book about his father (which only partially materializes, but not as a separate book within the novel), but they also engage in collaborative fantasy. His mother confesses to him that "she believed more and more that Fyodor's father was alive, that her mourning was ridiculous," halfway convincing Fyodor of this possibility, a prospect that unsettles him. On the same visit, the two often sit in silence, with Fyodor eventually realizing that they are, without speaking, "play[ing]" by "silently imagining to themselves that each was taking the same Leshino walk."[41] Both imagine themselves strolling the paths of their Russian family estate, Leshino, without verbally communicating their daydream to each other.

---

38 Ibid., 16; see Nabokov, *Speak, Memory*, 108 for Nabokov's description of his own insomnia.
39 Nabokov, *The Gift*, 13.
40 Ibid., 12.
41 Ibid., 87, 89.

Like Fyodor's own mother, Mrs. Chernyshevski, Fyodor's Jewish-Russian Berlin acquaintance, attempts to put Fyodor's writerly abilities to personal use by having him write about her late son, Yasha. Rather than sharing an imagined world with her, Fyodor allows the grieving mother to overestimate his interest in her son's life and poetry. Mrs. Chernyshevski misinterprets "the forced sounds of approbation [Fyodor] politely made" for "incoherent rapture." Fyodor never intends to write Yasha's story, hoping that Mrs. Chernyshevski will eventually give up, and "only much later [does] he understand [. . .] the irreproachable compositional balance" between the Chernyshevskis' "hope-suffused" grief for their late son and Fyodor's own grief for his disappeared father.[42]

Unlike *The Life of Chernyshevski*, which Fyodor writes and publishes within the novel, the aborted efforts of coauthorship with secondary female characters such as Fyodor's sister, mother, and Mrs. Chernyshevski, do not appear as distinct texts within the text. If we follow the argument most explicitly laid out by Blackwell, that text of *The Gift* is a product of Fyodor's collaboration with Zina, then Fyodor has *already* written both a story about Yasha and a story about his father. They are not, however, given the textual status of stand-alone pieces in *The Gift*.[43] While Fyodor has taken some liberties in his retellings of their respective stories, excluding the content of Yasha's poetry and fancifully inserting a version of himself into his father's adventures, the author(s) of *The Gift*—whomever we take them to be—has (have) textually materialized elements of both Yasha Chernyshevski and Konstantin Kirillovich Godunov-Cherdyntsev's lives. Consistent with Fyodor's polemical biography of Chernyshevski, these accounts demonstrate a certain irreverence toward their subjects (even Fyodor's father), with the subjects' views completely overwhelmed by the teller's own.

If this is evidence of the partial materialization of non-romantic collaboration, however, it *also* speaks to Nabokov's coauthorship with his protagonist. Within the narrative of *The Gift*, only Fyodor's complete published texts are read and received by other characters. While it is possible to conceive of the text of *The Gift* as a textual work authored by Fyodor, it is never fully acknowledged as such by the characters within the novel. It is implied at the end of the text that *The Gift* has been Fyodor's magnum opus all along, but if the characters on the same textual level as Fyodor are unable to recognize it, the authorship of the text

---

42 Ibid., 92.
43 Yasha's story was, however, eventually published as an excerpt in the *New Yorker*. See Nabokov, "Triangle Within Circle," *New Yorker*, March 15, 1963, 37–41.

must occur at least partially outside of the world Fyodor shares with the other characters. Thus our "real" world in which Nabokov is the author of *The Gift* is an "other" world to Fyodor.

Two recurring features of Nabokov's *The Gift* gesture toward an interpretation of Nabokov as coauthor with Fyodor. First is the book's slippage from first-to-third-person narration and back again with little acknowledgment of the transition. As noted earlier, one might attribute this to a distinction between a past and future Fyodor, but I would argue that this third person narrator is Nabokov's authorial presence. Second is Fyodor's repeated sense of fatedness, some unseen hand authoring his world. Fyodor "seem[s] to remember [his] future works," describes himself and Zina as "made to the measure of something not quite comprehensible," and asserts that he and Zina were brought together by fate's repeated attempts to introduce them.[44] Even though the life of Yasha Chernyshevski and the life of Konstantin Godunov-Cherdyntsev are partially materialized by Nabokov's fateful supervision, however, they are much less fully textualized than *The Life of Chernyshevski*. *Chernyshevski* exists both as text-within-a-text in our world—the world of Nabokov and the reader—and as Fyodor's published work in the textual world he shares with other characters. World-building and coauthorship reach their apotheoses through romantic love, which in the published complete text of *The Gift* Nabokov generously bestows upon Zina and Fyodor.

The Dissolution and Resurrection of Martin

To return to *Glory* and to Martin's anxieties of coauthorship and companionship, Toker argues that he is not a failed hero, but rather a hero incapable of comprehending his actual quest. He seeks to attain worldly glory, yet his predetermined quest is paradoxically aimed at both overcoming fear and achieving his own cancellation through his passage into the world of Zoorland.[45] Is it possible that, through Nabokov's intervention as author, Martin's dreams are transformed into something with an effect, be it the text of the novel he is living in or the world into which he disappears?

To recall the foreword, Nabokov follows his denial of Martin's relief from the "itch of being" with the admission that the authorial "temptation to perform [his]

44 Nabokov, *The Gift*, 194, 177, 363–64.
45 Toker, "Nabokov's *Glory*," 102.

own little exploit [...] prevailed."[46] From the very beginning, Nabokov's authorial will is for Martin to invent the world that he will dissolve into. Considering the connections that Nabokov's text establishes between play and artistic creation, Martin's author-diagnosed lack of talent marks him as a character who is destined never to reach textual maturity. By the end of the novel, his imaginative potential without a complementary artistic outlet comes across as hopelessly childish. This is best exemplified by Martin's final interaction with Darwin. Visiting at long last with his old Cambridge schoolmate, Martin expects to find the same eccentric and playful person he knew before. Instead, Darwin has outgrown his youthful mischievousness, and Martin is surprised that "he no longer composed those charming trifles about leeches and sunsets, but wrote articles on political and financial subjects."[47] When Martin tells Darwin of his plans to cross a border illegally, Darwin calls his plan "absurd and rather peculiar."[48] Unlike Martin, Darwin follows the trajectory of a Bildungsroman protagonist, accepting the societal pressure to evolve into an ordinary professional journalist at the expense of his extraordinary fictions.

If, as Shrayer asserts, "[i]n the novel's perfect ending [...] Nabokov undoes his characters but leaves a landscape, an art form that unravels in space,"[49] and, as Toker proposes, "the death of a fictional character is [...] his return to and dissolution into the 'involute abode' of the novelist's mind,"[50] then Martin's disappearance at the end of *Glory* allows for him to be recycled in Nabokov's literary world. Martin's history and his attributes, liberated from the character of Martin, are free to be reused and recontextualized across Nabokov's oeuvre. Nabokov's recycling of his characters is sometimes overt, as with Pnin's reappearance in *Pale Fire*. While the Pnin of *Pnin* leaves Waindell College defeated and undone, his resurrection as a successful yet minor character in *Pale Fire* shows him as apparently free from the weight of the alternate history of the novel to which Nabokov reassigns him.

I would therefore suggest that Nabokov resurrects some of Martin's personal characteristics and some elements of Martin's world in Fyodor's and his own. As a talented writer with a literary purpose, Fyodor is the artistically matured dreamer that Nabokov never allows Martin to be. Even physical elements of

---

46   Nabokov, *Glory*, xiii.
47   Nabokov, *Glory*, 198.
48   Nabokov, *Glory*, 200.
49   Shrayer," The Perfect Glory," 38.
50   Toker, "Nabokov's *Glory*," 99.

their respective environments migrate across texts. Consider these two parallel scenes, the first from the penultimate chapter of *Glory*:

> The late afternoon sky was a sunless cheerless blank [. . .] An open van passed by drawn by a pair of scrawny horses; upon it was heaped enough furniture to furnish a house: a couch, a chest of drawers, a gilt-framed seascape, and a lot of other melancholy chattels. A woman in mourning crossed the damp-dappled asphalt; she was pushing a pram, and in it sat a blue-eyed attentive infant. [. . .] "What's the matter, for goodness' sake,' thought Martin. "What's all this to me? I know I'm going to return. I must return."[51]

And the second from the opening of *The Gift*:

> One cloudy but luminous day, towards four in the afternoon [. . .] a moving van [. . .] pulled up in front of Number Seven Tannenberg Street, in the west part of Berlin [. . .] Running along its entire side was the name of the moving company in yard-high blue letters, each of which [. . .] was shaded laterally with black paint: a dishonest attempt to climb into the next dimension. On the sidewalk [. . .] stood two people who had obviously come out to meet their furniture. . .The woman, thickset and no longer young . . . brought a whiff of rather good but slightly stale perfume [. . .] Some day, he thought, I must use such a scene to start a good, thick old-fashioned novel.[52]

Alexandrov wonders if *The Gift*'s description of the moving van's lettering "raises the question of whether or not there are 'honest' attempts to move into another dimension."[53] Arguably, the motif of the moving van, delivering furniture on overcast afternoons in Weimar Berlin, is one such attempt at depositing the "baggage" of *Glory* in the world of *The Gift*. The moving van in *The Gift* picks up where the vehicle in *Glory* leaves off: the woman, once a widow with a baby, is "no longer young," and Martin's metafictional insistence that he will return is

---

51 Nabokov, *Glory*, 196.
52 Nabokov, *Gift*, 3–4.
53 Alexandrov, *Nabokov's Otherworld*, 109.

mirrored by Fyodor's thought that the moving scene will one day be the opening of his own novel and not only the novel he inhabits.

What purpose does this metaphysical-metafictional link between the two novels serve? In the years between the publication of the Russian-language versions of *Glory* and *The Gift*, Nabokov published three full-length novels: *Camera obscura* (significantly revised in English as *Laughter in the Dark*), *Despair*, and *Invitation to a Beheading*, as well as a number of shorter fictions. Although, as we have seen, the metaphysics of *Glory* and the literary texture of *The Gift* are ambitious, their ostensible focus on young male protagonists' coming-of-age is conventional in comparison to the experimental subjects of the intervening novels, such as Cincinnatus C.'s death sentence for "gnostical turpitude" in *Invitation to a Beheading*.[54] In the 1962 foreword to the English translation of *The Gift*, Nabokov writes that it was "the last novel [he] wrote, or [would] ever write, in Russian."[55] By revisiting the Bildungsroman as a *Künstlerroman*, Nabokov registers both the eternality of other worlds invented in—and inherited from—his Russian childhood and the finality of his Russian-language career as a fictionist.

Critics have compared both *Glory* and *The Gift* to a Möbius strip, with Toker noting *Glory*'s involution "between the fictional world and the implied author's mind."[56] *The Gift* ends on a far more optimistic note than *Glory*, with Fyodor and Zina on the threshold of consummating their relationship and Fyodor on the brink of creating his great novel that might well become *The Gift*. The young male protagonist previously embodied by Martin is given a chance at redemption through the materialization of his work and his romance. His story is rewritten as one of success, the "itch of being" relieved through writing. At the same time, Martin's liberation from his character is another kind of freedom; Nabokov releases him into the other world where he ceases to exist as Martin. If Fyodor's fate is not an outright negation of this freedom, it at the very least represents a late modernist ambivalence about character's freedom in fiction. Consider again the way *The Gift* concludes, with a sonnet written out as prose: "[...] the chords of fate itself continue to vibrate; and no obstruction for the sage exists where I have put The End: the shadows of my world extend beyond the skyline of the page, blue as tomorrow's morning haze—nor does this terminate the phrase."[57]

54 Nabokov, *Invitation to a Beheading*, 72.
55 Nabokov, *Gift*, Foreword.
56 Toker, "Nabokov's *Glory*," 88.
57 Nabokov, *Gift*, 366.

There is no definitive indication that this conclusion is in Fyodor's voice or Nabokov's, and it is readable as both simultaneously. The ending signals both the author's departure from this particular work and the fated eternity of his characters within the text and "beyond the skyline of the page." Martin is dissolved, but Fyodor is, as Nabokov states in his foreword, only "dismissed."[58] When Nabokov flees Germany for France, he leaves Fyodor and Zina in Berlin. What becomes of them? Do they continue to live out their lives in Germany—an almost certainly tragic fate for the half-Jewish Zina? Does the initial thrill of their romance succumb, at least at times, to the unhappiness Zina predicts?[59] If we accept the canonicity of Nabokov's unpublished sequel to *The Gift*, then Zina dies suddenly in an accident, as her marriage to Fyodor is apparently failing.[60] Or do they, as the Möbius strip metaphor suggests, slide back into the textual beginning, reliving and repeating the fated trajectory that Nabokov crafted for them?

If *Glory* is deceptively simple, *The Gift* (in its published form) is hauntingly optimistic, and it is at the discretion of the reader to judge which provides a more satisfying ending. The thrill in a Nabokov novel is, after all, the precipice: the train ride, the liminal moments before succumbing to sleep, the eager moment of sexual and intellectual excitement that Fyodor and Zina experience while locked out of the house. His characters experience "the weight and the threat of bliss."[61] The certainty of achieving one's bliss holds within it a threat: a dream realized is a dream no longer. Perhaps Martin's dissolution, his canceled existence on the precipice of the dream, offers a superior alternative to the assuredness of Fyodor's success and the burden of his endless existence.

Zina, Sonia, Véra

In the forewords to the Englished texts, Nabokov cautions readers not to read his novels as autobiographical accounts, "trust[ing] that wise readers [of *Glory*] will refrain from avidly flipping through his autobiography *Speak, Memory* in quest of duplicate items or kindred scenery."[62] Nabokov warns the readers that neither the fact that Nabokov had lived in Berlin at the same time as Fyodor

58   Ibid., Foreword.
59   Ibid., 365.
60   Jane Grayson, "Washington's Gift: Materials Pertaining to Nabokov's Gift in the Library of Congress," *Nabokov Studies* 1 (1994): 43.
61   Nabokov, *Gift*, 366.
62   Nabokov, *Glory*, xiv.

Godunov-Chernytsev, "nor my sharing of some of his interests, such as literature and lepidoptera, should make one say 'aha' and identify the designer with the design."[63] Despite his disclaimers and protests against narrowly autobiographical interpretations, however, Nabokov does not disguise the fact that he shares much of himself with his characters, and his very attempt to assert control over his personal and literary narratives backfires by drawing more attention to these parallels. Against Nabokov's wishes, I return to the final chapter of *Speak, Memory* as a potential gloss for reading the coauthorial relationships in *Glory* and *The Gift*. This is not to say that either of the protagonists serve as representatives of their author. Rather, Nabokov's stylized autobiography, more than revealing the previously unknown details of his life, supplements his fictional texts by revealing his model of coauthorship.[64]

Addressing Véra directly, Nabokov writes:

> Whenever I start thinking of my love for a person, I am in the habit of immediately drawing radii from my love—from my heart, from the tender nucleus of a personal matter—to monstrously remote points of the universe [. . .] the dreadful pitfalls of eternity, the unknowledgeable beyond the unknown, the helplessness, the cold, the sickening involutions and interpenetrations of space and time. [65]

To Nabokov, the experience of love is a gateway into frighteningly infinite worlds, alluring and monstrous all at once. Although the lone "I" in "[w]henever I start thinking" frames Nabokov's passage into such worlds as a solitary venture inspired by his love for another, his decision to open the chapter by telling Véra's "you" that "nobody will know what you and I know" reveals that they have shared the experience of other worlds. The "you and I" have ventured "beyond the unknown" to coauthor worlds "unknowledgeable" to anyone else. The historical Véra—like the fictional Sonia and Zina—was much more than a reader par excellence of Nabokov's work. She models not just Nabokov's ideal reader, but the ideal coauthor that he seeks to be to his characters—invested, conspiratorial, and quietly yet unmistakably present.

---

63 Nabokov, *Gift*, Foreword.
64 *For a discussion of Vladimir and Véra's co-creative relationship, see Ciara Spencer's essay in this volume (M. D. S.).*
65 Nabokov, *Speak, Memory*, 296.

Bibliography

Primary Sources

Nabokov, Vladimir. *The Gift*. Translated by Michael Scammel in collaboration with the author. New York: Vintage International, 1991.

———. *Glory*. Translated by Dmitri Nabokov in collaboration with the author. New York: Vintage International, 1991.

———. *Invitation to a Beheading*. Translated by Dmitri Nabokov in collaboration with the author. New York: Vintage International, 1989.

———. *Lectures on Literature*. Edited by Fredson Bowers. New York: Harcourt Brace Jovanovich/Bruccoli Clark, 1980.

———. *Speak, Memory: An Autobiography Revisited*. New York: Vintage International, 1989.

———. "Triangle within Circle." Translated by Dmitri Nabokov in collaboration with the author. *New Yorker*, March 15, 1963: 37–41.

Secondary Sources

Alexandrov, Vladimir E. *Nabokov's Otherworld*. Princeton, NJ: Princeton University Press, 1991.

Blackwell, Stephen H. *Zina's Paradox: The Figured Reader in Nabokov's "Gift."* New York: Peter Lang, 2000.

Grayson, Jane. "Washington's Gift: Materials Pertaining to Nabokov's Gift in the Library of Congress." *Nabokov Studies* 1 (1994): 21–67.

Johnson, D. Barton. *Worlds in Regression: Some Novels of Vladimir Nabokov*. Ann Arbor, MI: Ardis, 1985.

Morris, Paul D. "Zina's Paradox: The Figured Reader in Nabokov's Gift" [review of *Zina's Paradox*, by Stephen Blackwell]. *Nabokov Studies* 6 (2000–2001): 209–212.

Raeff, Marc. *Russia Abroad: A Cultural History of the Russian Emigration, 1919–1939*. New York: Oxford University Press, 1990.

Shrayer, Maxim D. *The World of Nabokov's Stories*. Austin: University of Texas Press, 1999.

———. "The Perfect Glory of Nabokov's Exploit." *Russian Studies in Literature* 35, no. 4 (October 1999): 29–41.

———. "Bunin's Tambourine: Echoes of the Old Master in His Disciple's Fourth Novel." *Nabokov Studies* 16 (2019): 1–11. Accessed March 25, 2024. https://muse.jhu.edu/article/747613.

Toker, Leona. *Nabokov: The Mystery of Literary Structures*. Ithaca, NY: Cornell University Press, 1989.

Other (Dis)enchanted Motels: Nabokov's Chronicles of Suburban America

Jared Hackworth

Nabokov in Suburban America

During the 1940s, the decade when Vladimir Nabokov immigrated to the United States of America, a new cultural system and vision of society took root. As a new American, Nabokov observed rapid suburbanization, which resulted in the ubiquity of single-family homes, automobiles, highways, and law enforcement. This suburbanization also superficially unified a community of white Americans that protected itself against outside influences. In his American novels of the 1950s, *Pnin* and *Lolita,* Nabokov resists the dominating cultural script of mid-century American suburbanization. By describing American suburbanization and critiquing its perceived virtues through outsider and immigrant protagonists, Nabokov shows that the outwardly monolithic suburban cultural imagination has always been fractured.[1]

That the two émigré protagonists—Humbert Humbert, a pedophile kidnapper, and Timofey Pnin, a politely awkward Russian intellectual—are near inversions of each other only strengthens Nabokov's critique of the suburbs' constitutive faults. Nabokov reveals the flaws in the suburban cultural scripts by performing idealized suburbanization and inverting it. With his detailed descriptions of physical spaces and attention to American tropes, Nabokov condemns the broken American infrastructure that both enables Humbert

---

1   For a discussion of cultural script theory, see Ann Swidler, "Culture in Action: Symbols and Strategies," *American Sociological Review* 51, no. 2 (1986): 273–286, accessed March 18, 2023, https://doi.org/10.2307/2095521.

Humbert to victimize Lolita and looks the other way as Timofey Pnin falters at Waindell.[2]

American suburbanization, while often understood today as a complex process with immense tradeoffs, was actively promoted in the late 1940s and 1950s. Suburban development rapidly transformed American life, with automobiles, law enforcement, houses of worship, and single-family homes creating insular communities distant from the city. Suburbanization was rapidly pivoted to favor single-family homes outside of the urban center, which one would reach not by public transportation but private automobiles driven on freeways.[3] In these communities, white cultural homogenization reigned supreme.[4] To protect this homogenization, under the guise of providing safe neighborhoods, suburban spaces increased their police forces exponentially.[5] Even family life transformed, with single-family homes designed for a male head of the household who commuted to work and a female spouse who worked in the home.[6] The ideal community of single-family homes would join together to attend (preferably Protestant) church on Sunday mornings. All of these suburban developments created, in the words of the cultural historian James Jacobs, "homogenized and stratified suburban worlds."[7] Writing in the late 1940s and early 1950s, Nabokov registered the challenges that American suburban space provided to its residents and strangers.

When Nabokov and his family fled France as the Nazis advanced toward Paris and came to the United States as refugees, his primary residence

---

2   In Nabokov scholarship, "Lolita" commonly refers to Humbert Humbert's creation of Lolita, instead of "Dolores," which is better suited to analysis of the character as a survivor of abuse. I use "Lolita" to emphasize the novel's subjective narration that enables a suburban critique.

3   See Eric Avila, *The Folklore of the Freeway: Race and Revolt in the Modernist City* (Minneapolis: University of Minnesota Press, 2014). Avila expands suburbanization to the roads, as decentralization had social and economic overtones.

4   Through the 1940s and 1950s, the definition of whiteness was moved from an implied common knowledge state to legal language; the suburban mythos expanded into racial categorization: the ideal American citizen became a white one with a white, middle-class nuclear family with two children and a car. For more information, see Ian López, *White by Law: The Legal Construction of Race* (New York: New York University Press, 1996).

5   Sarah A. Seo, *Policing the Open Road: How Cars Transformed American Freedom* (Cambridge, MA: Harvard University Press, 2019).

6   James Jacobs explores the relationship between gendered suburbanization and home development, arguing that class influenced home design and family structure. For more information, see James Jacobs, *Detached America: Building Houses in Postwar Suburbia* (Charlottesville: University of Virginia Press, 2015).

7   Ibid., 13.

shifted from cities to suburban and rural spaces.[8] Formerly of St. Petersburg, Cambridge (UK), Berlin, and Paris, Nabokov arrived in America in May 1940. After brief stays in New York City and Palo Alto, he resided first in Cambridge and Wellesley, Massachusetts, from 1941 to 1948, and then subsequently in Ithaca, New York, from 1948 until his return to Europe in 1959. Ithaca of the 1940s-1950s may come across as less a suburban space than a college town.[9] However, based on the predominance of suburban cultural values, citizens in small towns and near-urban spaces identified as suburbanites.[10] Nabokov depicts these suburban values across small towns, college towns, and suburbs, showcasing that Americans consider themselves suburbanites regardless of the legal density of their town.

Indeed, even in smaller towns, Americans aspired for a suburban lifestyle. In *Lolita*, Mrs. Haze's home, Ramsdale, despite being in a New England town built long before the 1940s, is actually described as a generalized suburban space. Humbert Humbert reflects on "a meddlesome suburban dog (one of those who lie in wait for cars)," and Mrs. Haze sends Lolita to summer camp, saying "is all so much more *reasonable* as I say than to mope on a suburban lawn."[11] Nabokov and his characters find themselves enmeshed in postwar American suburban mythology based on a faulty promise of homogeneity regardless of physical location. The uses of the word "suburb" are not just geographic descriptors; they indicate an aspirational lifestyle and a set of values.

In *Pnin*, Nabokov's setting may not seem initially suburban. Waindell, like many towns in New England and upstate New York, hardly resembles the suburbs around Boston and New York City. However, urban studies scholarship suggests the unique characteristics of the college town are best interpreted by considering its space as that of a suburb.[12] The growth development patterns are just "like suburbia" as the campus takes on the role of the central business district, with the surrounding town assuming the role of suburb.[13] These towns function as an "academic archipelago" resembling each other yet having immense differences

---

8   For an investigation of Nabokov's road trips in his American years, see Jane Grayson, *Vladimir Nabokov* (New York: Abrams Press, 2003); Robert Roper, *Nabokov in America* (New York: Bloomsbury USA, 2015); Brian Boyd, *Vladimir Nabokov: The American Years* (Princeton, NJ: Princeton University Press, 1991).

9   For the remainder of this essay, Cambridge refers to Cambridge, Massachusetts.

10 Blake Gumprecht, "The American College Town," *Geographical Review* 93. no 1 (2003): 51–80, accessed October 15, 2023, https://shibbolethsp.jstor.org/start?entityID=https%3A%2F%2 Fidp.bc.edu%2 Fopenathens&dest=https://www.jstor.org/stable/30033889&site=jstor.

11 Vladimir Nabokov, *Lolita* (New York: Vintage International, 1997), 36, 64.

12 Gumprecht, "The American College Town," 59.

13 Ibid.

from their surrounding regions. This uniqueness from the surrounding region explains the demographics unique to college towns as "they are alike in [. . .] their highly educated workforces, their relative absence of heavy industry, and the presence in them of cultural opportunities."[14] Culturally, these towns strive for an American dream of homogeneity based on the suburban ideal. Nabokov, in creating the fictional Waindell, leans into this suburban town's cultural identity, albeit with a diverse cohort of European expatriate professors surrounding the university. Even with a diverse demographic of academics, which includes foreigners and immigrants, the suburban norms and values are upheld, as rural college town residents shape a homogenizing narrative of unity for themselves.[15]

Single-family Homes and Suburban Towns in *Lolita*

In *Lolita*, Nabokov narrates the self-perceived suburban values of Mrs. Haze's home and of American motels at the same time as he destabilizes these values through Humbert Humbert's pathological and abusive relationship with a child. Nabokov's painfully cruel description of what happens to Lolita only furthers his subversion of the suburban culture; he peels back the suburban familial ideal and reveals evidence of domestic violence. In the novel, the residents of Ramsdale want to regard themselves as part of the American suburban narrative despite their status as a small New England town. Details such as the "suburban lawn" and the "suburban dog" throughout the text augment what to an American reader would be an idyllic image of American space—but Nabokov underscores it as the scene of sexual violence.[16]

Through Humbert Humbert's wry critique, Nabokov mocks the suburban ethos in the descriptions of the home's materials. Nabokov writes in Humbert Humbert's European voice, redolent of contempt for the American suburbs and their philistine residents: "I could not be happy in that type of household with bedraggled magazines on every chair and a kind of horrible hybridization between the comedy of so-called 'functional modern furniture' and the tragedy

---

14 Ibid., 51.
15 For Nabokov scholarship that touches on suburbanization, consider David Castronovo, "Humbert's America," *New England Review* 23, no. 2 (2002): 33–41, accessed November 7, 2023, http://www.jstor.org /stable/40244102; Mary Catanzaro, "The Car as Cell in *Lolita*," *Kansas Quarterly* 21, no. 4 (1989): 91–96; Yuri Leving, *Nabokov in Motion: Modernity and Movement* (New York: Bloomsbury Academic, 2022).
16 Nabokov, *Lolita*, 36, 64.

of decrepit rockers and rickety lamp tables with dead lamps."[17] With this description of the classic catalog furnishings, Nabokov mocks the setup of the suburban home. The single-family home is that of prefabricated, standardized design, and Mrs. Haze follows "the authoress of *Your Home Is You,* as she developed a hatred for little lean chairs and spindle tables" and replaces novels with "illustrated catalogs and homemaking guides."[18] For Nabokov, the vision that American culture projects as resplendent is merely a consumer-oriented veneer. Nabokov's work here, in *Lolita,* echoes his *Lectures on Literature,* where he composes an extended critique of Philistinism—or as he calls it—poshlust (based on the Russian *poshlost'*). Nabokov critiques poshlust as "not only the obviously trashy, but mainly the falsely important, the falsely beautiful, the falsely clever, the falsely attractive."[19] Nabokov's critique of the poshlust lifestyle is especially visible in his fiction of the 1950s—the false beauty of suburban façades exists to be debunked and mocked.

Nabokov represents the isolation of the suburban town through his descriptions of Humbert Humbert's and Mrs. Haze's church wedding. Of the couple's marriage, Nabokov writes, "When the bride is a widow and the groom is a widower; when the former has lived in our Great Little Town for hardly two years, and the latter for only a month [. . .] the wedding is generally a quiet affair."[20] With no other guests at the wedding, Nabokov parades the embarrassment of Humber Humbert, who wants no witnesses. The suburban lifestyle venerates the town itself; stylized with capital letters, its authority as the ideal "Great Little Town," thunders out any possible display of difference or dissent. The church continues to be present in the text as Humbert Humbert reflects, "a black thunderhead loomed above Ramsdale's white church tower when I looked around me."[21] The suburban environment creates a deepening sense of isolation for the duped Mrs. Haze, aided by Humbert's desire to keep the wedding secret.

Humbert Humbert: Suburbia's Enchanted Hunter

After Humbert Humbert's and Mrs. Haze's wedding, the novel further descends into darkness as Mrs. Haze is killed, Humbert kidnaps the twelve-year-old Lolita

---

17 Ibid., 37–38.
18 Ibid., 78.
19 Vladimir Nabokov, *Lectures on Russian Literature* (Boston, MA: Mariner Books Classics, 2002), 313.
20 Nabokov, *Lolita,* 74.
21 Ibid., 74.

from summer camp, drugs her, and rapes her. Nabokov inextricably connects the mechanisms of Humbert's abuse to the great American road trip.[22] The road trip, a new type of vacation made possible by suburban development, provides a unique isolation with no communal or public transport and anonymous, one-night motels. The connection between danger and suburban space is tied to Nabokov's critique of American suburbanization. When Mrs. Haze was still alive, she planned to take Humbert Humbert to The Enchanted Hunters Hotel because it is "quaint," "the food is a dream," and "nobody bothers anybody."[23] Nabokov immediately highlights the dangers of the motel's anonymity.

After Mrs. Haze's death, Humbert takes Lolita to the same motel, saying he "was agonizingly anxious to smuggle her into the hermetic seclusion of The Enchanted Hunters," again drawn to its ubiquitous anonymity.[24] The motel had no vacancies when they arrived due to "a religious convention" that had "clashed with a flower show in Briceland."[25] Through this pair of suburban, wholesome activities, Nabokov directly contrasts the drugging and rape with the prescribed delights of religion and flowers. The name signals danger-ous seclusion, as the "Enchanted Hunters" suggests a contradictory feeling of isolation, moving out of real world time, and active pursuit. Indeed, Lolita has been enchanted, drugged, and placed under the influence, while Humbert becomes the aggressive hunter.

Nabokov's depictions of Humbert Humbert's illicit crime made possible in the motel serve to counteract the suburban vision of seamless safety and white Christian purity. As Nabokov's protagonist drives toward the motel, he receives directions from strangers, gets continually lost, and remains commit-ted to finding The Enchanted Hunters instead of another motel, reflecting as he goes "along our route countless motor courts proclaimed their vacancy in neon lights, ready to accommodate salesmen, escaped convicts, impotents, family groups, as well as the most corrupt and vigorous couples."[26] With this depiction, Nabokov yet again highlights the allure of the place. The Enchanted Hunters, despite its emblematic nature in the text, is structurally interchangeable as American motels allow for the secure anonymity that Humbert Humbert desperately seeks. Finally, he receives directions from "a man and a girl, more or

22 See Roper, *Nabokov in America,* for a discussion of Nabokov's road trips across America. Roper (150) writes, "These years of *Lolita* were also the years of some of his most extensive, most joyous wanderings in the West."
23 Nabokov, *Lolita,* 93.
24 Ibid., 117.
25 Ibid., 118.
26 Ibid., 116.

less conjoined in a dark car," and this, once again, highlights the sexual activity hidden from the spotlight. The directions are received in "the Park [...] as black as the sins it concealed."[27]

As Humbert fantasizes about his original road trip, he writes to The Enchanted Hunters to book a room; he is denied the standard comfortable room he desires and offered only a basement room with four beds. The letterhead of the motel augurs a suburban fantasy; "THE ENCHANTED HUNTERS / NEAR CHURCHES / All Legal Beverages / NO DOGS."[28] With the coded message "near churches," Nabokov exposes the prejudice deeply embedded in the suburban imagination, wherein Jews face bigotry.[29] He wryly reflects on this prejudice and persecution, writing, "I also wondered if a hunter, enchanted or otherwise, would not need a pointer more than a pew."[30] With this, Nabokov showcases such coded religious discrimination as a failed act of forced cultural unification—the real hunters are at the motel with arrows drawn instead of in the pews of a local church. The Enchanted Hunters remains a symbol of perceived anonymous space, as Humbert Humbert remembers the first road trip and desires to return to "fall back on old setting in order to save what could be saved in the way of *souvenir, souvenir que me veux-tu?*"[31] Throughout the scenes of road trips, Nabokov punctuates this driving trip with sin and illicit lust—the nearby churches and the peaceful family atmosphere promised by suburban cultural scripts are nowhere to be seen.

Inversions of Suburban Town Scripts

Nabokov inverts the idealized road trip from a joyful familial adventure into a site of abuse. On the second road trip, Humbert arrives at Chestnut Court, and this motel also betrays the larger failure of suburban housing and culture to protect Lolita. Nabokov writes that Humbert Humbert finds a motel with "a pleasant little burg and [is] put up at Chestnut Court—nice cabins, damp

---

27 Ibid., 117.
28 Ibid., 261.
29 For a further discussion of Nabokov's relationship with antisemitic spaces throughout his American years, see Boyd, *Vladimir Nabokov: The American*; Maxim D. Shrayer, "Jewish Questions in Nabokov's Art and Life" in *Nabokov and His Fiction: New Perspectives*, ed. Julian W. Connolly (Cambridge: Cambridge University Press, 2012), 73–91.
30 Nabokov, *Lolita*, 261.
31 Ibid., 261.

green grounds, apple trees, and old swing—and a tremendous sunset which the tired child ignored."[32] In this idyllic scene, Nabokov observes, "from our window you could see the road winding down, and then running as straight as a hair [...] towards the pretty town, which looked singularly distinct and toylike in the pure morning distance."[33] Nabokov presents a perfect American scene idolized across the entire nation. There is an "elf-like girl on an insect-like bicycle, and a dog," as the small town imagery comes to complete fruition.[34] Walking through the town, Humbert Humbert engages in this picture of Americanness created by the motel and the small town, as he had "a cup of hot flavorless coffee, bought a bunch of bananas for my monkey" and got a "very mediocre haircut."[35] Over the course of two pages, Nabokov stacks and subverts picture after picture of American life, with new motel visitors and constant, outwardly tranquil scenes.

Nabokov shatters these images of American life when the perfect suburban space encases the sexual abuse of a child. When Humbert Humbert returns, Lolita is in the motel room with dusty sandals, leading him to believe she has snuck out. Looking around, Humbert Humbert sees that "all cars have disappeared" except the one neighbor, preparing to leave, as the scene becomes isolated.[36] Humbert Humbert has a "special suspicion" and "said nothing" but "pushed her softness back into the room and went in after her. I ripped her shirt off. I unzipped the rest of her."[37] Nabokov created this scene, perhaps one of the most shocking in the novel, to confront American suburban culture. This sexual attack subverts the suburban ethos—there is no safety in the American suburban space; Humbert Humbert's crimes against Lolita remain unnoticed and unobserved until he commits murder at the end of the novel by executing Quilty in his home. Nabokov shreds the perceived innocence of the town; this egregious violence could occur to any child across the nation.

As the novel concludes, Nabokov reflects on the constant presence of the motel as a site of harm for Lolita instead of a joyful vacation trip. Humbert Humbert reflects, "I have a memo here: between July 5 and November 18, when I returned to Beardsley for a few days, I registered, if not actually stayed, at 342 hotels, motels and tourist homes."[38] The emphasis on motels builds to the finale of the text when Humbert Humbert returns to Lolita, now the pregnant Mrs.

---

32 Ibid., 212.
33 Ibid.
34 Ibid.
35 Ibid., 213.
36 Ibid., 215.
37 Ibid.
38 Ibid., 242.

Richard F. Shiller. When he offers her cash, she immediately says, "'You mean,' [...] opening her eyes and raising herself slightly, the snake that may strike, 'you mean you will give [us] that money only if I go with you to a motel. Is *that* what you mean?'"[39] The site of sexual violence remains the American motel, and Humbert Humbert's declaration of love only exacerbates this profound disharmony. For Nabokov, the emphasis on families and churches is beside the point; Nabokov has exposed the American motel by stripping away its promise of middle-class propriety and safety.

Subversive Vehicular Homicide in *Lolita*

In addition to his critique of American suburban scripts regarding single-family homes, motels, and towns, Nabokov attacks the automobile. Highways, driveways, parking lots, mechanics, gas stations, and cars skyrocketed in prevalence in the mid-century.[40] The automobile was the predominant sign of American prosperity. By the time Humbert Humbert comes to America as an immigrant, cars dominate the nation's ideal vision, which Nabokov subverts by tying the automobile to death.

When Humbert Humbert arrives in Ramsdale, he is directed to the Hazes' house instead of the McCoos's house due to a fire; a neighbor then lets him borrow her "limousine, a marvelously old-fashioned, square-topped affair."[41] The ride continues: "Speaking of sharp turns: we almost ran over a meddlesome suburban dog (one of those who lie in wait for cars) as we swerved into Lawn Street."[42] Nabokov begins to couple the automobile-centered American cultural vision with death.

The linkage of the automobile with death instead of comfort allows Nabokov to crack the suburban veneer of safety. On the morning that Mrs. Haze discovers Humbert Humbert's desire for Lolita, he drives around town, and he "left in great spirits. Steering my wife's car with one finger, I contentedly rolled homeward."[43] With this description, Nabokov sets up the cultural script of the midday drive, a calm American activity. The day, too, is peaceful, as "Ramsdale had, after all,

---

39   Ibid., 278.
40   See Eric Avila, *The Folklore of the Freeway: Race and Revolt in the Modernist City* (Minneapolis: University of Minnesota Press, 2014).
41   Nabokov, *Lolita*, 35–36.
42   Ibid., 36.
43   Ibid., 95.

lots of charm" and "the cicadas whirred; the avenue had been freshly watered."[44] Everything about the New England scene is a perfect stereotyped image: the street is "so blue and green" and "as usual, as usual, the local paper was lying on the porch where it had just been hurled by Kenny."[45] With this poignant description, Nabokov portrays Ramsdale as perfectly conforming to a mid-century American script with a calm, leafy avenue and restful drive.

Nabokov undermines the suburban stereotype of the vehicle when Mrs. Haze discovers Humbert Humbert's morbid passion for her daughter through reading his journal. After confronting him, Mrs. Haze goes outside while Humbert Humbert mixes a drink. He receives a phone call that says, "Mrs. Humbert, sir, has been run over and you'd better come quick."[46] Nabokov catalogs Mrs. Haze's vehicular death but leaves out specific details. The description of the vehicular death tarnishes the script of the car. Consider Humbert Humbert's description: "I have to put the impact of an instantaneous vision into a sequence of words; their physical accumulation in the page impairs the actual flash."[47] The police arrive "due to their having been ticketing the illegally parked cars in a cross lane two blocks down the grade"—their focus has been on automobiles instead of sexual abuse.[48] The whole scene becomes a display of grotesque violence, mitigated through Humbert Humbert's role in the crime. Hearing about another failed vehicular murder later in the text, Humbert Humbert reflects, "Alas, the woman's battered body did not match up with only minor damage suffered by the car. I did better."[49] With this, Nabokov makes the death mysterious but leaves the common thread of the car, tying the suburban cultural norm of the automobile with sudden death.

Once Humbert kidnaps Lolita, Nabokov tirelessly links the automobile with violence and death, describing the roadkill the pair passes. While they are driving on the route, Nabokov notes that Humbert Humbert feels "an oppressive, hideous constraint as if I were sitting with the small ghost of somebody I had just killed," thus registering the weight of Lolita's melancholy.[50] While this occurs, Lolita "broke the silence" and commented, "Oh a squashed squirrel.

---

44   Ibid., 95–96.
45   Ibid., 95.
46   Ibid., 96.
47   Ibid., 97.
48   Ibid.
49   Ibid., 288.
50   Ibid., 140.

[...] What a shame."⁵¹ This attention to roadkill emphasizes death by automobile, as animal bodies begin to pile up around the car.

On the second road trip, Nabokov's pattern of linking the automobile with death continues. The road trips are a "joyride" for Humbert, free of the policing."⁵² Leaving Beardsley, the "breaks were relined, the waterpipes unclogged, the valves ground, and a number of other repairs and improvements were paid for by not very mechanically minded but prudent papa Humbert Humbert, so that the late Mrs. Humbert Humbert's car was in respectable shape when ready to undertake a new journey."⁵³ Through this recollection of the dead Mrs. Haze, the car continues to be both a site of death and destruction and a location of deadly and destructive memories. Nabokov pairs the memory of Mrs. Haze and the crushed animal as both incapable of survival. Animal, mother, and daughter all meet the same abysmal fate.

In addition to tying the automobile with death, Nabokov utilizes highway policing to expose the inability of law enforcement to protect *Lolita*. When Humbert Humbert first kidnapped Lolita, Nabokov registers the haste with which they drive as Lolita says, "You drive much faster than my mummy, mister," and Humbert reflects, "I slowed down from a blind seventy to a purblind fifty."⁵⁴ With this, Nabokov's protagonist pays attention to the danger and haste of the road—speeding may draw the attention of others. The interactions with the police on the road heighten as they have "still eighty miles to go, blessed intuition broke our embrace—a split second before a highway patrol car drew up alongside."⁵⁵ The police on the road, constantly monitoring automotive speed limits, do nothing in the face of his real crime, unable to notice it. Watching the change in speed limit from seventy to fifty, the police miss the pedophilia right under their gaze.

Nabokov emphasizes the police's failure to provide safety through the absence of Lolita's speech. This is Nabokov's—Humbert Humbert's—account of the interaction with a police officer: "Florid and beetle-browed, its driver stared at me: "Happen to see a blue sedan, same as yours, pass you before the junction?"⁵⁶ Nabokov doubles on this critique—the police are searching for another sedan, completely unrelated to the crime they are witnessing at that moment. Lolita speaks to the officer: "we didn't" and "but are you sure it was blue, because—,"

---

51 Ibid.
52 Ibid., 288.
53 Ibid., 208.
54 Ibid., 112.
55 Ibid.
56 Ibid., 113.

yet she is interrupted before she is able to share anything, and the police officer drives away.[57] Nabokov leaves open that Lolita may have attempted to tell the police about the crime, yet the cop "gave the little colleen his best smile and went into a U-turn," overlooking the crime.[58] Lolita then says, "The Fruithead [. . .] He should have nabbed *you*."[59] Lolita continues: "The speed in this bum state is fifty, and—No, don't slow down, you, dull bulb. He's gone now" and "that light was red. I've never seen such driving."[60] This superficially innocent conversation about a speeding ticket becomes infinitely more valuable in light of Humbert Humbert's real crime that the police cannot spot.

This farce of policing follows Humbert Humbert throughout the ride, as Nabokov's descriptions of highway patrol continue to overlook Humbert's pedophilia: "At inspection stations on highways entering Arizona or California, a policeman's cousin would peer with such intensity at us that my poor heart wobbled. 'Any honey?' he would enquire, and every time, my sweet fool giggled."[61] Nabokov displays the failure of the police to see actual crime on the American open road. In this novel, the police are not the protectors of the American suburban imagination. Instead, they pay attention to minor misdemeanors while true crimes are overlooked.

Pnin and the Suburban Architecture of Waindell

With depictions of single-family homes, motels, towns, automobiles, and the police in *Lolita*, Nabokov breaks the seal of the postwar American suburban cultural imagination, revealing ever-present crimes and the crimes' willing and accidental enablers. At first glance, *Pnin* comes across as the inverse of *Lolita*, a charming, episodic novel of an émigré professor's mishaps drastically differ from the darkness of *Lolita*. *Pnin*, however, functions as an heir to the suburban critique in *Lolita*; Nabokov continues to show the faults of suburbia through Timofey Pnin's alienation and exclusion from the local community.

When Pnin arrives in Waindell, the town's infrastructure highlights the isolation of the suburban space for those classified as "other." At the book's opening, Pnin works as a Russian professor at Waindell College. As a cultural outsider,

---

57 Ibid.
58 Ibid.
59 Ibid.
60 Ibid.
61 Ibid., 116.

Pnin struggles to find belonging. While some émigrés fit in with homogenous suburban culture by adhering to its norms, Pnin falters as he struggles to understand the social practices around him. The town is described as "the little town of Waindell—white paint, black pattern of twigs—was projected, as if by a child, in primitive perspective."[62] Although town residents perceive themselves mainly as suburbanites, Nabokov's description of the town fulfills an idyllic image of small-town American life. In the town, "everything was prettily frosted with rime; the shiny parts of parked cars shone; Miss Dingwall's old Scotch terrier, a cylindrical small boar of sorts, had started upon his rounds up Warren Street and down Spelman Avenue and back again; but no amount of neighborliness, landscaping, and change ringing could soften the season."[63] With this, Nabokov constructs an ideal suburban scene, with small-town life highlighting conventional pets and vehicles. Nabokov underlines that distant politeness, the standard cultural script of suburban "neighborliness" so valued by American suburbanites at mid-century, clashes with Pnin's immigrant behavior.[64]

For much of the novel, Pnin is seen as an outsider hopping between rented rooms. Not only an outsider, but as a Russian immigrant outsider during the Cold War,[65] Pnin is pushed even further to the margins of genteel society. Nabokov describes suburban single-family houses as "beautiful brick."[66] Pnin, though, formerly consigned to live in the "College Home for Single Instructors," tries to relocate into a rented room to shield himself from the noise, saying, "too many people [. . .] inquisitive people."[67] Due to the abundance of only single-family homes, Nabokov displays that Pnin does not fit into the fabric of the local community and is left to find his own temporary abodes or stay in a boarding house.

Here, Nabokov delves into the differences between a traditional American small town and a college town, where there are usually spaces for single instructors. Even with this provision from the university, however, Pnin is unable to homogenize his charming European eccentricities into the suburban American mainstream. Nabokov illustrates this through homes; "during the eight years Pnin had taught at Waindell College he had changed his lodgings—for one reason or another, mainly sonic—about every semester."[68] Pnin sticks out in the

---

62 Vladimir Nabokov, *Pnin* (New York: Vintage International, 1989), 29.
63 Ibid., 30.
64 Ibid.
65 *For a discussion of Nabokov's Cold War American contexts, see Samuel Peterson's essay in this volume (M. D. S.)*
66 Nabokov, *Pnin* 33.
67 Ibid., 34.
68 Ibid., 62.

sea of uniformity: "the accumulation of consecutive rooms in his memory now resembled those displays of grouped elbow chairs on show, and beds, and lamps, and inglenooks."[69] The blur of the sameness sticks out to Pnin as he moves between lodgings and around the town in "rooms for rent in private houses," jostled between spaces with little permeance, this in stark contrast to the stable uniformity of Miss Dingweld's dog, Warren Street, and the rest of the town's native residents.[70]

When Pnin is finally prepared to purchase a house, then, he feels he has achieved the suburban script of American homeownership—his "two-story house of cherry-red brick, with white shutters and a single roof [. . .] a rudimentary driveway along the south side of the house led to a small whitewashed garage for the poor man's car Pnin owned."[71] With this full description of the house, Nabokov parodies Pnin's belonging before forcibly removing it. Pnin, sitting with his German colleague Professor Hagen after his "house heating party," questions that "it signifies that they are firing me?" with the changes occurring in the department.[72] On the day of when "Vladimir Vladimirovich" [Nabokov] arrives into the stable community of single-family homeowners, he displaces Pnin. An outsider, Pnin is removed from the semblance of the community he believed to have finally gained. Nabokov anchors the single-family home as a centerpiece to Pnin's American failure; having failed to absorb and assimilate Pnin, the community now ousts him.

Pnin and The Pines

In the center of *Pnin*, Nabokov crafts a chapter removed from the larger trends of suburbanization. Pnin visits The Pines, an estate owned by a successful Russian American intellectual and his American-born wife. The Pines estate is filled with "émigré Russians" that were "swarming all over the place" in "every patch of speckled shade" and lie "suspended in hammocks with the Sunday issue of a Russian language newspaper over their faces in traditional defense against flies; sipping tea with jam on the veranda; walking in the woods and wondering about the edibility of local toadstools."[73] Nabokov crafts this country estate as an alternative to

---

69 Ibid.
70 Ibid., 63.
71 Ibid., 145.
72 Ibid., 169.
73 Ibid., 117.

American suburbanization, a private space where the expatriates, free from the confines of American uniformity, reunite with a modicum of prerevolutionary Russian culture. Varvara, the wife of Pnin's good friend Professor Chateau, felt she was entirely American. Nabokov writes of The Pines that its "birches and bilberries deceived her into placing mentally Lake Onkwedo, not on the parallel of, say, Lake Ohrida in the Balkans, where it belonged, but on that of Lake Onega in northern Russia, where she had spent her fifteen summers, before fleeing from the Bolsheviks to western Europe."[74] Because of the sprawling manor house on the estate, the natural beauty reminiscent of Russia, and the insular culture of the émigré residents, Nabokov recreates a living Russian space in America, allowing a brief reprieve from suburbanization.

The notion of an émigré's nostalgic respite from American space also highlights Nabokov's own biographical connections to The Pines and Pnin's newfound, temporary peace at the estate. Nabokov, in his first American summer of 1940, stayed at an estate owned by the Harvard historian Michael Karpovich in West Wardsboro, Vermont, where Karpovich and his family hosted Russian émigrés.[75] The Russian-style country estate that Nabokov observed and then fictionized here in Pnin provides Timofey Pnin with a space where he feels free to dwell in the recollections of the past—first pleasant and nostalgic, then increasingly traumatic.[76] Upon arrival at The Pines, Pnin feels at rest, as Nabokov describes that he "killed the motor and sat beaming at his friends."[77] The flights from suburban American space bring Pnin into an accepting community where he connects with his past. In a novel hemmed in by suburban life in every other chapter, The Pines provides a temporary escape from single-family homes and automobiles but also forces upon Pnin a torturous encounter with the death of his Russian beloved Mira Belochkin in the Shoah. This is the price he must pay for a measure of belonging.

Transportation in Pnin

In Pnin, Nabokov emphasizes the centrality of automobiles to suburban culture, contrasting the illusion of independence automobiles provide with an ultimate lack of social freedom in a suburbanized American town. In the first chapter,

---

74 Ibid., 120.
75 Boyd, *Vladimir Nabokov: The American Years*, 15–16.
76 For a study of Shoah memory in *Pnin*, see Maxim D. Shrayer "Nabokov, Religion, and the Holocaust," *Tablet Magazine*, September 7, 2023, accessed November 7, 2023, https://www.tabletmag.com/ sections/arts-letters/articles/nabokov-religious-conversion-holocaust.
77 Nabokov, *Pnin*, 122.

Pnin takes the wrong train, and Nabokov creates a farce of mixed-up translingual communications. Nabokov writes that Pnin receives a ride at the last minute after missing the bus in the wrong town and gets a ride from a kind man: "say, see those two guys loading that truck? They're going to Cremona right now. Just tell them Bob Horn sent you. They'll take you."[78] The car is the purported solution for the failure of the terrain and public transportation—exalted in the town's culture.

The descriptions of Pnin without a car stack up throughout the text, as Nabokov describes him as a Russian cultural outsider in contrast to his ex-wife, Liza Wind, who is also an immigrant yet much more Americanized and suburbanized than Pnin. When Pnin's ex-wife Liza appears, he has to wait for "five buses, and in each of them [he] clearly made out Liza waving to him through a window," but "then one bus after another was drained and she had not turned up."[79] With this deferral and Pnin's failure to meet her, Nabokov employs public transportation again to highlight Pnin's lack of fulfilling suburban expectations. Once she arrives, they take a "taxi" as "everything had happened before in this exact sequence."[80] After a short conversation, Liza asks, "And now where was the bathroom? And would he telephone for the taxi?"[81] Forced to use a shared bathroom and phone, Liza dreads the containment of Pnin's life and feels constrained without the suburban freedom of mobility and private space; in her eyes, Pnin, relegated to public and shared spaces, has not achieved much in America.

As the novel progresses, Pnin learns to drive but does so as a comedic outsider. When Pnin is driving to The Pines in his own private vehicle, Nabokov writes that someone

> [. . .] might have noticed an automobile that had turned off the highway just before reaching the bridge and was now nosing and poking this way and that in a maze of doubtful roads. It moved warily and unsteadily, and whenever it changed its mind, it would slow down and raise dust behind like a back-kicking dog. At times it might seem, to a less sympathetic soul than our imagined observer, that this pale blue, egg-shaped two-door sedan, of uncertain age and in mediocre condition, was manned by an

78 Ibid., 25.
79 Ibid., 53.
80 Ibid., 53.
81 Ibid., 57.

idiot. Actually its driver was Professor Timofey Pnin, of Waindell College.[82]

Nabokov preemptively confronts the average American reader, who may see Pnin as an impractical fool. In contrast with his position as a college instructor, his irregular and haggard driving makes him stick out—doubtful and unsure. Pnin's method of learning how to drive was that "he had been laid up with a sore back and had done nothing but study with deep enjoyment the forty-page *Driver's Manual* issued by the state."[83] Nabokov writes that "Pnin had been totally unable to combine perceptually the car he was driving in his mind and the car he was driving on the road. Now the two fused at last."[84] Having first put Pnin through a failed driving test, Nabokov paints Pnin's success as humorous and valorous while critiquing the American suburban reader for judging Pnin despite his many intellectual accomplishments.

Nabokov's narrator Vladimir Vladimirovich, a successful Russian-American author, punctuates the ending with a sense of Pnin's lack of belonging on the road:

> Hardly had I taken a couple of steps when a great truck carrying beer rumbled up the street, immediately followed by a small pale blue sedan with the white head of a dog looking out, after which came another great truck, exactly similar to the first. The humble sedan was crammed with bundles and suitcases; its driver was Pnin.[85]

Nabokov exhibits the irony of Pnin's departure; crammed between two beer trucks, each of them an American monstrosity, he is literally being squeezed out of the town, where he never belonged. However, Pnin escapes unscathed as "the little sedan boldly swung past the front truck and, free at last, spurted up the shining road, which one could make out narrowing to a thread of gold in the soft mist where hill after hill made beauty of distance and where there was simply no saying what miracle might happen."[86] Nabokov continues to critique American suburban scripts yet does so with a glimmer of hope for Pnin's future. Pnin exits American suburbia itself (and is subsequently resurrected in the American West as a minor character of *Pale Fire*).

---

82 Ibid., 112.
83 Ibid.
84 Ibid., 113.
85 Ibid., 191.
86 Ibid.

In Closing

In *Lolita* and *Pnin*, Nabokov set out to critique the new suburban landscape he discovered soon after immigrating to the United States. The suburban cultural imagination enveloped him—whether he was residing in an actual suburb, such as Wellesley, or in a college town like Ithaca, where he observed residents who embodied a homogenized suburban cultural imagination that emphasized white Anglo-Saxon Protestant values.[87] Nabokov envisioned the suburbs less as spaces of American cultural unification than spaces of isolation and injustice. In *Lolita*, Nabokov interrogates the isolation provided in single-family homes, motels, automobiles, and freeways.[88] Nabokov shows how these American sites and spaces permit a false suburban sense of safety and allow violent crimes to take place. In *Pnin*, its comical tone aside, the immigrant protagonist, an outsider, does not belong in the suburban communities. Yet again, Nabokov's technique emphasizes the spaces that engender this intolerance, Waindell's single-family homes and automobiles. And even at the rural summer estate where he briefly fits in, Pnin is haunted by the painful memory of the Shoah, perhaps to underscore his lack of stability and belonging.

In both novels, Nabokov portrays falsely idealized suburban scenes only to defamiliarize them by exposing the depravity lurking beneath their polished façades. Whether the target is single-family homes, uniformity of space design, motels, automobiles, freeways, or policing, Nabokov pierces the perfect bubble of the American cultural script. Nabokov never bought into the American suburban ideal; he saw it for what it was: an ill-founded, xenophobic, disenchanted myth.

Bibliography

Primary Sources
Nabokov, Vladimir. *Lolita*. New York: Vintage International, 1989
———. *Pnin*. New York: Vintage International, 1999.
———. *Lectures on Literature*. Edited by Fredson Bowers. New York: Harcourt Brace Jovanovich/ Bruccoli Clark, 1980.
———. *Lectures on Russian Literature*. Boston, MA: Mariner Books Classics, 2002.

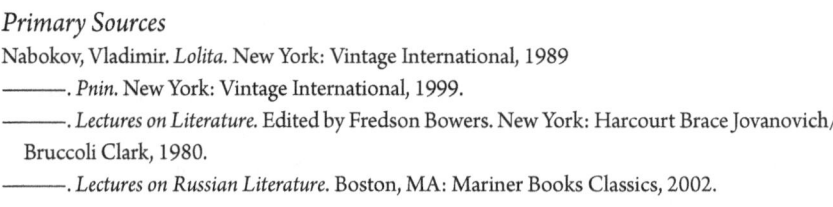

---

87 Some of Nabokov's American short stories, such as "The Vane Sisters," "Conversation Piece, 1945," and "Signs and Symbols," have urban rather than suburban settings and demand further critical attention.

88 *For a related discussion of suburbia in connection with American racism and antisemitism, see Samuel Peterson's essay in this volume (M. D. S.).*

Secondary Sources

Avila, Eric. *The Folklore of the Freeway: Race and Revolt in the Modernist City.* Minneapolis: University of Minnesota Press, 2014.

Boyd, Brian. *Vladimir Nabokov: The American Years.* Princeton, NJ: Princeton University Press, 1991.

Brodsky, Anna. "Nabokov's *Lolita* and the Postwar Emigre Consciousness." In *Realms of Exile: Nomadism, Diasporas, and Eastern European Voices,* edited by Dominica Radulescu, 49–66. Lanham, MD: Lexington Books, 2002.

Castronovo, David. "Humbert's America." *New England Review* 23, no. 2 (2002): 33–41. Accessed November 7, 2023. http://www.jstor.org/stable/40244102.

Catanzaro, Mary F. "The Car as Cell in *Lolita.*" *Kansas Quarterly* 21, no. 4 (1989): 91–96.

Grayson, Jane. *Vladimir Nabokov.* New York: Abrams Press, 2003.

Gumprecht, Blake. "The American College Town." *Geographical Review* 93, no. 1 (2003): 51–80. Accessed October 15, 2023. https://shibbolethsp.jstor.org/start?entityID=https%3A%2F%2Fidp.bc.edu%2Fopenathens&dest=https://www.jstor.org/stable/30033889&site=jstor.

Jacobs, James. *Detached America: Building Houses in Postwar Suburbia.* Charlottesville: University of Virginia Press, 2015.

Jenkins, Jennifer L. "Searching High and Lo: Unholy Quests for Lolita." *Twentieth Century Literature* 51, no. 2 (2005): 210–43. Accessed September 15, 2023. http://www.jstor.org/stable/20058762.

Leving, Yuri. *Nabokov in Motion: Modernity and Movement.* New York: Bloomsbury Academic, 2022.

López, Ian F. Haney. *White By Law: The Legal Construction of Race.* New York: New York University Press, 1996.

Manolescu-Oancea, Monica. "Inventing and Naming America: Place and Place Names in Vladimir Nabokov's *Lolita.*" *European Journal of American Studies* 4, no. 1 (2009): 1–47. Accessed March 18, 2023. https://journals.openedition.org/ejas/7550.

Norman, Will. *Transatlantic Aliens: Modernism, Exile, and Culture in Midcentury America.* Baltimore, MD: Johns Hopkins University Press, 2016.

Roper, Robert. *Nabokov in America: On the Road to Lolita.* New York: Bloomsbury USA, 2015.

Seo, Sarah A. *Policing the Open Road: How Cars Transformed American Freedom.* Cambridge, MA: Harvard University Press, 2019.

Shrayer, Maxim D. "Jewish Questions in Nabokov's Art and Life." In *Nabokov and His Fiction: New Perspectives,* edited by Julian W Connolly, 73–91. Cambridge: Cambridge University Press, 2012.

———. "Nabokov, Religion, and the Holocaust." *Tablet Magazine,* September 7, 2023. Accessed November 7, 2023. https://www.tabletmag.com/sections/arts-letters/articles/nabokov-religious-conversion-holocaust.

Swidler, Ann. "Culture in Action: Symbols and Strategies." *American Sociological Review* 51, no. 2 (1986): 273–86. https://doi.org/10.2307/2095521.

Questions of Style and Technique: Death and Immortality in the Works of Vladimir Nabokov

Katie Pelkey

Vladimir Nabokov's authorial persona has a distinct way of entering his prose by interrupting the narrative flow in order to offer first-person remarks about writerly decision-making and craft. Many of these authorial interruptions correspond with scenes where a character has died and/or has been extracted from the text by the author himself. Nabokov's self-insertion endows a character's death with ambiguity, leaving open the possibility that "death" can be negotiated without the text's universe, not just within it. Nabokov's own authorial commentary thus invites the reader to consider his character's death as a stylistic choice which tolerates metaphysical continuity and speculation beyond the text's physical ending.

A notable example of Nabokov's authorial interjections occurs in his first American novel, *Bend Sinister* (1947). At the end of the novel, a group of government thugs murders the protagonist, the philosopher Adam Krug, for his opposition to the totalitarian regime of the novel's fictitious European country of Padukgrad. Not long after the scene of Krug's murder, the familiar narrative voice dissolves and another voice makes reference to Nabokov's implied authorship: "I knew that the immortality I had conferred on the poor fellow was a slippery sophism, a play upon words. But the very last lap of his life had been happy and it had been proven to him that death was but a question of style."[1] Nabokov's authorial commentary in *Bend Sinister* extends to other deaths across

1   Vladimir Nabokov, *Bend Sinister* (New York: Vintage International, 1990), 241.

his literary works. He nudges the reader to explore interpretative possibilities in the metaphysical realm wherein death functions like an ellipsis, a stylistic device that promotes textual continuity.

A character's death in Nabokov's universe is metaphysically potent in its capacity to extend the character's existence beyond the paginated life of the novel. For Adam Krug, death is visceral and explicit in pedantically narrative terms; there is no ambiguity surrounding his murder by bullet. But as a meta-fictional device, his extraction from the text accords him paradoxical freedom from political oppression and tyranny. Is Krug's death the author's method of rescuing him from Padukgrad's dystopian turmoil by according him a form of immortality?

Once Nabokov declares that he "conferred" immortality on the "poor fellow," he draws attention to the novel as a constructed mechanism while also validating his authorship of a world wherein a character's existence, or nonexistence, is up to the author's artistic discretion. When Nabokov voices his decision to expunge Krug, his authorial self-insertion also expands beyond the physical realm the opportunities for what can and cannot happen within the novel. Furthermore, such a self-insertion—actually an authorial liberation of his privileged protagonist from the confines of physical death—defamiliarizes the role of Nabokov's omniscient, all-knowing yet absent narrator. Nabokov's authorial presence behind his "I" asserts him as both artistic director and performer of death.

Literary death for Nabokov is not merely defined by the physical characteristics that could be observed and measured–the undoing of a heartbeat, a fatal collapse. Death is also governed by the author's artistic rules, as per Nabokov's interjection in *Bend Sinister*: "[I]t had been proven to him that death was but a question of style."[2] Discernable characteristics of Nabokovian deaths recur across texts and genres. Take, for instance, the English-language poem "The Room" (1950), where the authorial "I" speaks of a character's death in an American hotel room: "A poet's death is, after all, / a question of technique, a neat / enjambment, a melodic fall."[3] Death, in this poem and elsewhere in Nabokov, transcends the physical world. The poet's death is not—or not only— a matter of organ failure; it is a device, matter of literary "technique."

This essay seeks to delineate some of the fundamental elements of style that give Nabokovian deaths their particular gloss. Foremost, the author's

2   Ibid.
3   Vladimir Nabokov, *Poems and Problems* (New York: McGraw-Hill, 1970), 105.

employment of death creates openings for metaphysical interpretations where characters, like Krug, are freed from textual hardships and the confines of linear and historical time, and also enabled to exist in ways that defy the physical properties of the conventional reality of the fictional world. In many of Nabokov's texts death, paradoxically, invites and promotes the reader's continued speculation of a text's or character's existence beyond the text's physical ending. Manifestations of death across Nabokov's works highlight his views on time and immortality, and perhaps, also point to his own postmortem literary legacy.

In this essay, the term "death" refers to Nabokov's authorial choice to extract a character from his work. After the Soviet-born émigré scholar Svetlana Boym, I too cushion "death" with quotation marks to reimagine the term as meaning more than a strictly visceral or physical experience. Relevant to the author's textual role, Boym writes of the figurative "death of the author," as one "emphasiz[ing] the irrelevance of the poet's biography, its almost accidental or insignificant relationship to the text, which develops according to its own textual laws."[4] Nabokov's texts stipulate death as a matter of artistic style, not a consequence of the artist's biography. Not limited to characters' physical, bodily expiration, Nabokovian deaths take the form of mysterious or ponderous disappearances and of character extractions, sometimes annunciated by the authorial persona.

The notion that death creates an opening in Nabokov's texts grows out of Maxim D. Shrayer's delineation of "open" versus "closed" textual endings. Shrayer explains that "[a]n open ending allows the reader to project narrative action in several directions, thereby creating a sense of indeterminacy since the reader is likely to speculate about 'what is going to happen?'"[5] To Shrayer's point, I add that part of this speculation involves the *evaluation* of what is logical within the context of the text, and what defies commonsense. For Nabokov, "Commonsense at its worst is sense made common, and so everything is comfortably cheapened by its touch."[6] His endings push against commonality and invite readers to form their own unique interpretations. To live in a world dictated by commonsense is to subvert creativity, a value in which Nabokov's texts revel. While his texts often leave behind scraps of questions, a reader's creativity fashions them together into a potential ending. For example, at the end of a

---

4   Svetlana Boym, *Death in Quotation Marks: Cultural Myths of the Modern Poet* (Cambridge, MA: Harvard University Press, 1991), 12.

5   Maxim D. Shrayer, *The World of Nabokov's Stories* (Austin: University of Texas Press, 1999), 8.

6   Vladimir Nabokov, "The Art of Literature and Commonsense," in *Lectures on Literature*, ed. Fredson Bowers (New York: Harcourt Brace Jovanovich/Bruccoli Clark, 1980), 372.

novel, the reader may probe the general question, "Has the character died?" A viable answer must comply with the reader's recognition of logical rules presiding over the text. In a Nabokovian text, it is within the realm of possibility to speculate that perhaps, the character has *not* expired. Instead, the character's essence has, for instance, been reintegrated with a nostalgic landscape painting, as is the case in the ending of the novel *Glory* (1932).

In contrast, closed endings are not as fit for speculative gymnastics. In Shrayer's view, "upon finishing a closed-ended story, the reader is unlikely to speculate about what happens beyond the closure. A closed ending offers a resolution of the actions in the story."[7] There is often less metaphysical or metaliterary potential here as the narrative is anchored by certainty. In many of Nabokov's Russian- and English-language works, death is marked by uncertainty and suffused with indeterminacy, which is why so many of his endings fall into the category of open-ended ones. Even after the book is closed, the story continues to take shape in the reader's mind; the projected, refinished story welcomes further interpretation.

Confronting texts that conclude so open-endedly with death scenes begs the question: how much pondering is expected from the reader after the initial act of reading is finished? A similar question was posed to Nabokov by Alfred Appel Jr. during a 1966 interview in Montreux: "Ideally, how should a reader experience or react to 'the end' of one of your novels, that moment when the vectors are removed and the fact of fiction is underscored, the cast dismissed?"[8] In response, Nabokov expressed a sense of delight over the question itself, calling it "charmingly phrased," then replied: "I think that what I would welcome at the close of a book of mine is the sensation of its world receding in the distance and stopping somewhere there suspended afar like a picture in a picture: *The Artist's Studio* by Van Bock."[9] The suspended imagery hints that Nabokov's endings are intended to hover, to last, and not to sink from the reader's mind. Equally worthy of pause is his creation and invocation of the name "Van Bock," which Appel points out is a near-anagram of the writer's own last name.[10] Just as Nabokov often does with his deployment of death, this statement further complicates the delineation between textual reality (of his creation and at least partial control) and the reality outside the text (outside his control).

---

7   Shrayer, *The World of Nabokov's Stories*, 8.
8   L. S. Dembo and Cyrena Pondrom, eds., *The Contemporary Writer: Interviews with Sixteen Novelists and Poets* (Madison: University of Wisconsin Press, 1972), 44.
9   Ibid., 45.
10 Ibid., 44.

Of Nabokov's presence in his receding worlds, D. Barton Johnson writes:

> Many, if not all, Vladimir Nabokov's novels contain more than
> one world in varying degrees of presence. This is not merely a
> stock literary metaphor: the world of the novel versus the world
> of the novelist. At the very least, what appears to be the world of
> the novelist is that of an author-persona, who, within the frame-
> work of the novel, creates and occasionally intrudes upon the
> world of his characters.[11]

The blurring of textual and extratextual worlds is, in part, what complicates
Nabokov's endings and makes their interpretation so user- (reader-) friendly.
The expansive number of possibilities of what may have *happened* ignite readerly imagination while also not confining it to the boundaries of physical reality.
Rather, the reader's imagination has ample room to ponder metaphysical possibilities and consider a conclusion where a character's death is not marked by
physical ruin, but charged with transformation, transcendence, or freedom.

When Nabokov's characters are permitted to leave the text or are expunged
from it, where do they go? With this question in mind, I turn to Nabokov's last
Russian-language short story, "Vasiliy Shishkov" (1939), where textual death
becomes a figure of disappearance, and the readers are left pondering the question posed by the story's narrator: "But where the deuce did he go?"[12] "He"
refers to the titular protagonist, a Parisian émigré poet named Vasiliy Shishkov.
As a Russian exile frustrated by his inability to gain traction with his poetry, he
converses with the narrator, an acclaimed émigré author, about "how to stop
things, how to get out."[13] Both the purpose and the means of "getting out" are
deliberately opaque. Might Shishkov escape, retire, retreat from society, or from
the world entirely? The story concludes with the poet's disappearance, and
the narrator is left wondering: "[W]hat did he have in mind when he said he
intended 'to disappear, to dissolve'? Cannot it actually be that in a wildly literal
sense, unacceptable to one's reason, he meant disappearing in his art, dissolving in his verse, thus leaving of himself, of his nebulous person, nothing but his
verse?"[14] The authorial narrator offers a plausible definition of what it means "to

---

11   Johnson, Donald Barton, *Worlds in Regression: Some Novels of Vladimir Nabokov* (Ann Arbor,
     MI: Artis, 1985), i.
12   Vladimir Nabokov, "Vasiliy Shishkov," trans. Dmitri Nabokov, in *The Stories of Vladimir
     Nabokov* (New York: Vintage International, 2008), 499.
13   Ibid.
14   Ibid.

die" in the context of the story: to disappear from the literary world. There is but a trace of causal agency here, no gunshot, ailment, or evidence of Shishkov's physical expiration. The physicality of death is not very relevant; instead, the disappearance of the poet is in itself the critical matter, one that inspires readerly speculation.

Paul Morris alludes to the "openness" of the story's ending: "Ultimately, however, interest in the story extends beyond the thematic contents and context of its inception [. . .]. 'Vasiliy Shishkov' also invites reading as a form of self-commentary by Nabokov on the state of his literary identity as a poet."[15] The knowledge that this was Nabokov's last short story before his escape to America and transition to English[16] sheds additional light on potential interpretations of the ending as related to Nabokov's own biography. Is there is a comparison to be made between the author and "Vasiliy Shishkov"? As several critics, notably Shrayer and Morris, indicate, both Nabokov and Shishkov perform exilic disappearance. For Shishkov, it is his physical *being* that gets extracted from the story. For the author, it is his Russian language that vanishes from most of his future literary works. Both Shishkov and Nabokov might be seen as, in a sense, as "dissolving" into their own texts. While there is certainly an implication of physical death for Shishkov, there might also be potential for metaphysical survival. Perhaps dissolving into one's art is an anti-death, a form of continuation that transcends the physical possibilities of the body and accords a refuge from textual containment.

Using Nabokov's later works as hermeneutic keys, one can trace the development of his use of death through his earlier Russian writings. In the pages below, I will briefly consider *The Defense* and *Glory*, two Russian novels that cemented Nabokov's literary reputation and served as a dress rehearsal of the device of death as disappearance. I will then return to Nabokov's early American years— all in anticipation of considering the question of death and immortality in *Lolita* and of a final discussion of the matter of Nabokov's literary legacy.

Nabokov already performed death as a disappearance that transcends the laws of physical reality in his third Russian novel, *The Defense* (book edition 1930). The main character, Aleksandr Ivanovich Luzhin, a chess grandmaster, meets his ending in the final line. In one moment, he is looking from a window onto the street below, where "the window reflections gathered together and

---

15   Paul D. Morris "Nabokov and the Short Story: The Lyric Heights of a Small Alpine Form," in *Vladimir Nabokov: Poetry and the Lyric Voice* (Toronto: University of Toronto Press, 2010), 242.

16   Shrayer, *The World of Nabokov's Stories*, 183.

leveled themselves out, the whole chasm was seen to divide into dark and pale squares . . ."[17] The image of the street below resembles that of a chessboard in an arrangement of black and white squares. This moment summons the reader to question Luzhin's ultimate fate. In Luzhin's final moments, a door opens and several voices call out for Aleksandr Ivanovich. And then the omniscient narrator declares: "But there was no Aleksandr Ivanovich."[18] The protagonist has vanished from the book, but whether he died in a physical, diagnosable manner is up for debate. The final image of the chessboard introduces the possibility that Luzhin becomes part of the chessboard itself, disappears in the transcendent art of chess.

Nabokov continued to experiment with both the text's open-endedness and the characters' mortality in *Glory* (book edition 1932), his fourth Russian-language novel. *Glory* recounts the experiences of a young émigré from the former Russian Empire, Martin Edelweiss, as he navigates the complexities of love and a life that stretches across cultures and languages. At the end of the novel, Martin undertakes the task of illegally reentering the Soviet Union, but the outcome is never obviated. The reader is left wondering whether Martin successfully carried out his dangerous expedition (*Podvig*, the original Russian title, means "exploit"). Even the characters in the novel who are closest to Martin are left uncertain of his final whereabouts. In the final pages, Martin is no longer part of the physical text. Again, the reader is left to ponder the question Nabokov would subsequently pose in "Vasiliy Shishkov": "But where the deuce did he go?" For an ending so encumbered with possibility at the metaphysical level, a specific physical or historical answer would seem rather untenable.

Wherever Martin went, whatever realm he disappeared into, the outcome remains hermeneutically ajar. The ending leaves room for metaphysical and fantastical readings,[19] and, in particular, one where Martin exits the text and (re)enters a nostalgia-infused watercolor depicting a path weaving into a thick forest. In the novel, the description of the painting is followed by a short anecdote: in Martin's Russian boyhood, his mother used to read to him a book about "such a picture with a path in the woods, right above the bed of a little boy, who [. . .] went from his bed into the picture onto the path that disappeared into the

---

17   Vladimir Nabokov, *The Defense* (London: Penguin Books, 1994), 256.
18   Ibid.
19   Different metaphysical interpretations of *Glory* are discussed in Leona Toker, "Nabokov's Glory: 'One Example of How Metaphysics Can Fool You,'" *Russian Literature* 21 (1987): 293–312; Edythe C. Haber, "Nabokov's Glory and the Fairy Tale," *Slavic and East European Journal* 21, no. 2 (Summer 1977): 214–224; and Maxim D. Shrayer, "The Perfect Glory of Nabokov's Exploit," *Russian Studies in Literature* 35, no. 4 (1999): 29–41.

woods."[20] The childhood storybook adumbrates Martin's later disappearance into a similar forest, or, perhaps, into the painting itself. Nabokov's foreword, composed for the English-language version of *Glory* in 1971, offers further support for the notion of Martin's disappearance into the forest painting: "The memory of childish reverie blends with the expectation of death. The perilous path that Martin finally follows [...] only continues to its illogical end the fairy-trail winding through the painted woods of a nursery-wall picture. 'Fulfillment' would have been, perhaps, an even better title for the novel."[21] The mysterious nature of Martin's disappearance allowed him to return to a place of childhood familiarity and thus "fulfill" Nabokov's quest for his potential as a character. Martin's expulsion from the physical text was the cost of his metaphysical continuity within the realm of art.

Martin's exit from *Glory* also provides what Shrayer calls "the perfect ending, where time is spatialized and forever vanquished."[22] As we recall the "picture in a picture," we are reminded that Nabokov desires literary lingering, where the text exists in a realm where time is not intrinsically important. Shrayer later proposes: "In the novel's perfect ending, the element of time is removed from the picture. Nabokov undoes his characters but leaves a landscape, an art form that unravels in space."[23] This interpretation echoes Nabokov's efforts to rescue characters from temporal boundaries. While this authorial desire will always precede disappointment in the physical conventional world, Nabokov's works, *Glory* included, can only be fully realized in contexts that reach beyond the confines of a timebound reality.

In *Nabokov: The Mystery of Literary Structures*, Leona Toker explored the metaphysical aspects of *Glory*'s ending. In Toker's assessment,

> [p]erhaps the most valuable aesthetic effect of the novel lies in the reader's regret that this sensitive and pathetically attractive human being should perish [...]. Nabokov achieves the purpose to which he alludes in the foreword, for this regret is tantamount to a reassertion of the thrill and glory of life, the supernatural supernaturalism that is no less sublime than the transcendental quest.[24]

---

20 Vladimir Nabokov, *Glory* (New York: McGraw-Hill Book Company, 1971), 4.
21 Ibid., xii.
22 Shrayer, "The Perfect Glory of Nabokov's Exploit," 29.
23 Ibid., 38.
24 Leona Toker, *Nabokov: The Mystery of Literary Structures.* (Ithaca, NY: Cornell University Press, 1989), 106.

Glory is remarkable in positioning the reader to experience a sense of continuation beyond the physical ending—a sense of metaphysical speculation. Martin's disappearance is logistically unclear until one acknowledges that the author's logic allows for authorial intervention and interpretation. Martin's essential quest is not for Russia under Bolshevik rule but for a return to his Russian childhood, to the origin of the "gentle nudge that jars the soul into motion and sets it rolling, doomed never again to stop."[25] Toker's apt description of the "reader's regret" delineates the manner in which Nabokov employs death. In her analysis, the regretful reader might take comfort in the fact that the painting betokens the closest thing to the lost motherland that Nabokov would provide for his character.

Nabokov's presentation of Martin Edelweiss's finale in *Glory* may be seen as a variation on one of the central themes of *The Defense*. In both cases, that of Martin's reintegration with his childhood painting and Luzhin's, with his sheltering chessboard, Nabokov's removal of these two characters from their respective novels hinges on the style in which he fashions death. Again, death is not necessarily a physical, measurable condition. Death is a manner of translating the world of the novel into a transcendent realm that calls to mind Nabokov's ideal of "picture in a picture"; an image that exists outside conventional space and historical time.

Nabokov's decision to detach his characters from linear time is closely related to his own fascination with John Dunne's theory of "serial Time," a fascination that Gennady Barabtarlo details in *Insomniac Dreams: Experiments with Time*. Working with the accounts of his dreams that Nabokov wrote down on index cards over the course of eight days in 1964–1965, Barabtarlo explicates the writer's experimentation with predictive dreaming based on Dunne's methodology. In brief, Dunne's theory negates the concept of linear time by positing that dreams consist of images of both past and future. Dunne believes that the state of being awake distorts one's ability to perceive time clearly.[26] According to Barabtarlo's interpretation, "Nabokov's own composing of 'long fiction' may be viewed as an extended, specialized experiment with Time whose ultimate goal was, if not to grasp then at least to touch the enigma of mortality—a highly pleasurable means to a wittingly unattainable end."[27] I believe these experimental

---

25 Nabokov, *Glory*, 4

26 Vladimir Nabokov, *Insomniac Dreams: Experiments with Time*, ed. and with commentary by Gennady Barabtarlo (Princeton, NJ: Princeton University Press, 2018), 12.

27 Nabokov, *Insomniac Dreams*, 160.

principles of composition apply to Nabokov's short fiction and poetry as well. Moreover, the deaths of many of Nabokov's characters betray an authorial resistance of linear time. Just as Dunne's theory of "serial Time" points to the possible existence of immortality as a continuation of the conscious mind after bodily death, Nabokov's technique of extracting characters from the text allows them to exist in perpetuity.

Nabokov systematizes his thoughts about time in his only memoir-cum-autobiography, known in its final English-language form as *Speak, Memory: An Autobiography Revisited* (1966). There, Nabokov's own discursive statement sheds light on how the deployment of death might function as a negation of linear time: "I confess I do not believe in time. I like to fold my magic carpet [...] in such a way as to superimpose one part of the pattern upon another. [...] And the highest enjoyment of timelessness—in a landscape selected at random—is when I stand among rare butterflies and their food plants."[28] To conceptualize time as a folding magic carpet is also to metaphorize the way time presents itself in a number of Nabokov's works of fiction, notably in the short story "Vasiliy Shishkov" and in the novels *The Defense* and *Glory*. In these works, characters enter and exit visual and composite images from the past and depart from their respective textual worlds, overcoming the boundaries of time and physical space. Nabokov's self-described disbelief in time as a fundamental category of being might be one of the artistic sources for his characters' quest for undoing or overcoming time—a quest in which the author helps liberate his characters from textual confinement.

The possibility of author-assisted liberation lies at the heart of Nabokov's use of death as a literary device. Just as the early American Nabokov freed Adam Krug from having to live in the oppressive society of *Bend Sinister*, so too had he previously liberated the protagonist of *Invitation to a Beheading* (first book edition 1938), his second to last full-length novel written in Russian. In the outset of this novel, Cincinnatus C. is sentenced to death for a crime he does not understand—"gnostical turpitude." He spends the final period of his confined life in the dystopian society, thinking about the arrival of his last day. The jailors disregard his requests for information and continue to torment the prisoner until his execution, which is staged as a spectacle.[29]

---

28 Vladimir Nabokov, *Speak Memory: An Autobiography Revisited* (New York: Vintage International, 1989), 139.

29 *See also Nina Khaghany's essay in this volume (M. D. S.).*

The linkages of death and liberation are riddled with allegorical complexities. The distinguished Russian émigré literary scholar Petr Bitsilli was arguably the first to pursue this line of inquiry in his essay "The Revival of Allegory" (1936), which Nabokov considered the best prewar critical study of his writings. Bitsilli asks: "[W]as Cincinnatus deprived of life or not? [. . .] Can we call that state in which Cincinnatus lived 'life'? Is it not all the same whether he was decapitated or not?"[30] In response to his own questions, Bitsilli goes on to suggest that the world in *Invitation to a Beheading* is "the world in general, just a Cincinnatus is man in general–everyman."[31] If the existence of Cincinnatus C. is allegorical, his death, too, must be representative of the allegorized, extratextual world. Bitsilli's proposition that *Invitation to a Beheading* is a work of allegory also implies that the termination of Cincinnatus C.'s character is representative of an extratextual reality. At the end of the novel, just before the execution, the atmosphere surrounding Cincinnatus C. disintegrates before the reader's eyes:

> Everything was coming apart. Everything was falling. A spinning wind was picking up and whirling: dust, rags, chips of painted wood [. . .] and amid the dust, and the falling things, and the flapping scenery, Cincinnatus made his way in that direction where, to judge by the voices, stood beings akin to him.[32]

Whether or not Nabokov assists Cincinnatus C. in escaping his execution remains a topic of critical debate. But it is revealing that Cincinnatus C. went to live *somewhere else*—to a space populated by other like beings, and also that such beings were not previously part of his life in the text. Nabokov's novel alludes to Cincinnatus C.'s life post-execution, but it does not textualize it. [33]

In reflecting on the way Nabokov's characters often escape the confines of the book, Brian Boyd wonders whether death for Nabokov is comparable to a freedom from existential confinement: "To the extent that Nabokov imagines passing through death—and that's to a very considerable extent—he sees it as

---

30 Petr M. Bitsilli, "The Revival of Allegory" [trans. Dwight Stephens], *TriQuarterly* 17 (Winter 1970), 114.

31 Ibid., 116.

32 Vladimir Nabokov, *Invitation to a Beheading*, trans. Dmitri Nabokov in collaboration with the author (London: Weidenfield and Nicolson, 1959), 208.

33 I am certainly aware of critical interpretations of *Invitation to a Beheading* that read Cincinnatus C.'s death in gnostical terms, but I will not consider them here. As an example, see Robert Grossmith, "Spiralizing the Circle: The Gnostic Subtext in Nabokov's *Invitation to a Beheading*," *Essays in Poetics: The Journal of the British Neo-Formalist School* 12, no. 2 (1987): 51–74.

a transition that hurtles the self into a state retaining accumulated selfhood but no longer subjected to 'the solitary confinement of the soul.'"[34] Boyd account suggests that Nabokov himself was not plagued by anticipation of death, rather, he felt that death harbors a sort of freedom from confinement. To that point one might also add that death for Nabokov actualizes his own notions of literary legacy and of immortality, that is, immunity to time.

As I think of *Lolita*, Nabokov's most famous American novel, where poetry is parodied and exulted—and ultimately condemned—I recall the last words of Humbert Humbert's soliloquy:

> And do not pity C. Q. [Clare Quilty, Humbert Humbert's antag-
> onist, whom he murders] One had to choose between him and
> H. H., and one wanted H. H. to exist at least a couple of months
> longer, so as to have him make you live in the minds of later gen-
> erations. I am thinking of aurochs and angels, the secret of dura-
> ble pigments, prophetic sonnets, the refuge of art. And this is the
> only immortality you and I may share, my Lolita.[35]

Out of context, it would be hard to believe these are the words penned by the sexual predator who repeatedly violates the young Dolores Haze ("Lolita") and destroys her childhood, often claiming that his behavior was out of other-worldly, nympholeptic love. It is also out of love—Humbert Humbert's morbid love for Lolita—that he decides to concretize his story by writing the memoir the reader presumably beholds while reading *Lolita*. Humbert Humbert's words deflate or reinforce, depending on the reader, the idea that Humbert Humbert, all along, was an artist who recaptured his love through writing—about—Lolita. Humbert Humbert's work is complete by the end of the novel because he and Lolita, though they both allegedly die of bodily causes in the text, do not suc-cumb to the brutality of linear time.

Of Lolita and Humbert Humbert's lasting togetherness, Ellen Pifer writes that Nabokov "evokes a realm of *timeless* existence and peoples it with shades who exist beyond the grave, the emphasis is not on sexual desire or ecstasy but rather upon love. It is love, I would suggest, that creates a point of contact, in Nabokov's universe, between the land of the living and the stylized representatives of

---

34   Brian Boyd, "Nabokov Lives On," *American Scholar* (Spring 2010), accessed November 30, 2023, https://theamericanscholar.org/nabokov-lives-on/.

35   Vladimir Nabokov, *Lolita* (New York: Vintage International, 1997), 309.

immortality."[36] Humbert Humbert's love is inexplicably enveloped in timeless-ness, foregrounding the style and technique of Nabokov's literary deaths. To dig deeply into *Lolita* is to unearth the love from Humbert Humbert's sick fixation with an innocent child. Humbert Humbert's deeply pathological love increas-ingly discourages a standard linear reading of the text as the novel summons a reading—rereading—of Humbert Humbert as artist.[37]

Nabokov not only invites a cyclical reading of *Lolita* to unhinge the familiarity of a linear reading of the novel. He also promotes what Gennady Barabtarlo calls "reverse reading, that is, going from effect to cause, ultimately from the end of the beginning—of a unit (chapter, part) and of the whole (novel.)"[38] Barabtarlo explains his point by revising a favorite dictum of Nabokov: "if a book is not worth retracing (checking hidden key points by backing up to the beginning) and rereading (now enlightened by the discoveries made by retrogressing), it is not worth reading the first time."[39] A *great* literary text, at least in Nabokov's perspective, does not die. It fosters rediscovery and does not have an expira-tion date. Thus, working through *Lolita* retroactively tends to reinforce a view of Humbert Humbert as an artist, adding shades of complexity to his depiction as a child predator. Nabokov advanced the notion that a character's death may not mean that their *time* has ended. Rather, Humbert Humbert and Lolita linger on "in the minds of later generations"[40]—with no ending in sight—for as long as readers continue to read and reread Nabokov's novel.

Not only do Nabokov's fictions portray death as a doorway to literary immor-tality, they also probe the endurance of authorial legacy. Consider Nabokov's English-language short story "A Forgotten Poet," originally published in the *Atlantic Monthly* in 1944.[41] The story is largely a pseudobiography of the fic-titious nineteenth-century Russian poet named Konstantin Perov. Nabokov's narrator enlivens Perov by recounting the details of his life and work. The final lines of the text theorize Perov's legacy: "No doubt a time will come when he will be republished and readmired; still, one cannot help feeling that, as things stand, people are missing a great deal. One also wonders what future historians will make of the old man and his extraordinary contention. But that, of course, is

---

36   Ellen Pifer, "Shades of Love: Nabokov's Intimations of Immortality," *Kenyon Review* 11, no. 2 (1989): 77.

37   *See also Kevin Ohi's essay in this volume (M. D. S.).*

38   Nabokov, *Insomniac Dreams*, 169.

39   Ibid., 172.

40   Nabokov, *Lolita*, 309.

41   Vladimir Nabokov, "A Forgotten Poet," *Atlantic Monthly*, October 1944, accessed December 3, 2023, "https://www.theatlantic.com/magazine/archive/1944/10/a-forgotten-poet/657366/.

a matter of secondary importance."[42] Although Perov's work is not well known, the narrator has hope that he will be rediscovered after his death. Thus, story's narrator (and perhaps Nabokov himself) believe in literature's capacity to allow the dead to linger beyond the boundaries of their lives. Fame is achievable, even postmortem, even though this idea is only implied in "A Forgotten Poet" and not actualized for Perov the poet. Petrov makes a tragicomical appearance at a commemoration of his own life and works, when the commemorators believe him to have died long ago. It is perhaps no coincidence that one of Nabokov's lesser short stories is about a little-known poet. In order for this text to have a sense of historical verisimilitude, Perov *must* be both unremembered and immortalized by his famous creator. Nabokov fuses the facts of his career with the fictions of his Russian literary past to the point where some readers might be lulled into thinking that Perov *is* the author's own nightmarish satire of literary oblivion.

Of the Nabokovian practice of conflating fiction with reality, his former student and *Lolita* commentator Alfred Appel Jr. writes, "By creating a reality which is fiction, but a fiction that is able to mock the reader, the author has demonstrated the fiction of 'reality' and the reader who accepts these implications may even have experienced a change in consciousness."[43] Even though Appel is referring to *Lolita*, something quite similar applies to Nabokov's other novels, stories and poems; reality within the text has a way of bleeding into the reader's own reality. Characters exist somewhere in between the boundaries of the textual world and the confines of the reader's world and can oscillate from one world to the other with a little help from the writer.

In Closing

For Nabokov, the boundary separating textual life and textual death makes for a blurry delineation, not a hard line. When he employs death as a means for extracting characters from the narrative, they die in one sense, while living on in another. Survival, for Nabokov, often entails a continuity or legacy. The notion of legacy recurs, not only in "A Forgotten Poet" but in a number of Nabokov's own poems. Composed in 1942 in Russian and Englished by the author himself, the poem "Fame" poignantly addresses the question of literary legacy and

---

42 Vladimir Nabokov, "A Forgotten Poet," in *The Stories of Vladimir Nabokov*, 579.
43 Alfred Appel Jr., "'Lolita: The Springboard of Parody," *Wisconsin Studies in Contemporary Literature* 8, no. 2 (1967): 218.

posthumous acclaim. This exilic poem allows its authorial voice to undertake a metaphorical crossing of the boundary that Nabokov would not transgress during his lifetime: the Soviet border, the "flame-licked night of my native land."[44] The moment at which an author's work exerts force on the world after his death is when the work takes on a life of its own: "I've read in myself how the self to transcend."[45]

For Nabokov, the author's extratextual, postmortem legacy is of little concern. In his first, transitional English-language novel, *The Real Life of Sebastian Knight* (first book edition 1941), Nabokov insists that to leave a legacy, there must be a worthy object of art to celebrate: "Fame in our day is too common to be confused with the enduring glow around the deserving book."[46] If this is to be taken as a sentiment that belongs not just to the novel's narrator but to Nabokov himself, then his idea of literary legacy hinges on the book's immortality, its potential to be reread and re-admired. In this way, Nabokov's bodily death in Switzerland in 1977 does not mark the death of his literary life. Rather, his death augurs an escape from physical existence and transience and a dissolution into metaphysical eternity. Nabokov is not the first or only writer to continue "living" in this way, but in his case, his death rings as a final note in its lifelong service as a textual device. Through death, Nabokov departs from physical reality, escapes linear time, "disappears in his art, dissolves in his verse.[47]

Bibliography

Primary Sources
Nabokov, Vladimir. *Bend Sinister*. New York: Vintage International, 1990.
———. *Glory*. Translated by Dmitri Nabokov in collaboration with the author. New York: McGraw-Hill Book Company, 1971.
———. *Insomniac Dreams: Experiments with Time by Vladimir Nabokov*. Edited and with commentary by Gennady Barabtarlo. Princeton NJ: Princeton University Press, 2018.
———. *Invitation to a Beheading*. Translated by Dmitri Nabokov in collaboration with the author. London: Weidenfield and Nicolson, 1959.
———. "The Art of Literature and Commonsense." *Lectures on Literature*, edited by Fredson Bowers, 371–380. New York: Harcourt Brace Jovanovich/Bruccoli Clark, 1980.
———. *Speak Memory: An Autobiography Revisited*. New York: Vintage International, 1989.

---

44 Nabokov, *Poems and Problems*, 105.
45 Ibid., 111.
46 Vladimir Nabokov, *The Real Life of Sebastian Knight* (New York: New Directions Publishing, 1959), 102.
47 Nabokov, "Vasiliy Shishkov," 499.

———. *The Defense*. Translated by Michael Scammell in collaboration with the author. London: Penguin Books, 1994.

———. *The Real Life of Sebastian Knight*. New York: New Directions Publishing, 1959.

———. "A Forgotten Poet." *Atlantic Monthly*, October 1944. Accessed December 3, 2023. https://www.theatlantic.com/magazine/archive/1944/10/a-forgotten-poet/657366/.

———. "A Forgotten Poet." In *The Stories of Vladimir Nabokov*, [edited by Dmitri Nabokov], 565–575. New York: Vintage International, 2008.

———. "Vasiliy Shishkov." In *The Stories of Vladimir Nabokov*, [edited by Dmitri Nabokov], 490–495. New York: Vintage International, 2008.

———. *Poems and Problems*. New York: McGraw-Hill, 1970.

Secondary Sources

Appel, Alfred, Jr. "'Lolita: The Springboard of Parody." *Wisconsin Studies in Contemporary Literature* 8, no. 2 (1967): 204–241.

Bitsilli, Petr M. "The Revival of Allegory." [Trans. Dwight Stephens]. *TriQuarterly* 17 (Winter 1970): 102–118.

Boym, Svetlana. *Death in Quotation Marks: Cultural Myths of the Modern Poet*. Cambridge, MA: Harvard University Press, 1991.

Boyd, Brian. "Nabokov Lives On." *American Scholar* (Spring 2010). Accessed November 30, 2023. https://theamericanscholar.org/nabokov-lives-on/.

Dembo, L. S., and Cyrena Pondrom. *The Contemporary Writer: Interviews with Sixteen Novelists and Poets*. Madison: University of Wisconsin Press, 1972.

Grossmith, Robert. "Spiralizing the Circle: The Gnostic Subtext in Nabokov's *Invitation to a Beheading*." *Essays in Poetics: The Journal of the British Neo-Formalist School* 12, no. 2 (1987): 51–74.

Haber, Edythe C. "Nabokov's Glory and the Fairy Tale." *Slavic and East European Journal* 21, no. 2 (Summer 1977): 214–224

Johnson, Donald Barton. *Worlds in Regression: Some Novels of Vladimir Nabokov*. Ann Arbor, MI: Ardis, 1985.

Morris, Paul D. "Nabokov and the Short Story: The Lyric Heights of a Small Alpine Form." In *Vladimir Nabokov: Poetry and the Lyric Voice*, 241–276. Toronto: University of Toronto Press, 2010.

Pifer, Ellen. "Shades of Love: Nabokov's Intimations of Immortality." *Kenyon Review* 11, no. 2. (1989): 75–86.

Shrayer, Maxim. "The Perfect Glory of Nabokov's Exploit." *Russian Studies in Literature* 35, no. 4 (Fall 1999): 29–41.

———. *The World of Nabokov's Stories*. Austin: University of Texas Press, 1999.

Toker, Leona. "Nabokov's Glory: 'One Example of How Metaphysics Can Fool You.'" *Russian Literature* 21 (1987): 293–312

———. *Nabokov: The Mystery of Literary Structures*. Ithaca, NY: Cornell University Press, 1989.

Nabokov, the Poetics of Religious Conversion, and the Post-Shoah Reckoning

Maxim D. Shrayer

Introduction: "Hebrews not accommodated"

For a Russian aristocrat of his standing,[1] Nabokov inherited a diversity of past religious backgrounds, notably the Lutheranism of the German ancestors

This research was partially supported by a Boston College Research Expense Grant.

I would also like to express my gratitude to the following archivists for their help with my research: Richard D. Davies at the Leeds Russian Archive, Brotherton Collection, Leeds University Library; Nadezhda Spivak at the Amherst Center for Russian Culture, Amherst College; Julie Carlsen, Emma Davidson, and Carolyn Vega of the Albert A. Berg Collection of English and American Literature, The New York Public Library. Kevin Writing, Executive Director of the Chatham Historical Society, Chatham, MA kindly arranged for me to work with archival materials on the history of Chatham's hotels. Last but not least, I would like to thank Anne Kenny and Nina Bogdanovsky, both of the O'Neill Library, Boston College, for their generous assistance.

Early versions of this essay were presented at Hidden Nabokov: An International Conference at Wellesley College, 17 June 2022, and Twenty-Eighth Annual Jewish-American and Holocaust Literature Symposium (JAHLIT), Miami, 13 November 2023. Early sections previously appeared in "Jewish Questions in Nabokov's Art and Life," in *Nabokov and His Fiction: New Perspectives*, ed. Julian W. Connolly (Cambridge: Cambridge University Press, 1999), 73–91; "Evreiskie voprosy v zhizni i tvorchestve Nabokova," *Wiener Slawistischer Almanach* 43 (1999): 109–128; "Nabokov, Religion, and the Holocaust," *Tablet Magazine*, 7 September 2023, https://www.tabletmag.com/sections/arts-letters/articles/nabokov-religious-conversion-holocaust;, accessed 20 October 2023; Shrayer, *Nabokov e o Judaísmo—História e Memória antes e depois do Holocausto*, trans. into Portuguese by Sandra Aparecida Faria de Almeida et al., ed. and with introduction by Jimmy Sudário Cabral (São Paulo: Editora Recriar, 2023).

Unless stated otherwise, all translations from the Russian are my own literal translations (M. D. S.).

1   I rely in this essay on the wealth of information in Brian Boyd, *Vladimir Nabokov: The Russian Years* (Princeton, NJ: Princeton University Press, 1990) and his *Vladimir Nabokov: The*

on the side of his paternal grandmother, Maria Baroness von Korff, and Judaism on the side of his maternal great-grandfather, Nikolai I. Kozlov.[2] There was also a sectarian streak in the family, and not only owing to the Old Believers roots of Nabokov's maternal grandfather, Ivan Rukavishnikov of the gold-mining fortune. In exile, Nabokov's mother, Elena I. Nabokova, embraced Christian Science.[3] Less known is the fact that Nabokov's maternal uncle Vasily Rukavishnikov was a Pashkovian, as they called the followers of Granville Waldegrave, the Third Baron Radstock, one of the founders of the evangelical movement in Russia.[4]

Nabokov's departure from formal Orthodox Christian observance had pre-dated meeting the St. Petersburg-born Jewish-Russian émigrée Véra Slonim in 1923 in Berlin,[5] as did the young writer's curiosity about the Hebrew language,[6] Judaism, and Jewish-Christian relations. Véra and Vladimir were married in a civic ceremony in Berlin at Rathaus Wilmersdorf on April 15, 1925. In the words of Véra's biographer Stacy Schiff, "Nabokov's [paternal] grandmother had but one question concerning the new addition to the family [...]: 'Of what religion is she?'"[7] Véra's course was drawn upon loyalties of memory, blood, and spirit.

Nabokov himself never stopped identifying as an Orthodox Christian. In a letter to his Jewish wife, dated June 2, 1926, he described receiving a note from the German tax office regarding the collection of a mandatory "church tax": "Tell them [...] that I'm not Catholic but Russian Orthodox, and so they

---

American Years (Princeton, NJ: Princeton University Press, 1991). For Nabokov's family tree, see Dieter E. Zimmer, "Nabokov Family Web [July 2000]," accessed June 10, 2022, http://dezimmer.net/NabokovFamilyWeb/nfw_toc.htm. I discuss some of Nabokov's Jewish biographical connections in Shrayer, "Jewish Questions." Stacy Schiff's biography of Véra Nabokov (Slonim) is a great source of information about Véra's origins and Jewishness: Schiff, *Véra (Mrs. Vladimir Nabokov)* (New York: The Modern Library, 1999). Last but not least, Nabokov's literary autobiography *Speak, Memory: An Autobiography Revisited* (New York: G. P. Putnam's Sons, 1966), as well as its English- and Russian-language antecedents, should be plumbed for pertinent information about his ancestry and family,

2   See Svetlana Malysheva, "Praded Nabokova, pochetnyi chlen Kazanskogo universiteta," *Ekho vekov* [Kazan'] 1/2 (1997): 31–134.

3   Nabokov, *Speak, Memory*, 39; Boyd, *The Russian Years*, 354.

4   See Sergey Nabokov (Nabokov's first cousin), letter to Z. Shakhovskaia, February 29, 1979, Shakhovskoy Family Papers, Amherst Center for Russian Culture.

5   Schiff, *Véra*, 44–45; on Véra's Jewish identity, see also ibid., 99–100, 261.

6   See Maxim D. Shrayer, "Nabokov's Use of Hebrew in 'Easter Rain,'" *Nabokov Online Journal* 4 (2010), accessed October 23, 2023, https://www.academia.edu/35528824/NABOKOV_S_USE_OF_HEBREW_IN_EASTER_RAIN.

7   Schiff, *Véra*, 44–45; on Véra's Jewish identity, see also ibid., 99–100, 261.

wouldn't bother me again."[8] And yet, Véra's Judaic loyalty and pride continued to resonate in the inner chambers of the Nabokov marriage and family. In searching for Nabokov's records in the Ellis Island passenger database, one comes across the manifest of the SS *Champlain*, the vessel that carried the writer, his wife and son from Saint-Nazaire to America in May 1940. In the column "race or people," "Vladimir Nabokoff" and "Dimitri Nabokoff" are listed as "Russian," whereas "Véra Nabokoff" is registered as "Hebrew."[9]

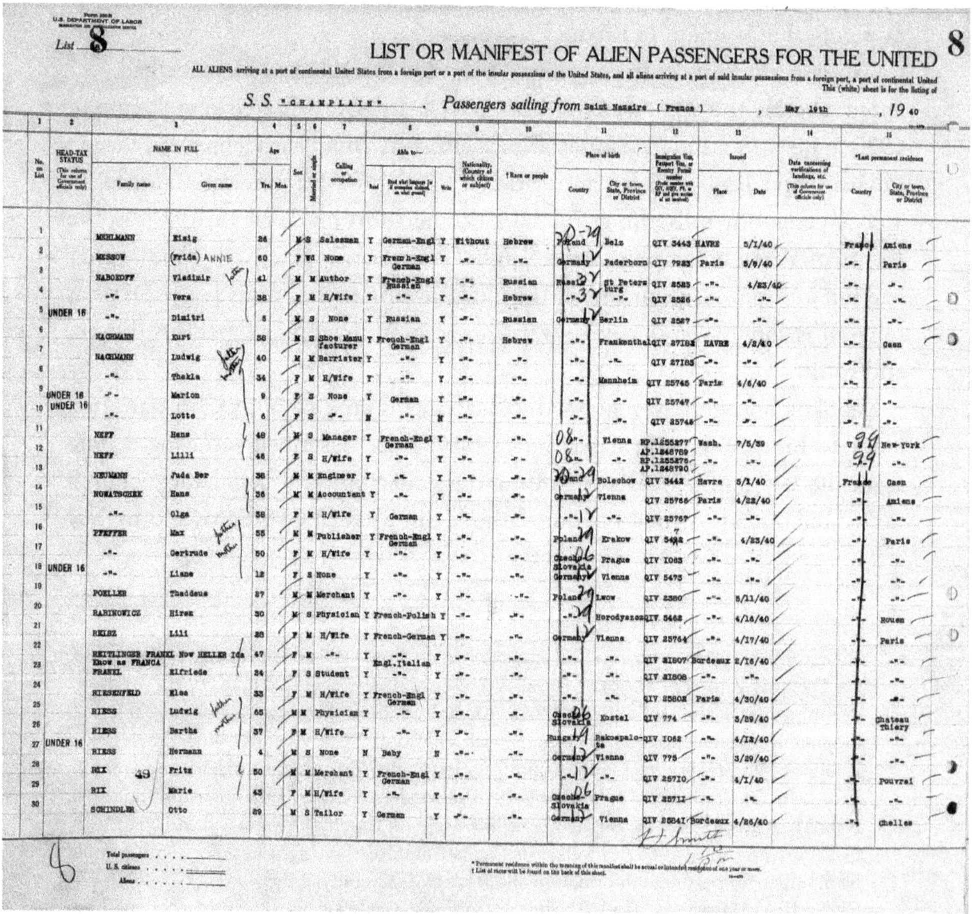
U.S. DEPARTMENT OF LABOR

List 8

LIST OR MANIFEST OF ALIEN PASSENGERS FOR THE UNITED 8

ALL ALIENS arriving at a port of continental United States from a foreign port or a port of the insular possessions of the United States, and all aliens arriving at a port of said insular possessions from a foreign port, a port of continental United

This (white) sheet is for the listing of

S. S. "CHAMPLAIN" Passengers sailing from Saint Nazaire (France), May 19th, 1940

1 No. on List	2 Head-tax status	3 Name in full: Family name	Given name	4 Age: Yrs.	Mos.	5 Sex	6 Married or single	7 Calling or occupation	8 Able to: Read	Read what language	Write	9 Nationality (Country of which citizen or subject)	10 † Race or people	11 Place of birth: Country	City or town, State, Province or District	12 Immigration Visa, Passport Visa, or Reentry Permit number	13 Issued: Place	Date	14 Data concerning verifications of landings, etc.	15 *Last permanent residence: Country	City or town, State, Province or District
1		MEHLMANN	Eisig	26		M	S	Salesman	Y	German-Engl	Y	Without	Hebrew	Poland	Belz	QIV 3443	HAVRE	5/1/40		France	Amiens
2		MESSOW	(Frida) ANNIE	60		F	Wd	None	Y	French-Engl German	Y	-"-	-"-	Germany	Paderborn	QIV 7923	Paris	5/9/40		-"-	Paris
3		NABOKOFF	Vladimir	41		M	M	Author	Y	French-Engl Russian	Y	-"-	Russian	Russia	St Petersburg	QIV 2525	-"-	4/23/40		-"-	-"-
4		-"-	Vera	38		F	M	H/Wife	Y	-"-	Y	-"-	Hebrew	-"-	-"-	QIV 2526	-"-	-"-		-"-	-"-
5	UNDER 16	-"-	Dimitri	5		M	S	None	Y	Russian	Y	-"-	Russian	Germany	Berlin	QIV 2527	-"-	-"-		-"-	-"-
6		NACHMANN	Kurt	38		M	S	Shoe Manufacturer	Y	French-Engl German	Y	-"-	Hebrew	-"-	Frankenthal	QIV 27182	HAVRE	4/2/40		-"-	Caen
7		NACHMANN	Ludwig	40		M	M	Barrister	Y	-"-	Y	-"-	-"-	-"-	-"-	QIV 27183	-"-	-"-		-"-	-"-
8		-"-	Thekla	34		F	M	H/Wife	Y	-"-	Y	-"-	-"-	-"-	Mannheim	QIV 25745	Paris	4/6/40		-"-	-"-
9	UNDER 16	-"-	Marion	9		F	S	None	Y	German	Y	-"-	-"-	-"-	-"-	QIV 25747	-"-	-"-		-"-	-"-
10	UNDER 16	-"-	Lotte	6		F	S	-"-	N	-"-	N	-"-	-"-	-"-	-"-	QIV 25748	-"-	-"-		-"-	-"-
11		NEFF	Hans	48		M	S	Manager	Y	French-Engl German	Y	-"-	-"-	-"-	Vienna	RP.1255277 AP.1248789	Wash.	7/5/39		U S A	New-York
12		NEFF	Lilli	46		F	S	H/Wife	Y	-"-	Y	-"-	-"-	-"-	-"-	RP.1255276 AP.1248790	-"-	-"-		-"-	-"-
13		NEUMANN	Juda Ber	38		M	M	Engineer	Y	-"-	Y	-"-	-"-	Poland	Bolechow	QIV 3442	Havre	5/1/40		France	Caen
14		NOWATSCHEK	Hans	36		M	M	Accountant	Y	-"-	Y	-"-	-"-	Germany	Vienna	QIV 25766	Paris	4/22/40		-"-	Amiens
15		-"-	Olga	38		F	M	H/Wife	Y	German	Y	-"-	-"-	-"-	-"-	QIV 25767	-"-	-"-		-"-	-"-
16		PFEFFER	Max	55		M	M	Publisher	Y	French-Engl German	Y	-"-	-"-	Poland	Krakow	QIV 5492	-"-	4/23/40		-"-	Paris
17		-"-	Gertrude	50		F	M	H/Wife	Y	-"-	Y	-"-	-"-	Czecho Slovakia	Prague	QIV 1063	-"-	-"-		-"-	-"-
18	UNDER 16	-"-	Liane	12		F	S	None	Y	-"-	Y	-"-	-"-	Germany	Vienna	QIV 5473	-"-	-"-		-"-	-"-
19		POELLER	Thaddeus	37		M	M	Merchant	Y	-"-	Y	-"-	-"-	Poland	Lwow	QIV 2380	-"-	5/11/40		-"-	-"-
20		RABINOWICZ	Hirsz	30		M	S	Physician	Y	French-Polish	Y	-"-	-"-	-"-	Horodyszcz	QIV 5462	-"-	4/16/40		-"-	Rouen
21		REISZ	Lili	28		F	M	H/Wife	Y	French-German	Y	-"-	-"-	Germany	Vienna	QIV 25764	-"-	4/17/40		-"-	Paris
22		REITLINGER FRANKL Now HELLER Know as FRANCA	Ida	47		F	M	-"-	Y	-"- Engl.Italian	Y	-"-	-"-	-"-	-"-	QIV 21807	Bordeaux	2/16/40		-"-	-"-
23		FRANKL	Elfriede	24		F	S	Student	Y	-"-	Y	-"-	-"-	-"-	-"-	QIV 21808	-"-	-"-		-"-	-"-
24		RIESENFELD	Else	33		F	M	H/Wife	Y	French-Engl German	Y	-"-	-"-	-"-	-"-	QIV 25802	Paris	4/30/40		-"-	-"-
25		RIESS	Ludwig	65		M	M	Physician	Y	-"-	Y	-"-	-"-	Czecho Slovakia	Kostel	QIV 774	-"-	3/29/40		-"-	Chateau Thiery
26		RIESS	Bertha	37		F	M	H/Wife	Y	-"-	Y	-"-	-"-	Hungary	Rakospalota	QIV 1062	-"-	4/12/40		-"-	-"-
27	UNDER 16	RIESS	Hermann	4		M	S	None	N	Baby	N	-"-	-"-	Germany	Vienna	QIV 775	-"-	3/29/40		-"-	-"-
28		RIX	Fritz	50		M	M	Merchant	Y	French-Engl German	Y	-"-	-"-	-"-	-"-	QIV 25710	-"-	4/1/40		-"-	Pouvrai
29		RIX	Marie	43		F	M	H/Wife	Y	-"-	Y	-"-	-"-	Czecho-Slovakia	Prague	QIV 25711	-"-	-"-		-"-	-"-
30		SCHINDLER	Otto	29		M	S	Tailor	Y	German	Y	-"-	-"-	Germany	Vienna	QIV 25841	Bordeaux	4/26/40		-"-	Chelles

Total passengers . . . . .

U.S. citizens . . . . .

Aliens . . . . . .

* Permanent residence within the meaning of this manifest shall be actual or intended residence of one year or more.

† List of races will be found on the back of this sheet.

Figure 1. List 8 of the manifest of the SS *Champlain*, May 19, 1940. Ellis Island Records.

8 Nabokov, letter to Véra Nabokov, June 2, 1926, in Nabokov, *Pis'ma k Vere*, ed. Brian Boyd and Olga Voronina (Moscow: KoLibri, 2014), 92. On the same topic, see also Schiff, *Véra*, 99; Ioann Shakhovskoi's letter to Anna Shakhovskaia, October 2, 1926, in Arkhiepiskop Ioann Shakhovskoi, *Biografiia iunosti, Ustanovlenie edinstva* (Paris: YMCA-Press, 1977), 118.

9 SS *Champlain*, List or Manifest of Alien Passengers, May 19–27, 1940, List 8, Passenger Search, Ellis Island Records, The Statue of Liberty and Ellis Island Foundation, accessed October 23, 2023, https://heritage.statueofliberty.org.

Very soon, in their travels across New England, the Nabokov family would encounter not only coded signs such as "near churches" or "gentile clientele" but also openly antisemitic verbiages such as "Hebrews not accommodated."[10]

A Russian Orthodox Christian (although not a practicing one) married to an unconverted (though unobservant) Russian Jew, Vladimir Nabokov regularly returned to the topics of religious transformation and religious conversion in his letters and autobiographical writing. Nabokov's views of religious conversion would be less interesting to his readers if these views did not set some of the central axes of his Russian- and English-language fiction. Aspects of mimicry in nature fascinated and excited him as "signs and symbols" of complexity and beauty. Mimicry in society, and especially religious mimicry, from dissimulation to conversion, reminded him of the unresolved—unresolvable—contradictions of his own family and marriage. Forming an imperfectly monosyllabic pair in both of Nabokov's main languages, two of Nabokov's great novels, the Russian-language *The Gift* (*Dar*, partially serialized 1937–1938, complete book edition 1952) and the English-language *Pnin* (partially serialized 1953–1955, complete book edition 1957), clamor to be recognized for their dynamic exploration of the religious conversion of Jews born in the former Russian Empire. Structural differences and compositional ambitions apart, in a number of ways *The Gift*, including its abandoned second part, could be considered a pre-Shoah dress rehearsal of *Pnin*.

"O terra addio": *The Gift* between Hope and Despair

Set in Weimar Berlin, although also taking readers on real and imaginary trips to Russia, Siberia, and Central Asia, *The Gift* documents the artistic and personal growth of the Russian émigré aristocrat Fyodor Godunov-Cherdyntsev. Fyodor's success as a writer is inextricably linked to his relationship with Zina Mertz, a Russian émigrée and product of a mixed Jewish and Russian marriage. (Zina, whose first name in Russian suggestively rhymes with Mnemosyne, serves as Fyodor's most ecstatic reader.)[11] In *The Gift* Nabokov explicitly connects mixed marriages and Jewish conversion with the trajectory of his quasi-autobiographical protagonist by placing Fyodor in close contact with the

---

10   Dmitri Nabokov, recorded interview, December 11, 2011, unpublished. See also Boyd, *The American Years*, 107; Shrayer, "Jewish Questions," 76–77.

11   *About Zina as Fyodor's reader and coauthor, see Fiona Steacy's essay in this volume (M. D. S.).*

The Hawthorne House
CHATHAM, MASSACHUSETTS

MRS. IRENE J. BOYD
Proprietor

'Phone 8079

The rates—from $12.00 to $18.00 per week according to rooms—are very reasonable. Special terms may
be made in case of families or large parties making
extended stay, and for first of season to July 1st. A cash
deposit is respectfully requested from new patrons when
rooms are engaged. Hebrews not accommodated.

Season: June 1st to September 10th.

Automobiles can be accommodated. A new Garage
has been built this season.

Chatham is reached by the New York, New Haven &
Hartford Railroad from New York, Boston and other
points on its system. Close connections are made by it
with the Fall River Line steamers from New York at
Fall River. Time by Train from Boston, about three hours.

Carriages are in waiting at the Chatham Station
to convey guests to the house.

For any further information address

MRS. IRENE J. BOYD, Chatham, Mass.

FIGURES 2a and b. Information brochure of The Hawthorne House, Chatham, Cape Cod, circa mid-1950s. Courtesy of the Chatham Historical Society.

Chernyshevski family of Jewish Russian émigrés and by endowing his love for Zina Mertz with vatic significance.

The Jewish grandfather of the fictional Alexander Chernyshevski is said to have been baptized by a proselytizing Russian Orthodox priest, the father of the historical Nikolai G. Chernyshevski (1828–89), utilitarian aesthetician and prominent radical of 1860s Russia, whose critical martyrology Fyodor writes, and Nabokov includes as a chapter, in their novel. As a part of the conversion, Chernyshevski the priest apparently lent the new Orthodox Christian his last name. For Alexander Chernyshevski—and for about seventy thousand Jews who were baptized into the Russian Orthodox Church throughout the nineteenth century, as the historian Michael Stanislawski famously calculated[12]—their acquired religion amounted to an illusory ticket to the mainstream. Culturally a Russian, and spiritually an agnostic, the exile Chernyshevski hovers between his ancestral Judaic past and his assimilated and displaced present. Despite a stated materialism and secularism, the fictional exile Chernyshevski, who goes insane following his queer son's suicide, becomes Nabokov's agent for exploring the metaphysics of death.

Chernyshevski, a secularized Orthodox Christian of Jewish extraction, voices skepticism about Christian notions of the afterlife through a parodic evocation of the Sermon on the Mount: "If the poor in spirit enter the heavenly kingdom I can imagine how gay it is there. I have seen enough of them on earth. Who else makes up the population of heaven? Swarms of screaming revivalists, grubby monks, lots of rosy, shortsighted souls of more or less Protestant manufacture—what deathly boredom!"[13] On the eve of his death, in a "moment of lucidity," Chernyshevski utters: "What nonsense. Of course there is nothing afterwards." With "extreme distinctness," he repeats: "There is nothing. It is as clear as the fact that it is raining."

One of the surprises Nabokov has in stock for us is that Chernyshevski "turned out at the last minute to be a Protestant,"[14] and in the Russian original, Nabokov specifies that Chernyshevski was a Lutheran. Towards the end of the funeral service for Chernyshevski, Fyodor goes out onto the street. Behind the crematorium, he spots "turquoise turrets of a mosque" and "green cupolas of a white Pskovan-type church."[15] (Pskov is an ancient Russian city.) What is the meaning

---

12 Stanislawski, Michael, "Jewish Apostasy in Russia: A Tentative Typology," in *Jewish Apostasy in the Modern World*, ed. Todd M. Endelman (New York: Holmes and Meier, 1987), 189–205.

13 Nabokov, *The Gift*, trans. from the Russian by Michael Scammel with the collaboration of the author (New York: Vintage International, 1991), 312.

14 Ibid.

15 Ibid., 313–314.

of these references to Islam and Russian Orthodoxy, and of the missing reference to the Judaism of Chernyshevski's ancestors? Does Chernyshevski's religious affiliation with Protestantism, and not Russian Orthodoxy, highlight his pro forma Christianity, his conversion in a minor key, through a ritual that does not require a public disavowal of one's ancestors as mandated in an Eastern Christian conversion? It is possible that Chernyshevski's Lutheranism also betokens the experience of Russian Jews—such as Nabokov's former tutor Filip Zelenski,[16] a Lutheran by necessity—who sought to bypass the official czarist quotas yet were not prepared to go through with a Russian Orthodox conversion? Osip Mandelstam, who attended the same private high school as Nabokov, became a Methodist in 1911, the year he entered St. Petersburg University. But that was the Russian Empire in 1911, and this was Weimar Germany in the 1920s. Is it possible that Chernyshevski's Lutheranism signals Nabokov's disapproval of the opportunism of a new member of the Russian Orthodox Church who has Jewish roots and becomes a Lutheran in Germany so as to assimilate further, to blend in and survive? If so, such authorial vexation with doubly the convert living in Weimar Berlin must be tempered with the afterknowledge of what would have befallen Chernyshevski if he had remained in Nazi Berlin in 1935–1938 when Nabokov actually wrote *The Gift*.

A great deal has been said about the role of Zina Mertz in Fyodor's formation. Over twenty-five years ago I wrote of Zina as Fyodor's Jewish muse; I have since come to feel that it might have been a wishful oversimplification. The entire novel becomes, in the words of its protagonist, "a kind of declaration of love." And yet it is hard to read these words without anticipatory bitterness, just as it is difficult to dispel thoughts about the Shoah while reading the passage in *Speak, Memory* where Nabokov describes watching trains, with his Jewish wife and young son, in Berlin in 1936–1937 and in Paris in 1938–1940: "But whatever the truth may be, we shall never forget, you and I, we shall forever defend, on this or some other battleground, the bridges in which we spent hours waiting with our little son (aged anything from two to six) for a train to pass below."[17]

In the course of the novel, Fyodor rents a room in the Berlin apartment where Zina lives with her mother and stepfather, Boris Shchyogolev, whom Zina's mother married after the death of her first husband and Zina's father, Oscar Mertz. Upon seeing Shchyogolev for the first time, Fyodor thinks that his new landlord has "one of those open Russian faces whose openness is almost indecent."[18] A former prosecutor, Shchyogolev exemplifies the repugnantly burlesque Russian antisemitism of Jewish jokes, mock-Yiddishisms, and leisurely meanderings on the subject of international Jewish conspiracy. At one point, believing Fyodor to be a one-hundred-proof Russian open to antisemitic talk, Shchyogolev offers him an analysis of the Jews' impact on his wife and stepdaughter: "My better half [. . .] was for twenty years the wife of a kike and got mixed up with a whole rabble of Jew in-laws [tselym kagalom]. [. . .] Zina (he alternately called his stepdaughter either this or Aïda, depending on the mood), thank God, doesn't have anything specific—you should see her cousin, one of these fat little brunettes, you know, with a fuzzy upperlip."[19] Aïda is a double play on the Yidish a id, a Jew, and on the name of the captive Ethiopian's girl in Giuseppe Verdi's eponymous opera. Shchyogolev even speculates that Zina is a progeny of her mother's extra-marital affair with an ethnic Russian. Zina, in turn, imparts to Fyodor quite a different image of her father: "In her version the image of her father took on something of Proust's Swann." She fashions her deceased father as a Jewish aristocrat, a "refined, noble, intelligent and kindly man" who recited "Homer by heart."[20]

While the prewar, "Russian" Nabokov lacks the vocabulary to express that, halachically speaking, Zina would not even be considered Jewish, he shows with precision that religion barely surfaces in her discussions of her identity. In fact, the wife of Alexander Chernyshevski points out to Fyodor that Zina does not care "very much to admit her origins," which would discordantly place Zina in the same category as other assimilated Jews whom Nabokov chides for their self-abnegation. He also notes that Zina's sense of Jewishness betrays contradictions and that she has a complicated relationship with her own Jewish roots. To Zina, her Jewish boss was "a German Jew, i.e. first of all a German."[21] Looking for vestiges of the historical Véra Nabokov, whose father refused to convert even if it meant giving up law practice in czarist Russia, may result in disappointment. I do not think it has been noted that Nabokov's novel knows, without being overexplicit about it, that Zina's Jewish-born father would have had to convert in order to be able to marry Zina's Russian Orthodox mother, and that Zina was likely born to two Christian parents.

---

18 Nabokov, *The Gift*, 364.
19 Ibid., 187; cf. *Dar*, in Nabokov, *Polnoe sobranie sochinenii russkogo perioda v piati tomakh*, vol. 4, ed. N. I. Artemenko-Tolstaia (St. Petersburg: Simpozium, 2000), 168.
20 Nabokov, *The Gift*, 187–188.
21 Ibid., 188.

This does not necessarily mean that Zina could not return to Judaism, and in fact Nabokov would have heard of the Jewish reaffirmation of Arnold Schoenberg, who had converted to Lutheranism in 1898; Marc Chagall served as the composer's witness in 1933 in Paris.

There are many reasons why *The Gift* starts and ends in Weimar Berlin. Even though Nabokov had completed the novel in January 1938, nine months before *Kristallnacht*, he chose to give Fyodor and Zina a chance at the kind of tremulous happiness that the ending communicates. In Weimar Berlin Fyodor and Zina could be married in a civil ceremony, the way Vladimir and Véra had been married in 1925. Neither the fictional Fyodor and Zina nor the historical Vladimir and Véra could marry after the passage of Nuremberg Laws in 1935. A historical scrutiny of *The Gift* reveals gestures of preemptive fear and despair that Nabokov also performed in his other fiction of the 1930s.

Nothing in Nabokov's pre-1940 work offers such a crushing defeat of hope as the surviving archival pages of Part Two of *The Gift*, which he most likely penned in Paris in the months preceding the escape to America—although some scholars do not rule out that he wrote it already in America soon after having arrived there as a refugee with his "Hebrew" wife and "Russian" son.[22] The Nabokovs' own marital discord, framed by the advent of World War II and the Shoah, seeps into Part Two, the manuscript of which the London-based scholar Jane Grayson had originally described and the Ukrainian-born translator and critic Andrei Babikov subsequently published and annotated. Zina and her husband Fyodor are living in Paris in the late 1930s; they are poor and childless and their marriage is on the rocks; Fyodor is having an affair with a French prostitute by the name of Yvonne.[23] Zina, whose own sense of Jewishness has acquired combative dimensions, rebuffs a Russian fascist, who visits to see her husband, by telling him she is "a Jewess." In the autumn of 1938 Zina dies in Paris, run over

22 The text of the unfinished Part 2 of *The Gift* has been published in Russian but not yet in English: Vladimir Nabokov, *Dar. II chast'*, publication and commentary by Andrei Babikov, *Zvezda* 4 (2015): 157–175. For details, see Jane Grayson, "Washington's Gift: Materials Pertaining to Nabokov's *Gift* in the Library of Congress," *Nabokov Studies* 1 (1994): 21–67 and Andrei Babikov, "'Dar' za chertoi stranitsy," *Zvezda* 4 (2015), accessed October 23, 2023, https://zvezdaspb.ru/index.php?page=8&nput=2481. For a polemical exchange between Andrei Babikov and Alexander Dolinin, see Dolinin, "O pagubakh diletantizma," *Zvezda* 9 (2015), https://zvezdaspb.ru/index.php?page=8&nput=2580; Babikov, "Publikatsia vtoroi chasti 'Dara' Nabokova i ee kritika," *Novyi zhurnal* 281 (2015), accessed October 23, 2023, https://magazines.gorky.media/nj/2015/281/publikacziya-vtoroj-chasti-dara-nabokova-i-ee-kritika.html.

23 *See also Ciara Spencer's discussion in her essay in this volume (M. D. S.).*

by a car—perhaps more of an authorial rescue from encroaching history than an authorial punishment for the historical demise of Nabokov's earlier fatidic design. What, indeed, awaited a Russian refugee of partially Jewish descent in the occupied Paris? Perhaps survival and escape? But more likely, Vél d'Hiv, deportation to Drancy, Pithiviers, or Beaune-la-Rolande and then a transport to Auschwitz. With Zina's death, Nabokov's novel, too, has nowhere to go, and the story of a mixed, Jewish Russian marriage gains a devastating, dispiriting finale.

Pnin *"from sentimental reasons"*

During the interwar years, Nabokov generally regarded religious apostasy as an act of violence against one's origins and true self—in much the same way he would later consider Freud and Freudianism to be "crude" and "medieval."[24] In America, after World War II and the Shoah, Nabokov became less judgmental about religious conversion, and his novel *Pnin* offers unparalleled evidence of his writing under the burden of guilt and trauma.

Set in the early 1950s, mainly on a college campus on the Eastern Seaboard, and striated with émigré recollections and reconstructions, *Pnin* is simultaneously a wry campus comedy, an immigrant chronicle of translingual perils and pleasures, and one of the first American novels about the memory of the Shoah. After the war Nabokov learned of the two arrests, in Nazi Berlin, of his Anglophilic, queer brother Sergey Nabokov and of his subsequent death, in January 1945, of illness and inanition at the Neuengamme concentration camp. [25] *Pnin* originated, emotionally, in Nabokov's guilt over —and expanding knowledge about —the deaths of his brother and of a number of Jewish-Russian émigré authors, some of them Jewish converts to Christianity, in the Nazi camps and prisons. They included the Parisian poets Yuri Felzen and Yuri Mandelstam and the Parisian editor and philanthropist Ilya Fondaminsky (Bunakov), all three of whom were sent, in 1942–1943, from Drancy to their deaths in Auschwitz. Nabokov took some of the tangible features of Mira Belochkin, the novel's

---

24 Nabokov's comments at the beginning of Robert Hughes and Terence Macartney Filgate, dirs., *Vladimir Nabokov*, video, 28:25, accessed September 11, 2024, https://youtu.be/V8O wyqvSh2g?si=SU4jkVgcwSZieXtG.

25 See "Sergey Nabokov," Wikipedia, last modified April 19, 2024, accessed October 24, 2023, https://en.wikipedia.org/wiki/Sergey_Nabokov.

female heroine and Professor Pnin's youthful love, and of her family members from his former Berlin acquaintances, the poet and medievalist Raisa Bloch (Gorlin) and her husband Mikhail Gorlin, a literary scholar and author. In July 1942 Mikhail Gorlin was taken from Pithiviers to Auschwitz, where he was murdered on September 5, 1942. Raisa Bloch attempted to cross the Swiss border from France on October 18, 1943. After the Swiss border police returned her to France, she was taken to Drancy, from where she was deported on November 20, 1943. She was probably gassed upon arrival in Auschwitz; as the extensive research of the Vienna-based scholar Fedor Poljakov demonstrates, the exact record of Bloch's death remains unknown.[26]

In the judgment of Brian Boyd, "of all Nabokov's novels, *Pnin* seems the most amusing, the most poignant, the most straightforward."[27] I am not sure I would agree with the third part, especially when it comes to the novel's presentation of questions of Jewish identity, Jewish conversion, and marriages between Jews and Christians. While in the published Part One of *The Gift* Nabokov is overexplicit about the origins of Fyodor Godunov-Cherdyntsev in the pre-Petrine Russian nobility and a little uncertain about the contours of Zina Mertz's Jewish identity, he delivers the information about the ancestry and identity of Professor Timofey Pnin only gradually and in puzzle pieces that, when we finally put them together, form a picture that is hardly straightforward.

I propose to challenge the established tradition of regarding—regaling— Timofey Pnin as both a quintessential Russian *intelligent* and Nabokov's idealized Gentile. In a 1955 letter to the editor of Harper & Brothers, which rejected the novel, Nabokov wrote about his Pnin: "A man of great moral courage, a pure man, a scholar and a staunch friend, serenely wise, faithful to a single

---

26 For details and bibliography, see Maxim D. Shrayer, "Raisa Blokh as an Historical, Literary and Emotional Source for Nabokov's *Pnin*," in *Skreshcheniia sudeb. Literarische und kulturelle Beziehungen zwischen Russland und dem Westen. A Festschrift for Fedor B. Poljakov*, ed. Lazar Fleishman, Stefan Michael Newerkla, and Michael Wachtel, *Stanford Slavic Studies* 49 (Berlin: Peter Lang, 2019), 619–656. See Fedor Poljakov, "'Der steinerne Boden des Exils': Materialien zu Leben und Werk des Dichterpaares Michail Gorlin und Raisa Bloch," in *Slavistische Forschungen. In memoriam Reinhold Olesch*, ed. Angelika Lauhus and Bodo Zelinski (Köln-Weimar-Wien: Bohlau Verlag, 2005), 219–234; Fedor Poljakov, "'Tragicheskaia i neiskupimaia sud'ba': Svidetel'stva o gibeli Mikhaila Gorlina," in *Avoti. Trudy po balto-rossiiskim otnosheniiam i russkoi kul'ture. V chest' 70-letiia Borisa Ravdina*, part 2, ed. Irina Belobrovtseva, Aurika Meimre, and Lazar Fleishman (Stanford, CA: Stanford Slavic Studies, 2012), 212–233.

27 Boyd, *The American Years*, 271.

love, he never descends from a high plane of life characterized by authenticity and integrity."[28] Critics—and I myself have been guilty of this—have linked Pnin's moral trepidation with his survival as a non-Jew. Pnin experiences profound guilt over living more or less comfortably in a world in which the murder in a death camp of Mira Belochkin, his Jewish beloved, was permitted. A closer inspection of Pnin's origins suggests that Nabokov gives the reader just enough—or perhaps more than enough—to discover that his protagonist may be a product of a mixed marriage and the son of a Jew who converted to Russian Orthodoxy.[29]

From what is stated in the final version of the novel, Pnin's father, an ophthalmologist with the Chekhovian first name and patronymic Pavel Antonovich Pnin (which hints at reversals of origin), is married to Valeria, daughter of the revolutionary Umov and of a German woman from Riga. (This, by the way, hints oddly at the origins of Viktor Shklovsky, whose early work, both theory and fiction, Nabokov closely followed since their shared time in Berlin.) A close friend of Pnin's father is the Jewish pediatrician Yakov Grigorievich Belochkin, father of Mira. From their prerevolutionary encounters, notably with the young aristocrat Vladimir Vladimirovich, we get the distinct sense that they belong to a different social stratum, which I am inclined to define as the milieu of Jewish university graduates, some of whom had to convert in the 1880s-1890s so as to circumvent the anti-Jewish quotas.[30] In fact, in the first installment of *Pnin*, printed in the *New Yorker* in 1953, the last name of

---

28   Nabokov, letter to Cass Canfield, December 8, 1955, in *Selected Letters 1940–77*, ed. Dmitri Nabokov and Mathew J. Bruccoli (New York: Vintage, 1989), 180.

29   *Pnin's* first Russian translator Gennady Barabtarlo, born in Moscow to Jewish-Russian parents, subsequently became a Christian; see "Gennady Barabtarlo, 70, of Columbia died peacefully at home on February 24, 2019," Dignity Memorial, accessed October 23, 2023, https://www.dignitymemorial.com/en-ca/obituaries/columbia-mo/gennady-barabtarlo-8183494; St. Luke the Evangelist Orthodox Church, Columbia, Missouri, accessed October 23, 2023, https://saintlukecolumbia.org. In his book-length commentary to *Pnin*, Barabtarlo does not touch on questions of religious conversion or consider the possibility of Pnin's Jewish origin; see Gennadi Barabtarlo, *Phantom of Fact: A Guide to Nabokov's* Pnin (Ann Arbor, MI: Ardis, 1989).

30   On the Jewish numerus clausus in prerevolutionary Russia, see "Protsentnaia norma," World ORT: Elektronnaia evreiskaia entsiklopediia, accessed June 15, 2022, https://eleven.co.il/diaspora/judeophobia-anti-semitism/13338/. On the Jews of St. Petersburg, see "Sankt-Peterburg," World ORT: Elektronnaia evreiskaia entsiklopediia, accessed June 15, 2022, https://eleven.co.il/diaspora/communities/12415/.

the "best friend" of Pnin's father is "Sokolov," which Nabokov subsequently changed to the much more explicitly Jewish last name "Belochkin."[31]

According to the research of the Russian-Israeli historian Mikhail Beizer, in the 1910s, about 17 percent of all doctors in St. Petersburg were Jewish.[32] My own examination of Petrograd's directory for 1916 (the city had been renamed after the start of World War I), the year of Timofey Pnin and Mira Belochkin's romance, revealed that some 30 percent of the ninety-one ophthalmologists had likely Jewish names.[33] Pnin's father, Nabokov's narrator tells us, once treated Leo Tolstoy, and this may also be an allusion to Dr. Grigorii Birkengeim, a Jewish doctor who attended to Tolstoy's family.[34]

Pnin's last name, not easily pronounceable for a native speaker of English, is usually treated as a truncated one (from Re*pnin* or Chere*pnin*, and perhaps signaling his ancestor's having been a nobleman's illegitimate son) or as one derived from the Russian noun *pen'* (tree stump).[35] However, the last name Pnin also suggests a Hebrew origin and a meaningful connection with Pnina (Peninnah פְּנִנָּה *Pəninnā*; "pnina" means "pearl" in Hebrew), a character in the Hebrew Bible. (While composing his novel in English in early 1950s America, Nabokov, who had toyed with the Hebrew alphabet as a young writer, must have had in mind Peninnah (Пнина) of the Hebrew Bible rather than Fennana (Феннана), the name's Greek-influenced Church Slavonic transliteration.) In 1 Samuel, we read of Elkanah and his two wives, Hannah and Peninnah. Peninnah has children, whereas Hannah, whom Elkanah loves, is initially childless.[36]

---

31 Nabokov, "Pnin," *New Yorker*, November 28, 1953, 46; see also Barabtarlo, *Phantom of Fact*, 76–77.

32 Mikhail Beizer, *Evrei Leningrada. 1917–1939. Natsional'naia zhizn' i sovetizatsiia* (Moscow: Mosty kul'tury/Jerusalem: Gesharim, 1999), 14.

33 See A. P. Shashkovskii, ed., *Ves' Petrograd na 1916 god. Adresnaia i spravochnaia kniga g. Petrograda* (Petrograd: Izdanie t-va A. S. Suvorina – "Novoe vremia," 1916), 716–717 (data on pediatricians and ophthalmologists). Some Germanic names could belong not to Ashkenazi Jews but to Baltic Germans.

34 See Valerii Porudominskii, "Evreiskie stranitsy biografii L'va Tolstogo," *Zametki po evreiskoi istorii*, June 2009, accessed October 20, 2023, https://berkovich-zametki.com/2009/Zametki/Nomer10/Porudominsky1.php.

35 See "Znachenie i proiskhozhdenie familii Pnin," NEOLOVE, accessed October 25, 2023, https://names.neolove.ru/last_names/15/pn/pnin.html; Barabtarlo, *Phantom of Fact*, 55–56, 267.

36 *Tanakh: The Holy Scriptures*, The New JPS Translation According to the Traditional Hebrew Text (Philadelphia, PA: Jewish Publication Society, 1988), 417–420.

Figure 3. Meester van de Vederwolken, *Elkanah and His Two Wives Returning to Ramah*, circa 1467. Wikimedia.

Different Midrashic sources regard Peninnah as either spiteful or as the one who helps Hannah conceive and give birth to Samuel, future prophet and seer.[37] Phonetically, the connection is brought out already in the novel's opening pages, during Pnin's reading at Cremona, when he is introduced as "Professor Pun-neen."[38] Nabokov may have heard—perhaps through his Parisian émigré connections or the musical studies of his son Dmitri—of the great Israeli pianist Pnina Salzman, who was born in Tel Aviv in 1922 to Jews from the former Russian Empire and who studied in Paris in the 1930s as a child prodigy.[39] (Since the 1940s Pnina has become a more common modern Israeli Hebrew name—as in Pnina Lahav, a biographer of Golda Meir, or Pnina Tornai, an Israeli fashion designer.) In fact, in an overlooked comment from a 1965 interview, Nabokov might be hinting at the Pnin-Pnina conection. The interviewer Robert Hughes asks: "How about the name of your extraordinary creature, Professor P-N-I-N?" Nabokov replies:

> The "p" is sounded, that's all. But since the "p" is mute in English words starting with "pn," one is prone to insert a supporting "uh" sound—"Puh-nin"—which is wrong. To get the "pn" right, try the combination "Up North," or still better "Up, Nina!," leaving out the initial "u." Pnorth, Pnina, Pnin. Can you do that? . . . That's fine.[40]

37   Tamar Kadari, "Peninnah: Midrash and Aggadah," Shalvi/Hyman Encyclopedia of Jewish Women, December 31, 1999, https://jwa.org/encyclopedia/article/peninnah-midrash-and-aggadah. Lillian Klein, "Peninnah: Bible," Shalvi/Hyman Encyclopedia of Jewish Women, December 31, 1999, accessed June 7, 2022, https://jwa.org/encyclopedia/article/peninnah-bible.

38   On punning in *Pnin*, see the classic study by Omry Ronen, "Dva poliusa paroniomazii," in *Russian Verse Theory. Proceedings of the 1987 Conference at UCLA*, ed. Barry P. Sherr and Dean S. Worth, UCLA Slavic Studies 18 (Columbus, OH: Slavica, 1989), 289–291.

39   See "Pnina Salzman," Wikipedia, last modified December 31, 1999, accessed October 20, 2023, https://en.wikipedia.org/wiki/Pnina_Salzman; Ronit Seter, "Pnina Salzman," Shalvi/Hyman Encyclopedia of Jewish Women, accessed October 20, 2023, https://jwa.org/encyclopedia/article/salzman-pnina.

40   Nabokov, *Strong Opinions* (New York: Vintage International, 1990), 52.

Figure 4. Palestine Orchestra information page featuring Paul Ben-Haim and Pnina Salzman, circa 1936. Wikimedia.

At the same time, as if to underscore the contrapositions of a Jewish-Gentile marriage, Timofey Pnin's first name, patronymic, and background suggest a vital connection with Saint Timothy of Ephesus[41] and with conversion of Jews. Timótheos (Τιμόθεος, "God has honored") is the exact Greek equivalent of the

---

41 On Saint Timothy of Ephesus, see Rev. S[abine] Baring-Gould, "S. Timothy, B. of Ephesus," in *The Lives of the Saints*, vol. 1, new and rev. ed. (Edinburgh: John Craft, 1914), 359–361, accessed October 25, 2023 https://www.gutenberg.org/files/46947/46947-h/46947-h.htm#Page_359; Shaye J. D. Cohen, "Was Timothy Jewish (Acts 16:1–3)? Patristic Exegesis, Rabbinic Law, and Matrilineal Descent," *Journal of Biblical Literature* 105, no. 2 (June 1986): 251–268; "Saint Timothy of Ephesus (ca. 17–79 C.E.)," Wikipedia, last modified June 18, 2024, accessed October 25, 2023, https://en.wikipedia.org/wiki/Saint_Timothy; "Sviatoi Apostol Timofei," Patriarchia.ru, accessed October 20, 2023, http://www.patriarchia.ru/db/text/909840.html; "Sviatoi Apostol Timofei," Brooklyn-church.org, accessed June 11, 2022, http://www.brooklyn-church.org/svyatoj-apostol-timofej.html; "Timofei," *Illiustrirovannaia polnaia populiarnaia bibleiskaia entsiklopediia.* ed. Nikanor, Arkhimandrit (Moscow: Tipografia E. I. Snegirevoi, 1891. Rpt. Moscow, 1990), 697.

Hebrew Johannon (יְהוֹחָנָן). Several Nabokovians, among them the émigré scholar Gennady Barabtarlo, the American poet and critic Matthew Roth,[42] and the British researcher Erik Eklund, have noted Nabokov's reliance on the six-teen-volume compendium *The Lives of the Saints*, by Rev. S[abine] Baring-Gould, specifically on the 1914 Edinburgh edition. To quote the article on St. Timothy of Ephesus in Baring-Gould's *Lives*,

> Saint Timothy, the beloved disciple of S. Paul, was born at Lystra in Lycaonia. His father was Gentile, but his mother, Eunice, was a Jewess. She, with Lois, his grandfather, embraced Christianity, and S. Paul commends their faith. S. Timothy made the writings of the Old Testament his study from infancy. S. Paul took the young man as the companion of his labours, but he first had him circumcised at Lystra, as a condescension to the prejudices of the Jews. [...] When S. Paul was compelled to quit Beræa, he left Timothy behind him to confirm the new converts. [...] During the subsequent imprisonment of S. Paul Timothy appears to have been with him. He was ordained Bishop of Ephesus, prob-ably in the year 64. [...] S. Timothy was afterwards [after the death of S. Paul] associated with S. John; and in the Apocalypse he is the Angel, or Bishop, of the Church of Ephesus, to whom Christ sends His message by S. John.[43]

Baring-Gould and other commentators discuss the conversion of the Jews and stress Paul's fatherly religious love for Timothy, to whom he refers to as "true-born son in the faith" (1 Tim. 1:2).[44]

Inverting the story of St. Timothy's genetic and religious origins, Nabokov may have given Timofey Pavlovich Pnin a Jewish converted father and Gentile mother to rhyme with Zina Mertz's origins in *The Gift*. Son of a Jewish mother and Greek father, St. Timothy was baptized by St. Paul to become his close associate. Two of Paul's letters to Timothy are part of the New Testament, and the book of Acts devotes significant attention to Timothy. A separate, apocryphal text, focuses on Timothy's acts. Paul, himself a Jewish convert whose name was once Saul, serves as Timothy's spiritual father. In Chapter 4 of Nabokov's novel, Victor, son of

---

42 Matthew Roth, "A Source of Character Names in *Pale Fire*," *Nabokovian* 59 (2007): 5–9.
43 Baring-Gould, "S. Timothy, B. of Ephesus."
44 *The Revised English Bible with the Apocrypha* (Oxford and Cambridge: Oxford University Press and Cambridge University Press, 1989), 187.

Pnin's casually antisemitic ex-wife, a young man for whom the childless Pnin feels a surge of fatherly affection, visits Pnin in the college town of Waindell. During Victor's visit Pnin says to Victor in English: "'My name is Timofey [. . .] Timofey Pavlovich Pnin,' which means 'Timothy the son of Paul.'"[45] This Nabokovian clue has been curiously overlooked by Nabokov's students. Only the Hungarian critic Márta Pellérdi has discussed Pnin's connection to St. Timothy and St. Paul, although without reference to the former's Jewish origins and conversion.[46]

Twice in the novel, Pnin, whose name may be anagrammatically linked to "epiphany" and "nimb," is referred to as a "saint,"[47] on one of these occasions by "Desdemona, the old colored charwoman," who serves as a transposed sign of alterity. Thinking of Timothy, a martyred early Christian saint at a time when many Christians came from Jewish communities, also puts the reader in conversation about the lot Pnin has escaped by fleeing Europe and about Pnin's failed attempts to dwell in the survivor's silence of unremembrance. Not only Mira Belochkin's death in the Shoah but the deaths of close friends and colleagues haunt Pnin. At the end of Chapter 4, he has a dream of "pacing a desolate strand with his dead friend Ilya Isidorovich Polyanski as they waited for some mysterious deliverance to arrive in a throbbing boat from beyond the hopeless sea."[48] Yuri Leving originally noted that the name Ilya Isidorovich memorializes Ilya Isidorovich Fondaminsky (Bunakov).[49] In Chapter 5, at a colorful gathering of émigrés at The Pines estate, Pnin encounters the survivors Samuil Lvovich and Roza Abramovna Shpolyanski, in whose last name one hears an echo of Pnin's deceased friend Polyanski. Against Pnin's wishes, Madame Shpolyanski forces him to remember Mira.[50] Visions of the Shoah pursue Pnin, and he sees "ditches and even ravines gaping on either side"[51] of the road as he drives up to The Pines. The Shoah context links Pnin to the martyrdom of his émigré loved ones who were Russian Jews.

---

45 Nabokov, *Pnin*, 104; cf. explanation of Russian patronymics in "'Pavel Pavlovich,' Paul, son of Paul," in Nabokov, *Look at the Harlequins!* (New York: McGraw-Hill, 1970), 249.

46 See Márta Pellérdi, "Nabokov's Russian Professor: *Pnin*," *Studia Russica* 14–15 (1991): 421–420; Pellérdi, *Nabokov's Palace: The American Novels* (Cambridge: Cambridge Scholars Press, 2010), 64–65.

47 Nabokov, *Pnin*, 40, 184.

48 Ibid., 109.

49 Yuri Leving, "Samuel Izrailevich: Pnin's Character, Nabokov's Friend," *Nabokovian* 39 (Fall 1997): 13–17.

50 For a detailed discussion, see Shrayer, "Raisa Blokh as an Historical, Literary and Emotional Source for Nabokov's *Pnin*."

51 Nabokov, *Pnin*, 115.

January 24.

S. TIMOTHY, *B. M., at Ephesus,* A.D. 97.
SS. BABYLUS, *B., and* COMPANIONS, *MM., at Antioch, 3rd cent.*
S. FELICIAN, *B. M. of Foligni, in Italy,* A.D. 250.
S. MACEDONIUS, *H., in Syria, beginning of 5th cent.*
S. EUSEBIA, *V., at Mylasa, in Caria (Asia Minor), 5th cent.*
S. CADOC, *Ab., in Wales, and M., 6th cent.*
S. ZOZIMUS, *B. of Babylon, in Egypt, 6th cent.*

S. TIMOTHY, B. OF EPHESUS.

(A.D. 97.)

[By almost all the ancient Latin Martyrologies, S. Timothy is com-
memorated on this day, but by the Greeks on Jan. 22. The Martyrology
called by the name of S. Jerome on Sept. 27. That of Wandelbert on
May 16, possibly because of some translation of relics. Authorities: the
Epistles of S. Paul, and the Acts of S. Timothy, by Polycrates, Bishop of
Ephesus (210), which, however, we have not in their original form, but in a
recension of the 5th or 6th century; other Acts of S. Timothy, also in
Greek, and a life in Metaphrastes.]

AINT TIMOTHY, the beloved disciple of S.
Paul, was born at Lystra in Lycaonia. His
father was a Gentile, but his mother, Eunice, was
a Jewess. She, with Lois, his grandmother,
embraced Christianity, and S. Paul commends their faith.
S. Timothy had made the writings of the Old Testament
his study from infancy.[1] S. Paul took the young man as the
companion of his labours,[2] but first he had him circumcised
at Lystra, as a condescension to the prejudices of the
Jews. He would not suffer S. Titus, born of Gentile
parents, to be brought under the law, but Timothy, on
account of his Jewish mother, to avoid scandal to the Jews,
he submitted to circumcision.

When S. Paul was compelled to quit Beræa, he left

[1] 2 Tim. iii. 14.   [2] 1 Thess. iii. 2; 1 Cor. iv. 17.

FIGURES 5a and 5b. The first page of and illustration to the entry on Saint Timothy of Ephesus
from *The Lives of the Saints,* by Rev. S[abine] Baring-Gould.

S. TIMOTHY.
From a Window of the Eleventh Century at Neuweiler.

Jan., p. 360.]   [Jan. 24.

In his autobiographies, Nabokov spoke of Fondaminsky, who had been an early herald of his talent and his benefactor, as "a saintly and heroic soul," and in the foreword to *Glory*, penned in 1970, Nabokov specified Fondaminsky's conversion: "He was a Social-Revolutionist, a Jew, a fervent Christian [...] later murdered by the Germans in one of their concentration camps."[52] Fondaminsky, who hesitated to take baptism for several years after his wife's death in 1935, became a member the Orthodox Church in the Royallieu-Compiègne internment camp in 1941.[53] According to some evidence, Fondaminsky refused to

Figure 6. Ilya Fondaminsky, 1925. Wikimedia.

52   Nabokov, *Speak, Memory*, 286–287; cf. Nabokov, *Conclusive Evidence* (New York: Harper and Row, 1951), 216. Note that in *Drugie berega* (Other shores), the Russian-language version of the autobiography, Nabokov puts it differently: "His political and religious interests were alien to me"—Nabokov *Drugie berega*, in *Polnoe sobranie sochinenii russkogo perioda v piati tomakh*, vol. 5, ed. N. I. Artemenko-Tolstaia (St. Petersburg: Simpozium, 2000), 316. Also see Nabokov, *Glory*, trans. Dmitri Nabokov in collaboration with the author (New York: Vintage, 1991), x.

53   About Fondaminsky, see "Blessed Martyr Elias (Fondaminsky)," *Heavy Anglophile Orthodox* (blog), Novemeber 6, 2015, accessed October 20, 2023, http://heavyangloorthodox. blogspot.com/2015/11/blessed-martyr-elias-fondaminsky.html; Matthew Cooper, "Saint Ilya Fondaminsky and the Spiritual Awakening of Asia," Academia.edu, accessed June 8, 2022, https://www.academia.edu/40929087/Saint_Ilya_Fondaminsky_and_the_spiri-tual_awakening_of_Asia; Aleksandr Kumbarg, "Obyknovennyi podvig. K 140-letiiu so dnia rozhdeniia Il'i Fondaminskogo," *Evreiskaia panorama* 3 (March 2020): 47, https://evrejskaja-panorama.de/issue.2020-03.pdf; Natal'ia V. Osipova, "Il'ia Isidorovich Fondaminskii (doklad na konferentsii 'Religioznaia deiatel'nost' russkogo zarubezh'ia)," zarubezhje.narod.ru, November 9–10, 2005, accessed October 20, 2023, http://zarubezhje.narod.ru/texts/stfond. htm; "Saint Elias Fondaminsky of Paris," Orthodox Christianity Then and Now, November 6, 2017, accessed June 8, 2022, https://www.johnsanidopoulos.com/2017/11/saint-elias-fondaminsky-of-paris-1942.html; Oleg Korostelev, "Fondaminskii Il'ia Isidorovich," in *"Sovremennye zapiski" (Parizh, 1920-1940). Iz arkhiva redaktsii*, vol. 1, ed. Oleg Korostelev and Manfred Shruba (Moscow: Novoe literaturnoe obozrenie, 2011), 29–31.

entertain the possibility of an arranged escape because he wanted to remain with fellow Jews. He was murdered in Auschwitz on November 19, 1942. In 2003 Elias (Ilya) Fondaminsky of Paris was pronounced Saintly Martyr by the Ecumenical Patriarch of Constantinople, along with three Russian Orthodox émigrés who in 1941–1942 actively assisted with the rescue of Jews, were arrested, and died in Nazi camps—Mother Maria (Skobtsova), her son Yuri Skobtsov, and Father Dimitri Klepinin. In the last chapter of the novel, where the narrator Vladimir Vladimirovich reconstructs his prewar meetings with Pnin, he describes

> the apartment of a famous émigré, a social revolutionary, one of those informal gatherings where old-fashioned terrorists, heroic nuns, gifted hedonists, liberals, adventurous young poets, elderly novelists and artists, publishers and publicists, free-minded philosophers and scholars would represent a kind of special knighthood, the active and significant nucleus of an exiled society which during the third of a century it flourished remained practically unknown to American intellectuals.[54]

While the description intersects with Nabokov's preface to the Englished text of *The Gift*, it also links Fondaminsky ("a social revolutionary") and Mother Maria ("heroic nuns"), thus contextually acknowledging their deaths at the hands of the Nazis.

One wonders how Nabokov would have reacted if he had lived to see his Jewish-born friend Ilya Fondaminsky canonized as an Eastern Orthodox Saintly Martyr? I believe Nabokov would have found offensive the postwar comments by those émigrés who spoke of Fondaminsky's "expiatory" path to Christianity. In her diary entry for September 3, 1945 Vera Muromtseva-Bunina, second wife of Nabokov's Russian master Ivan Bunin, who in 1933 became the first Russian writer to receive the Nobel Prize in Literature, records a conversation with another émigrée about Fondaminsky's last months in the transit camp and his death in Auschwitz: "Muza is also certain that Ilyusha willingly embraced the suffering, regarded it as a redemption."[55] In 1965 Nabokov's lashed out at his friend Roman Grinberg, editor of a New York-based émigré magazine, for publishing Vladislav Khodasevich's epigrammatic fable from the 1930s that had

---

54 Nabokov, *Pnin*, 184.
55 Vera Muromtseva-Bunina, diary, September 3, 1945, Ivan Bunin Papers, Leeds Russian Archive, Brotherton Collection, Leeds University Library.

been aimed at Raisa Bloch and Mikhail Gorlin: "given the tragic and inexpiable fate of the Gorlins [prinimaia vo vnimanie tragicheskuiu i neiskupimuiu sud'bu Gorlinykh], it probably should not have been published."[56]

Aside from Nabokov's morbid if principled dislike of Boris Pasternak's supercessionism as coming from a Soviet Jew who in the 1940s-1950s fashioned himself as an Orthodox Christian),[57] the Nabokov of the American and Swiss years became less condemnatory of converts and conversion. *Pnin* shows that while retaining a measure of skepticism about the ethics of religious apostasy, Nabokov was prepared to regard it in a more gentle, more forgiving way. Consider the scene where Pnin goes for a swim in the country. The episode is doubly marked by the presence of Professor Chateau, Pnin's close friend with a Kafkaesque last name, and a "score of butterflies," implying the witnessing absence of Vladimir Vladimirovich:

> "Oh no," said Chateau. "You will lose it some day," he added, pointing to the Greek Catholic cross on a golden chainlet that Pnin had removed from his neck and hung on a twig. Its glint perplexed a cruising dragonfly.
>
> "Perhaps I would not mind losing it," said Pnin. "As you well know, I wear it merely from sentimental reasons. And the sentiment is becoming burdensome. After all, there is too much of the physical about this attempt to keep a particle of one's childhood in contact with one's breast bone."
>
> "You are not the first to reduce faith to a sense of touch," said Chateau, who was a practicing Greek Catholic and deplored his friend's agnostic attitude.[58]

While especially touching, Pnin's (mis)use of the preposition *from*—"from sentimental reasons"—also highlights two possibilities: Pnin's impulse to reject his father's apostasy and reclaim his Jewishness, and the opposite of it, a baptismal

56 Nabokov, letter to Roman Grinberg, January 30, 1965, quoted in Shrayer, "Raisa Blokh as an Historical, Literary and Emotional Source for Nabokov's *Pnin*," 636.

57 Nabokov characterized Pasternak's *Doctor Zhivago* as a "very mediocre concoction, badly written, trite, old-fashioned [...] and quite in keeping with the provincial banality of Soviet letters of the past forty years"; see Nabokov, diary entry, March 12, 1959, Vladimir Nabokov Papers, The Henry W. and Albert A. Berg Collection of English and American Literature, The New York Public Library. See also Nabokov, *Strong Opinions*, 57. This interview, recorded in Montreux in 1965, appears in Robert Hughes and Terence Macartney Filgate, dirs., *Vladimir Nabokov*, video, 28:25, accessed September 11, 2024, accessed October 23, 2023, https://youtu.be/V8OwyqvSh2g?si=SU4jkVgcwSZieXtG. Nabokov's view of Pasternak's poetry was favorable.

58 Nabokov, *Pnin*, 127–128.

immersion and a symbolic reaffirmation of his Christianity. Nabokov's nunced treatment of Jewish conversion in *Pnin* may be understood as a post-Shoah tribute to the reluctant choices some Russian Jews had to make in czarist Russia.

In a letter of July 18, 1926, sent from Berlin to a sanatorium in St. Blasien in the Black Forest, where Véra Nabokov was undergoing treatment most likely after a miscarriage, Nabokov mentioned relaxing in the Grunewald and encountering a boy, who saw a cross on his neck and said one word: "Christ."[59] We do not know exactly when Nabokov stopped wearing his Russian Orthodox cross,[60] but we do know how he fundamentally felt, even after World War II and the Shoah, about renouncing one's origins—one's parents and their religion.

Bibliography

Primary Sources

Nabokov, Vladimir. *Conclusive Evidence*. New York: Harper and Row, 1951.

——. "Pnin." *New Yorker*, November 28, 1953, 42–48.

——. "Pnin's Day." *New Yorker*, April 23, 1955, 31–38.

——. "Victor Meets Pnin." *New Yorker*, October 15, 1955, 38–45.

——. "Pnin Gives a Party." *New Yorker*, November 12, 1955, 46–55.

——. *Speak, Memory: An Autobiography Revisited*. New York: G. P. Putnam's Sons, 1966.

——. *Look at the Harlequins!* New York: McGraw-Hill, 1970.

——. *The Gift*. Translated from the Russian by Michael Scammel with the collaboration of the author. New York: Vintage International, 1991.

——. *Pnin*. New York: Vintage International, 1989.

——. *Selected Letters 1940–77*. Edited by Dmitri Nabokov and Mathew J. Bruccoli. New York: Vintage, 1989.

——. *Strong Opinions*. New York: Vintage International, 1990.

——. *Bend Sinister*. New York: Vintage International, 1990.

——. *Glory*. Translated by Dmitri Nabokov in collaboration with the author. New York: Vintage, 1991.

——. *The Stories of Vladimir Nabokov*. [Edited by Dmitri Nabokov]. New York: Alfred A. Knopf, 1995.

——. *Drugie berega*. In *Polnoe sobranie sochinenii russkogo perioda v piati tomakh*. Edited by N. I. Artemenko-Tolstaia, 140–335. Vol. 5. St. Petersburg: Simpozium, 2000.

——. *Dar*. In *Polnoe sobranie sochinenii russkogo perioda v piati tomakh*. Vol. 4. Edited by N. I. Artemenko-Tolstaia, 189–541. St. Petersburg: Simpozium, 2000.

——. *Pis'ma k Vere*. Edited by Brian Boyd and Olga Voronina. Moscow: KoLibri, 2014.

---

59 Nabokov, letter to Véra Nabokov, July 18, 1926, in *Pis'ma k Vere*, 170.

60 A discussion of Nabokov's cross is also found in Gavriel Shapiro, "Some Observations on Nabokov's Faith," *Nabokov Online Journal* 15 (2022), accessed September 11, 2024, http://www. nabokovonline.com/uploads/2/3/7/7/23779748/vol._16_shapiro_on_nabokovs_faith.pdf.

———. *Dar. II chast'*. [Publication and commentary by Andrei Babikov]. *Zvezda* 4 (2015): 157–175.

Secondary Sources

Babikov, Andrei. "'Dar' za chertoi stranitsy." *Zvezda* 4 (2015). Accessed October 23, 2023, https://zvezdaspb.ru/index.php?page=8&nput=2481.

———. "Publikatsia vtoroi chasti 'Dara' Nabokova i ee kritika." *Novyi zhurnal* 281 (2015). Accessed October 23, 2023. https://magazines.gorky.media/nj/2015/281/publikaciya-vtoroj-chasti-dara-nabokova-i-ee-kritika.html.

Barabtarlo, Gennadi. *Phantom of Fact: A Guide to Nabokov's* Pnin. Ann Arbor, MI: Ardis, 1989. "Gennady Barabtarlo, 70, of Columbia died peacefully at home on February 24, 2019." Dignity Memorial. Accessed October 23, 2023. https://www.dignitymemorial.com/enca/obituaries/columbia-mo/gennady-barabtarlo-8183494.

Baring-Gould, S[abine], Rev. *The Lives of the Saints*. Volume the First. New and rev. ed. Edinburgh: John Craft, 1914.

———. "S. Timothy, B. of Ephesus." In Rev S[abine] Baring-Gould, *The Lives of the Saints*, Volume the First, 359–361. New and rev. ed. Edinburgh: John Craft, 1914. 2023. Accessed October 25, 2023. https://www.gutenberg.org/files/46947/46947-h/46947-h.htm#Page_359.

Beizer, Mikhail. *Evrei v Peterburge*. Jerusalerm: Biblioteka-Aliia, 1990.

———. *Evrei Leningrada. 1917–1939. Natsional'naia zhizn' i sovetizatsiia*. Moscow: Mosty kul'tury/Jerusalem: Gesharim, 1999.

———. "Blessed Martyr Elias (Fondaminsky)." *Heavy Anglophile Orthodox* (blog), November 6, 2015. Accessed October 25, 2023. http://heavyangloorthodox.blogspot.com/2015/11/blessed-martyr-elias-fondaminsky.html.

Boyd, Brian. *Vladimir Nabokov: The Russian Years*. Princeton, NJ: Princeton University Press, 1990.

———. *Vladimir Nabokov: The American Years*. Princeton, NJ: Princeton University Press, 1991.

Cohen, Shaye J. D. "Was Timothy Jewish (Acts 16:1–3)? Patristic Exegesis, Rabbinic Law, and Matrilineal Descent." *Journal of Biblical Literature* 105, no. 2 (June 1986): 251–268.

Cooper, Matthew. Saint Ilya Fondaminsky and the Spiritual Awakening of Asia." Academia.edu. Accessed June 8, 2022. https://www.academia.edu/40929087/Saint_Ilya_Fondaminsky_and_the_spiritual_awakening_of_Asia.

Dolinin, Aleksandr. "O pagubakh diletantizma." *Zvezda* 9 (2015). Accessed June 8, 2022. https://zvezdaspb.ru/index.php?page=8&nput=2580.

Eklund, Erik. "The Gist of Masks: Notes on Kinbote's Christianity and Nabokov's Authorial Kenosis." *Nabokov Online Journal* 15 (2021). Accessed October 23, 2023. http://www.nabokovonline.com/uploads/2/3/7/7/23779748/1-1__eklund_gist_of_the_matter_final.pdf.

Grayson, Jane. "Washington's Gift: Materials Pertaining to Nabokov's *Gift* in the Library of Congress," *Nabokov Studies* 1 (1994): 21–67.

Hughes, Robert, and Terence Macartney Filgate, dirs. *Vladimir Nabokov*. Accessed September 11, 2024. Video, 28:25., https://youtu.be/V8OwyqvSh2g?si=SU4jkVgcwSZieXtG.

Kadari, Tamar. Peninnah: Midrash and Aggadah." Shalvi/Hyman Encyclopedia of Jewish Women. December 31, 1999. Accessed June 7, 2022. https://jwa.org/encyclopedia/article/peninnah-midrash-and-aggadah.

Klein, Lillian. S.v. "Peninnah: Bible." Shalvi/Hyman Encyclopedia of Jewish Women. December 31, 1999. Accessed June 7, 2022. https://jwa.org/encyclopedia/article/peninnah-bible.

Korostelev, Oleg. "Fondaminskii Il'ia Isidorovich." In *"Sovremennye zapiski" (Parizh, 1920–1940). Iz arkhiva redaktsii*, vol. 1, edited by Oleg Korostelev and Manfred Shruba, 29-31. Moscow: Novoe literaturnoe obozrenie, 2011.

Kumbarg, Aleksandr. "Obyknovennyi podvig. K 140-letiiu so dnia rozhdeniia Il'i Fondaminskogo." *Evreiskaia panorama*, nr. 3, March 2020, 47. Accessed June 7, 2023. https://evrejskaja-panorama.de/issue.2020-03.pdf.

Leving, Yuri [Iurii Leving]. "Phantom in Jerusalem: Or, the History of an Unrealized Visit." *Nabokovian* 37 (Fall 1996): 30–44.

———. "Samuel Izrailevich: Pnin's Character, Nabokov's Friend." *Nabokovian* 39 (Fall 1997): 13–17.

Malysheva, Svetlana. "Praded Nabokova, pochetnyi chlen Kazanskogo universiteta." *Ekho vekov* [Kazan'] 1/2 (1997): 31–134.

Mikhail Beizer, *Evrei Leningrada. 1917–1939. Natsional'naia zhizn' i sovetizatsiia* (Moscow: Mosty kul'tury/Jerusalem: Gesharim, 1999), 14.

Osipova, V. Natal'ia. "Il'ia Isidorovich Fondaminskii (doklad na konferentsii 'Religioznaia deiatel'nost' russkogo zarubezh'ia')." zarubezhje.narod.ru, November 9–10, 2005. Accessed October 20, 2023. http://zarubezhje.narod.ru/texts/stfond.htm.

Pellérdi, Márta. "Nabokov's Russian Professor: *Pnin*." *Studia Russica* 14–15 (1991): 416–430.

———. *Nabokov's Palace: The American Novels*. Cambridge: Cambridge Scholars Press, 2010.

Poljakov, Fedor. "'Der steinerne Boden des Exils': Materialien zu Leben und Werk des Dichterpaares Michail Gorlin und Raisa Bloch." In *Slavistische Forschungen. In memoriam Reinhold Olesch*, edited by Angelika Lauhus and Bodo Zelinski, 219–234. Köln-Weimar-Wien: Bohlau Verlag, 2005.

———. "'Tragicheskaia i neiskupimaia sud'ba': Svidetel'stva o gibeli Mikhaila Gorlina." In *Avoti. Trudy po balto-rossiiskim otnosheniiam i ruskoi kul'ture. V chest' 70-letiia Borisa Ravdina*, edited by Irina Belobrovtseva, Aurika Meimre, and Lazar Fleishman, Part 2, pages 212–233. Stanford, CA: Stanford Slavic Studies, 2012.

Porudominskii, Valerii. "Evreiskie stranitsy biografii L'va Tolstogo." *Zametki po evreiskoi istorii*, June 2009. Accessed October 20, 2023. https://berkovich-zametki.com/2009/Zametki/Nomer10/Porudominsky1.php.

Proffer, Ellendea, comp. and ed. *Vladimir Nabokov: A Pictorial Biography*. Ann Arbor, MI: Ardis, 1991.

The Revised English Bible with the Apocrypha. Oxford and Cambridge: Oxford University Press and Cambridge University Press, 1989.

Ronen, Omri. "Dva poliusa paroniomazii." In *Russian Verse Theory. Proceedings of the 1987 Conference at UCLA*, edited by Barry P. Sherr and Dean S. Worth, 289–291. UCLA Slavic Studies 18. Columbus, OH: Slavica, 1989.

Roth, Matthew. "A Source of Character Names in *Pale Fire*." *Nabokovian* 59 (2007): 5–9.

"Saint Elias Fondaminsky of Paris (+1942.)" Orthodox Christianity Then and Now. November 6, 2017. Accessed June 8, 2022. https://www.johnsanidopoulos.com/2017/11/saint-elias-fondaminsky-of-paris-1942.html.

"Sankt-Peterburg." World ORT: Elektronnaia evreiskaia entsiklopediia. Accessed June 15, 2022. https://eleven.co.il/diaspora/communities/12415/.

Schiff, Stacy. *Véra (Mrs. Vladimir Nabokov)*. New York: The Modern Library, 1999.

Seter, Ronit. "Pnina Salzman." Shalvi/Hyman Encyclopedia of Jewish Women. Accessed October 20, 2023. https://jwa.org/encyclopedia/article/salzman-pnina.

Shapiro, Gavriel. "Some Observations on Nabokov's Faith." *Nabokov Online Journal* 16 (2022). Accessed October 20, 2022. http://www.nabokovonline.com/uploads/2/3/7/7/23779748/vol._16_shapiro_on_nabokovs_faith.pdf.

Shrayer, Maxim D. [Maksim D. Shraer]." *The World of Nabokov's Stories*. Austin: University of Texas Press, 1999.

———. Jewish Questions in Nabokov's Art and Life." In *Nabokov and His Fiction: New Perspectives*, edited by Julian W. Connolly, 73–91. Cambridge: Cambridge University Press, 1999.

———. "Evreiskie voprosy v zhizni i tvorchestve Nabokova." *Wiener Slawistischer Almanach* 43 (1999): 109–128.

———. "Nabokov's Use of Hebrew in 'Easter Rain,'" *Nabokov Online Journal* 4 (2010). Accessed October 23, 2023. https://www.academia.edu/35528824/NABOKOV_S_USE_OF_HEBREW_IN_EASTER_RAIN_.

———. "Spasenie evreisko-russkogo mal'chika: rasskazy Nabokova v ozhidanii katastrofy." Translated by Vera Polishchuk with the author. *Nabokovski sbornik* 1 (2011): 76–89.

———. "I Am Talking to You Like King Solomon." *Jewish Review of Books* (Fall 2015). Accessed January 22, 2022. https://jewishreviewofbooks.com/articles/1870/i-am-talking-to-you-like-king-solomon.

———. "Pis'ma evreiskoi muze: Zhizn' Vladimira Nabokova i Very Slonim kak literatura i istoriia." Colta.ru, February 7, 2018. Accessed Jaunuary 22, 2022. https://www.colta.ru/articles/literature/17272.

———. "Raisa Blokh as an Historical, Literary and Emotional Source for Nabokov's *Pnin*." In *Skreshcheniia sudeb. Literarische und kulturelle Beziehungen zwischen Russland und dem Westen. A Festschrift for Fedor B. Poljakov*, edited by Lazar Fleishman, Stefan Michael Newerkla, and Michael Wachtel, 619–656. Stanford Slavic Studies 49. Berlin: Peter Lang, 2019.

———. "Nabokov, Religion, and the Holocaust." *Tablet Magazine*, September 7, 2023. Accessed October 20, 2023. https://www.tabletmag.com/sections/arts-letters/articles/nabokov-religious-conversion-holocaust.

———. *Nabokov e o Judaísmo – História e Memória antes e depois do Holocausto*. Translated into Portuguese by Sandra Aparecida Faria de Almeida et al., edited and with introduction by Jimmy Sudário Cabral. São Paulo: Editora Recriar, 2023.

Stanislawski, Michael. "Jewish Apostasy in Russia: A Tentative Typology." In *Jewish Apostasy in the Modern World*, edited by Todd M. Endelman, 189–205. New York: Holmes and Meier, 1987.

"St. Luke the Evangelist Orthodox Church." Saint Luke Columbia. Accessed October 23, 2023. https://saintlukecolumbia.org.

"Sviatoi Apostol Timofei." Patriarchia.ru. Accessed October 20, 2023. http://www.patriarchia.ru/db/text/909840.html.

"Sviatoi Apostol Timofei." Brooklyn-church.org. Accessed June 11, 2022. http://www.brooklyn-church.org/svyatoj-apostol-timofej.html.

Tanakh: The Holy Scriptures. The New JPS Translation according to the Traditional Hebrew Text. Philadelphia, PA: Jewish Publication Society, 1988.

"Timofei." *Illiustrirovannaia polnaia populiarnaia bibleiskaia entsiklopediia*. Edited by Nikanor, Arkhimandrit, 697. Moscow: Tipografiia E. I. Snegirevoi, 1891. Rpt. Moscow, 1990.

Ves' Petrograd na 1916 god. Adresnaia i spravochnaia kniga g. Petrograda. Edited by A. P. Shashkovskii. Petrograd: Izdanie t-va A. S. Suvorina – "Novoe vremia," 1916.

Zimmer, Dieter. "Nabokov Family Web [July 2000]." Accessed June 10, 2022. http://dezimmer.net/NabokovFamilyWeb/nfw_toc.htm.

"Znachenie i proiskhozhdenie familii Pnin." NEOLOVE. Accessed June 7, 2022. https://names.neolove.ru/last_names/15/pn/pnin.html.

"She stands before me as a living child": Aestheticism, Sentimentality, and Desire in *Lolita*

Kevin Ohi

And thereupon my heart is driven wild:
She stands before me as a living child.

—Yeats, "Among School Children"[1]

The first little throb of *Lolita* went through me late in 1939 or early in 1940, in Paris, at a time when I was laid up with a severe attack of intercostal neuralgia. As far as I can recall, the initial shiver of inspiration was somehow prompted by a newspaper story about an ape in the Jardin des Plantes, who, after months of coaxing by a scientist, produced the first drawing ever charcoaled by an animal: this sketch showed the bars of the poor creature's cage. The impulse I record had no textual connection with the ensuing train of thought, which resulted, however, in a prototype of the present novel.

—Nabokov, "On a Book Entitled *Lolita*"[2]

The present essay is an excerpt from a chapter originally published in *Innocence and Rapture: The Erotic Child in Pater, Wilde, James, and Nabokov* (New York: Palgrave Macmillan, 2005), 155–90. It is excerpted without major revisions. The essay benefited greatly from Cynthia Chase's response to it.

1   W. B. Yeats, "Among School Children," in *W. B. Yeats: The Poems, Revised*, ed. Richard J. Finneran (New York: Macmillan Publishing Company, 1989), 216.
2   Nabokov, "On a Book Entitled *Lolita*," in *The Annotated Lolita*, ed. Alfred Appel Jr., rev. ed. (New York: Vintage, 1991), 311.

W. B. Yeats's image for the poet's sudden schoolroom yearning condenses, Anita Sokolsky suggests, the poem's "eroticized sentimentality."[3] Its sentimentality derives not only from the ostentatious self-display of a heart "driven wild" that refuses to censor its grief and its claims upon our sympathy, but also from a personification in which the "living child" implicitly evokes a dead one reanimated by the poet's yearning. This recovery relies on nostalgia's power to convert *before* from a temporal marker to a spatial one asserting recovered presence: "she stands before me as a *living* child" (italics added). The spatial and temporal oscillation of *before* (and of *thereupon*) marks the stanza's sense that the poet has been blindsided by his own yearning, by his expressive capacities for evincing loss. This rhythm of recovery and loss marks the ambivalence of the animating trope. One's heart is perhaps driven wild because the "living child" threatens to dissolve the aging poet who witnesses the resurrection. "Before me" threatens to shift from a claim of recovered presence to an annihilating anteriority, making the living child an uncanny harbinger of a time before the poet's birth—or before the poem. This anteriority gives the *living child* precedence over the poem purporting to resurrect it and suggests that the child might exceed the claims of poet and poem in a way radically unsettling to both. Presenting a reminder that the poem—and the poet's consciousness—might not have been, this erotic gaze derives its not insignificant charge from the child's power to emblematize its own recovery and vanishing—and that of the poetic voice resurrecting it.

Yeats's poem can be said to deploy rather than to embody sentimentality because of its self-consciousness about the contradictory effects on poetic utterance of gazing at the child. No such circumspection waylays erotic innocence: the adult spectator is expected to melt at the sight of the proffered child. The threat to childhood's spectator registered by Yeats is disavowed in contemporary ideology of sexual innocence, its dispropriating potential menacing instead the innocence one would protect.[4] The thinly veiled aggression toward children exceeds the understandable resentment aroused by the perpetual pageant of innocence—by beings who seem to possess what we have lost: wholeness, innocence, exemption from desire. Erotic innocence produces its violence by blindly inhabiting the sentimental structure elucidated by Yeats's image: a proleptic self-annihilation rooted in animating the child on whose behalf one speaks. This child in need of our rhetorical resources makes possible the

---

3   Anita Sokolsky, "The Resistance to Sentimentality: Yeats, de Man, and the Aesthetic Education," *The Yale Journal of Criticism* 1, no. 1 (Fall 1987), 67.
4   On this ideology, see James R. Kincaid, *Erotic Innocence: The Culture of Child Molesting* (Durham, NC: Duke University Press, 1998).

eroticized alternation between presence and absence of "she stands before me as a living child."

Vladimir Nabokov's account of the "first little throb of *Lolita*," which occurred not long before his escape to America, deploys the sentimental in ways similar to these lines from Yeats and explores a temporal logic central to *Lolita's* eroticism. While the ape narrative tempts as an allegory of verisimilitude—the imprisoned creature depicts the bars but misses the world beyond—the image's foreshortened myopia activates, above all, the seductions of imagining a misery so fixated that it sees nothing but its imprisonment: the image luxuriates in the failure to transcend one's predicament. For the ape's destitution extends beyond its mere imprisonment; it cedes to another the task of imagining a world beyond its captivity and thus of making comprehensible the compass of its misery. The image centering Nabokov's account of *Lolita's* genesis is sentimental insofar as its inarticulate sorrow all but coerces words on its behalf. Coerced into speech, the spectator then feels speech's failure to do justice to such a predicament and, compromised, risks becoming not the liberator of the poor creature's speech but the scientist who "coaxes" the drawing out of it. The sentimental allure lies in this experience of speech's failure, which paradoxically mirrors the ape's own misery. The dogged attempt to make the mute speak produces an image whose pathos exorbitantly exceeds the scientist's mimetic interest in simian communication, uncovering no sketches with proto-realistic aspirations, but an emblem that merges with the imprisoning enclosure—like the motto that, according to Walter Pater, Leonardo's patron Ludovico wove in and out, repetitively, "in great letters," on his prison walls: *"Infelix Sum"* (I am unhappy).[5]

Nabokov's account craftily distances "Vladimir Nabokov" from the anecdote's sentimentality. Hedging it about with equivocation—"as far as I can recall, . . . inspiration was somehow prompted"—he also denies a direct "textual connection" to *Lolita*: "The impulse I record had no textual connection with the ensuing train of thought, which resulted, however, in a prototype of my present novel, a short story some thirty pages long."[6] It is perhaps unclear whether this "impulse" refers to the ape's drawing or to the author's "shiver of inspiration"; nor is it clear what a "textual connection" would entail. In any event, another layer of mediation intervenes: by unspecified means, the ape inspires not *Lolita*

---

5   Walter Pater, "Leonardo da Vinci," in *The Renaissance: Studies in Art and Poetry, the 1893 Text,* ed. Donald L. Hill (Berkeley: University of California Press, 1980), 96.
6   Nabokov, *The Annotated Lolita,* 311

but its "prototype," his "short story," or the novella *The Enchanter*.[7] Obliquities and severed "textual connection," however, replay the story by rendering the novel's genesis as mute and equivocal as that ape, its lost charcoaled intentions subject to a similarly vicarious recovery. Nabokov invokes his own implication in this structure by questioning the possibility of a first-person "authorial" voice: "After doing my impersonation of suave John Ray [. . .] any comments coming from me may strike one—may strike me, in fact—as an impersonation of Vladimir Nabokov talking about his own book."[8]

The discovery that speech subjects one to an experience of internal vicariousness—explicit in Nabokov's hope that the "autobiographic device may induce mimic and model to blend" (311)—is an unnerving insight that follows from *Lolita*'s inhabiting of the sentimental. Embarrassing in its compromising ambition to convey as immediate an experience it insists is unshared and inexpressible, sentimentality alternates between a universalization verging on banality and an overly intimate idiosyncrasy (too personal a confession that presumes it describes a shared experience); it attempts to generalize the absolutely private and thereby embodies the vicariousness it denies. The embarrassment is perhaps less a failure to communicate emotion than an intimation in its very power to move that the emotion was already vicarious, even for the person originally feeling it. The embarrassment of sentimentality—of its power to seduce even those of us who know better—is largely this willful blindness to its own exorbitance: to this vicarious structure of emotion, to its banality, to its uncertain status as shared. Sentimentality proves corrosive to sincerity itself: "Customarily we are embarrassed by sentimentality because it affronts our sense of sincerity and decorum. Too much emotion is given away; sincerity verges on self-parody. The sophisticated ear is disturbed by the grotesque, impish quality of awareness, of calculation, in the sentimental at the moment when one professes the most unselfconscious sincerity and directness of feeling."[9]

Sentimental calculation produces a queasy uncertainty that one's most intimate emotions are not hammily preening themselves for the benefit of others;

---

7   Nabokov claims that he destroyed *The Enchanter* "sometime after moving to America in 1940" (ibid., 312); according to Appel, it "unexpectedly turned up among his papers in 1964" (453 [Appel's note in ibid., 312/1]). Appel writes that two passages from the novella were "made available" to Andrew Field. Brian Boyd gives a similar account of the text that differs in certain details. See Boyd, *Vladimir Nabokov: The American Years* (Princeton, NJ: Princeton University Press, 1991), 379. For other precursors to *Lolita*, see Maxim D. Shrayer, "Nabokov's Sexography," *Russian Literature* 48 (2000): 507–8.

8   Nabokov, *The Annotated Lolita*, 311.

9   Sokolsky, "The Resistance to Sentimentality," 83.

for many sentimental texts, the calculation, and its exposure of itself, *is* the effect. That self-betrayal is part of sentimentality's power to move us. *Lolita* stages sentimentality's clandestine gratifications, its bad faith, and makes both the basis for a virtuosic display. The sentimentality of erotic innocence—parading its victims like so many caged apes—lacks this canny self-knowledge, and shores up identities through a cultivated blindness to its own effects. Suggesting that this sentimentality contains the potential for its own disruption, *Lolita* also suggests that demystification alone will not accomplish such disruption. The knowing effects in Nabokov's anecdote point to sentimentality's curious immunity to demystification, which can intensify, rather than diminish, its effect. Sentimentality might therefore help conceptualize the multivalent effects of the novel's knowing, and knowingly demystified narrative voice, and to chart the seduction it achieves.

Lionel Trilling writes in his compelling account of the novel, "in recent fiction no lover has thought of his beloved with so much tenderness, ... no woman has been so charmingly evoked, in such grace and delicacy, as Lolita; the description of her tennis game ... is one of the few examples of rapture in modern writing."[10] To James Kincaid, Stanley Kubrick's 1962 film adaptation suggests that this rapture is what unsettles readers: "The pedophile is driven not by lust but by rapture, capturing the most subversive feature of Nabokov's original work: here is the great, the only, American novel about dizzying, transforming love."[11] Most troubling about the pleasures of guilt and love is perhaps simply that they are pleasures. And they are pleasures, Humbert Humbert makes manifest, like those of reading and writing; more subversive than the pedophile's lust is the rapture of his language. Humbert Humbert suggests that one may confess not for truth, redemption, remorse, restitution, or retribution, but simply for its own sake. More troublingly, he suggests that any narrative of truth, redemption, remorse, restitution, or retribution might be, at best, a merely fortuitous outcome of, or, at worst, a self-serving rationale for, the guilty pleasure of confession for its own sake. One (sentimental) name for this decadent economy of confession is love. Another is writing.

This decadence is a large part of the novel's unsettling power, and Humbert Humbert's relishing of self-accusation and guilt irritates critics, for whom his sentimental insincerity is perhaps his most serious crime. I would argue, following Trilling and Kincaid, that *Lolita* is a great love story not in spite of its cloying sentimentality, its insincerity, the ever-visible calculation behind its more

---

10   Lionel Trilling, "The Last Lover: Vladimir Nabokov's *Lolita*," in *Vladimir Nabokov's* Lolita, ed. Harold Bloom (New York: Chelsea House, 1987), 9–11.
11   Kincaid, *Erotic Innocence*, 125.

dazzling stylistic effects, but because of these things.[12] The seductiveness of this love story is made apparent by the compulsive need of critics to distance themselves from Humbert Humbert's manifestly terrible crimes, most often by setting themselves the task of adjudicating his redemption; to read the novel, these accounts suggest, is to weigh the sincerity of his remorse, which alone can prove that he has transcended his pedophilic fixation. Such evaluations expect Humbert Humbert's confessions to conform to Paul de Man's characterization of confession: "To confess is to overcome guilt and shame in the name of truth: it is an epistemological use of language in which ethical values of good and evil are superseded by values of truth and falsehood. . . . By stating things as they are, the economy of ethical balance is restored and redemption can start in the clarified atmosphere of a truth that does not hesitate to reveal the crime in all its horrors."[13] *Lolita* plays on just this expectation; moralistic readings must cultivate an obliviousness to the novel's remarkable language and its transformation of confessed remorse into aesthetic rapture. The need to ignore the novel's language registers an awareness that the linguistic seduction and the erotic seduction are one; critics' leaden readings seek to contain the novel's erotic subversiveness.[14]

Lolita makes manifest, however, confession's potential to up-end the certainties it ought to secure, above all by displaying confession's pleasure. As Michael Wood writes, *Lolita*, "littered with expressions of compunction," is about a guilt that "both glorifies itself and grovels in self-accusation."[15] Among the novel's loveliest passages are those of self-flagellating penitence, and efforts to adjudicate their sincerity are vexed from the outset. What happens, therefore, if we suspend the question of innocence and guilt; what complexities of style and tone, what intricacies of guilt, confession, desire, and pleasure, can be traced in these moving and often highly sentimental passages? In one of the most famous epiphanies of guilt and absence Humbert awaits the police after killing Clare

12 Ellen Pifer makes a related argument, suggesting that "love [. . .] creates a point of contact, in Nabokov's universe, between the land of the living and the stylized representatives of immortality" (77). I find it difficult to share her opposition between "lust" and "love," and, as will become clear, my sense of the relation of the novel's moral epiphanies to Humbert Humbert's desire differs from hers in many respects. Ellen Pifer, "Shades of Love: Nabokov's Intimations of Immortality," *Kenyon Review* 11, no. 2 (1989): 75–86.

13 Paul de Man, "Excuses (Confessions)," in *Allegories of Reading: Figural Language in Rousseau, Nietzsche, Rilke, and Proust* (New Haven, CT: Yale University Press, 1979), 279.

14 For an illuminating account of Nabokov's writing about sex, see Shrayer, "Nabokov's Sexography."

15 Michael Wood, "The Language of Lolita," in *The Magician's Doubts: Nabokov and the Risks of Fiction* (Princeton, NJ: Princeton University Press, 1994), 137 and 107.

Quilty in a car rolled to a stop "among surprised cows." Evoking "a last mirage of wonder and hopelessness,"[16] he remembers stopping on a mountain pass just after Lolita's disappearance:

> A very light cloud was opening its arms and moving toward a slightly more substantial one belonging to another, more sluggish, heavenlogged system. As I approached the friendly abyss, I grew aware of a melodious unity of sounds rising like vapor from a small mining town that lay at my feet, in a fold of the valley. One could make out the geometry of the streets between blocks of red and gray roofs, and green puffs of trees, and a serpentine stream, and the rich, ore-like glitter of the city dump, and beyond the town, roads crisscrossing the crazy quilt of dark and pale fields, and behind it all, great timbered mountains. [. . .] And I soon realized that all these sounds were of one nature, that no other sounds but these came from the streets of the transparent town, with the women at home and the men away. Reader! What I heard was but the melody of children at play, nothing but that, and so limpid was the air that within this vapor of blended voices, majestic and minute, remote and magically near, frank and divinely enigmatic—one could hear now and then, as if released, an almost articulate spurt of vivid laughter, or the crack of a bat, or the clatter of a toy wagon, but it was all really too far for the eye to distinguish any movement in the lightly etched streets. I stood there listening to that musical vibration from my lofty slope, to those flashes of separate cries with a kind of demure murmur for background, and then I knew that the hopelessly poignant thing was not Lolita's absence from my side, but the absence of her voice from that concord.[17]

To Alfred Appel Jr., the passage shows that Humbert "has transcended his solipsism"; "aesthetic, moral, and communal perspectives have cohered, as ideally they should."[18] "For the first time in the novel," the remorse "is in no way undercut by parody or qualified by irony"; quoting "foolish" John Ray Jr. (who "turns out to be right"), Appel calls this passage the novel's "moral apotheosis".

---

16 Nabokov, *The Annotated Lolita*, 306–307.
17 Ibid., 307–308.
18 Ibid., 450–451, 308/1.

Wood, in contrast, finds Humbert's uttering of a "morally correct" perception "mawkish and self-regarding, altogether too good to be true": "Humbert's fussy prose [...] here manages to seem both artful and hackneyed."[19]

This does not strike me as a passage "in no way undercut by parody or qualified by irony"; perhaps most undercut is the yearning for a convergence of "aesthetic, moral, and communal perspectives."[20] "Communal perspectives," for instance are explicitly parodied. Its skirting of kitsch might be the "hackneyed," "mawkish and self-regarding" quality Wood objects to: he reacts against a sentimentality Appel ignores. The passage's sentimentality so overinflates any yearned-for coherence of moral, aesthetic, and communal judgments that its claims are rendered suspect. This moment of sentimental exorbitance also marks a culmination of Humbert Humbert's devotion to Lolita, transforming loss, absence, and remorse into love.

Most accounts focus on the passage's closing insight—"the hopelessly poignant thing was the absence of her voice from that concord"—partly because it provides a condensed expression of a remorse whose sincerity can be evaluated. Childhood's vanishing is perhaps always premature, and presents a reliable source of pathos; Lolita's final absence, moreover, is framed by a series of distancing or abstracting aestheticizations. Humbert's "lofty perch," which leaves him too remote "to distinguish any movement in the lightly etched streets," makes the children's voices beautiful by abstracting particular voices and content, renders their laughter "almost articulate," but not quite. The aestheticizing effects are also sentimental ones, breaking down any opposition between distancing aestheticizations and the proximities of sentimentality. The discomfort of critics with Humbert Humbert's seductiveness might be illuminated by the way this passage makes an aestheticizing, distancing effect complicit in a self-consciously sentimental one, articulates the "lightly etched streets" with the voices of children at play.

The first image, of "a very light cloud ... opening its arms," evokes the earlier projections on the lovely, trustful, dreamy American landscape. Its knowingly sappy pathetic fallacy offers the possibility of seeing Lolita in the "very light cloud" and Humbert in the "more substantial ... sluggish system." The saccharin image of a cloud "opening its arms" melodramatically renders the realization that Lolita will never again open her arms to him. The melodrama redoubles the alienation by deflating its claims, skirting the ludicrous by finding one's misery reflected in the clouds; the passage parodies the correspondence between nature

19   Ibid., 280.
20   Ibid., 450–n308/1.

and internal human states on which it simultaneously relies. Similarly, the wryly domesticated "friendly abyss" also renders its attraction and uncanny familiarity. The "sluggish . . . system" indicates blockage in the aestheticizing imagery, a "slug" that interrupts the workings of anthropomorphizing projection. Appel is perhaps right about *heavenlogged*'s connotations of "harmonious authorial patterning"; I think we should also hear "waterlogged"—as a cloud might be—in Humbert Humbert's neologism. The "heavenlogged" cloud tempts us as an image for Humbert's sated rapture and grief. At the same time, "heavenlogged" also renders a "sluggish . . . system" that cannot stop generating insights, sentences that begin: "then I knew [. . .]." Glutted with transcendence, the image also suggests that Humbert Humbert's "hopelessly poignant" insight is generated not by his more or less sincere remorse, but by a habit of aestheticizing landscapes as he does here.

Heavenlogged's saturation reappears in the pile-up of descriptive detail. The movement outward—from the "geometry of the streets" and the "serpentine stream" to the fields "beyond the town" and "behind it all, great timbered mountains"—suggests a saturation of the field of vision, which is nevertheless engulfed by the "fold of the valley." The writing is similarly sated in its lush detail and relished sounds. "Roofs" becomes "green puffs," and the passage almost overdoes its repeated sounds: "between blocks," "serpentine stream," "roads crisscrossing the crazy quilt," a pattern of repetition culminating in the all-but-stuttering fluency of "demure murmur." Relishing its funny words—*roofs, puffs, glitter, crisscrossing, crazy*—it transmutes them into limpid prose, a slithery serpentine stream lithe enough to work even *dump* into its harmonies.

The passage is thus about its own fluency, about language's power to aestheticize and seduce. It is the writing's beauty that persuades us of the "melodious unity of sounds." That unity, which leads to Humbert Humbert's moral insight, is self-consciously built on negation: "*no other sounds but these* came from the streets . . . What I heard was *but* the melody of children at play, *nothing but that*" (italics added here and hereafter). The assertion of a child-like simplicity that had, nevertheless, been overlooked, serves to naturalize as perception a process of unification through negation or exclusion: "I *grew aware* of a melodious unity of sounds." Asserting this discovery obscures the work of unification: "within this vapor of blended voices, majestic and minute, remote and magically near, frank and divinely enigmatic." The synthesis is less achieved than asserted, its seduction again at least partly in the sound, the initial and internal alliteration, particularly of *m* and *n*, that makes the unification seem pre-given. The mellifluous language replays and naturalizes the "melodious unity of sounds" it discovers, a synthesis propped thematically on children praised in a vocabulary borrowed from the appreciation of nature's beauty. The passage points to its seductive power by leaving its repeated sounds, lavish language and the allure of children to overcome its lack of unity on the level of sentence structure. The sentence staging this unification ("What I heard was but the melody of children at play . . .") is a strangely wily one, largely because of the dash in the middle, which leads one to expect, in this symmetrically structured sentence about discovered symmetries, a second one that never arrives, leaving uncertain, until the very end, whether "one could hear now and then" is the continuation of "so limpid was the air that" or a parenthetical interruption of that thought. The syntax remains unsettlingly suspended until the final period, even as meaning is rendered almost irrelevant by the accretion of phrases and details, the "or . . . or" construction a structural analogue to the earlier repeated *and*s, linking the accretion this conjunction enables to the "ore-like glitter of the city dump." "Ore-like glitter" thereby figures, again, language's power, in repeated words or constructions, to transform and aestheticize.

To read this passage as the final unification of "aesthetic, moral, and communal perspectives" not only misses its over-inflated, even "mawkish and self-regarding" language. Foregrounding a rhetorical power to naturalize such unifications and their engendered insights, it disrupts the category of the aesthetic education—which allows a reader to move, as Appel does, from beautiful prose to the closing moral insight to the unification of aesthetic, moral, and communal registers. That the aesthetic education is in question—and is subjected to parody—is suggested by the surname (namely, Schiller) of Lolita's simpleton husband at the end of the novel. *Lolita* brings out an exorbitance that, perhaps implicit in the sentimental, has the potential to interrupt the totalizing perceptions that underlie the ideology of the aesthetic education.[21] Humbert Humbert's roadside epiphany of overheard childish concord presents an insight of great pathos— "then I knew . . ."—generated, I have suggested, by an aestheticizing habit and creating an effect of remorse. The emergence of a pathetic fallacy figures a sentimental exorbitance internal to the passage's aestheticizing pleasures: to its "concord," and to its own harmonious sounds, its repeated nasal consonants, for instance. The passage's final insight presents not the culmination of the aesthetic education but a sentimental overinflation of its yearning. The discovery

---

21 For a detailed account of aesthetic education in Friedrich Schiller, and de Man's critique, see the extended version of this essay as it appears in my book *Innocence and Rapture*. The extended version relies heavily on Cynthia Chase, "Trappings of an Education," in *Responses: On Paul de Man's Wartime Journalism*, ed. Werner Hamacher, Neil Hertz, and Thomas Keenan (Lincoln, NE: University of Nebraska Press, 1989), 44–79.

of pre-given unities or pseudo-dialectical syntheses—voices "majestic and minute, remote and magically near, frank and divinely enigmatic," for instance, or
the blending and abstracting in Humbert Humbert's valley—stages an aesthetic
education making Humbert capable of moral insight, of subordinating his loss
to Lolita's. Yet the insight is undermined not only by the mechanical, routinized
quality that makes remorse seem incidental, intimating that the aestheticizing
machine can dispense with the contrite subjectivity it is supposed to excuse. The
self-abnegation is also self-indulgent, relishing its sentimental excess. The passage suggests that insinuated intimacy is not opposed to, but may be inextricably
bound up with, effects of aestheticizing abstraction—lightly etched streets and
serpentine streams.

To my mind, Humbert Humbert has not, as Appel puts it, "transcended his
solipsism"; such transcendence is presented as a yearned-for impossibility,
achieved only by the self-blinding will of assertion. This failed transcendence,
moreover, is not a moral problem; its unrepentant desublimations, its rendering of self-abnegation as a form of self-absorption is cast as love's sentimental
appeal. After his roadside epiphany, Humbert Humbert writes of his introspection ("At this or that twist of it I feel my slippery self eluding me, gliding into
deeper and darker waters than I care to probe"), and of not using the book for his
legal defense because he "could not parade living Lolita."[22] This ostensibly moral
decision in effect parades dead Lolita, and allows Humbert the self-consciously
sentimental gesture of addressing a dead lover from the grave in the book's final
paragraph:

> Thus, neither of us is alive when the reader opens this book.
> But while the blood still throbs through my writing hand, you
> are still as much part of blessed matter as I am, and I can still
> talk to you from here to Alaska. Be true to your Dick. Do not let
> other fellows touch you. Do not talk to strangers. I hope you will
> love your baby. I hope it will be a boy. That husband of yours, I
> hope, will always treat you well, because otherwise my specter
> shall come at him, like black smoke, like a demented giant, and
> pull him apart nerve by nerve. And do not pity C. Q. One had to
> choose between him and H. H., and one wanted H. H. to exist
> at least a couple of months longer, so as to have him make you
> live in the minds of later generations. I am thinking of aurochs

22 Nabokov, *The Annotated Lolita*, 308.

and angels, the secret of durable pigments, prophetic sonnets, the refuge of art. And this is the only immortality you and I may share, my Lolita.[23]

Lolita's absence from the concord of children's voices and Humbert Humbert's self-abnegation are thus made sentimental by the pathos of writing. The sentimentality lies, in part, in the second-person address to the dead, in desire's willful abolishing of mortality: "I can still talk to you from here to Alaska," where speech relies simultaneously on asserted continuity and acknowledged vanishing, on *here*'s deictic reference both to the ephemeral scene of its enunciation and to a proleptic nostalgia anticipating that later reference. As in the oscillations in Yeats's image for the power of poetic utterance to invoke its vanishing, Humbert Humbert, by making their deaths the condition of the book's being read both asserts an animating, communicating power and luxuriates in its failure.

The "refuge of art" is then not simply writing's promise of immortality. Like Shakespeare's Sonnets, Humbert Humbert invokes a much more ambivalent structure that finds death encrypted within immortality itself. "My American sweet immortal dead love":[24] it is not merely that one has to be dead to become immortal. Living "in the minds of later generations" comes at the cost of deferring one's existence until after it is over. Thus, beyond the *a* that they share with angels, aurochs move with their beauty because, unlike the North American buffalo, they are extinct. And when Humbert writes not of "durable pigments" but of "the secret of durable pigments," the secret is always already lost, the refuge constituted by the secret's inaccessibility. Likewise, prophetic sonnets are legible only in retrospect, when their truth can finally be judged; belated in relation to themselves, prophetic sonnets thus condense the temporality of all writing.

To call this invoking of writing's belatedness *sentimental* is one way to characterize the passage's self-conscious willfulness about diffusing the threat of that ambivalent structure. Like "I can still talk to you from here to Alaska," Humbert Humbert's remark that we prefer to have him "exist at least a couple of months longer, so as to have him make you live in the minds of later generations" offers a wry acknowledgment of writing's expropriating potential. The passage further domesticates the threat of death by transferring—in a parody of psychoanalytic castration—the aggression to "Dick," who risks being pulled apart "nerve by nerve." Humbert's threat to avenge himself on the hapless Dick for future neglect reasserts art's power to transcend death by parodying both the power

23 Ibid., 308–309.
24 Ibid., 280.

and the yearning for it, and diffuses writing's lethal threat by transferring it to a trivial character. Humbert Humbert relishes invoking an impossible communion so that its impossibility might be willed away through his writing's tonal and rhetorical resources, the pathos of impossibility adding pleasure to the asserted immortality.

The direct address simultaneously invokes Lolita's absence ("neither of us is alive . . .") and asserts her recovery ("my Lolita"). Recovery is, from the outset, acknowledged to be impossible, and acknowledged impossibilities often structure the pleasures of Humbert Humbert's writing. His moral epiphanies discover Lolita's irremediable absence, achieve pained realizations that he never understood her. To adjudicate the sincerity of such moments is to miss nothing short of Humbert's desire; the insight restates the desire for which critics would have him feel remorse, repeating (and prefiguring) the elegy that ends the novel.[25] Among the most lavishly repentant passages are those of Chapter 32 of Part Two, which—just preceding Quilty's murder, the remembered concord of children's voices, and the novel's closing address to Lolita—turn to a retrospective glance at Humber Humbert's love and Lolita's pain. All of these passages depict his agonized memory (and newfound recognition) of earlier failures of perception.

Chapter 32 begins, after a parody of confession (in the previous chapter) has disrupted sincerity and, with it, beauty's essential relation to morality, and it begins having linked failures of articulation or perception to Humbert Humbert's desire for Lolita. Humbert calls the chapter's guilty *tableaux vivants* "smothered memories, now unfolding themselves into limbless monsters of pain,"[26] evoking not only the dismembered, naked mannequins he sees with Lolita in Wace ("Look, Lo . . . Is not that a rather good symbol of something or other?")[27] and Dick Schiller's one-armed friend Bill ("It was then noticed that one of the few thumbs remaining to Bill was bleeding [not such a wonder-worker after all]"),[28] but also Nabokov's remarks about his relation to Humbert Humbert's desires. Calling it "childish" to study literature for information about a country, a social

25 I name some of these critics (and discuss their arguments in more detail) in the extended version of this essay. That "moralizing" critics can nevertheless be discerning about the novel is evidenced by, for example, Leland de la Durantaye, *Style Is Matter: The Moral Art of Vladimir Nabokov* (Ithaca, NY: Cornell University Press, 2007) and Elizabeth Freeman, "Honeymoon with a Stranger: Pedophiliac Picaresques from Poe to Nabokov," *American Literature* 70, no. 4 (December 1998): 863–97.

26 Nabokov, *The Annotated Lolita*, 284.

27 Ibid., 226.

28 Ibid., 273.

class, or an author, Nabokov reports that one of his "very few intimate friends" was worried that "I (I!) should be 'living among such depressing people'—when the only discomfort I really experienced was to live in my workshop among discarded limbs and unfinished torsos."[29] His characters, Nabokov suggests, are not people with whom one may associate, but lifeless parts awaiting animation. A statement of aesthetic distance, the image is a curiously lurid one of dismemberment and bodily assembly, imagining a violence akin to that of "aesthetic formalization" in de Man. The echo suggests that the "limbless monsters of pain" be read as analogous "discarded limbs," as assembled (but incomplete, limbless) aesthetic parts. Nabokov's incredulity at his "intimate friend" asserts that his "discomfort" is not that of the prude forced to associate with "depressing persons"; rather, it is an aesthetic one, of the impossibility of completing a work of art, the discomfort of parts yet to cohere in an organic unity comparable to the human form. He is not "living among such depressing people" but living in his "workshop among discarded limbs and unfinished torsos," and Nabokov's interpolated repetition (I[I!]) suggests that these unassembled parts might include those of the author explicitly in question in this savvy response to "a book entitled *Lolita*."

Humbert Humbert's smothered memories "unfold themselves into limbless monsters of pain"; in light of Nabokov's "workshop," the image evokes an unfolding (like paper, or, figuratively, a narrative) into something that pains because it is incomplete. The remembered *tableaux vivants* are thus figured as incomplete or dismembered bodies; to discover in them moral and aesthetic registers unified by sincere remorse reassembles those bodies and, forgetting their fragmentation, confuses "dismemberment of language by the power of the letter with the gracefulness of a dance."[30] Humbert anticipates this confusion by correlating aesthetic incompletion with imperfect understanding (of Lolita). The chapter's four tableaux all depict her distance or unguessed pain and Humbert's agonies of guilt perceiving his failure of perception.

I will focus on the second tableau. Walking behind Lolita "on a sunset-ending street," Humbert overhears her say:

> "You know, what's so dreadful about dying is that you are completely on your own"; and it struck me, as my automaton knees went up and down, that I simply did not know a thing about my darling's mind and that quite possibly, behind the awful juvenile

---

29   Nabokov, "On a Book Entitled *Lolita*," in Nabokov, *The Annotated Lolita*, 316.
30   Paul de Man, "Aesthetic Formalization: Kleist's *Über das Marionettentheater*," in *The Rhetoric of Romanticism* (New York: Columbia University Press, 1984), 290 (essay: 263–90).

clichés, there was in her a garden and a twilight, and a palace
gate—dim and adorable regions which happened to be lucidly
and absolutely forbidden to me, in my polluted rags and miser-
able convulsions; for I often noticed that living as we did, she
and I, in a world of total evil, we would become strangely embarrassed whenever I tried to discuss something she and an older
friend, she and a parent, she and a real healthy sweetheart, I and
Annabel, Lolita and a sublime, purified, analyzed, deified Harold
Haze, might have discussed—an abstract idea, a painting, stip-
pled Hopkins or shorn Baudelaire, God or Shakespeare, anything
of a genuine kind. Good will! She would mail her vulnerability in
trite brashness and boredom, whereas I, using for my desperately
detached comments an artificial tone of voice that set my own
last teeth on edge, provoked my audience to such outbursts of
rudeness as made any further conversation impossible, oh my
poor, bruised child.[31]

The image of a twilight garden manages a delicate equipoise between a calculat-
ing distance and its overwhelmed, sentimental dissolution. Humbert Humbert's
reminiscences stage remorse's power to produce aesthetic wholes—complete,
unlike Nabokov's "unfinished torsos." Emphasizing that these are limbless
monsters of *pain* helps obscure that they are limbless. Hence, the passage's wry,
distancing touches seem meant ostentatiously to fail, seem defensive, the self-
consciously staged symptoms of a tortured sincerity, which seek to ward off the
wounding perceptions that leave Humbert an "automaton." In this light, the
closing apostrophe—"oh my poor, bruised child"—marks (or simulates) a resur-
gence of remorse against which Humbert has no rhetorical defenses.

The description addressed to the reader suddenly punctured by the apostrophe to Lolita is an apt emblem for the novel's equivocal remorse; apostrophe at
once asserts distance's annihilation (Lolita made present to hear it) and relies,
for its pathos, on the acknowledged failure of recovery. Evoking the alterna-
tions in the image from "Among School Children," apostrophe opens the novel:
"Lolita, light of my life, fire of my loins. My sin, my soul. Lo-lee-ta."[32] If the resur-
gence of emotion in the later passage comes across as knowing or staged, it is
because an apostrophe is a self-consciously formal, rhetorical gesture. This formal gesture, which, presiding over the novel's opening, appears in nearly every

---

31 Nabokov, *The Annotated Lolita*, 284.
32 Ibid., 9.

crucial passage, is the master trope of Humbert Humbert's yearning. Lolita is made present to hear expressions of remorse uttered too late; we overhear words delivered to dead ears beyond the reach of consolation. This effect is compounded at the novel's opening when the apostrophe (Lolita, light of my life) becomes something more like apostrophe's citation, an elegiac decomposition of Lolita's name (Lo-lee-ta) that, evoking her disappearance into language, her vanishing as anything but name, is also the eroticization of the name as sound.

Humbert Humbert's apostrophes bring out a sentimental quality, exacerbated rather than attenuated by the trope's formal quality—its knowing address to an absent or fictional figure. Remorse's pathos, and the complex staging of emotional rawness and ironic distance more generally, thus replay what occasions the guilt in the first place: Lolita's inaccessibility and Humbert's willful ignorance of her thoughts and desires ("I simply did not know a thing about my darling's mind"). This inaccessibility is the focus of the passage's loveliest images: "quite possibly [...] there was in her a garden and a twilight, and a palace gate—dim and adorable regions which happened to be lucidly and absolutely forbidden to me." The hopelessly poignant thing is Humbert's sense of having missed what was most beautiful about Lolita, but this failure is vexed by the novel's refusal to reify what he missed: figuring the inaccessible, the palace gate, far from locating, even figurally, a place, instead redoubles the exile, giving us not a lost palace but only its gate. Other figures of liminality echo this one. "Lucidly," for instance, marks not only Lolita's conscious securing of her privacy, but also a translucence, a suffusion of light that contrasts with the lovely but fading garden "twilight." It is therefore unclear what would constitute a more genuine access to Lolita's mind, for the loveliness forbidden Humbert Humbert is defined by its isolation and resistance to perception. To perceive her "true" self would be to perceive—lucidly—that self's resistance to being seen—to enter not a palace but its garden, to arrive not inside it but at its gate. To "know" Lolita is thus to realize that one has not known her, precisely what Humbert Humbert does; the ostensible "goal" was to have been achieved only by failing to reach it. The pathos of suddenly realizing Lolita's loneliness—"You know, what's so dreadful about dying is that you are completely on your own"—becomes, by the end, what is most desirable about her and what is most anguishing about loving her. Her remoteness, the impossibility of further conversation, makes possible the compensations of the doubled structure of yearning and impossible address— of heart-rending presence and eviscerating absence—in the apostrophe to "my poor, bruised child."

So thoroughly disoriented is any notion of a "real" Lolita whom Humbert Humbert was to have known that any moralizing effort to condemn his willful ignorance of her is destined to incoherence. The remorse; the staged dissolution and distance; the melancholy impossibility of conversation, address, and redress all lead to one of the novel's most sentimental and moving declarations of love: "I loved you. I was a pentapod monster, but I loved you. I was despicable and brutal, and turpid, and everything, *mais je t'aimais, je t'aimais!* And there were times when I knew how you felt, and it was hell to know it, my little one. Lolita girl, brave Dolly Schiller."[33] The impossible address to "my poor bruised child" becomes a more rapturously extended proclamation of thwarted love, again structured by an irremediable guilt. Its pathos is partly its wastefully expended emotion, its overwrought, sated declaration of love to the dead. As Humbert Humbert writes of a moment when he thought Lolita had left him: "'Lo! Lola! Lolita!' I hear myself crying from a doorway into the sun, with the acoustics of time, domed time, endowing my call and its tell-tale hoarseness with such a wealth of anxiety, passion, and pain that really it would have been instrumental in wrenching open the zipper of her nylon shroud had she been dead. Lolita!"[34] This passage (with its equivocations of tone—"nylon," "instrumental") dramatizes Humbert's use of apostrophe's proleptic recovery and proleptic loss to indulge retrospectively his failure to recover what he has not yet lost. "She stands before me as a living child": Lolita is Lazarus to Humbert's Christ, called back from the dead by his yearning address.

The compensations of pathos—anticipating an address to the dead—and the structure of redoubled guilt are similar in the passage above ("I loved you . . ."). It is not merely that Humbert was a "pentapod monster," or that he was "despicable and brutal, and turpid, and everything." Rather, he knows now that he knew then that he was these things, and he knows that he knew that he caused her suffering without expressing contrition or striving to assuage her pain. The repeated *but* makes the retrospective contrition all but equivalent to love. I knew how you felt, but I did nothing; I was a pentapod monster, but I loved you. The parallelism implies a convergence of love and the inaction occasioning the guilt—the riveted sense of atonement's impossibility. Guilt merges with love through a temporality guaranteeing that no restitution will be possible, isolating realization from any action that could be adequate to it. This guilty confession thus offers another version of the mind—"a garden and a twilight, and a palace gate" ("despicable and brutal, and turpid, and everything")—whose inaccessibility Humbert Humbert desires, paradoxically, to bring within reach. Love is

---

33 Ibid., 284–285.
34 Ibid., 236.

not only tied emotionally and mnemonically to the agony of remembered guilt;
it also has the same structure of impossible yearning.

This eroticized structure of yearning inflects what is often read as Humbert
Humbert's redemption in his final meeting with a pregnant Dolly Schiller, where
critics have gratefully discovered a repentant Humbert redeemed by renouncing
his pedophilia. Such accounts register a palpable relief when the novel's apparent denunciation of its seductively charted desire can finally be said to vindicate
the critic's morality. Humbert, these accounts often assert, finally renounces his
desire for a group (nymphets) and arrives at a morally valorized desire for an
individual, for Lolita as she "really" is—a bizarre contention about this record
of an overmastering, life-destroying passion for one particular person, a novel
that begins and ends with the word *Lolita*. The encounter with a pregnant Lolita
frames that love through the remorse, nostalgia, and inaccessibility that have all
along characterized his desire:

> there she was with her ruined looks and her adult, rope-veined
> narrow hands and her goose-flesh white arms, and her shallow
> ears, and her unkempt armpits, there she was (my Lolita!), hope-
> lessly worn at seventeen, with that baby, dreaming already in her
> of becoming a big shot and retiring around 2020 A. D.—and I
> looked and looked at her, and knew as clearly as I know I am
> to die, that I loved her more than anything I had ever seen or
> imagined on earth, or hoped for anywhere else. She was only the
> faint violet whiff and dead leaf echo of the nymphet I had rolled
> myself upon with such cries in the past; an echo on the brink of
> a russet ravine, with a far wood under a white sky, and brown
> leaves choking the brook, and one last cricket in the crisp weeds
> . . . but thank God it was not that echo alone that I worshipped.
> What I used to pamper among the tangled vines of my heart,
> *mon grand péché radieux*, had dwindled to its essence: sterile and
> selfish vice, all *that* I cancelled and cursed. You may jeer at me,
> and threaten to clear the court, but until I am gagged and half-
> throttled, I will shout my poor truth. I insist the world know how
> much I loved my Lolita, *this* Lolita, pale and polluted, and big
> with another's child, but still gray-eyed, still sooty-lashed, still
> auburn and almond, still Carmencita, still mine; *Changerons de
> vie, ma Carmen, allons vivre quelque part où nous ne serons jamais
> séparés*; Ohio? The wilds of Massachusetts? No matter, even if
> those eyes of hers would fade to myopic fish, and her nipples

swell and crack, and her lovely young velvety delicate delta be tainted and torn—even then would I go mad with tenderness at the mere sight of your dear wan face, at the mere sound of your raucous young voice, my Lolita.[35]

Anticipating the remorseful tableaux of Chapter 32 and the epiphanic concord of children's voices, the passage's closing turn to overwhelmed apostrophe also links it structurally to those at the novel's beginning and end. This is no renunciation of pedophilia achieved by eroticizing an adult pregnant woman; it is a passage about ruin and ruin's centrality to the love Humbert Humbert has professed from the outset. Lolita's decay realizes the proleptic nostalgia of the novel's many epiphanies of regret. The final transition to the second person not only stages a passionate address extorted by overwhelming emotion; its equivocal animation also returns us to the loss inherent in apostrophe, the death that would be structural to this address even were we not told of Lolita's death before the novel begins. The lovely passage of self-conscious disavowal—"even if those eyes of hers would fade to myopic fish . . ."—foregrounds this anticipation of Lolita's vanishing. The disavowal of Lolita's death denies what its apostrophe knows to be true—like the pathos of hopes known to be useless, like that yet-to-be-stillborn baby's dreams of being a big shot. The nostalgia, the sentimentality, of the final address invokes a recovery of her lost youth it knows to be impossible in order that ruin might be remembered before it has happened. Humbert Humbert's reference to "the coffin of coarse female flesh in which my nymphets are buried alive"[36] does not simply testify to a sexual revulsion felt toward adult women. It also anticipates the structure of desire he finds in a "pale and polluted," "ruined," "hopelessly worn" Lolita who is nonetheless "still gray-eyed, still sooty-lashed, still auburn and almond, still Carmencita, still mine." The recovery asserted by the anaphoric *still* relies on a melancholy structure of proleptic loss, a rediscovery of her youth in the form of what will have been her ruin (the epiphany of "there she was"), which renders Lolita both young and old, virginal and ruined, desirable as the rediscovery, in ruin, of her youth as the harbinger of age and loss. This paradoxical coalescence of youth and its vanishing appears, as "dear wan face" and "raucous young voice" are made almost synonymous, an effect reinforced by parallelism—"at the mere sight . . . at the mere sound." And the

---

35   Ibid., 277–278.
36   Ibid., 75.

sentence ties this coalescence to an impossible, overwhelmed address: "my Lolita," "my American sweet immortal dead love."[37]

Like earlier moments of sentimental projection, the passage finds Lolita's ruined looks in nature, in autumnal ruin: "she was only the faint violet whiff and dead leaf echo ... an echo on the brink of a russet ravine." Movingly rendering Humbert Humbert's loss in a figure of displacement or dispersal—Lolita as an autumn landscape, a delicate, disappearing element in the landscape of Humbert's memory—the description, like the "palace gate" passage, nevertheless does not posit a "real" Lolita to be recovered; she disappears into a series of fainter and more fragile figures for the poignancy of Humbert's loss. Her loss is also self-consciously literary; the passage invokes a traditional trope (in Homer, Virgil, Dante, and, later, in Shelley) that figures the souls of the dead as leaves blown by the wind.[38] Lolita's ruin is thus also her disappearance into a traditional trope, one that, moreover, the passage dares to offer again—and that is moving, in spite of, even because of, this cited quality, which redoubles, intensifies, stands in for, Lolita's ruin. The "echo" figures both the citation and the finding of correspondences for human emotions in nature: the last cricket's desolation and loneliness, and the "choking brook" with its sympathetic mirroring of Humbert's own choking grief. Neither cricket nor brook can truly take cognizance of its loneliness; the sentimental structure of projection and vicarious emotion repeats, in another register, the impossible recovery and proleptic loss and the overwhelmed address to a dead Lolita. As self-conscious yet affecting projections, the finding of natural correspondences—known to be illusory—and literary allusion—known to be all but clichéd—thus replays Humbert Humbert's desire for Lolita.

Imagining an address to the dead, the passage gives us speech overwhelmed by aphasia, imagined in turn as external constraint: "You may jeer at me, and threaten to clear the court, but until I am gagged and halfthrottled, I will shout my poor truth."[39] Beyond the self-indulgent melodrama, Humbert Humbert's

---

37 Ibid., 280.
38 See Homer, *Iliad* 6, ll. 146–49; Virgil, *Aeneid* 6, ll. 414–20 and *Georgics* 2, ll. 82; Dante, *Inferno* 3, ll. 112–17; and, perhaps most immediately for this passage, the opening of Percy Shelley, "Ode to the West Wind": "O wild west wind, thou breath of Autumn's being, / Thou, from whose unseen presence the leaves dead / Are driven, like ghosts from an enchanter fleeing .. ." (221), in *Shelley's Poetry and Prose*, ed. Donald Reiman and Sharon B. Powers (New York: W. W. Norton and Company, 1977), 221–223.
39 Roman Jakobson's famous theorization of metaphor and metonymy was, of course, occasioned by a study of aphasia. See Jakobson, "Two Aspects of Language and Two Types of Aphasic Disturbances, in Roman Jakobson and Morris Halle, in *Fundamentals of Language*, trans. Morris Halle (The Hague: Mouton, 1956), 69–96.

imagining of himself gagged and throttled (like the "choking brook") relishes the impediments to an unlawful passion's revelation and relishes, too, the fluency it inspires. The evoked difficulty of speech—and its contrast with Humbert's manifest eloquence—replays the structure of retrospective prolepsis and the declaration of love to the dead. Speech made impossible by death or throttled by a court, its muting makes it all the more moving (and its rhetorical power all the more striking), and the pleasures of impossibility and negation inflect the assertions of guilt and cancelled lust. The extended sentence structures and the alliterative phrases—from "faint violet whiff and dead leaf echo" to "her lovely young velvety delicate delta . . . tainted and torn"—point to ways that the profession of cancelled lust replays that lust. The renunciation of lust takes the same form as Lolita's imagined ruin. "What I used to pamper among the tangled vines of my heart . . . had dwindled to its essence: sterile and selfish vice"; the sin, the lust dwindles to its essence much as Lolita does. In the context of the quotation from Verlaine through which Humbert proclaims his sin—*"mon grand péché radieux"*[40]—"selfish and sterile vice" is less the moral judgment for which it is often taken than a decadent celebration of the aesthetic thrills of sin and vice, and of the (desire-fueling) exhaustion of desire. "Cancelled" vice then evokes a protesting lover "gagged and half-throttled"; the erotically inflected structure of yearning renunciation; the lovely, exhausted figure of autumnal ruin repeated from Homer, Virgil, Dante, and Shelley; and the proleptic loss and its impossible address to the dead. These elements are united—in a strikingly decadent manner—as forms of writing, a link suggested, from the outset, by the (possibly motivating) alliteration of "cancelled and cursed" and the compositional connotations of "cancelled" (as in a cancelled verse). Writing makes possible the structures of anticipated retrospective loss, sentimental vicarity, and impossible address that constitute—and immortalize—Humbert's desire, love, and loss. The passage marks the becoming-*Lolita* of Lolita: the transformation does not transcend Humbert Humbert's desire so much as restate it.

I confess that I like Humbert Humbert, that I am ready to be seduced by him, not only because he is a beautiful writer, but because he is queer. I confess that I am helplessly, sentimentally, simply moved because he volubly celebrates a forbidden, illegal passion, because his desire and his prose are energized by

---

40 Paul Verlaine, "Laeti et Errabundi," *Parallèlement* (Paris: Leon Vanier, 1894), 114 (poem: 109–115). This section of the poem about his travels with Rimbaud glories in the poet's suffering, concedes death, wallows in it, and claims to overcome it through memory, melancholy incorporation, and the (potentially aggressive) assimilation of the loved one into culture and language ("Quoi, le miraculeux poème / Et la toute-philosophie, / Et ma patrie et ma bohème / Morts ? Allons donc ! tu vis ma vie !" [115]).

the world's disapproval, because he transforms everything he encounters into an aspect, sign, monument, or portent of his passion, because he is riven and obsessed, self-loathing and self-aggrandizing, proud and ashamed, mawkish and ironic, conflicted and arrogant in his refusal to stop talking about a love that disgusts the world. He invites my presumption in thinking that his predicament is a terribly familiar one. What if, in lieu of moralizing efforts to evaluate Humbert Humbert's sincerity, we unreservedly relinquish ourselves to the seduction of desire as a form of aestheticism or decadence, of Humbert's love as founded on an impossibility or loss structural to writing? Thus to give oneself over to seduction, to Humbert's deployment of sentimentality, marks a choice perhaps analogous to what Lee Edelman suggests is the "ethical" response to certain homophobic figurations of queerness: to accede to the charge of death-bearing antisociality and thereby to disrupt the given terms of the social.[41]

The child, Edelman suggests, is the "emblem" for an identification constituting a political realm synonymous with a futurity claiming to recover a phantasmatic past of imaginary wholeness. This yearning—one precisely "sentimental" in Schiller's sense[42]—marks the desire to overcome the constitutive division of subjects insofar as they are subjects of the signifier, to bring into self-presence a subject constituted by a deferral of presence and a division from itself. The imaginary past that structures the political is a fantasy of form, of a wholeness that, constitutively divided from itself by its retrospective construction, holds out a promised future of totalization. The innocent child might therefore serve as an emblem for the aesthetic education as it does for the political structure Edelman diagnoses.[43] In this light, *queerness* indexes the novel's deployment of sentimentality as an irrecuperable yearning within the aesthetic education: it interrupts the coerced forgetting of its impossibility—the impossibility of rediscovering an imaginary past in a symbolic future, or lost innocence on the far side of reason.

Erotic innocence inflames and assuages our anxieties by allowing us to confess and secretly to enjoy our guilt. Guilt and confession endlessly proliferate; *Lolita* does not so much demystify that process as overinflate it, making manifest its erotic structure of yearning. "Excuses," de Man writes,

---

41 See Lee Edelman, *No Future: Queer Theory and the Death Drive* (Durham, NC: Duke University Press, 2004); Edelman, *Bad Education: Why Queer Theory Teaches Us Nothing* (Durham, NC: Duke University Press, 2022).

42 See Friedrich Schiller, "Naïve and Sentimental Poetry," in *Naïve and Sentimental Poetry and On the Sublime*, trans. Julius A. Elias (New York: Frederick Ungar, 1966), 81–190. See also Schiller, *The Aesthetic Education of Man in a Series of Letters*, trans. Reginald Snell (New York: Frederick Ungar, 1965).

43 See also Edelman, *Bad Education*.

generate the very guilt they exonerate, though always in excess
or by default.... No excuse can ever hope to catch up with such
a proliferation of guilt. On the other hand, any guilt, including
the guilty pleasure of writing the *Fourth Reverie*, can always be
dismissed as the gratuitous product of a textual grammar or a
radical fiction: there can never be enough guilt around to match
the text-machine's infinite power to excuse. Since guilt, in this
description, is a cognitive and excuse a performative function
of language, we are restating the disjunction of the performative from the cognitive: any speech act produces an excess of
cognition, but it can never hope to know the process of its own
production (the only thing worth knowing). Just as the text can
never stop apologizing for the suppression of guilt that it performs, there is never enough knowledge available to account for
the delusion of knowing.[44]

Whatever the pathos of this moment, these disjunctions also ensure that "the
linguistic model cannot be reduced to a mere system of tropes."[45] Like a certain
deployment of sentimentality, they might also help prevent us from forgetting
the impossibility of the aesthetic education. De Man then turns, at the close of
Allegories of Reading, to irony, "the permanent parabasis of an allegory (of figure)
[...] the undoing of the deconstructive allegory of all tropological cognitions,
the systematic undoing, in other words, of understanding" that ensures the per-
petuation and endless "aberration" of the "tropological system." That "aberration" denotes, for de Man, the permanent erroneousness of language's effort to
refer, and the pessimistic rigor of de Man's account of irony might also offer a
way to conceptualize the ambivalent resources Nabokov finds in an unabashed,
canny deployment of sentimentality's blind yearning. Rather than resolving the
question of guilt and excuse, confession and sincerity, in a definitive moral statement revealing, at last, the "real" wounded Lolita and Humbert Humbert's sincere or indubitably faked remorse, his sentimentality endlessly proliferates its
guilt and excuses, perpetuating the guilty pleasures of their mismatch. "Who
can say," Humbert asks, "what heartbreaks are caused in a dog by our discon-
tinuing a romp?"[46] Who can say: the endlessly inventive prose of this novel turns
on an erotics of falling mute. Humbert Humbert shamelessly identifies with

---

44 De Man, *Allegories of Reading*, 299–300.
45 Ibid., 300.
46 Nabokov, *The Annotated Lolita*, 238.

everything he encounters, shamelessly enjoys the posing of such unbearable questions, shamelessly enjoys the shame and agony and beauty of his love.

Bibliography

Primary Sources

Nabokov, Vladimir. *The Annotated Lolita*. Edited by Alfred Appel Jr. Rev. ed. New York: Vintage, 1991.

Secondary Sources

Boyd, Brian. *Vladimir Nabokov: The American Years*. Princeton, NJ: Princeton University Press, 1991.

Chase, Cynthia. "Trappings of an Education." In *Responses: On Paul de Man's Wartime Journalism*, edited by Werner Hamacher, Neil Hertz, and Thomas Keenan, 44–79. Lincoln, NE: University of Nebraska Press, 1989.

De la Durantaye, Leland. *Style Is Matter: The Moral Art of Vladimir Nabokov*. Ithaca, NY: Cornell University Press, 2007.

De Man, Paul. "Excuses (Confessions)." In *Allegories of Reading: Figural Language in Rousseau, Nietzsche, Rilke, and Proust*, 278–301. New Haven, CT: Yale University Press, 1979.

———. "Aesthetic Formalization: Kleist's *Über das Marionettentheater*." In *The Rhetoric of Romanticism*, 263–290. New York: Columbia University Press, 1984.

Edelman, Lee. *No Future: Queer Theory and the Death Drive*. Durham, NC: Duke University Press, 2004.

———. *Bad Education: Why Queer Theory Teaches Us Nothing*. Durham, NC: Duke University Press, 2022.

Freeman, Elizabeth. "Honeymoon with a Stranger: Pedophiliac Picaresques from Poe to Nabokov." *American Literature* 70, no. 4 (December 1998): 863–97.

Jakobson, Roman. "Two Aspects of Language and Two Types of Aphasic Disturbances." In Roman Jakobson and Morris Halle, *Fundamentals of Language*, 69–96. (The Hague: Mouton, 1956).

Kincaid, James. *Erotic Innocence: The Culture of Child Molesting*. Durham, NC: Duke University Press, 2000.

Ohi, Kevin. *Innocence and Rapture: The Erotic Child in Pater, Wilde, James, and Nabokov*. New York: Palgrave Macmillan, 2005.

Pater, Walter. *The Renaissance: Studies in Art and Poetry, the 1893 Text*. Edited by Donald L. Hill. Berkeley: University of California Press, 1980.

Pifer, Ellen. "Shades of Love: Nabokov's Intimations of Immortality." *Kenyon Review* 11, no. 2 (1989): 75–86.

Schiller, Friedrich. *The Aesthetic Education of Man in a Series of Letters*. Translated by Reginald Snell. New York: Frederick Ungar, 1965.

———. "Naïve and Sentimental Poetry." In *Naïve and Sentimental Poetry and On the Sublime*, translated by Julius A. Elias, 81–190. New York: Frederick Ungar, 1966.

Shrayer, Maxim D. "Nabokov's Sexography." *Russian Literature* 18 (2000): 495–516.

Shelley, Percy Bysshe. *Shelley's Poetry and Prose*. Edited by Donald Reiman and Sharon B. Powers. New York: W. W. Norton and Company, 1977.

Sokolsky, Anita. "The Resistance to Sentimentality: Yeats, de Man, and the Aesthetic Education." *Yale Journal of Criticism* 1, no. 1 (Fall 1987): 67–86.

Trilling, Lionel. "The Last Lover: Vladimir Nabokov's *Lolita*." In *Vladimir Nabokov's* Lolita, edited by Harold Bloom, 9–11. New York: Chelsea House, 1987.

Verlaine, Paul. *Parallèlement*. Paris: Leon Vanier, 1894.

Wood, Michael. "The Language of Lolita." In *The Magician's Doubts: Nabokov and the Risks of Fiction*, 103–42. Princeton, NJ: Princeton University Press, 1994.

Yeats, W. B., "Among School Children." In *W. B. Yeats: The Poems, Revised*, edited by Richard J. Finneran, 215–18. New York: Macmillan Publishing Company, 1989.

Vladimir Nabokov and the Fruits of Fiction

Brendan McCourt

Introduction: (R)eat/ding Nabokov

"Like the post-structuralist text," Terry Eagleton reminds us, "food is endlessly interpretable, as gift, threat, poison, recompense, barter, seduction, solidarity, suffocation."[1] Few other writers of the twentieth century championed the literary power of food more than Vladimir Nabokov. Throughout his works, Nabokov explored the multiple meanings of food and eating to extreme and often divergent ends. For instance, we might consider the jelly jars of "Signs and Symbols" (1958), that "dainty and innocent trifle"[2] bought by a Jewish-Russian émigré couple as a birthday present for their suffering son. Despite the vast critical attention given to this story, the importance of the jellies as food item, as gift have been largely understated. Instead, and perhaps in contradistinction to the story's hermeneutic framework, readers frequently locate within these five jars of jelly a secret, hidden meaning that dulls whatever the husband found so "luminous"[3] about them in the first place.

Consider also the oft-cited passage in which Humbert Humbert drapes his pathological desire for the young Lolita in language spun in sugar and excess: "I felt proud of myself. I had stolen the honey of a spasm without impairing the morals of a minor. Absolutely no harm done. The conjurer had poured milk, molasses, foaming champagne into a young lady's new white purse; and lo, the purse was intact."[4] Humbert Humbert's carnal appetites push euphemism to the

---

1   Terry Eagleton, "Edible ecriture," *Times Higher Education*, October 24, 1997, https://www.timeshighereducation.com/features/edible-ecriture/104281.article.
2   Vladimir Nabokov, "Signs and Symbols," in *The Stories of Vladimir Nabokov*, [ed. Dmitri Nabokov] (New York: Vintage, 2008), 598.
3   Ibid., 603.
4   Vladimir Nabokov, *Lolita* (New York: Vintage, 1997), 62.

bounds of comprehensibility, so much so that the inseparability of sex from eating renders the action indeterminate. While some critics may argue that cutting through the morass of representation reveals the awful reality of Humbert Humbert's abuse, what remains certain is how the narrative frequently adopts food and eating, like the overloaded images of milk and honey, to highlight connections between sex and eating, and as a result, to obfuscate the boundaries between them.

Examinations into the gastronomic dimension of Nabokov's works have only recently begun to emerge. Critics influenced by the growing interdisciplinary field of food studies have returned to the "endlessly interpretable" depictions of food in the fictions of Nabokov for a variety of reasons and interests. In her essay "Some Foodnotes to Nabokov's Works," Lara Delage-Toriel remains perplexed by this previous omission, wondering how it is that "much has been said about the visual and tactile delights" of his fiction while, at the same time, "no substantial case has been made in favor of its gustatory pleasures."[5] While functionally operating as a surveyor more concerned with tracing broad themes—a fondness for chocolate, the frequency of meals to drive a plot—across many of Nabokov's works, Delage-Toriel nevertheless ratifies food and eating as important sites for critical inquiry. Concurrently, Beci Carver, in "Nabokov's American Gut," historicizes Nabokov's vexed relationship with food as demonstrative of his ambivalent acclimatization to American cultural habits. For Carver, Nabokov's American works, in conjunction with his correspondences with Edmund Wilson, especially abundant during Nabokov's first years in America, evince a reconsideration of food's potential. Beyond operating as a staging device for his literary works, food, in Carver's estimation, became "a kind of politically flavoured poison,"[6] and one in which the ills of consumerism, now on the rise in post-war America, could be made apparent on the page.

Even though neither Vladimir Nabokov nor his wife Véra Nabokov (née Slonim) considered themselves skillful cooks or culinary connoisseurs, food and eating nevertheless occupies a notable place in his fiction. More often than not, these instances perform specific aesthetic tasks in a novel or short story, but so too do they highlight the historical, political, and sexual domains of his writing. Given the number of gustatory references and the consistency of them across all periods of his career, one can safely say that food and eating was, in one

---

5   Lara Delage-Toriel, "Some Foodnotes to Nabokov's Works," in *Nabokov Upside Down*, ed. Brian Boyd and Marijeta Bozovic (Evanston, IL: Northwestern University Press, 2017), 69.
6   Beci Carver, "Nabokov's American Gut," *Textual Practice* 34, no. 11 (2020): 1888.

fashion or another, a *fruitful* motif for Nabokov. For instance, in "The Seaport," an early short story from 1924, a restaurant for Russian émigrés—wherein "a solitary old fellow [. . .] was making smacking and sucking noises as he lapped borscht from his spoon"[7]—frames the story's central encounter. In *The Defense*, Luzhin removes a mysterious peach pit from his pocket mere moments before the novel's ambiguous ending. (I will return to the peach motif in the pages below.) In *Glory*, Martin Edelweiss marvels at the "pastry of every imaginable color" offered in Rose's tea room in Cambridge, the place where one could continue "devouring cake after cake till one's innards got glued together, in the ever-present hope of at last discovering something good."[8] *The Real Life of Sebastian Knight* speaks romantically of "sugar-coated violets"[9] and undecorated dining rooms, the latter prompting V. to submit this endlessly quotable maxim: "food is our chief link with the common chaos of matter rolling about us."[10] And *Pale Fire*'s Charles Kinbote has been called cruel and narcissistic, but his vegetarianism disrupts both the neatness of those monikers and the assumptions of character based upon one's eating habits. (For instance, both Tolstoy and Hitler were devout vegetarians.) Nabokov's continual return to food and eating thus clamors for more attention.

My interest in the literary-gastronomic thread in Nabokov is one of both history and method. By the time Nabokov wrote what would come to be known as "the davenport scene" of *Lolita*, with its poisoned apple of the nympholept's love, he had already relied on the libidinous connotations of eating to aestheticize sexual desire.[11] In a sense, the shockingly perverse depictions here and throughout *Lolita* can be understood less as anomalies and more as inheritors to a long-standing body of work nearly twenty years in the making. Mapping the textual genealogy of this aspect of Nabokov's writings through his earlier Russian fictions offers insight into his creative laboratory. And while Carver has argued for how "in the 1940s, Nabokov changed his tune about eating,"[12] I suggest that the tune did not change so much as it reached a fever pitch. Nabokov's

---

7   Vladimir Nabokov, "The Seaport," trans. Dmitri Nabokov in collaboration with the author, in *The Stories of Vladimir Nabokov*, 61.
8   Vladimir Nabokov, *Glory*, trans. Dmitri Nabokov in collaboration with the author (New York: Vintage, 1991), 102.
9   Vladimir Nabokov, *The Real Life of Sebastian Knight* (New York: Vintage, 1992), 8.
10 Ibid., 35.
11 *See also Kevin Ohi's essay in this volume (M. D. S.).*
12 Carver, "Nabokov's American Gut," 1886.

"gustatory qualms"[13] may have gained additional valences by way of his flight from Europe to America, but the penchant to use the figurative language of food and eating to represent desire, longing, and displacement had already been an established feature of his early writings. Put differently, understanding the textual genesis of *Lolita* and the amount of carnal metaphors plotted throughout the novel helps to show how they are both conventional and exceptional, novel in English and established in Russian.

In addition to the historical and textual plates, thinking through food and eating in Nabokov has methodological significance, particularly for the way it invites opportunities to rethink the disciplinary principles that regulate reading and elicit interpretation. If Eagleton is in some sense correct when he indexes food and the "post-structuralist text," thus honoring ambiguity, indeterminacy, and prolificity, then why does so much of the criticism dedicated to Nabokov's use of food privilege fixed and stable meaning? Why do critics desire decoding the signs and symbols of "Signs and Symbols?" What methodological insights are afforded when, as Gitanjali G. Shahani writes, "tasting, chewing, and digesting" serves "as a kind of theme and method?"[14]

After all, Nabokov himself imagined reading in exactly these terms. In his *Lectures on Russian Literature*, he avows the association between reading and eating when he enjoins his students to read as the gourmand might savor a choice piece of fruit: "Literature must be taken and broken to bits, pulled apart, squashed—then its lovely reek will be smelt in the hollow of the palm; it will be munched and rolled upon the tongue with relish; then, and only then, its rare flavor will be appreciated at its true worth."[15] Delage-Toriel describes this passage as "one of [Nabokov's] choicest morsels on literature,"[16] and for good reason; implicit in its metaphorization of eating and reading is the idea that food and literature go hand in hand. With his emphasis on slow and attentive savoring, Nabokov clues us in to a highly aestheticized theory of reading that he at some point endorsed, but so too does he point toward the possible challenges of interpretive reading—uncovering a work's "true worth"—that food and/as literature ultimately seeks to redress.

13 Ibid., 1888.
14 Gitanjali G. Shahani, Introduction, *Food and Literature*, ed. Gitanjali G. Shahani (New York: Cambridge University Press, 2018), 2.
15 Vladimir Nabokov, *Lectures on Russian Literature*, ed. Fredson Bowers (New York: Harcourt Brace Jovanovich/Bruccoli Clark, 2017), 105.
16 Delage-Toriel, "Some Foodnotes to Nabokov's Works," 79.

Whither Lolita?: Sex and Eating in "Spring in Fialta" and *Invitation to a Beheading*

That Nabokov settled on the images of food and feasting as aesthetic representations of sexual desire is not surprising in the slightest. "The connection between
food and sex," writes Antje Lindenmeyer, "can be a cliché."[17] Against the backdrop of the banality or tiredness of the connection, and especially so in early
modernism, the particular innovation that Nabokov makes evident throughout
Lolita is how the figuration itself becomes suffused with perversion. The vividness of Nabokov's gustatory imagery is almost too good, too powerful, to remain
purely metaphorical.[18] Critics are therefore right to point out how the excess of
Lolita's narration implicates figuration itself in what Mark Greif (begrudgingly)
calls "Nabokov's allegories of the seductions of aestheticism, which transfigures
the forbidden into the beautiful."[19] But at the same time, Nabokov's variation
on this theme began long before the composition of *Lolita*. In fact, two earlier
Russian works composed in the middle of the 1930s—the short story "Spring in
Fialta" (1936) and the novel *Invitation to a Beheading* (1935–1936)—anticipate
Lolita thematically and linguistically. I suggest historicizing *Lolita*'s food imagery
within his Russian works.[20]

Although the literary and cultural influences of "Spring in Fialta" have been
well established,[21] it is worth returning to the story's manipulation of food imagery in the context of sexual transgression. Before there were the "honey-hued
shoulders"[22] of Humbert Humbert's nymphet, there was first the "honey-stained

---

17 Antje Lindenmeyer, "'Lesbian Appetites': Food, Sexuality and Community in Feminist
    Autobiography," *Sexualities* 9 no. 4 (2006): 471.
18 Delage-Toriel guides our attention to how this modernist preoccupation meets its apex in
    Lolita, where perverted sexual desire is traced directly onto "the nymphet's body as it is
    compared to various sweet edibles," specifically, Humbert's baleful descriptions of Lolita's
    physique, her "apricot midriff," her "peach-cleft," masks its perversion through creative and
    figurative language.
19 Mark Greif, "Afternoon of the Sex Children." *n+1* 4 (2006), accessed October 6, 2023,
    https://www.nplusonemag.com/issue-4/essays/afternoon-of-the-sex-children/.
20 Nor am I alone in this line of thought. See also Alexei Lalo, "Nabokov's *Lolita* and Its
    Precursors," in *Libertinage in Russian Culture* (Boston, MA: Brill, 2011), 219–251, as well
    as Maxim D. Shrayer, "Nabokov's Sexography," *Russian Literature* 48 (2000): 495–516.
    Shrayer's textual history is particularly salient for its analysis on the multidimensionality of
    sexual imagery in Nabokov's Russian works.
21 See, for instance, Thomas Siefried, "Nina's Endings: Some Subtexts of Nabokov's 'Spring in
    Fialta,'" *Nabokov Online Journal* 14 (2020), 1–29.
22 Nabokov, *Lolita*, 39.

knife"[23] of "Spring in Fialta," in which the married Russian expatriate named Victor (Vasen'ka in the original Russian) narrates his sexual encounters with the married émigrée Nina. Upon entering Nina's Parisian hotel room, Victor notices "a tray with the remains of breakfast—a honey-stained knife, crumbs on the gray porcelain."[24] On the one hand, this detail operates like much of Nabokov's gastronomic language, that is, as indicating sex and desire. The repeated use of honey throughout *Lolita* makes this certain. While the "honey-stained knife" was left over from an earlier meal, it also recalls the presence of Ferdinand, Nina's husband. In a sense, the image performs double work for Nabokov, as a signal of sex and a reminder of adultery. This hotel scene, after all, brings us back to Ferdinand, but so too does it bring us back to food and the places of eating: "from the hotel I accompanied her to [. . .] to the café where her husband was holding session with his court at the moment."[25]

Invitation to a Beheading likewise makes use of gustatory language to punctuate erotic desire and adultery.[26] Nabokov marks the anxieties of Cincinnatus C.'s relationship with his wife Marthe by the language of food and eating. The earliest such mention occurs in Chapter Five when Cincinnatus C. becomes seized by the memory, the "endless torture"[27] of her many affairs. Cincinnatus C. remarks how he would "talk at dinner with one or another of her lovers, appear cheerful, crack nuts, crack jokes,"[28] knowing full well what was going on behind the scenes, or rather beneath the table. The social performance of the meal calls attention to the publicity of Cincinnatus C. as a cuckolded husband, a role he begrudgingly yet consistently upholds. At the same time, during such performances Marthe's "eating" metaphorically disguises the exhibitionism of her desires. And as the "young man visible down the waist at table, peacefully feeding and chatting,"[29] gives way to the "writhing, raging quadruped" beneath, the notion of animal compulsions and bestial impulses collapse food and eating as distinctly carnal. But appearances are of course deceiving, as feeding, both literal and figurative, occurs above and below the table.

---

23 Nabokov, "Spring in Fialta," trans. Vladimir Nabokov and Peter Pertzoff, in *The Stories of Vladimir Nabokov*, 419.
24 Ibid.
25 Ibid., 420.
26 *Also see Ciara Spencer's essay in this volume (M. D. S.).*
27 Vladimir Nabokov, *Invitation to a Beheading*, trans. Dmitri Nabokov in collaboration with the author (New York: Vintage, 1989), 64.
28 Ibid.
29 Ibid,

Later in the novel, the metaphorization of sex and eating reaches its apex when, in a letter to Marthe, Cincinnatus C. describes in graphic detail what he saw when she performed oral sex on another man. The vividness of its representation borders on literary licentiousness:

> Your and his kisses, which most resembled some sort of feeding, intent, untidy, and noisy. Or when you, with eyes closed tight, devoured a spurting peach and then, having finished, but still swallowing, with your mouth still full, you cannibal, your glazed eyes wandered, your fingers were spread, your inflamed lips were all glossy, your chin trembled, all covered with drops of the cloudy juice, which trickled down onto your bared bosom, while the Priapus who had nourished you suddenly, with a convulsive oath, turned his bent back to me, who had entered the room at the wrong moment. "All kinds of fruit are good for Marthe," you would say with a certain sweet-slushy moistness in your throat [. . .].[30]

The scene's sumptuousness, its emphasis on fruitful sweetness, even its linguistic and grammatical excess all anticipate *Lolita*'s "davenport scene." But what distinguishes this "spurting peach" scene from what goes on during the "davenport scene," and even from the dinner table scene earlier in *Invitation to a Beheading*, is how blunt the former is, how it eschews euphemistic language. Cincinnatus C. begins this passage by noting the resemblance of Marthe's "kisses" to "some sort of feeding," but by the end, the resemblance is so apt, the representation so descript, that the semantic divide between signifier and signified disintegrates, rendering the metaphor inoperable—or literally climactic. In *Invitation to a Beheading* the figurative and structural parallels between eating and sex are pushed to their limits, so much so that the central conceit—to make palatable what is obviously sexual—remains both thwarted and actualized to completion.

Perhaps most telling is the instance when Cincinnatus C. calls Marthe "you cannibal," which literalizes the relationship between gastronomic and sexual consumption. Delage-Toriel has taken up the idea of cannibalism and sexuality in Nabokov's fiction, but only insofar as it relates to *Lolita*. If, as Delage-Toriel argues, we should regard Humbert Humbert's cannibalism for Lolita as figurative of "total appropriation," since "food satisfies us because it does not

---

30 Ibid., 141. *See also Nina Khaghany's discussion of the scene in her essay on Nabokov and Joyce in this volume (M. D. S.).*

refuse itself to us,"[31] then how are we to make sense of Marthe's cannibalism in *Invitation to a Beheading*? For Humbert, the paradigm of food as "triumph over otherness"[32] remains consistent with his nympholeptic desire; yet for Marthe, it is not entirely clear what or whom she becomes master over, except maybe herself and her own erotic dissent.

Additionally, it is worth mentioning how, alongside sex, food and eating often function alongside Nabokov's theory of reading. Lest we forget the opening to *Invitation to a Beheading*, the narration ironizes the anticipation of the mortal closure pronounced in the novel's opening (death) sentence by reminding the reader how much of the book still remains unread: "So we are nearing the end. The right-hand, still untasted part of the novel, which, during our delectable reading, we would lightly feel, mechanically testing whether there were still plenty left [. . .] has suddenly, for no reason at all, become quite meager."[33] The narration emphasizes the language of taste and touch in order to render the act of reading explicit. Not only does it cleverly prompt the reader to pass their thumb along the book's recto pages for tactile reassurance that the story will not conclude so soon after it has begun ("and our fingers were gladdened by the placid, faithful thickness"),[34] but the narration even goes so far as to metaphorize the pleasures of reading as recognizably gustatory. What remains of the novel is "untasted," and the reading to occur will be "delectable." A few lines later, Nabokov amplifies the association between literary and gastronomic consumption through the image of spoiled cherries: "O horrible! The heap of cherries, whose mass had seemed to us such a ruddy and glossy black, had suddenly become discrete drupes: the one over there with the scar is a little rotten, and this one has shriveled and dried up around its stone."[35] Likening Cincinnatus C.'s bathetic death sentence to the ripeness of stone fruit, *Invitation to a Beheading*, from its very outset, foregrounds a preoccupation with the objects and features of gastronomy.

We might therefore wonder whether Nabokov means to constellate reading and sex as well, with food and eating as intermediaries of the act. One possible unifying factor is the basic feeling of pleasure garnered. To this end, Rodney Giblett has convincingly argued for understanding *Lolita* in the context of Roland Barthes's notion of textual *jouissance* as outlined in the *The Pleasure of*

---

31 Delage-Toriel, "Some Foodnotes to Nabokov's Works," 74.
32 Ibid.
33 Vladimir Nabokov, *Invitation to a Beheading*, 12.
34 Ibid.
35 Ibid.

the Text. For Giblett, here walking in Barthes's footsteps, *Lolita* "discomforts and unsettles the reader's cultural assumptions" of sexual desire and its "relation with language through its use of irony and parody,"[36] though the same could also be said for *Invitation to a Beheading*. From its very beginning, the novel sets up the reading to be pleasurable and "delectable," but Cincinnatus C.'s representation of Marthe's sexual affairs complicates the agreeableness of textual pleasures. On the one hand, the peach passage is "delectable" in so far as the reader appreciates the intricacies of its figuration, the lyricism of its prose. On the other hand, that which is described, the literal climax of an adulterous affair with Cincinnatus C. as witness, is at odds with the notion of pleasure as banal or uncritical. The appalling underside to both Humbert Humbert's and Cincinnatus C.'s representations, as Giblet notes, does "not produce a good belly laugh" we might expect from pleasure, but "a wry smile at his excesses, his ironic naivety."[37]

In sum, "Spring in Fialta" and *Invitation to a Beheading* reveal an understanding of carnal appetites as gustatory, erotic, and also traumatic—in anticipation of *Lolita*. For fear of sounding too teleological, I will conclude this section by mentioning that, at the very least, by rooting Lolita's fruits in their Russian-language precursors, we have, in Nabokov's own words, "taken and broken to bits, pulled apart, squashed" the text of his most famous American novel. I will now return to those fateful little jam jars of "Signs and Symbols" and redirect the joys and dangers of reading back to 1958, the year *Lolita* was published in America.

The (Gastronomic) Pleasures and Discontents of Reading: "Signs and Symbols"

Early in "Signs and Symbols," an old immigrant couple living in New York purchases for their son an oddly specific birthday present, "a dainty and innocent trifle: a basket with ten different fruit jellies in ten little jars."[38] Their reasoning is sound enough. The son, suffering from a mental illness described later in the story as "referential mania," considers all things fabricated or humanly crafted to be "either hives of evil, vibrant with a malignant activity that he alone could perceive, or gross comforts for which no use could be found in his abstract world."[39] The jars of jelly strike them as a safe bet, or, at the very least, so far afield

---

36   Rodney Giblett, "Writing Sexuality, Reading pleasure," *Paragraph* 12, no. 3 (1989): 233.
37   Ibid., 235.
38   Vladimir Nabokov, "Signs and Symbols," in *The Stories of Vladimir Nabokov*, 598.
39   Ibid.

from what their son might deem threatening or encroaching. In the parents' estimation, things synthetic or technological were off the table—"anything in the gadget line for instance was taboo."[40] And yet, many readers tend to disagree with the Jewish-Russian couple and choose instead to take the (deceptively?) innocuous inclusion of these fateful little jellies as clues to an encoded yet concealed meaning. Alarmingly, the son's birthday present remains central to a community of Nabokov's readers dedicated to deciphering the story's hidden, cryptic message, a message that the right interpretive tools will reveal. To find this message, one must gloss over the story's rich middle section and also disregard the brief yet particularly meaningful references to the couple's traumatic emigration from Europe and the looming threat of Nazi violence,[41] and focus one's attention solely on the ending.

To be fair, it would be difficult to come up with a reading of the story that does not engage the ending, and for good reason. The third and final section of "Signs and Symbols" is mysterious and alluring, and one of the most emotive scenes Nabokov ever wrote. But because of the ending, the story's closest readers instruct us to treat this ending, the father's reading of the names on the jars, with suspicion. Carol M. Dole stresses Nabokov's "fondness for puns and puzzles"[42] as ratification of one's imperative to read between the lines, of one's hope to find a linguistically concealed clue that would guide the reader toward a discovery of the story's meaning. Joanna Trzeciak justifies a similar interpretive approach, arguing that the veiled meaning of the jellies "escapes close scrutiny unless attended to from the standpoint of the story's silences."[43] Dole and Trzeciak align themselves with John V. Hagopian, who rejects reading the end indeterminately on the grounds that "[t]he post-modernists must not be allowed to kidnap Nabokov."[44]

While the works of Vladimir Nabokov are not the only landing sites for the riddle-minded reader, they are nevertheless paradigmatic. My point in enumerating some of the story's interpretations is to highlight a critical tradition of reading not only "Signs and Symbols," but also much of Nabokov's fiction,

---

40 Ibid.
41 See Maxim D. Shrayer, "Jewish Questions in Nabokov's Life and Art," in *Nabokov and His Fictions: New Perspectives*, ed. Julian W. Connolly (New York: Cambridge University Press, 1999), 73–91. As Shrayer details here, biographical details like Nabokov's marriage to Véra Slonim inform the themes of death and antisemitism in *The Gift* (1938) and Shoah memory in *Pnin* (1957).
42 Carol M. Dole, "Five Known Jars," in *Anatomy of a Short Story: Nabokov's Puzzles, Codes, "Signs and Symbols,"* ed. Yuri Leving (New York: Continuum, 2012), 139.
43 Joanna Trzeciak, "The Last Jar," in Leving, *Anatomy of a Short Story*, 143.
44 John V. Hagopian, "Decoding 'Signs and Symbols,'" in Leving, *Anatomy of a Short Story*, 303.

as a puzzle in need of being solved. At the same time, more recent critical studies have been calling for a different approach. Eric Naiman notes the "painful psychic damage"[45] that Nabokov's other famous English-language story of this time, "The Vane Sisters," has exacted on the readings of "Signs and Symbols." Remarking on the twinned reception of these two American short stories, Naiman wonders: "[D]id [Nabokov] mean that most of his work necessarily revolved around a hidden message which the reader was supposed to decode?"[46] Whereas Naiman puzzles over what it is about Nabokov's texts that invites such obsessive deciphering practices, I would like to pose related questions. What is it about ourselves as readers that deems cracking, breaking, and solving Nabokov's textual code—supposing one even exists—as appropriate, even important? And what other discursive methods can critics attend to? What would it mean, for instance, to read "Signs and Symbols" not as a puzzle, but as a meal, a feast?

Allow me, then, to turn to the story's ending to suggest what is at stake in reading Nabokov against the interpretive grain. After a moment of sustained clarity in which the immigrant couple decides, no matter what the consequences, to bring their son home as soon as possible, they share a brief moment of comfort:

> They sat down to their unexpected festive midnight tea. The birthday present stood on the table. He sipped noisily; his face was flushed; every now and then he imparted a circular motion to his raised glass so as to make the sugar dissolve more thoroughly. [...] While she poured him another glass of tea, he put on his spectacles and reexamined with pleasure the luminous yellow, green, red little jars. His clumsy moist lips spelled out their eloquent labels: apricot, grape, beech plum, quince. He had got to crab apple, when the telephone rang again.[47]

This ending has produced a record number of interpretations—too many, in fact, to credit here. Accordingly, I will limit myself only to those readings of "Signs and Symbols" that focus on the jars of jelly. Carol M. Dole insists on how the reader "must join the father in spelling"[48] to understand fully what Nabokov

---

45 Eric Naiman, "Lynchers at Heart: De-Ciphering 'Signs and Symbols,'" *Nabokov Studies* 17 (2020–2021): 97.
46 Ibid.
47 Nabokov, "Signs and Symbols," 603.
48 Dole, "Five Known Jars," 139.

is playing at and how he plays. Dole notes how the names of the jellies contain a message which can be revealed by taking the final letter of each name and reorganizing them. Taking the final letter of each of the five named jellies, apricot, beech plum, grape, quince, and reorienting the letters reveals the word "theme." What is particularly compelling about Dole's revelation of the anagram is how it connects back to the earlier diagnostic description of the young man's referential mania: "Everything is a cipher and of everything he is the theme."[49] While other critics, among them Joanna Trzeciak or, more recently, Graeme Arkell, have attempted anagrammatical readings of either this last passage or the jars themselves, Dole who comes closest to what is critically at stake when one pursues the possibility of the hidden message. "Might [Nabokov] be taunting us," Dole offers, "for hunting symbols in a way that is suspiciously like the maniac son's?"[50] Rather than take the gesture as Nabokov playfully soliciting his reading into decoding, Dole helps reinterpret the clues as traps, the express purpose of which is to make conspicuous the practice of symptomatic reading. Perhaps it is best not to take Nabokov's bait altogether. As Dole mentions, the revelation of the word "theme" seeks to align "reader, writer, and referential maniac,"[51] indicating further the deep psychoanalytic underpinnings of both the story itself and the methods it forces upon the reader.

I cannot help but think that detail becomes more apparent when we abandon puzzles and codes and revisit "Signs and Symbols" as an immigrant fiction by an immigrant author. Earlier in the story, the father's reading of the jelly labels is situated during an act of eating, this time a Shabbat dinner—fried fish—which the mother dutifully prepares. "He read his Russian-language newspaper while she laid the table. Still reading, he ate the pale victuals that needed no teeth."[52] The association between eating and reading is, of course, made particularly apparent here. But equally important is the language in which the father reads. As an émigré, he comfortably reads in Russian, but most certainly not English, the language in which the names on the jars are to be printed. Perhaps, then, it is not so much that the father is divining, in real time, alongside the reader, a hidden or secret message from the names of the jars, but remarking on the transliteration of them. If we take the joys of the final scene to be those of the name as read from a

49 Nabokov, "Signs and Symbols," 599.
50 Graeme Arkell, "Mislaid or Misdial: Misplacement of the Jelly Jars in Nabokov's 'Signs and Symbols," *Nabokov Online Journal* 10–11 (2016–2017), accessed December 6, 2024, http://www.nabokovonline.com/uploads/2/3/7/7/23779748/21_notes_signs_and_symbols.pdf; Dole, "Five Known Jars," 138.
51 Ibid., 139.
52 Nabokov, "Signs and Symbols," 600.

transnational, perhaps even translingual Jewish émigré, then the reader's joy too is of a similar kind—the particularity of the names and their contents. This fact would then draw the reader's attention back to the circumstances in which their escape to America occurred, the horrific particulars "Signs and Symbols" only alludes to. What is, on the outside, a supremely aesthetic connection quickly reveals its historical and political importance. Take, too, the couple's moment of comfort, a brief respite in the tragedy of their past and present, not as escape, but as a radical act of pleasure—or *jouissance*—which, this story, published in the shadow of the Shoah, tolerates only briefly. Hence the status of this pleasure as small, transient, "dainty and innocent," just as the fruit jellies that the couple's son will likely never taste.

In Closing: Eating with Nabokov

From the figurative language of eating and sex found on both sides of the Atlantic, we can create a throughline between Nabokov's European and American years. From the jam jars of "Signs and Symbols," we can understand food's historical and political significance when we begin to recognize its importance beyond symbolic or associative functions. True, "food is endlessly interpretable," but that should not mean that we abandon the detail of the description that brings us closer to meaning. What is so distinctive about reading food in "Signs and Symbols," *Lolita*, "Spring in Fialta," or *Invitation to a Beheading*? As much as we are horrified by what Nabokov's gustatory metaphors represent, we must contend with both the pleasures and the qualms of eating with Nabokov. Whether indeterminate and suggestive, or downright conclusive in their imbrication of desire and eating, the fruits of his fiction are garnering their proper attention. Or at least, Nabokov would have wanted so, for in the process, his words "will be munched and rolled upon the tongue with relish [. . .] its rare flavor" to be savored once and for all time.

Bibliography

Primary Sources
Nabokov, Vladimir. *Glory*. Translated by Dmitri Nabokov in collaboration with the author. New York: Vintage, 1971.
———. "Interview with Anne Guerin for *L'Express* (1961)." In *Think, Write, Speak*, edited by Brian Boyd and Anastasia Tolstoy, 298–300. New York: Knopf, 2019.

———. *Invitation to a Beheading.* Translated by Dmitri Nabokov in collaboration with the author. New York: Vintage, 1989.

———. *Lolita.* New York: Vintage, 1997.

———. *The Real Life of Sebastian Knight.* New York: Vintage, 1992.

———. *The Stories of Vladimir Nabokov.* Edited by Dmitri Nabokov. New York: Vintage, 2006.

Secondary Sources

Arkell, Graeme. "Mislaid or Misdial: Misplacement of the Jelly Jars in Nabokov's 'Signs and Symbols.'" *Nabokov Online Journal* 10–11 (2016–2017). Accessed December 6, 2024. http://www.nabokovonline.com/uploads/2/3/7/7/23779748/21_notes_signs_and_symbols.pdf.

Carver, Beci. "Nabokov's American Gut." *Textual Practice* 34, no. 11 (2020): 1885–1904.

Delage-Toriel, Lara. "Some Foodnotes to Nabokov's Works." In *Nabokov Upside Down*, edited by Brian Boyd and Marijeta Bozovic, 69–83. Evanston, IL: Northwestern University Press, 2017.

Dole, Carol M. "Five Known Jars." In *Anatomy of a Short Story: Nabokov's Puzzles, Codes, "Signs and Symbols,"* edited by Yuri Leving, 137–139. New York: Continuum, 2012.

Eagleton, Terry. "Edible ecriture." *Times Higher Education*, October 24, 1997. Accessed October 6, 2023. https://www.timeshighereducation.com/features/edible-ecriture/104281.article.

Giblett, Rodney. "Writing Sexuality, Reading Pleasure." *Paragraph* 12, no. 3 (1989): 229–238.

Greif, Mark. "Afternoon of the Sex Children." *n+1* 4 (2006). Accessed October 6, 2023. https://www.nplusonemag.com/issue-4/essays/afternoon-of-the-sex-children/.

Hagopian, John V. "Decoding 'Signs and Symbols.'" In *Anatomy of a Short Story: Nabokov's Puzzles, Codes, "Signs and Symbols,"* edited by Yuri Leving, 298–303. New York: Continuum, 2012.

Lalo, Alexei. "Nabokov's *Lolita* and Its Precursors." In *Libertinage in Russian Culture*, 219–251. Boston: Brill, 2011.

Lindenmeyer, Antje. "'Lesbian Appetites': Food, Sexuality and Community in Feminist Autobiography." *Sexualities* 9, no. 4 (2006): 469–485.

Naiman, Eric. "Lynchers at Heart: De-ciphering 'Signs and Symbols.'" *Nabokov Studies* 17 (2020–2021): 97–113.

Siefried, Thomas. "Nina's Endings: Some Subtexts of Nabokov's 'Spring in Fialta.'" *Nabokov Online Journal* 14 (2020): 1–29.

Shahani, Gitanjali G. Introduction to *Food and Literature*, edited by Gitanjali G. Shahani, 1–33. New York: Cambridge University Press, 2018.

Shrayer, Maxim D. "Jewish Questions in Nabokov's Art and Life." In *Nabokov and His Fiction: New Perspectives*, edited by Julian W. Connolly, 73–91. New York: Cambridge University Press, 1999.

———. "Nabokov's Sexography." *Russian Literature* 48 (2000): 495–516.

———. *The World of Nabokov's Stories.* Austin: Unversity of Texas Press, 1999.

Trzeciak, Joanna. "The Last Jar." In *Anatomy of a Short Story: Nabokov's Puzzles, Codes, "Signs and Symbols,"* edited by Yuri Leving, 143. New York: Continuum, 2012.

Negotiating Nabokov within America's Political and Social Context

Samuel Peterson

> I will contend until I am shot that art as soon as it is brought into
> contact with politics inevitably sinks to the level of any ideological trash.
> —Vladimir Nabokov, "Spring in Fialta" (1936)[1]

Introduction: The American Nabokov

After nearly two decades of living in the United States, Vladimir and Véra
Nabokov moved back to Europe, and eventually settled in Montreux, Switzerland
in 1961.[2] During a 1967 interview, Nabokov famously told Herbert Gold: "I
am as American as April in Arizona."[3] In this essay about Nabokov's American
experience, I explore the tensions between his émigré routes and his uniquely
American literary output. I will examine how Nabokov interacted within his
adoptive society, both in the political and social realms, and how those interactions manifested in his work of the American and Swiss years. Nabokov's
engagement with antisemitism, racial prejudice, and Cold War-era political

---

1   Vladimir Nabokov, "Spring in Fialta," trans. Peter A. Pertzoff and Vladimir Nabokov, in
    The Stories of Vladimir Nabokov, [ed. Dmitri Nabokov] (New York: Vintage International,
    2008), 427.
2   Brian Boyd, "Chronology of Nabokov's Life and Main Works," *Nabokovian*, last modified
    2018, accessed April 1, 2023, https://thenabokovian.org/chronology.
3   Herbert Gold, "The Artist in Pursuit of Butterflies" [*Saturday Evening Post*, 1967], in
    Conversations with Vladimir Nabokov, ed. Robert Golla (Jackson: University Press of
    Mississippi, 2017), 110–119.

conversations around communism were particularly important in shaping his perspective on the United States, and thus, his writing.

Nabokov Writes about Antisemitism and Racism in America

By the time Nabokov arrived on American shores in May of 1940, he was no stranger to Jews or the experience of antisemitism.[4] During his childhood, he "attended the cosmopolitan Tenishev School, where two of his close friends were Jewish." Nabokov's father, Vladimir Dmitrievich Nabokov, "was an out-spoken opponent of antisemitism in pre-1917 Russia."[5] In 1925, Nabokov married Véra Slonim, a Jewish woman who was very proud of her ancestors and did not convert to Christianity. After their union, in the words of Maxim D. Shrayer, "opposition to antisemitism became a leitmotif of Nabokov's living."[6]

Nabokov's acclimation to American society owed itself in part to his relationship with Edmund Wilson, a leading literary critic who helped Nabokov gain a foothold in prominent American journals and publishing houses.[7] They met on October 9, 1940. Within a few months they had become friends even despite vast political and social differences, and by April 9, 1941, Nabokov began to address Wilson as "Bunny" in their personal correspondence.[8] Eventually, Wilson became Nabokov's closest American literary friend, in no small part because Wilson was not openly antisemitic at a time when, in Robert Roper's words, "prominent English-language authors—[T. S.] Eliot, [Ezra] Pound, [Ernest] Hemingway, [F. Scott] Fitzgerald, many others—signaled a sham gentility by disdaining Jews."[9]

In 1942, having not yet received a renewal offer to teach at Wellesley College, Nabokov undertook a whistle-stop tour of the South, lecturing mainly on Russian literature.[10] This tour, Nabokov's first trip below the Mason-Dixon line, was a watershed moment for his understanding of his new country's deeply

---

4   Boyd, "Chronology."
5   Maxim D. Shrayer, "Jewish Questions in Nabokov's Art and Life," in *Nabokov and His Fiction: New Perspectives*, ed. Julian W. Connolly (Cambridge: Cambridge University Press, 1999), 74–91.
6   Shrayer, "Jewish Questions."
7   Boyd, "Chronology."
8   Simon Karlinsky, ed., *Dear Bunny, Dear Volodya. The Nabokov-Wilson Letters: Correspondence between Vladimir Nabokov and Edmund Wilson 1940–1971* (New York: Harper and Row, 1979), 41.
9   Robert Roper, *Nabokov in America: On the Road to Lolita* (New York: Bloomsbury, 2015), 73.
10 Boyd, "Chronology."

rooted racial prejudices. Just as Nabokov was becoming aware of American anti-semitism—something he understood well in the European context, especially having lived in Nazi Berlin in 1933–1937—he was also introduced to deeply entrenched racism and racial segregation. The first and most thorough record of his interactions with systemic American racism comes from this journey across the Southern states.

While at Coker College for Women, a small, rural institution nestled in Hartsville, South Carolina, Nabokov wrote to his Jewish wife of his discontent upon hearing the white residents speak of the Black laborers who worked in their cotton fields: "It is picking time now—and the '*darkies*' (an expression that jars on me, reminding me [...] of the patriarchal 'Yid' of western Russian landown-ers) pick in the fields, getting a dollar for a hundred 'bushels'" of cotton."[11] That Nabokov says the slur "stuck mechanically in [his] ears" illustrates that he could not help but make a connection between the habitual and institutional anti-semitism in czarist Russia and what he now observed in the American South.[12] Beyond the legally disenfranchised Jews and the Pale of Settlement, Nabokov's only measuring stick for such language was the Russian peasants who had been enslaved serfs until 1861, in a parallel to American slaves.[13] That these observa-tions come at Coker College for Women is notable because it shows Nabokov engaging with the historical racism of the United States. The man whose name Coker College for Women (now Coker University) still bears today is Major James Lide Coker.[14] However, Coker was not an officer in the American armed forces—he served as the captain of the Ninth South Carolina Regiment in the Confederate Army, before he was injured by a cannonball, became a Union pris-oner of war, and returned to the South, where he was readily elected to state government and given the honorary title of major.[15] Coker's history, one defined by the legacy of slavery, is not explicitly elucidated in Nabokov's letters, but the

11 To Véra Nabokov, October 2–3, 1942, in Vladimir Nabokov, *Letters to Véra*, ed. and trans. Olga Voronina and Brian Boyd (New York: Vintage International, 2017), 465.
12 To Véra Nabokov, October 2–3, 1942, in Nabokov, *Letters to Véra*, 465.
13 Roper, *Nabokov in America*, 90; For details about the emancipation of the serfs in the Russian Empire, see: "Emancipation Manifesto," *Encyclopedia Britannica*, last modified February 24 2023, accessed May 11, 2023, https://www.britannica.com/event/Emancipation-Manifesto.
14 "Presidential Prospectus," Coker University, accessed November 15, 2023, https://www.coker.edu/wp-content/uploads/PresidentialProspectus/CokerUniversity_PresidentialProspectus.pdf.
15 Susan Asbury and Ryan Semmes, "James Lide Coker Papers: Biographical Sketch," University of South Carolina, accessed November 15, 2023, https://archives.library.sc.edu/repositories/3/resources/40.

historical significance of the school is critical in contextualizing the entrenched forces of prejudice that he encountered on his tour.

Nabokov had other eye-opening experiences during his travels. For instance, he learned why most Southern couples with children rarely went out in the evenings, even if they could afford it. Here Nabokov reports his observations to Véra on October 2–3, 1942. "They have no one to leave the kids with—Negro servants never sleep over in the whites' homes—it is not allowed—and they cannot have white servants because they cannot work with blacks."[16] During his tour, Nabokov also spoke at Spelman College, an historically Black, women's school in Atlanta, Georgia. In his biography, Brian Boyd remarks that Nabokov had been "depressed by the Uncle Tomism he had already witnessed in the [South]."[17] When he arrived at Spelman, Nabokov was "delighted" to spend time at a school he regarded as a "black Wellesley."[18] While lecturing on Pushkin, Nabokov emphasized the great poet's African roots, which at the time were believed to be Abyssinian. Nowadays, it is accepted that Pushkin's ancestor, Abram (Abraham) Petrovich Hannibal, originally came from Central Africa.[19] Nabokov stated that "Pushkin provides a most striking example of mankind at its very best when human races are able to freely mix."[20] In quite a contrast to his takeaways from Coker College for Women, Nabokov told his wife, with whom he did not have to pretend or be politically correct, that this lecture "was greeted with almost comical enthusiasm."[21]

Spelman's president Florence Matilda Read became a friend of the Nabokov family.[22] During the visit, Nabokov breakfasted with Read every morning, their meals punctuated "with conversations about the Negro problem and telepathy."[23] In the evenings, she would invite "various leading Negro figures" to come to dinner, as Nabokov described the meals to Véra on October 11, 1942. Robert Roper notes that these meetings were with "iconic African Americans,

16 To Véra Nabokov, October 2–3, 1942, in Nabokov, *Letters to Véra*, 467.
17 Brian Boyd, *Vladimir Nabokov: The American Years* (Princeton, NJ: Princeton University Press, 1991), 35–57.
18 Boyd, *Vladimir Nabokov: The American Years*, 35–57; To Véra Nabokov, October 7, 1942, in Nabokov, *Letters to Véra*, 469.
19 Lilian Thuram, Bernard Fillaire, Laurent Dubois, Charles Forsdic, and Aedín Ní Loingsigh, "General-in-Chief of the Russian Imperial Army: Abraham Petrovich Hannibal 1696–14 May 1781," in *My Black Stars: From Lucy to Barack Obama*, ed. David Murphy (Liverpool: Liverpool University Press, 2021), 34–36, accessed November 15, 2023, https://www.jstor.org/stable/j.ctv1pfqnct?turn_away=true.
20 Boyd, *Vladimir Nabokov: The American Years*, 35–57.
21 To Véra Nabokov, October 11, 1942, in Nabokov, *Letters to Véra*, 470.
22 Boyd, *Vladimir Nabokov: The American Years*, 35–57.
23 To Véra Nabokov, October 11, 1942, in Nabokov, *Letters to Véra*, 471.

among them W. E. B Du Bois."[24] These experiences in the South were formative in shaping Nabokov's view of racial relations in America, and they solidified in him what Roper describes as a "disgust" for segregation.[25]

On November 24, 1942, soon after returning to the Boston area, Nabokov wrote an extraordinary letter to Wilson. It features six paragraph-length vignettes of American life that he "collected during [his] tour."[26] This letter is one of the first distinct examples of Nabokov's interactions with his adoptive country's sociopolitical problems, and to some degree, also one of his first forays into American political satire. The letter's sixth paragraph—sixth slice of life—details the following encounter on the train:

> Old man in the "lounge" (really, lavatory) of the Pullman [. . .].
> Horrible eyes, black fingernails. Somehow reminded me of the
> militant type of Russian "chernosotenetz." And as if in answer
> to my passing thought he started on a wild attack against Jews.
> "They and their pissing children," he said. Then he spat into the
> wash basin and missed by several inches.[27]

Nabokov, whose father was a leading liberal politician in prerevolutionary Russia, likens the American "militant type" to a member of the "Black Hundreds," a vile, antisemitic organization.[28] Despite being an immigrant of less than three years, Nabokov had internalized that antisemitism and antisemitic attitudes were commonplace in the United States; the old man had such gall that he voiced his hatred in a public space.

In these early reflections on antisemitic attitudes in the United States, Nabokov cannot help but relate his experiences here to his prerevolutionary Russian and interwar émigré past. He is still seeing American worlds through the eyes of an expatriate. This comes across in the allusion he plants—both in his letter to Wilson and in the letter to his wife with its poignant reflections on Coker College for Women. As Nabokov describes the American bigot, he characterizes the repugnant old man he observed on the train as a boor. While Nabokov disdained those who held antisemitic views, in the letter he wondered whether it was a symptom of poor education, poor morals, or both.

---

24 Ibid.; Roper, *Nabokov in America*, 90.
25 Roper, *Nabokov in America*, 90.
26 Karlinsky, *The Nabokov-Wilson Letters*, 87.
27 Ibid., 88.
28 Ibid., 98n3.

In three of the letter's six shorts, Nabokov discusses race. The letter to Wilson offers a window into the way travel across America, especially in the segregated South, contributed to Nabokov's understanding of racial prejudice. In the third short, Nabokov mentions W. E. B. Du Bois: "[c]elebrated Negro scholar and organizer [. . .] brilliant talker with an old-world touch. *Très gentilhomme.*"[29] In the fifth we meet "Big heavy man, College President. [. . .] Talked very entertainingly about his grandfather, a Confederate hero. [. . .] Otherwise a most tremendous gentleman as egocentrical as I."[30] And in the fourth Nabokov offers a little more detail about "[m]an in shirtsleeves at my hotel. [. . .] Began telling me, with copious details, all about his sugar business in Florida, his reasons of coming to Valdosta (to hire colored labor) and lots of extravagant particularities about his factory."[31] Nabokov's letter travels the spectrum of racial relations. He demonstrates the knowledge he has gained about the exploitative economic conditions that many Black people faced during the Jim Crow era, but he also alludes to interactions with white southerners who were proud of their Confederate roots. This catalogue of human experience that Nabokov dispatched to Wilson, at the time his principal American interlocutor, helps us understand how strongly Nabokov felt about the societal injustices he witnessed in his travels. Moreover, Nabokov's epistolary reports from the South—both to his Jewish wife and to his Christian white literary colleague—highlight the intertwined nature of racism and antisemitism that was on display during Nabokov's early exploration of America.

Nabokov's first lengthy reflection on antisemitism appears in one of his finest American short stories "Conversation Piece, 1945." Published in the *New Yorker* as "Double Talk" on June 23, 1945 and later renamed, this story is ripe for interpretation.[32] As Nabokov's first story to appear in the *New Yorker*, it was also one of his first longform texts read by a wide American audience. While Nabokov had previously published poetry in the magazine, a full-length story represents a different level of engagement with the American readership. Amid his lecture tour in the South, Nabokov wrote to his wife that "a great many of the people have read my little pieces in the *Atlantic* and the *New Yorker*—and in general the atmosphere here is the same middle-brow one as at Wellesley,"[33] That is to say,

---

29   Ibid., 88.
30   Ibid.
31   Ibid.
32   "Nabokov Under Glass: American Stories," New York Public Library, accessed November 15, 2023, http://web-static.nypl.org/exhibitions/nabokov/amer.htm.
33   To Véra Nabokov, October 2–3, 1942, in Nabokov, *Letters to Véra*, 466.

many of the people whose antisemitism and racism were on full display during his travels were a part of his audience and intended targets of the story's verdict.

Upon the story's acceptance in April 1945, Nabokov received $817.50 for it (the 2023 equivalent of nearly fourteen thousand dollars), the highest sum for any short story in his career.[34] As Shrayer observes: "this is one of the earliest statements on the Holocaust in all of American fiction."[35] The story was written and printed just as the American public was becoming informed of the atrocities committed by the Nazis and their accomplices during the Shoah (Holocaust). Although there had been news accounts of Nazi death and concentration camps, especially starting in the summer of 1944, it was not until May 1945 that *Life* magazine photojournalists "shocked and horrified the American public" with their images from the Buchenwald, Dachau, and Bergen-Belsen concentration camps, liberated, respectively, by American, British, and Canadian troops.[36] While the *New Yorker* story came before the widely covered liberation of Nazi camps by Allied troops, it postdates the liberation of Nazi death camps in Poland by Soviet troops in 1944 and early 1945. By the time the story appeared, its American audience certainly had some knowledge of the genocide of European Jewry committed by the Nazis.

In "Conversation Piece, 1945," we not only get fuller access to Nabokov's true feelings about American antisemitism than in his epistolary reflections of the early 1940s, but we also encounter a more insidious type of upper-class white Anglo-Saxon Protestant antisemitism. At the center of the story is a "dinner party" that showcases members of intellectual and academic circles in Cambridge, Massachusetts. Unlike Nabokov's reflections on the American South, this story operates within the world that Nabokov knew best, among the people he regularly encountered as a professor and author living in the Northeast. In this pointed commentary on his New England neighbors and colleagues (and, by extension, many members of his literary audience), Nabokov is not only writing as a White Russian émigré but also speaking from the perch of a politically conscious American.

34   Boyd, "Chronology." For an inflation calculator, see "CPI Inflation Calculator," US Bureau of Labor Statistics, accessed April 25, 2023, https://www.bls.gov/data/inflation_calculator.htm.
35   Shrayer, "Jewish Questions."
36   Maxim D. Shrayer, "Raisa Blokh as an Historical, Literary and Emotional Source for Nabokov's *Pnin*," in *Skreshcheniia sudeb. Literarische und kulturelle Beziehungen zwischen Russland und dem Westen. A Festschrift for Fedor B. Poljakov*, ed. Lazar Fleishman, Stefan Michael Newerkla, and Michael Wachtel, *Stanford Slavic Studies* 49 (2019): 619–656. For greater historical context of the period, see "The United States and the Holocaust 1942–45," Holocaust Encyclopedia (United States Holocaust Memorial Museum, Washington, DC), last modified March 30, 2023, accessed October 9, 2023, https://encyclopedia.ushmm.org/content/en/article/the-united-states-and-the-holocaust-1942–45.

The first-person narrator begins his tale, and reveals the subject matter at hand, by recalling a story about a Russian library in interwar Prague demanding he return the copy of *Protocols of the Wise Men of Zion* he had borrowed. This is the infamous antisemitic screed that had been "wistfully appreciated by the Tsar," and the same text that Nabokov's Russian émigré roommate at Cambridge once tried to "foist upon him."[37] The story flashes through several memories in Europe before pivoting to the United States. Much like Nabokov, the authorial narrator settles in the Boston area after arriving in America. The narrator receives a surprise phone call from a Mrs. Sybil Hall, inviting him to a gathering at her fancy Cambridge apartment. The narrator walks into a "bourgeois salon" of about a dozen people, where he is introduced to "the guest of honor," "a professor of German, or music, or both, somewhere in the Middle West."[38] The narrator assigns the German expatriate a rather comical, probably Americanized last name: Shoe. (Could it have once been Schuh?) Very quickly, it becomes apparent that the narrator has stumbled—through a case of mistaken identity—into a room of Nazi sympathizers. Dr. Shoe, self-described as being "of pure Bavarian stock, though a loyal citizen of this country," is the center of attention when he deliberately and eloquently makes his remarks:

> "And that was Adolf Hitler's mistake. Being mad, he failed to take into account the scheming of irresponsible politicians. Being mad, he believed that other governments would act in accordance with the principles of mercy and common sense."
>
> "I always think of Prometheus, said Mrs. Hall. "Prometheus who stole fire and was blinded by the angry gods."
>
> [...] Dr. Shoe lowered his eyelids for a moment. "The answer is a terrible one," he said with an effort [...]. "Germans"—the soft-lashed eyes were half-closed again—"Germans are dreamers."[39]

By now the narrator, surrounded by American Germanophiles, has realized that he is in a "nightmare"; he is stunned that what he is witnessing is "not a Punch-and-Judy show."[40] However, before he can extricate himself from this performance of Holocaust-denial, the dialogue takes an even darker turn. "The

---

37 Vladimir Nabokov, "Conversation Piece, 1945," in *The Stories of Vladimir Nabokov*, 587; Shrayer, "Jewish Questions," 75.
38 Nabokov, "Conversation Piece, 1945," 588–589.
39 Ibid., 588–590.
40 Ibid.

tragedy of Germany [. . .] is also the tragedy of cultured America," Dr. Shoe
tells the room, as they bemoan the destruction of cultural sites such as the city
of Dresden. To Dr. Shoe's grateful American audience, it is inconceivable that
Germans would do anything as heinous as destroy a "sacred historical" land-
mark.[41] The final salvo in this barrage comes when the room, led by Dr. Shoe,
collectively rejects the report about the annihilation of Jews, which has already
reached American shores. It is important, Dr. Shoe professes, that his audience
know that "propaganda, exaggeration, faked photographs, and so on are the
tools of modern war" and "the workings of the vivid Semitic imagination which
controls the American press."[42] After finishing his diatribe, Dr. Shoe ends on an
invocation: "Let the phoenix of Europe spread its eagle wings again, and God
bless America. [. . .] First of all, I will play the 'Star Spangled Banner.'"[43]

In this text, Nabokov registers his understanding of the insidious antisemitism
within America's privileged, white Protestant class. Unlike the raving old man in
the bathroom of the train car, at the Cambridge party Nabokov's authorial representative observes a shockingly and absurdly different scene. In a room of the
literate and the wealthy, antisemitic prejudice was just as prevalent, and perhaps
more toxic because of its veneer of cultural sophistication. Nabokov rejected the
majority of the edits that the New Yorker staff brought to him, reminding his edi-
tors that "the average reader does not read" the publication and stating that he
had "gone as far as my conscience permits in accepting alterations."[44] Nabokov
tailored this story to the comfortably established American intelligentsia, exactly
the kind of people he dealt with on a regular basis, including Edmund Wilson
himself. In all likelihood, the characters in the story are the types who read the
New Yorker, something Nabokov's comments suggest between the lines. In his
short story debut in the magazine, Nabokov taps into a distinct, and not all
together hidden, current within the American sociopolitical fabric.

Throughout the 1940s and 1950s, Vladimir, Véra, and Dmitri Nabokov
encountered many expressions, both subtle and explicit, of antisemitism.[45]
It was an ambient characteristic of their social environment, and it informs
Nabokov's principal American novels of the 1950s Pnin and Lolita. In both
works, we can see references to the Nabokovs' lived experiences, from the cam-
puses to the roadway motels, and both works are compilations, in a sense, of

41   Ibid., 591.
42   Ibid.
43   Ibid., 594–595.
44   Boyd, Vladimir Nabokov: The American Years, 77–92.
45   Ibid.; Shrayer, "Jewish Questions"; Shrayer, "Raisa Blokh."

his political reality. Partly serialized in the *New Yorker* in 1953–1955 prior to its book publication in 1957, *Pnin* includes a scene reminiscent of the gathering depicted in "Conversation Piece, 1945."[46] At a college party Dr. Hagen, chair of the German Department at Waindell College, where Nabokov's émigré protagonist Pnin teaches, tells "grinning Thomas the latest story about Mrs. Idelson," a woman with a distinctly Jewish last name.[47] When Pnin hears the story, he makes a "disgusted" gesture and remarks, "I have heard quite the same anecdote thirty-five years ago in Odessa, and even then I could not understand what is comical in it."[48] The antisemitism in this instance is veiled, perhaps genteel, but it is certainly there. Commenting on the scene, Nabokov told Katherine White, his editor at the *New Yorker*, that "the Idelsons had not come [to the party] because they discovered the Hagens had been invited too."[49] However "faint," in Nabokov's own words, the scene captures the habitual prejudice of the world of private American colleges and universities, where Jewish students and Jewish professors alike felt unwelcome.[50] This episode is also reminiscent of an event in Nabokov's own life. At a party he hosted while teaching at Cornell in the mid-1950s, Nabokov stood "stricken" after one of his guests defended an accused antisemite, protesting that the charges were false.[51] Nabokov pulled aside his Cornell colleague M. H. Abrams, a distinguished literary scholar and one of the first Jewish professors at an Ivy League university, and said of the other guest, "I am going to have to throw him out of my house."[52] Although Abrams calmed the situation, Nabokov remained "shocked by the casual anti[semitism] he found among his academic colleagues [and] remained hypersensitive to any hint of a slur."[53]

Beyond scenes of antisemitism, both from Americans and Russian émigrés, *Pnin* also represents what Shrayer describes as "the pinnacle of Nabokov's Jewish theme."[54] The presence of Mira Belochkin, Pnin's youthful love who was

---

46 "Nabokov Under Glass: *Pnin*. Garden City, New York, 1957," New York Public Library, accessed November 15, 2023, http://web-static.nypl.org/exhibitions/nabokov/pnin.htm; Boyd, "Chronology."

47 Nabokov, *Pnin* (New York: Vintage International, 1989), 160.

48 Ibid.

49 Boyd, *Vladimir Nabokov: The American Years*, 271–287.

50 Ibid.

51 Ibid., 288–317.

52 Daniel R. Schwarz, "Eating Kosher Ivy: Jews as Literary Intellectuals," *Shofar* 21, no. 3 (2003): 16–28, accessed October 2, 2023, http://www.jstor.org/stable/42943317; Boyd, *Vladimir Nabokov: The American Years*, 288–317.

53 Ibid.

54 Shrayer, "Jewish Questions."

murdered in the Shoah, is felt throughout the entire work, reaching a crescendo in Chapter 5. There, Pnin (and the reader) is transported to the overwhelming scene of Pnin's imagining—reconstructing—different scenarios of Mira's death:

> If one were quite sincere with oneself, no conscience, and hence no consciousness, could be expected to subsist in a world where such things as Mira's death were possible [. . .]. And since the exact form of her death had not been recorded, Mira kept dying a great number of deaths in one's mind, and undergoing a great number of resurrections, only to die again and again, led away by a trained nurse, inoculated with filth, tetanus bacilli, broken glass, gassed in a sham shower bath with prussic acid, burned alive in a pit on a gasoline-soaked pile of beechwood [...].[55]

Indeed, as Shrayer's research demonstrates, "[w]hen Nabokov worked on *Pnin*, the American-liberated Buchenwald played a role in the American popular imagination that was much greater" than its place on the map of the Shoah. While the camp Nabokov describes was a "composite" of a number of Nazi death and concentration camps, Nabokov's artistic decision for "Pnin's beloved Mira Belochkin to perish in Buchenwald [...] was a testament [...] to the American context of his novel."[56]

Lolita's Lens

In *Lolita* (1955; British and American first editions 1958), as in *Pnin*, we are able to see the connective tissue between Nabokov's own experiences and the Middle America on display. When Humbert Humbert first tries to check into The Enchanted Hunters Hotel, he is informed there are no rooms available.[57] In reply, Humbert "coldly" tells the receptionist that his name "is not Humberg."[58] After the suspicion of his Jewish origin is dispelled, a room miraculously becomes free. Later, it is revealed that in The Enchanted Hunters' advertising material, the

---

55 Nabokov, *Pnin*, 135–136.
56 See Shrayer, "Raisa Blokh."
57 Vladimir Nabokov, *Lolita* (New York: Vintage International, 1997), 118.
58 Ibid.

dog-whistle "near churches" is featured, something that Boyd characterizes as "a discreet code in mid-century America that only Gentiles were welcome."[59]

Stacey Schiff, author of Véra Nabokov's biography, also stresses that "since the arrival in America, [Vladimir Nabokov] had been fascinated by the hotels that advertised 'restricted colonies' or 'exclusive clientele' in the pages of *The New Yorker*."[60] In *Lolita* more so than in *Pnin*, examples of run-of-the-mill antisemitism punctuate the American reality of socially acceptable prejudice, which Nabokov experienced personally alongside his family. Schiff contends that antisemitism was "a prejudice to which [Vladimir] was more sensitive than his wife."[61]

In *Lolita*, American antisemitism and racism work in tandem. Prior to the death of Charlotte Haze, she and Humbert Humbert regularly go to Hourglass Lake during their shared July. En route to one of their near-daily swims, "Charlotte remarked that Jean Farlow [...] had seen Leslie taking a dip 'in the ebony' (as John had quipped) at five o'clock in the morning last Sunday [...] He is subnormal, you see."[62] John Farlow's racist joke is yet another normative element of the American political landscape that Nabokov is living in and recreating in his texts. In analyzing this scene, Steven Belletto observes that a standard, suburban day is "characterized by casual racist quips and middlebrow aesthetics."[63]

Just as anti-Black racism and antisemitism were linked in Nabokov's understanding of America so were other forms of bigotry and intolerance, particularly anti-immigrant rhetoric. In the English-language *Lolita*, those sentiments are explicitly against Italian Americans. When discussing the school and community of Ramsdale, John Farlow offers the following criticism: "'Of course, too many of the tradespeople here are Italians,' said John, 'but on the other hand we are still spared—'I wish,' Jean [interrupted] with a laugh."[64] Spared whom, the reader wonders? Jews most immediately, given the small-town New England context, but also Black people in the big picture, all-American sense. In the Russian-language edition of the text, there no ambiguity with this em-dash. The phrase stops with "... and Yi—."[65] In this American instance, Jews and Italians are

---

59 Ibid. 261; Brian Boyd, *Vladimir Nabokov: The American Years*, 227–254.

60 Stacy Schiff, *Véra (Mrs. Vladimir Nabokov)* (New York: The Modern Library, 1999), 134.

61 Ibid.

62 Nabokov, *Lolita*, 82.

63 Stephen Belletto, "Of Pickaninnies and Nymphets: Race in *Lolita*," *Nabokov Studies* 9 (2005): 1–17, accessed May 10, 2023, https://sites.lafayette.edu/belletts/files/2010/06/9.1belletto.pdf.

64 Nabokov, *Lolita*, 79.

65 I thank Professor Maxim D. Shrayer for this comment.

bunched together, with Jews as a greater corrosive agent on the community. Jean Farlow quickly interrupts her husband because they are not sure how exactly Humbert Humbert identifies himself. He is a European immigrant; in her mind, Humbert Humbert could be a Jew or partially Jewish.[66]

Let us return to The Enchanted Hunters, which allegorizes American middle-class culture of the late 1940s and early 1950s. When Humbert Humbert and Lolita exit the car, he describes "a hunchbacked and hoary Negro [. . . who] took our bags."[67] After Humbert clarifies the spelling of his name, and is granted a room for the night, the room key is "handed over to Uncle Tom" and a "handsome young Negress slipped open the elevator door," leading to the room.[68] When it is time for Humbert Humbert to tip the bellman, he considers placing a "five-dollar bill in that sepia palm, but thought the largesse might be misconstrued."[69] He instead gives the man fifty cents. When reading Lolita, it is important to be very precise about the audience Humbert Humbert prepares to address in a court of law—a white middle-class audience of small-town New Englanders. Belletto argues that in this scene, "Humbert has positioned himself as discriminator rather than discriminatee" with his pejorative use of the phrase "Uncle Tom" along with his dehumanization of the man to a "synecdochic wanting black hand."[70] In a short essay titled "On a Book Entitled Lolita," which became the novel's afterword, Nabokov explains why the American publishing community avoided his book to such a degree that he had to find a firm in Europe:

> Their refusal to buy the book was based not on my treatment of the theme but on the theme itself, for there are at least three themes which are utterly taboo as far as most American publishers are concerned. The other two are: a Negro-White marriage which is a complete and glorious success resulting in lots of children and grandchildren; and the total atheist who lives a happy and useful life, and dies in his sleep at the age of 106.[71]

66 Many have speculated to this point. See Mark Ford, "Is Humbert Humbert Jewish?" New York Review of Books, June 6, 2013, accessed November 15, 2023, https://www.nybooks.com/articles/2013/06/06/is-humbert-humbert-jewish/.
67 Nabokov, Lolita, 117.
68 Ibid., 118–119.
69 Ibid., 119.
70 Belletto, "Race in Lolita," 1–17.
71 Vladimir Nabokov, "On a Book Entitled Lolita" [1956], in Lolita (New York: Vintage International, 1997), 311–317.

All three of these themes are representative of suburban attitudes and the pulse of the American body politic in the America that Nabokov now considered his home. It is noteworthy, though, that Nabokov chose to wade into these troubled waters, particularly with regard to questions of race. In closing his most controversial work with a potentially inflammatory statement against racism— over a decade before interracial marriage was legalized nationwide—Nabokov reaffirmed his belief in racial equality and civil rights.[72]

Vestiges of Racism in Pale Fire

In *Pale Fire*, Nabokov's postmodernist masterpiece, published in 1962, at the tail end of his American years, at least two moments in the poetry of John Shade are coded within the language of civil rights. In one of the final stanzas of the long poem also titled *Pale Fire*, near the conclusion of the fourth canto, Shade writes: "now I shall speak of evil as none has / Spoke before. I loathe such things as jazz; / The white hosed moron torturing a black / Bull, rayed with red; abstractist bric-a-brac."[73] Is it possible that in these lines, in which Shade details evil, he is channeling some of his creator's own likes and dislikes? Boyd wondered the same thing, contending that "Nabokov's feelings for Russia are plainly—albeit enchantedly—reflected" in the text.[74] However, it is also true that Nabokov's feelings about America are hardwired into *Pale Fire*. In 1962 Nabokov conceded that while Shade "does borrow some of my own opinions," a reader would be a "clown" to ascribe all of Shade's traits to those belonging to his creator.[75]

Today's reader would be likely to discern two meanings in the clause "[. . .] the white hosed moron torturing a black / Bull [. . .]." The first reading would take stock of Nabokov's own distaste for bullfighting.[76] However, today's reader is also likely to garner a second meaning in this enjambment: "The white hosed moron torturing a black." In the context of the 1960s, this line conjures up the

---

72 Loving v. Virginia, which legalized interracial marriage, was decided on June 12, 1967. For details, see: "Loving v. Virginia 1967," Oyez, accessed May 11, 2023, https://www.oyez.org/cases/1966/395.

73 Vladimir Nabokov, *Pale Fire* (New York: Vintage International, 1989), 67.

74 Boyd, *Vladimir Nabokov: The American Years*, 425–456.

75 Peter Duval Smith, "Vladimir Nabokov on His Life and Work" [for the *Listener*, 1962], in *Conversations with Vladimir Nabokov*, 62–69.

76 See Vladimir Nabokov, *Speak, Memory: An Autobiography Revisited* (New York: Vintage International, 1989), 256, where Nabokov refers to his brother Kirill, who "loathed, as much as I do, bullfighting."

famous images of firefighters in Birmingham, Alabama training their hoses on peaceful Black demonstrators during the protests in May 1963.[77]

Figure 1. White firefighters disperse protestors and onlookers with fire hoses, Chattanooga, Tennessee, February 1960. Chattanooga History Center.

Yet, there is a slight problem with this logic: for all his linguistic wizardry and historical foresight, Nabokov was not capable of knowing the future. The famous, nationally covered fire-hose violence took place in 1963, one year after the publication of *Pale Fire*. However, it is possible, and even likely, that Nabokov was referencing fire-hose-based crowd dispersal techniques, which had been employed in 1960 when Black high schoolers sought to desegregate the lunch counters in Chattanooga, Tennessee.[78] While the enduring images of the

---

77 For an image, see Charles Moore, "Alabama Fire Department Aims High-Pressure Water Hoses at Civil Rights Demonstrators," *Smithsonian*, May 1963, accessed May 9, 2023, https://nmaahc.si.edu/object/nmaahc_2011.49.1.

78 For reference and photos of the 1960 Chattanooga sit-ins, see Alex Q. Arbuckle, "February 1960 Chattanooga sit-ins," Mashable, accessed November 16, 2023, https://mashable.com/feature/chattanooga-sit-ins; "February 1960: The Beginning of the End of Segregation," Chattanooga History, accessed June 5, 2023, https://chattanoogahistory.com/february1960.php.

fire-hosed Black protestors come from Alabama, the incidents in Chattanooga in 1960 were reported when they occurred. Considering Nabokov's recorded opinions about segregation, it is possible that he inscribed into the text of *Pale Fire* something he had seen or heard in the news.

Another layer to this charged sentence is the standalone word "Bull." There is reason to believe that in the context of the civil rights movement, Nabokov was referring to Bull Connor, the segregationist leader from Birmingham, Alabama. Connor served as the commissioner of public safety in Birmingham for twenty-two years.[79] During Bull Connor's tenure in city government, his violent responses to civil rights demonstrations, which featured the aforementioned firehoses and ferocious dogs, became infamous and helped to put the civil rights movement on the national stage.[80]

Equally ponderous is a couplet from Canto One which initially strikes the reader as a simple pun. "A curio: *Red Sox Beat Yanks 5–4 / On Chapman's Homer*, thumbtacked to the door."[81] In Major League Baseball, there was indeed once a baseball player named Chapman whose home run defeated the Yankees. At a secondary level, Nabokov has also managed to work in a reference to the poem "On First Looking into Chapman's Homer," by John Keats. Kinbote says as much in his commentary on this line.[82] Boyd notes that Kinbote knows "too little about obvious Americana to understand the joke" about baseball, as in the commentary it is referred to as one of the text's "misprints."[83] But there does appear to be another dimension here, one that is too fortuitously coincidental to write off. While in *Nabokov's Dark Cinema*, Alfred Appel Jr. claims that the sports headline was "unearthed by Nabokov in the stacks of a Cornell library," an analysis by the *Los Angeles Times* concludes that there is no chance this was a real headline from a real game.[84] Yet the line refers to a real-life ballplayer, Ben Chapman, whom Nabokov could have come across in a headline. While it has been established that

79 "Connor, Theopilus Eugene 'Bull,'" The Martin Luther King, Jr. Research and Education Institute, Stanford University, accessed November 12, 2023, https://kinginstitute.stanford.edu/connor-theophilus-eugene-bull.

80 "Connor, Theopilus Eugene 'Bull'"

81 Nabokov, *Pale Fire*, 36.

82 Ibid., 116.

83 Boyd, *Vladimir Nabokov: The American Years*, 425–456; Nabokov, *Pale Fire*, 116.

84 Alfred Appel Jr., *Nabokov's Dark Cinema*, (New York: Oxford University Press, 1974), 30; Brian Croning, "Sports Legend Revealed: Did Vladimir Nabokov Work an Actual Baseball Headline into His Novel 'Pale Fire'?" *Los Angeles Times*, February 16, 2011, accessed May 11, 2023, https://www.latimes.com/archives/blogs/sports-now/story/2011-02-16/sports-legend-revealed-did-vladimir-nabokov-work-an-actual-baseball-headline-into-his-novel-pale-fire.

Nabokov was not a fan of popular American sports—even though he was once followed around by a *Sports Illustrated* reporter, "baseball [...] meant nothing to him"—we also know that Nabokov was meticulous with his details. Additionally, Nabokov's son Dmitri Nabokov was a passionate athlete and, as a teenager growing up in New England and upstate New York, played different sports.[85]

Ben Chapman was not a random player on a random Red Sox roster. He is notorious as being "the most bigoted man in baseball."[86] Chapman was the manager of the Philadelphia Phillies when Jackie Robinson broke the Major League Baseball color barrier in 1947, and he is remembered for having "ordered his players to harass Robinson with a barrage of racial insults so venomous that [Robinson] came close to a nervous breakdown."[87] Chapman's vitriol was so extreme it helped unite the Brooklyn Dodgers, and even the broader baseball world, around Robinson. Jonathan Eig, a biographer of Jackie Robinson, told the *New York Times* that Chapman's behavior "was the first time a lot of white people and white reporters in particular noticed the abuse Robinson was taking."[88] Moreover, before the integration of baseball, when he was an all-star player, Chapman's violently antisemitic attitude was also well documented. He often launched antisemitic insults against Jewish fans, and as legend has it, "he nearly sparked a riot in 1933 when he slid into the Washington Senators' Jewish second baseman Buddy Myer" and reportedly "cut a swastika with his spikes on Myer's thigh."[89] When Nabokov's heightened attention to details is considered, it is unlikely that the invocation of this particularly polarizing player was gratuitous. Much like the racism and racial dynamics on display in *Lolita*, Chapman's inclusion gives further evidence of how Nabokov recorded his sociopolitical American environment on the printed page.

---

85   Boyd, *Vladimir Nabokov: The American Years*, 77–92; Boyd, *Vladimir Nabokov: The American Years*, 356–390.

86   See "The Most Bigoted Man in Baseball," *Sports History Weekly*, October 7, 2022, accessed May 11, 2023, https://www.sportshistoryweekly.com/stories/the-most-bigoted-man-in-baseball,1116 and Allen Barra, "What Really Happened to Ben Chapman, the Racist Baseball Player in 42?" *Atlantic*, April 15, 2013, accessed May 11, 2023, https://www.the-atlantic.com/entertainment/archive/2013/04/what-really-happened-to-ben-chapman-the-racist-baseball-player-in-i-42-i/274995/.

87   Stephen H. Norwood and Harold Brackman, "Going to Bat for Jackie Robinson: The Jewish Role in Breaking Baseball's Color Line," *Journal of Sport History* 26, no. 1 (1999): 115–41, accessed November 12, 2023, http://www.jstor.org/stable/43611720.

88   Marc Tracy, "69 Years Later, Philadelphia Apologizes to Jackie Robinson," *New York Times*, April 14, 2016, accessed July 28, 2023, https://www.nytimes.com/2016/04/15/sports/baseball/philadelphia-apologizes-to-jackie-robinson.html.

89   Norwood and Brackman, "Going to Bat for Jackie Robinson."

Nabokov and Cold War Politics

It would take an entire article—or book—to do justice to how the Cold War and the postwar Soviet Union fit into the paradigms of Vladimir Nabokov's engagement with and participation in the American political realm. What can be said with brevity, though, is that Nabokov's feelings about the Soviet Union are of particular importance not only because of his roots and staunch anti-Bolshevism, but also because they help to explain why he wanted to come across as a proud American.

While Vladimir Nabokov and Edmund Wilson enjoyed good interpersonal commerce, it is also true that there was an ocean of separation between their views on the Soviet Union and political philosophy. Stacy Schiff says it well: "Vladimir and Edmund Wilson fought like cocks on the subject."[90] Whereas Nabokov was outspokenly opposed to the Soviet Union on principled grounds, Wilson's *To The Finland Station* touts his Marxist interests and sympathy for the revolutionary cause. Wilson describes Lenin as one whose "ultimate aims were of course humanitarian, democratic, and anti-bureaucratic" but got overwhelmed by the practical realities of governance.[91] Wilson expresses his disappointment that Marxism has not been implemented in the correct way, concluding *To The Finland Station* by telling his readership that "to accomplish such a task [i.e. the creation of a Marxist system] will require of us an unsleeping adaptive exercise of reason and instinct combined."[92] It is this acknowledgment, that the Soviet Union was deeply flawed, that likely saved the friendship between the two writers. While at Wellesley, Nabokov did not keep quiet about his opinions on the Soviet Union. Prior to the USSR and the USA becoming allies, "Nabokov had publicly equated Nazi Germany and the Soviet Union."[93] Nabokov remained "unable to praise" the Soviet Union after the Anglo-Soviet Agreement was signed; but after Pearl Harbor, he was hard-pressed to deride the Soviet publicly.[94] In early February 1942, Nabokov addressed the Wellesley community, and offered the following remarks, which appeared in *Wellesley Magazine*:

> Democracy is humanity at its best, not because we happen to
> think that a republic is better than a king and a king is better than

---

90   Schiff, *Véra*, 131.
91   Edmund Wilson, *To the Finland Station: A Study in the Writing and Acting of History* (New York: Doubleday & Company, 1940), 480.
92   Ibid., 484.
93   Boyd, *Vladimir Nabokov: The American Years*, 35–57.
94   Ibid.

nothing and nothing is better than a dictator, but because it is the natural condition of every man ever since the human mind became conscious not only of the world but of itself. Morally, democracy is invincible.[95]

These words convey the sincerity with which Nabokov valued his freedom. In 1964, he summarized his world view, stating that since age nineteen, "[his] political outlook has remained as bleak and changeless as an old gray rock. It is classical to the point of triteness. Freedom of speech, freedom of thought, freedom of art. [...] No torture and no executions."[96] The desire for "freedom," the deep, visceral identification with that word, is one of the keys—rusty keys—to American politics. It has had an amorphous definition and has been appropriated by both sides of the political aisle.[97] Nabokov's identification with such tenets of democracy is more evidence of his status as an American, and if we take him at his word, and boil his politics down to a desire to be free, he is participating in a tradition shared by many millions in his adopted country—both those who had achieved it and who were striving for it.

Nabokov's urge for freedom—his urge to speak his truth—led to his eventual exit from Wellesley, where a high-ranking administrator told him to "tone down his classroom criticism of Soviet writers," remarking, as Nabokov recalled in 1971, "they are our allies you know."[98] Of all the writers that Nabokov interacted with in his various circles, Appel alleges that "only Robert Frost seemed to share his [highly negative] opinion of Communism."[99] While the academic arena in which Nabokov operated was left-leaning, it is also true that Nabokov's own opinions about the Cold War were quite extreme. In 1949, Nabokov wrote to Katherine White, wishing that it would be possible to "invade the Bears' territory at once" and advocating for "a preventative war against Russia before Stalin built up a nuclear arsenal and the power to destroy the world."[100] Famously, Vladimir

95 Quoted in ibid., 41; 679n19.
96 Alvin Toffler, "Playboy Interview: Vladimir Nabokov," *Playboy Magazine* (1964), in *Conversations with Vladimir Nabokov*, 70–89.
97 For a contemporary reflection, see Angela De Djin, "'Freedom' Means Something Different to Liberals and Conservatives. Here's How the Definition Split—And Why That Still Matters," *Time*, August 25, 2020, accessed May 11, 2023, https://time.com/5882978/freedom-definition-history/.
98 Alfred Appel Jr., "Nabokov: A Portrait," for the *Atlantic Monthly*, 1971, in *Conversations with Vladimir Nabokov*, 161–179.
99 Appel, "Nabokov: A Portrait," 161–179. *For a photo of the house the Nabokovs briefly rented from Frost in 1952, see Matthew Lyberg's photo essay in this volume (M. D. S.).*
100 Brian Boyd, *Vladimir Nabokov: The American Years*, 129–148.

and Véra Nabokov did not completely reject Senator Joseph McCarthy and his brand of politics as anti-democratic. In Boyd's analysis, while "they disapproved of McCarthy's random accusations and unscrupulous cross-examinations of alleged Communists, the Nabokovs believed many of his charges were correct, that there was serious Communist infiltration in high places in American officialdom."[101]

These political sentiments are not part of the central dynamic in *Lolita* or *Pnin*. Although *Lolita* does not have the Cold War at its epicenter, the scope of the narrative, 1947–1952, is notable. Douglas Anderson comments that the timeline matches up with eerie precision to the period of the most intense nuclear tests in the United States and Soviet Union. He observes that the Manhattan Project officially ended in 1947, just when the plot begins.[102] In 1949, after two years of Humbert Humbert's control of Lolita, everything falls apart. This, too, has a nuclear mirror according to Anderson:

> By 1949, when Humbert's monopolistic grip on Lolita's life came to an end—and when the United States too discovered, with the detection of atmospheric radiation from a Soviet atomic test, that it had been overtaken by its own Red Aztec convertible— this hopeful period was over. When the hydrogen bomb tests took place at Eniwetok in 1952, followed within months by a successful Soviet thermonuclear test, the critical variables of the post-war decades were established. What Humbert Humbert, referring to the death of Charlotte Haze, described as the "ulti- mate sunburst" had quite literally taken place.[103]

In this hidden meaning of the text, negatives of the Cold War era are developed and printed.

Soon after meeting the Haze family, Humbert Humbert witnesses Lolita argue with her mother about bedtime. Lolita's argument for why she ought to be allowed to stay awake is that "This is a free country."[104] The atmosphere of open- ness and freedom is palpable in the text, which is perhaps the greatest irony in this novel about child sexual abuse, as even the open expanse of the American West is turned into a veritable prison for Lolita. When Nabokov was writing

---

101 Ibid., 166–198.
102 Douglas Anderson, "Nabokov's Genocidal and Nuclear Holocausts in 'Lolita,'" *Mosaic: An Interdisciplinary Critical Journal* 29, no. 2 (1996): 73–90, accessed May 10, 2023, http:// www.jstor.org/stable/44029747.
103 Ibid., 88.
104 Nabokov, *Lolita*, 46.

Lolita, he undoubtedly heard about the political issue of building an interstate highway network. It was not until 1956 that President Dwight D. Eisenhower finally passed the National Interstate and Defense Highways Act, the then-largest infrastructure bill in American history.[105] This act is relevant because of that key word, "Defense," in its title. The bill was designed to build these roads, in part, to ensure that easy travel would be available in the case of a Soviet nuclear attack.[106] Those soon to be rebuilt and refurbished highways are the ones on which Humbert Humbert and Lolita drive for thousands of miles. Even if the Cold War rhetoric is below the asphalt, it is certainly present, as it was yet another feature of American life during this period.

In *Pale Fire*, a Cold War dimension is also at play. In terms of the more occluded connections to the Cold War, Belletto argues that Kinbote's homosexuality, something that is unlocked through the commentary, "makes him the object of persecution by a Cold War community that displaces a patriotism based on anti-communism with a patriotism based on something equally pernicious—homophobia."[107] Not all references are so theoretical. For instance, in the middle of Shade's poem, a couplet reads "Thunder above the Jungle. 'No, not that!' / Pat Pink, our guest (antiatomic chat)."[108] These dueling images allude to the Cold War. Was Nabokov invoking the earlier stages of the American involvement in Vietnam when he discussed "Thunder above the Jungle"? The "antiatomic chat" needs no explanation. What these two images offer is another reminder of how Nabokov intertwines the political with the ordinary; they are one and the same, as these topics were subjects of conversation in homes across America. These homes—the families and people created in Nabokov's fiction—are, for the most part, situated in the suburbs. They are the middle class. Outside of the world of fiction, these were people who were experiencing the greatest upward mobility, along with their country, in the postwar period, something equally reflected in *Pale Fire*. In his commentary, Kinbote remarks at an early juncture that "taxation had become a thing of beauty. The poor were getting a little richer and the rich a little poorer."[109] Nabokov was a participant in this model of optimism. Some

105 "National Interstate and Defense Highways Act (1956)," National Archives, last modified February 8, 2022, accessed May 8, 2023, https://www.archives.gov/milestone-documents/national-interstate-and-defense-highways-act/.

106 "Highways Act (1956)," National Archives, accessed September 12, 2024, https://www.archives.gov/milestone-documents/national-interstate-and-defense-highways-act.

107 Steven Belletto, "The Zemblan Who Came in from the Cold, or Nabokov's 'Pale Fire', Chance, and the Cold War," *ELH* 73, no. 3 (2006): 755–80, accessed May 10, 2023, http://www.jstor.org/stable/30030034.

108 Nabokov, *Pale Fire*, 49.

109 Ibid., 74.

three years after *Pale Fire*'s publication, when President Lyndon B. Johnson had his gallbladder removed in 1965, Nabokov sent the president a telegram in which he wished him a "'speedy return to the admirable work you are accomplishing' in containing Communist expansion and promoting civil rights."[110] While swaths of the country disagreed with the Vietnam War, Nabokov himself was a supporter.[111]

In Place of a Conclusion: The American Suburbs, or Where It All Comes Together

For the American Nabokov the political world, including its unappealing features and qualities, is knowable through the socioeconomic status of the people about whom—and to whom—he is writing. These are the suburbanites, the educated people of means in whose society Nabokov participated and existed.[112] This social world, this cultural landscape, one that was experiencing an unprecedented boom following the end of World War II, affected Nabokov's political experiences in the United States to such a degree that he felt—or at least publicly behaved—like a proud American until the end of his days. It is important to appreciate Nabokov's bitter comment that when people call *Lolita* anti-American, it is a charge "that pains me significantly more than the idiotic accusation of immorality."[113] How could Nabokov, a relatively recent immigrant to America, write so compellingly about this environment, most notably in *Lolita*? Anna Brodsky argues that "Humbert recognizes rot when he sees it. His depiction of American suburbia—smug, genteel, racist—is not just an exhilarating background. There exists a kind of complicity between it and Humbert."[114]

Nabokov's interactions with the landscape of American life changed over time. From the beginning of his life in the United States, he took great pleasure in attacking the popular authors of the day, typically from a lecturing pulpit. In early 1941, Nabokov told Wilson that his lectures had been "a purring success. Incidentally, I have slaughtered Maxim Gorky, Mr. Hemingway—and a

---

110 Douglas Brinkley, "Bookend; The Other Vietnam Generation," *New York Times*, February 28, 1999, accessed May 11, 2023, https://www.nytimes.com/1999/02/28/books/bookend-the-other-vietnam-generation.html.

111 Brinkley, "Bookend."

112 *For a detailed investigation of American suburban cultural scripts in Nabokov's works, see Jared Hackworth's essay in this volume (M. D. S.).*

113 Nabokov, "Book Entitled *Lolita.*"

114 Anna Brodsky, "Nabokov's *Lolita* and the Postwar Émigré Consciousness," in *Realms of Exile: Nomadism, Diasporas, and Eastern European Voices*, ed. Domnica Radulescu (Lanham, MD: Lexington Books, 2002): 49–66.

few others—corpses impossible to identify."[115] That pattern continued through the rest of Nabokov's public life. He disliked most authors. In 1960, he called Joseph Conrad and Ernest Hemingway "writers for little boys."[116] At the same time, Nabokov was happy to admit that he found J. D. Salinger to be the best American novelist of the younger generation.[117] In a later interview, in 1966, Nabokov amended his list to include John Updike, whom he called, along with Salinger, "the finest [American] artists in recent years."[118]

Nabokov's strong opinions about popular culture did not endear him to some of his American readers. In 1944, he published his first project of length written in the United States, *Nikolai Gogol*. At the end of Nabokov's study of the great Ukrainian Russophone writer, he includes a chapter titled "Commentary." In this addendum to the text, Nabokov reveals that during the editing process, his publisher wanted to make the work less intellectually rigorous:

> I said that an intelligent person could always look up dates and things in a good encyclopedia or in any manual of Russian literature. He said that a student would not be necessarily an intelligent person and would resent the trouble of having to look up things. I said there were students and students. He said that from a publisher's point of view there was only one sort.[119]

In the end, the publisher, James Laughlin of New Directions, won, but Nabokov was still able to keep in the final text the comment that "this chronology is meant for the indolent reader" who does not want to take the effort to read the whole text.[120] In Leona Toker's eyes, Nabokov, as usual, was work-

---

115 Karlinsky, *The Nabokov-Wilson Letters*, 40. On Nabokov's engagement with Hemingway, see Yuri Leving, "Nabokov and Hemingway: The Fish That Got Away," in *Revising Nabokov Revising*, ed. Mitsuyoshi Numano and Tadashi Wakashima (Kyoto: The Nabokov Society of Japan, 2010), 137–144.

116 Helen Lawrenson, "The Man Who Scandalized the World" [for *Esquire*, 1960], in *Conversations with Vladimir Nabokov*, ed. Robert Golla (Jackson: University Press of Mississippi, 2017), 47–58.

117 Alan Nordstrom, "My Child *Lolita*" [for *Ivy Magazine*, 1959], in *Conversations with Vladimir Nabokov*, 18–20.

118 Robert Hughes, "Why Nabokov Detests Freud" [interview for the National Education Television Network], New York Times Archive, January 30, 1966, https://archive.nytimes.com/www.nytimes.com/books/97/03/02/lifetimes/nab-v-freud.html?_r=1&oref=slogin#:~:text=Well%2C%20seldom%20more%20than%20two,finest%20artists%20in%20recent%20years.

119 Vladimir Nabokov, *Nikolai Gogol* (New York: New Directions, 1944), 151–155.

120 Nabokov, *Gogol*, 151–155.

ing on a multidimensional level in his composition of the text. Toker points to "Nabokov's trope-rich digressions and his contraband epithets" as evidence that he was "engaged in a different project. Nabokov focused on Gogol's features that were relevant to his own work."[121] In this sense, *Nikolai Gogol* was also a reflection on American life and politics, not just the czarist Russia of Gogol's time.

Beyond Nabokov and his first American publisher's arguments about *Nikolai Gogol*, every day that Nabokov lived in his adoptive country was further immersion in the body politic that shaped his English-language works. On D-Day, 1944, Nabokov was hospitalized with a nasty case of food poisoning. He described these experiences to Edmund Wilson in a letter postmarked 9 June 1944:[122]

> I had been transferred (in spite of my protests) to the general ward, where the radio kept emitting hot music, cigarette ads (in a juicy voice from the heart) and gags without interruption until (at 10 p.m.) I bellowed to the nurse to have the bloody thing stopped (much to the annoyance and surprise of the staff and of the patients). This is a curious detail of American life—they do not actually listen to the radio, in fact everybody was talking, retching, guffawing, wisecracking, flirting with the (very charming) nurses—all the time—but apparently the impossible sounds coming from the apparatus (it is really the first time that I have heard the radio, except for very brief spasms in other people's houses and in the saloon cars during my travels) somehow acted as a "life-background" for the occupants of the ward, for as soon as it was stopped complete quiet ensued and I soon fell asleep.[123]

In this anthropological gold mine from the mid-1940s, we are given access to Nabokov's bewilderment and frustration with both the news and the advertisements on the radio—what he described to Véra Nabokov three days later as "zoological sounds."[124] Booming commercialism, a definitive trait of the postwar era, is also on full display in *Lolita*. Barbara Wyllie argues that the radio "has a greater evocative power even than cinema, since it demands active participation

---

121 Leona Toker, "Nabokov's *Nikolai Gogol*: Doing Things in Style," in *Nabokov at Cornell*, ed. Gavriel Shapiro (Ithaca, CT: Cornell University Press, 2003), 136–147.

122 The letter to Edmund Wilson is quoted in Brian Boyd, *Vladimir Nabokov: The American Years*, 58–76.

123 Ibid.

124 To Véra Nabokov on 11 June 1944, in Nabokov, *Letters*, 492.

on behalf of the listener. [. . .] For Humbert Humbert, radio music signifies Lolita's presence, close or distant."[125] Wyllie's analysis tracks with Nabokov's own thoughts on the radio broadcasts he heard. In addition to music, *Lolita* is filled with signs and symbols of postwar American suburban culture, stretching from limitless shopping trips to, as Humbert Humbert puts it, "those American ads where schoolchildren are pictured in a subtle ratio of races" to celebrity culture and everything in between.[126] As Roper asks, "if he is not writing a novel of midcentury America, what *is* he writing?"[127]

In a sense, the same could hold true for *Pnin*—it is a Holocaust novel of American life, rich with reflective details and images. And as the text reveals, even Pnin's own assimilation is underway: "[He] walked to the little tavern in Liberty Lane for a large portion of Virginia ham and a good bottle of beer."[128] What could be more American than that?

Bibliography

Primary Sources

Nabokov, Vladimir. "Conversation Piece, 1945." In *The Stories of Vladimir Nabokov*, [edited by Dmitri Nabokov], 587–597. New York: Vintage International, 2008.

———. *Letters to Véra*. Edited and translated by Olga Voronina and Brian Boyd. New York: Vintage International, 2017.

———. *Lolita*. New York: Vintage International, 1997.

———. *Nikolai Gogol*. New York: New Directions, 1944.

———. "On a Book Entitled *Lolita*" [Published 1956]. In *Lolita*, 311–317. New York: Vintage International, 1997 [1956].

———. *Pale Fire*. New York: Vintage International, 1989.

———. *Pnin*. New York: Vintage International, 1989.

———. *Speak, Memory*. New York: Vintage International, 1989.

———. "Spring in Fialta." Translated by Peter A. Pertzoff and Vladimir Nabokov. In *The Stories of Vladimir Nabokov*, [edited by Dmitry Nabokov], 413–429. New York: Vintage International, 2008.

---

125 Barbara Wyllie, "Popular Music in Nabokov's Lolita, Or Frankie and Johnny: A New Key to Lolita?" *Revue Des Études Slaves* 72, no. 3/4 (2000): 443–52, accessed May 10, 2023, http://www.jstor.org/stable/43271909.

126 Nabokov, *Lolita*, 80.

127 Roper, *Nabokov in America*, 161.

128 Nabokov, *Pnin*, 79.

Secondary Sources

Anderson, Douglas. "Nabokov's Genocidal and Nuclear Holocausts in 'Lolita.'" *Mosaic: An Interdisciplinary Critical Journal* 29, no. 2 (1996): 73–90. Accessed May 10, 2023. http://www.jstor.org/stable/44029747.

Alan Nordstrom, "My Child *Lolita*" [for *Ivy Magazine*, 1959], in *Conversations with Vladimir Nabokov*, 18–20.

Appel, Alfred, Jr. *Nabokov's Dark Cinema*. New York: Oxford University Press, 1974.

Arbuckle, Alex Q. "February 1960 Chattanooga sit-ins." Mashable. Accessed November 16, 2023. https://mashable.com/feature/chattanooga-sit-ins.

Asbury, Susan, and Ryan Semmes. "James Lide Coker Papers: Biographical Sketch." University of South Carolina. Accessed November 15, 2023. https://archives.library.sc.edu/repositories/3/resources/40.

Barra, Allen. "What Really Happened to Ben Chapman, the Racist Baseball Player in 42?" *Atlantic*, April 15, 2013. Accessed May 11, 2023. https://www.theatlantic.com/entertainment/archive/2013/04/what-really-happened-to-ben-chapman-the-racist-baseball-player-in-i-42-i/274995/.

Belletto, Steven. "Of Pickaninnies and Nymphets: Race in *Lolita*." *Nabokov Studies* 9 (2005): 1–17. Accessed May 11, 2023. https://sites.lafayette.edu/belletts/files/2010/06/9.1belletto.pdf.

———. "The Zemblan Who Came in from the Cold, or Nabokov's 'Pale Fire', Chance, and the Cold War." *ELH* 73, no. 3 (2006): 755–80. Accessed May 10, 2023. http://www.jstor.org/stable/30030034.

Boyd, Brian. "Chronology of Nabokov's Life and Main Works." *The Nabokovian*. International Nabokov Society. Last modified 2018. Accessed April 1, 2023. https://thenabokovian.org/chronology.

———. *Vladimir Nabokov: The American Years*. Princeton, NJ: Princeton University Press, 1991.

Brinkley, Douglas. "Bookend; The Other Vietnam Generation." *New York Times*, 28 February 1999. Accessed May 11, 2023. https://www.nytimes.com/1999/02/28/books/bookend-the-other-vietnam-generation.html.

Brodsky, Anna. "Nabokov's *Lolita* and the Postwar Émigré Consciousness." In *Realms of Exile: Nomadism, Diasporas, and Eastern European Voices*, edited by Domnica Radulescu, 49–66. Lanham, MD: Lexington Books, 2002.

Coker University. "Presidential Prospectus." Accessed November 15, 2023. https://www.coker.edu/wp-content/uploads/PresidentialProspectus/CokerUniversity_PresidentialProspectus.pdf.

"CPI Inflation Calculator." US Bureau of Labor Statistics. Accessed April 25, 2023. https://www.bls.gov/data/inflation_calculator.htm.

Croning, Brian. "Sports Legend Revealed: Did Vladimir Nabokov Work an Actual Baseball Headline into His Novel 'Pale Fire'?" *Los Angeles Times*, 16 February 2011. Accessed May 11, 2023. https://www.latimes.com/archives/blogs/sports-now/story/2011-02-16/sports-legend-revealed-did-vladimir-nabokov-work-an-actual-baseball-headline-into-his-novel-pale-fire.

De Djin, Angela. "'Freedom' Means Something Different to Liberals and Conservatives. Here's How the Definition Split—And Why That Still Matters." *Time*, August 25, 2020. Accessed May 11, 2023. https://time.com/5882978/freedom-definition-history/.

"Emancipation Manifesto." Encyclopedia Britannica. Last modified February 24, 2023. https://www.britannica.com/event/Emancipation-Manifesto.

"February 1960: The Beginning of the End of Segregation." Chattanooga History. Accessed June 5, 2023. https://chattanoogahistory.com/february1960.php.

Ford, Mark. "Is Humbert Humbert Jewish?" *New York Review of Books*, June 6, 2013. Accessed June 5, 2023. https://www.nybooks.com/articles/2013/06/06/is-humbert-humbert-jewish/.

Golla, Robert, ed. *Conversations with Vladimir Nabokov*. Jackson: University Press of Mississippi, 2017.

Hughes, Robert. "Why Nabokov Detests Freud." New York Times Archive, January 30, 1966. Accessed November 15, 2023. https://archive.nytimes.com/www.nytimes.com/books/97/03/02/lifetimes/nab-v-freud.html?_r=1&oref=slogin#:~:text=Well%2C%20seldom%20more%20than%20two,finest%20artists%20in%20recent%20years.

Karlinsky, Simon, ed. *Dear Bunny, Dear Volodya. The Nabokov-Wilson Letters: Correspondence Between Vladimir Nabokov and Edmund Wilson 1940–1971*. New York: Harper and Row, 1979.

Leving, Yuri. "Nabokov and Hemingway: The Fish That Got Away." In *Revising Nabokov Revising*, edited by Mitsuyoshi Numano and Tadashi Wakashima, 137–144. Kyoto: The Nabokov Society of Japan, 2010.

"Loving v. Virginia 1967." Oyez. Accessed May 11, 2023. https://www.oyez.org/cases/1966/395.

The Martin Luther King, Jr., Research and Education Institute. "Connor, Theopilus Eugene 'Bull.'" Accessed November 12, 2023. https://kinginstitute.stanford.edu/connor-theophilus-eugene-bull.

Moore, Charles. "Alabama Fire Department Aims High-Pressure Water Hoses at Civil Rights Demonstrators" [Photographed May 1963]. Smithsonian Museum of African American History & Culture. Accessed May 9, 2023. https://nmaahc.si.edu/object/nmaahc_2011.49.1.

"The Most Bigoted Man in Baseball." *Sports History Weekly*, October 7, 2022. Accessed May 11, 2023. https://www.sportshistoryweekly.com/stories/the-most-bigoted-man-in-baseball,1116.

National Interstate and Defense Highways Act (1956). National Archives. Last modified February 8, 2022. Accessed May 8, 2023. https://www.archives.gov/milestone-documents/national-interstate-and-defense-highways-act/.

———. "Nabokov Under Glass: Pnin. Garden City, New York, 1957." Accessed November 15, 2023. http://web-static.nypl.org/exhibitions/nabokov/pnin.htm.

New York Public Library. "Nabokov Under Glass: American Stories." Accessed November 15, 2023. http://web-static.nypl.org/exhibitions/nabokov/amer.htm.

Nordstrom, Alan. "My Child Lolita" [for *Ivy Magazine*, 1959]. In *Conversations with Vladimir Nabokov*, edited by Robert Golla, 18–20. Jackson: University Press of Mississippi, 2017.

Norwood, Stephen H., and Harold Brackman. "Going to Bat for Jackie Robinson: The Jewish Role in Breaking Baseball's Color Line." *Journal of Sport History* 26, no. 1 (1999): 115–41. Accessed November 12, 2023. http://www.jstor.org/stable/43611720.

Roper, Robert. *Nabokov in America: On the Road to Lolita*. New York: Bloomsbury, 2015.

Schiff, Stacy. *Véra (Mrs. Vladimir Nabokov)*. New York: The Modern Library, 1999.

Schwarz, Daniel R. "Eating Kosher Ivy: Jews as Literary Intellectuals." *Shofar* 21, no. 3 (2003): 16–28. Accessed October 2, 2023. http://www.jstor.org/stable/42943317.

Shrayer, Maxim D. "Jewish Questions in Nabokov's Art and Life." In *Nabokov and His Fiction: New Perspectives*, edited by Julian W. Connolly, 74–91. Cambridge: Cambridge University Press, 1999.

———. "Raisa Blokh as an Historical, Literary and Emotional Source for Nabokov's Pnin," in *Skreshcheniia sudeb. Literarische und kulturelle Beziehungen zwischen Russland und dem Westen. A Festschrift for Fedor B. Poljakov*, ed. Lazar Fleishman, Stefan Michael Newerkla, and Michael Wachtel. *Stanford Slavic Studies* 49 (2019): 619–656.

Smith, Peter Duval. "Vladimir Nabokov on His Life and Work" [for the *Listener*, 1962]. In *Conversations with Vladimir Nabokov*, edited by Robert Golla, 62–69. Jackson: University Press of Mississippi, 2017.

Thuram, Lilian, Bernard Fillaire, Laurent Dubois, Charles Forsdic, and Aedín Ní Loingsigh. "General-in-Chief of the Russian Imperial Army: Abraham Petrovich Hannibal 1696–14 May 1781." In *My Black Stars: From Lucy to Barack Obama*, edited by David Murphy, 34–36. Liverpool: Liverpool University Press, 2021. Accessed November 15, 2023. https://doi.org/10.2307/j.ctv1pfqnct.11.

Toffler, Alvin. "Playboy Interview: Vladimir Nabokov" [for *Playboy Magazine*, 1964]. In *Conversations with Vladimir Nabokov*, edited by Robert Golla, 70–89. Jackson: University Press of Mississippi, 2017.

Toker, Leona. "Nabokov's *Nikolai Gogol*: Doing Things in Style." In *Nabokov at Cornell*, edited by Gavriel Shapiro, 136–147. Ithaca, CT: Cornell University Press, 2003.

Tracy, Marc. "69 Years Later, Philadelphia Apologizes to Jackie Robinson." *New York Times*, April 14, 2016. Accessed July 28, 2023. https://www.nytimes.com/2016/04/15/sports/baseball/philadelphia-apologizes-to-jackie-robinson.html.

"The United States and the Holocaust 1942–45." United States Holocaust Memorial Museum, Washington DC. Last modified March 30, 2023. Accessed October 9, 2023. https://encyclopedia.ushmm.org/content/en/article/the-united-states-and-the-holocaust-1942–45.

Wilson, Edmund. *To The Finland Station*. New York: Doubleday & Company, 1940.

Wyllie, Barbara. "Popular Music in Nabokov's Lolita, Or Frankie and Johnny: A New Key to Lolita?" *Revue Des Études Slaves* 72, no. 3/4 (2000): 443–52. Accessed May 10, 2023. http://www.jstor.org/stable/43271909.

Nabokov in Boston:
A Photo Essay

———

Matthew Lyberg

Introduction: Mapping Nabokov's Boston

My relationship with Nabokov's Boston began unexpectedly. It was a morning filled with regret for what could have been, and dread for what was about to happen. I had not typed a single word of my original senior thesis topic. Now it was the due date for the draft. I arrived late with nothing to present.

I expected a thrashing. Professor Shrayer suggested a stroll.

On the walk, he pondered the many people living happy lives without having completed a thesis. He shared how a good thesis bursts out of you, almost writing itself. A bad thesis is misery, inflicted on professor and student alike—it is better to not write at all than pursue one for pure form's sake. Hoping for some redemption, I shared how at least my photography seemed to be improving. Professor Shrayer stopped abruptly, looked straight ahead for a seeming eternity. Then he turned to me, slowly, and said: "You know, Nabokov lived in Boston. What if you attempted a photo essay. . . ?" It felt like an electric shock. I think I said, "Yes, this."

What follows is the resulting attempt to capture Nabokov's Boston. We start with the mundane landmarks of daily life; a home in Wellesley, lecture halls, museum buildings, an apartment in Cambridge, and a few more rentals scattered about Harvard Square. From these points, we tease out the connecting threads. I mean that literally; with the help of retired transit operator Ernest Ringer, who drove many of the same routes, I sketched Nabokov's likely train, bus, and street-car commutes between Wellesley and Cambridge, even now arduous affairs. Practically, I wanted to understand the physical realities of Nabokov's life in the Boston area—how much time was required for his commute between Wellesley and Cambridge, was it loud on the bus, how cold or warm was the walk from the nearest stop. In another sense, I hoped that exposure to these shared sensations would provide either a connection with Nabokov's works, or even a glimpse into the kind of "otherworld" which has been described as "a space where love and memory are in harmony, where past and future, life and death, cease to be antinomies."[1]

The approach here is also the intent—to find the connections between the everyday and the transcendent, to which various "signs and symbols" within Nabokov's works guide the reader. The language of Nabokov is a poetic portal onto eternity, where the otherworld "is a domain that exists synchronically with and influences the mundane world."[2] For my project, I focused on the "this-world" components of Nabokov's Boston period. Focusing on the quotidian, I hoped to encounter the eternal.

For me, Nabokov's poetics of what Shrayer calls "mapping narrative space"[3] is deeply rooted in St. Petersburg, the city of the author's birth. I experienced this first hand through an elective "Artistic Photography" class I took while doing a Boston College study abroad program in St. Petersburg in 1999. It was a frenetic time in Russia. The ruble had just collapsed, coalitions were fomenting democracy, and disparate criminal organizations were vying for control of local fiefdoms. My intention to study Russian literature became a casualty to my new passion for photography. Instead of a jam-packed introductory class, I was apprenticed to Vladimir Semyonovich Antoshchenkov,[4] a professor of architecture and urban studies and renowned photographer of St. Petersburgh. Vladimir Semyonovich emphasized a strong command of St. Petersburg geography. For the two months before I was allowed to pick up a camera, my (graded) exams consisted of providing the exact street address for any of the five thousand-plus images Professor Antoshchenkov had taken of the Admiralty region over the past thirty years. The images ranged from rooftop cityscapes to small architectural details. If there was natural light in the photograph, I had to know the approximate time of day. To prepare for these exams, I spent as much time as possible walking and studying these buildings. As a result, I gained an intimate knowledge of the area surrounding the Nabokovs' former mansion at 47 Bol'shaia Morskaia Street. Professor Antoshchenkov's goal was for me not to look, but to see.

While getting to know the city of Nabokov's youth, I also wondered what it would have meant for Nabokov to lose that entire world as he fled from the Bolsheviks, and then to surrender more or less established lives in flight from the

---

1   Maxim D. Shrayer, *The World of Nabokov's Stories* (Austin: University of Texas Press, 1999), 70.

2   Ibid., 21.

3   Ibid., 71–86.

4   "Antoshchenkov Vladimir Semenovich," Wikipedia, accessed November 28, 2023, https://ru.wikipedia.org/wiki/Антощенков,_Владимир_Семёнович.

Nazis. Upon my return to Boston, I proceeded to investigate Nabokov's spaces in the Boston area. Perhaps at a minimum, I thought the writer and his family might gravitate at least to an American middle-class equivalent of comfort. A walled palace of sorts, a refuge from the cacophony of urban life. Their first residence on 19 Appleby Road in Wellesley was just such a place—a spacious home nestled on a sleepy street a few minutes' walk from Nabokov's teaching post at Wellesley College. Quiet. Solitude. Fall leaves drifting down on rolling hills. Spared the daily drudgery of commuting. Just silence, and the pen. Why trade this for stuffy train cars, roaring busses with fogged glass, or rain-soaked streetcar queues for the inevitable delay? What on earth could draw one of the great writers from his sanctuary?

Dusty butterflies.

Soon after moving to the Boston area in 1941, Nabokov volunteered to catalogue and reorganize the butterfly collection at Harvard's Museum of Comparative Zoology. And they needed the help; as Bryan Boyd notes, "the collection was in frightful disarray [. . .] old world butterflies were left exposed to dust and museum mites with no glass case."[5] Nabokov's once a week visit to the museum became twice a week, twice a week became more frequent. By the time the family moved to a two-bedroom apartment at 8 Cragie Circle in Cambridge, Nabokov was spending sometimes twelve hours or more a day studying and classifying butterflies. And then he would work late into the night upending American literature. According to one friend, "I never knew any family who cared less about possessions, food, anything. Their only luxury was [their son] Dmitri."[6]

Part of me wanted Nabokov walled off, producing great works of literature. He possessed one of the most active minds and souls of his century, yet was able to sit for twelve hours, occupied only by the meticulous, manual work of butterfly study. So incongruous with artistic creation, I thought as I ventured to reconstruct the Nabokovs' family walks or to reenact Nabokov's excruciatingly long commute from Cambridge to Wellesley and back. And then this dull gray fabric would be pierced by a moment of transcendence.

One such moment was in the middle of the night, in March of 2000, as my friend Patrick Hess and I set off for Harvard Square. A most spectral fog rolled in. The Weeks Footbridge, spanning the Charles River from Allston to Cambridge, emerged as a gateway from the streetlamps reflecting in the vapor droplets. The bridge was built in 1929, thirty years before the traffic-bearing Elliot Bridge.

---

5 Brian Boyd, *Vladimir Nabokov: The American Years* (Princeton: Princeton University Press, 1991), 37.
6 Ibid., 46.

Perhaps Nabokov had seen something similar on a late evening stroll. All of a sudden, we had found ourselves in the world of *Bend Sinister*, the bulk of which Nabokov composed in Boston "in the winter and spring of 1945–1946," during what he referred to as "a particularly cloudless and vigorous period of life."[7] Some of the images from that night remain among my most treasured ones. Fortunately, even at 4:00 am, there was plenty of burly foot traffic to help stage the scene of Nabokov's novel, where Krug is stopped by Ekwilist soldiers. My friend Patrick patiently posed as Krug while I tried to calibrate my camera for the pitch-black night and sheer white fog. Hence a confluence of our puckish departure, the fog, and the resulting image of a scene Nabokov himself may have seen in the 1940s nighttime Cambridge.

On many occasions, Nabokov stressed the importance of physically connecting with the geography of literary works. In the introduction to *Lectures on Literature*, Fredson Bowers shares Nabokov's insistence that "instructors should prepare maps of Dublin with Bloom's and Stephen's intertwining itineraries clearly traced," and that, "unless the façade of Dr. Jekyll's house is distinctly reconstructed in the student's mind, the enjoyment of Stevenson's story cannot be perfect."[8]

At a minimum, the images attempt to provide some echo of Nabokov's Boston—both places where he lived and places informing the setting of his novel *Bend Sinister* and his short story "The Vane Sisters" (1952). It is my hope that some of the images might connect with those spaces where Nabokov's characters experienced moments of joy and terror, existential dread, and soaring love. Perhaps these were places and moments of transcendence for the author himself, and in connecting, we might experience the same.

—December 2023

Photographs

In the captions, I incorporate some of the information from Brian Boyd's *Vladimir Nabokov: The American Years*. The page references below are to the following editions of Vladimir Nabokov's works: *Bend Sinister* (New York: Vintage, 1990) and *The Stories of Vladimir Nabokov*, [edited and translated by Dmitri Nabokov] (New York: Vintage, 1997).

---

7   Vladimir Nabokov, *Bend Sinister* (New York: Vintage, 1990), xi.
8   Fredson Bowers, editor's forward to *Vladimir Nabokov, Lectures on Literature*, ed. Fredson Bowers (New York, Harvest Brace Jovanovich/Bruccoli Clark, 1980), viii.

19 Appleby Road, Wellesley, Massachusetts. The Nabokovs lived here from September 1941 to September 1942, during the first year of Nabokov's teaching at Wellesley College. A short walk from campus, the house would have provided a quiet, convenient refuge.

The Museum of Comparative Zoology, 26 Oxford Street, Cambridge, Massachusetts. Nabokov first visited the butterfly collection at Harvard's Museum of Comparative Zoology in the fall of 1941. Many will recognize this building as the Harvard Museum of Natural History. Established in 1998, the museum houses the public collections for the Museum of Comparative Zoology, The Herbaria, and the Mineralogical and Geological Museum. The building was originally constructed in 1859 to house the Museum of Comparative Zoology.

8 Craigie Circle, Cambridge, Massachusetts. The Nabokovs lived in a third-floor apartment from September 1942 until July of 1948. The two-bedroom unit was small, but less than a ten-minute walk from the Museum of Comparative Zoology. At least twice a week, Nabokov would commute to his teaching post at Wellesley, which comprised the family's primary income source. During these years, Nabokov completed "The Assistant Producer," *Nikolai Gogol, Bend Sinister,* "Time and Ebb," the collection of verse translations for *Three Russian Poets,* "Conversation Piece 1945" (originally "Double Talk"), and "Signs and Symbols." In the introduction to *Bend Sinister,* Nabokov places the novel's last scene in this apartment.

9 Maynard Place, Cambridge, Massachusetts. Nabokov lived here while he was a visiting lecturer at Harvard University in the spring of 1952. It is about a fifteen-minute walk from campus along the Charles River.

35 Brewster St., Cambridge, Massachusetts. The Nabokovs found this house, which belonged to Robert Frost, to be altogether too uncomfortable. They stayed for all of two weeks before decamping to a hotel. Frost had linoleum placed in the bedrooms. According to Warren Little, as of the spring of 2000, the house was still quite draughty.

"He walked through a spasmodic fog down the cobbled Omigod Lane towards the embankment" (*Bend Sinister*, 5). Acorn St., Beacon Hill, Boston, Massachusetts.

"'I am not interested in politics,' he said. 'And I have the only river to cross'"
(*Bend Sinister*, 5). The Weeks Footbridge, Cambridge, Massachusetts.

"As Krug, trudging steadily, approached, two Ekwilist soldiers barred his way"
(*Bend Sinister*, 6). The Weeks Footbridge, Cambridge, Massachusetts.

"[…] but as soon as the camera clicked everything started to move, to gush, and he walked on, jerkily […] he felt an intimate connection with the black lacquered water lapping and heaving under the stone arches of the bridge" (*Bend Sinister*, 10). The Weeks Footbridge, Cambridge, Massachusetts.

"Doomed to walk back and forth on a bridge which has ceased to be one since neither bank is really attainable" (*Bend Sinister*, 10). The Weeks Footbridge, Cambridge, Massachusetts.

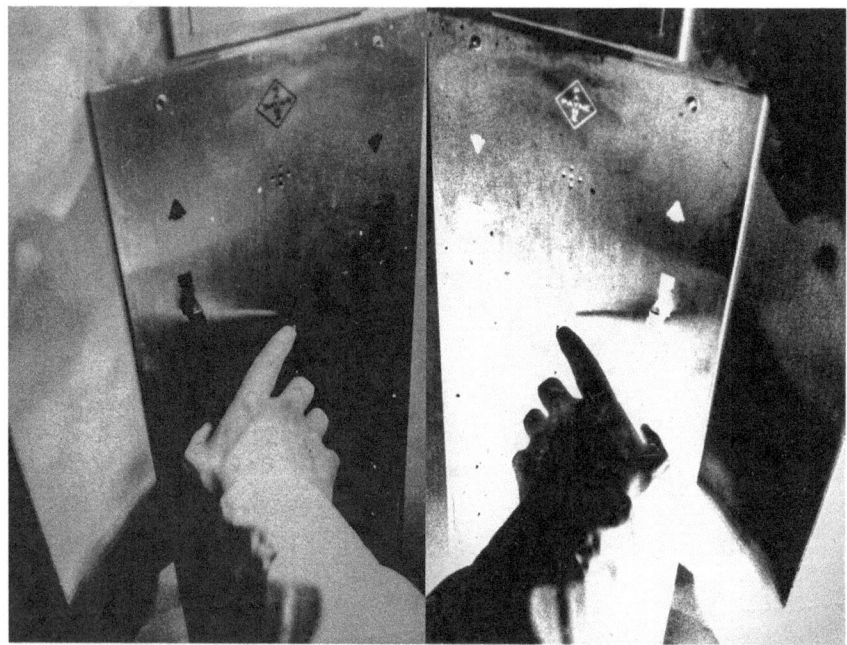

"He entered the elevator which greeted him with the small sound he knew, half stamp, half shiver, and its features lit up. He pressed the third button. The brittle, thin walled, old fashioned little room blinked but did not move. He pressed again "(*Bend Sinister*, 20).

"[...] in one of those express elevators manned by delicate hands—my own in a negative picture—of dark skinned men with sinking stomachs and rising hearts [...]" (*Bend Sinister*, 38). Building elevator, Boston, Massachusetts.

"The street seemed to be full of bookshops and dim little pubs" (*Bend Sinister*, 160). Boston, Massachusetts.

"I remember sitting next day at my raised desk in the large classroom where a mid-year examination in French Lit. was being held on the eve of Sybil's suicide" ("The Vane Sisters," in *The Stories of Vladimir Nabokov*, 621). Pendleton Hall 112, Wellesley College, Wellesley, Massachusetts.

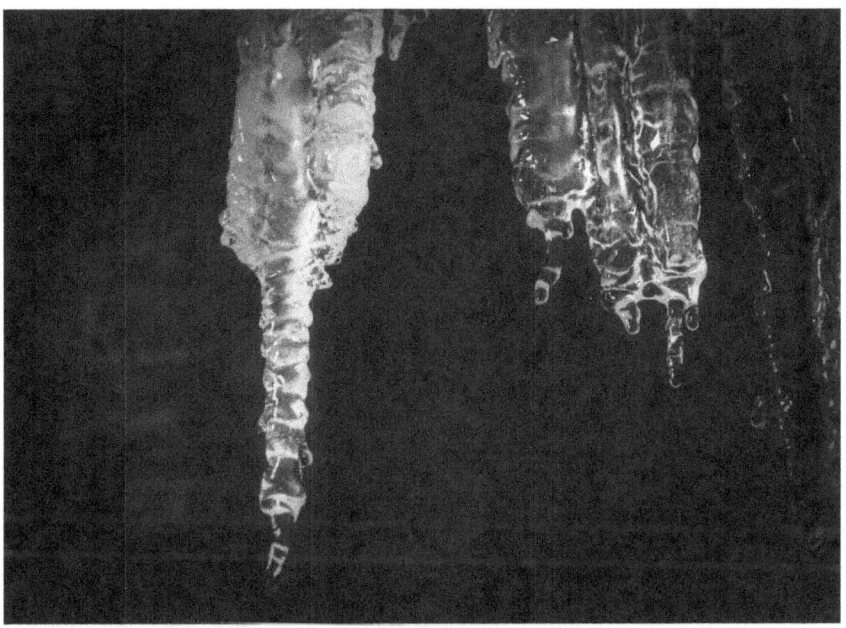

"In the midst of my usual afternoon stroll through the small hilly town attached to the girls' college where I taught French Literature, I stopped to watch a family of brilliant icicles drip-dropping from the eaves of a frame house" ("The Vane Sisters," *The Stories of Vladimir Nabokov*, 619). Wellesley College, Wellesley, Massachusetts.

Acknowledgments

In a way, this project has been in the works since 1996, when I had the good fortune of joining the Boston College community.

While my interests have changed and evolved, Vladimir Nabokov has remained both a protagonist in my research and a recurrent subject of my teaching. My esteemed colleague Michael J. Connolly, who was chair of the Department of Slavic and Eastern Languages and Literatures when I arrived on the Heights, encouraged me to offer a course on Nabokov, and over the years it has developed into a research seminar. The majority of the essays gathered in this volume began as research papers by the talented undergraduate and graduate students who participated in my Nabokov seminar in the spring of 2023. I would like to thank all of them for their contributions, for their passion and enthusiasm—and also for adhering to draconian deadlines.

A separate word of great appreciation goes to Matthew Lyberg, who studied Nabokov, graduated from Boston College with a BA in Russian in 2000, went on to have a successful career in finance, but never gave up his project of documenting Nabokov's sites in Boston.

It has been my privilege to gain fellow Nabokovians in my English Department colleagues at BC, Kevin Ohi and Eric Weiskott, both of whom contributed essays to this book. I would also like to thank the dedicated librarians who generously assisted with the work on this volume: Christian Dupont, associate university librarian for scholarly resources and Burns librarian, and Anne Kenny, interlibrary loan librarian, O'Neill Library, as well as the staff of the John J. Burns Library and the O'Neill Library at Boston College.

I would like to express my deep gratitude to Dean Gregory Kalscheur, S.J., Morrissey College of Arts & Sciences, and Provost David Quigley, both of Boston College, for their support of this project from the moment of its inception all the way to its publication.

Professor Leona Toker, a major Nabokov scholar, generously commented on the manuscript and suggested a number of important corrections.

Last but not least, the staff of Academic Studies Press has been particularly welcoming and enthusiastic, and I would especially like to thank Stuart Allen, Alessandra Anzani, Matthew Charlton, Kira Nemirovsky, and Ilya Nikolaev.

—M. D. S.
Lyons Hall, Boston College
November 2024

Index

Contributors

Nicholas Adler is an English PhD student at Boston College. He specializes in gender and sexuality studies, particularly the burgeoning field of asexuality studies. After graduating from the University of Vermont, he taught middle school math before returning to UVM to pursue an MA in English. The work he did during that time earned him the Graduate Teaching Assistant of the Year award from his department and the Leon Edel Prize from *The Henry James Review*. A longtime chess player and Nabokov reader, he is excited to combine those passions in his essay in this volume.

Megumi DeMond has a background in teaching and literature. She recently received her MA in English at Boston College, where her research focused on transnational Japanese literature, Asian American literature, and ecocriticism. She has given talks on the role of the natural environment in both Japanese and American literature and film, and her creative writing has been published in *The Smart Set*. Megumi currently lives in Seattle, WA, where she continues to write about multiculturalism, language crossings, home, and displacement.

Jared Hackworth is a PhD student in English at the University of Illinois, Chicago, where he studies the connections between literature and urbanization. He is particularly interested in how the forms of twentieth-century American literature respond to our increasingly urban and suburban world. Before beginning his PhD, Jared received his MA in English at Boston College and a BA in urban studies and English from Wheaton College. He has presented his work at the Modern Language Association, the American Comparative Literature Association, and the American Literature Association.

Nina Khaghany graduated from Boston College in 2024 with a double major in English and Classics. She grew up in Bloomfield Hills, Michigan, before moving to Boston for college. At Boston College she worked on James Joyce's *Ulysses* in digital humanities and did research on the nineteenth-century Irish immigrant experience. She served as an editor of Boston College's *Stylus*, a literary magazine where she also contributed poetry. Nina studied Latin and Attic Greek and wrote her senior undergraduate thesis on T. S. Eliot's "Sweeney," a character featured in Eliot's poetry and verse drama. Nina is presently pursuing an MA in literature at Columbia University.

Matthew Lyberg is a quantitative developer with Manulife Investment Management, where he applies statistical models to derive investment insights across asset classes. Previously, Matthew photographed the rebirth of Orthodox Monasticism on a Fulbright Fellowship to Ukraine. Matthew holds an MS in computational finance from Carnegie Mellon University, a BS in mathematics from Boston University, an MBA from Hult Business School, and a BA in Russian language and literature from Boston College. He is a reviewer for the *Journal of Asset Management* and for the US-Ukraine Fulbright Selection Committee. Matthew edited the English translation of *While We Remember* (Russian, *Poka my pomnim*), by Dr. Mark Ginzburg.

Brendan McCourt is a writer and critic whose scholarly interests range from cultural representations of food to the impact of formalism and psychoanalysis on twentieth-century American literature. A Philadelphia native, he received his MA in English from Boston College and currently lives and writes in Boston, Massachusetts.

Kevin Ohi is professor of English at Boston College. The recipient of fellowships from the National Humanities Center, the Cornell Society for the Humanities, and the Guggenheim Foundation, he is the author of *Innocence and Rapture: The Erotic Child in Pater, Wilde, James, and Nabokov* (2005); *Henry James and the Queerness of Style* (2011); *Dead Letters Sent: Queer Literary Transmission* (2015); and *Inceptions: Literary Beginnings and Contingencies of Form* (2021). He has recently completed a book on the equivocal personhood of narrators and characters in modern fiction.

Katie Pelkey is a poetry student in the creative writing MFA program at Syracuse University. Her work defamiliarizes everyday experiences and invites readers to embrace the poems living among us. Her recent scholarly interests include poetics, instructional design, composition and rhetoric, and the impact of artificial intelligence on creativity as we know it. She currently lives in upstate New York where she teaches composition and is writing her first book.

Samuel L. Peterson is in the undergraduate class of 2025 at Boston College. He is a member of the Gabelli Presidential Scholars Program, double majoring in English and Hispanic studies, with a minor in Jewish studies. While at

BC, he has been selected as a Clough Center for the Study of Constitutional Democracy Undergraduate Correspondent, interned at Boston College Law School's Innocence Program, and written for the *College Basketball Times*. He has studied in Israel, Ireland, and Spain and plans to attend law school. He hails from the Washington, DC metro area.

Maxim D. Shrayer, the editor of this volume, is professor of Russian, English, and Jewish Studies at Boston College, where he has been teaching since 1996 and co-founded the Jewish Studies program. Shrayer is the author and editor of almost thirty books of criticism, nonfiction, fiction, poetry, and translations, most recently the memoir *Immigrant Baggage* and the collection of poetry *Kinship*. Shrayer has published four books about Vladimir Nabokov and regularly teaches Nabokov seminars at Boston College.

Ciara Spencer is from Melbourne, Florida. She graduated from Rollins College with a BA in English in 2020, completing an honors thesis titled "The Implications of an Active Protagonist in Bruce Miller's Hulu Adaptation of Margaret Atwood's *The Handmaid's Tale*." In 2023, she graduated from Boston College with an MA in English. She is a former bookseller, an avid jigsaw puzzler, and usually carries a film camera. She lives in Boston, where she is now a student at Boston University School of Law.

Fiona Steacy holds an MA in English from Boston College and a BA in literature from Bard College. Her research interests include modernism and American literature with a focus on themes of regional and familial inheritance. Originally from Cape Cod, Fiona now lives in Boston.

Eric Weiskott is professor of English at Boston College. He is the author, most recently, of the poetry chapbook *Chanties: An American Dream* (Bottlecap Press, 2023) and the scholarly monograph *Meter and Modernity in English Verse, 1350–1650* (University of Pennsylvania Press, 2021). He is working on a new monograph that brings Nabokov's fiction into the orbit of the enigmatic styles of fourteenth- and twenty-first-century poetries. Eric's note on Nabokov's *Ada or Ardor* appears in the *Nabokovian*, and a book review in *Nabokov Online Journal*.

www.ingramcontent.com/pod-product-compliance
Lightning Source LLC
Chambersburg PA
CBHW050923030726
47503CB00007BB/2438